BARRON'S

AP*

EUROPEAN HISTORY

6TH EDITION

James M. Eder
Former Social Studies Teacher
Northport High School
Northport, New York

Seth A. Roberts
Former A.P. and I.B. European History Teacher
Social Studies Teacher Specialist
Frederick County Public Schools
Frederick, Maryland

BARRON'S

DEDICATION

To the students at Northport High School

To those from whom I have learned the most, the students and teachers
of Frederick County, Maryland, and to my wife, Michelle.

All inquiries should be addressed to:
Barron's Educational Series, Inc.
250 Wireless Boulevard
Hauppauge, New York 11788
www.barronseduc.com

ISBN (book): 978-0-7641-4697-8
ISBN (book & CD-ROM Pkg.): 978-1-4380-7124-4
ISSN (book): 2164-4519
ISSN (book & CD-ROM Pkg.): 2164-4586

PRINTED IN THE UNITED STATES OF AMERICA

9 8 7 6 5 4 3 2 1

10%
POST-CONSUMER
WASTE
Paper contains a minimum
of 10% post-consumer
waste (PCW). Paper used
in this book was derived
from certified, sustainable
forestlands.

Contents

As you review the content in this book to work toward earning that **5** on your AP European History Exam, here are five things that you **MUST** know above everything else:

Barron's Essential 5

1 **Know the important European Dynasties and Rulers.** This is a huge subject on the AP exam! There are almost always specific multiple-choice questions on the most important rulers and ruling families and how their power and decisions have a reach through the ages to today.
- ✔ Know the Hapsburgs with special attention to Charles V, Philip II, and Marie Teresa
- ✔ Know the Romanovs with attention to Peter I, Catherine II, and Nicholas II
- ✔ Know the Valois and Bourbon Dynasties with special attention to Henry II, Henry III, Louis XI, Louis XIV, Louis XVI, and Napoleon.
- ✔ Know the English succession with attention to Henry VIII, Elizabeth I, Charles I, Oliver Cromwell, Charles II, and William and Mary.
- ✔ Know the Hohenzollern line including Frederick William, Frederick II, Kaiser Wilhelm I and Kaiser Wilhelm II.

2 **Know the details about the transition from Monarchies to Democracies across Europe.** The subject of how different countries evolved politically and socially is a very big one for the exam and there are usually many questions on the subject.
- ✔ Study England as the first nation to move toward democratic principles.
- ✔ Compare England's political evolution to that of France including the revolution of 1789 and the other uprisings in 1830 and 1848.
- ✔ Understand the impact of 1848 and how even after revolutions failed, they did lead to more democratic state institutions.
- ✔ This should include the creation of modern nations such as Germany and Italy under Bismarck and Cavour respectively.

3 **Practice preparing for the Document-Based Question.** The DBQ is a hugely important indicator of your success on the AP exam. In the weeks leading up to the test, practice at least a few complete DBQ responses. You won't know what the DBQ question is going to be, but the thoroughness of your response, your ability to show point of view in the documents, and the amount of detail used in high-scoring responses is what you need to concentrate on. Have your teacher or classmates help on this.
- ✔ Practice your Point of View commentary on document authors.
- ✔ Group your documents into at least three groups and explain the groupings.
- ✔ ANSWER THE QUESTION with a strong thesis and good support. Stay on track and do not go off on a tangent.

4 **Be sure to know the important figures in the twentieth century.** This is essentially a modern history course and knowing the importance of many figures of the last century is key to success on the exam. Figures such as Kaiser Wilhelm II, Otto von Bismarck, Winston Churchill, Mohandas Gandhi, Margaret Sanger, Adolf Hitler, Vladimir Lenin, and Mikhail Gorbachev should be known.
- ✔ The exam is focusing more and more on recent history.
- ✔ The wars of the twentieth century are great fodder for questions.
- ✔ The fights for minority rights is also a big topic for multiple-choice questions.

5 **Know your Revolutions.** You need to be familiar with all of the revolutions in European History. There are many turning points when a great change came about politically, socially and economically. These revolutions include but are not limited to the Agricultural Revolution and Enclosure, the Scientific Revolution and Enlightenment, the English Civil War, The French Revolution, The Industrial Revolution, Revolutions of 1830 and 1848, Nationalist Movements, the Russian Revolution and Decolonization.

PART ONE

INTRODUCTION

Using This Book

This book is designed primarily to prepare you for the AP European History exam. It provides

- Systematic Methods for Studying History
- A Guide to the AP European History exam
- Review chapters including sample and practice questions on the various periods of European history
- Two complete model AP exams with answers

To the Teacher and the Student

This book can be used as a supplement to your classwork and study material, or as a review book to help you refresh your memory on what you learned throughout the year. However you choose to use the book, creating a study plan to suit your needs is simple and easy.

Beginning on page 5 with "Systematic Methods for Studying History," you will learn how to recognize the logical order of history materials; how to pre-read; how to frame the big picture; how to read, take notes, and highlight; and how to connect event by using chronology. These skills are all essential for helping you understand history, make sense of it, and retain the most relevant bits of information needed to excel on the exam.

Next we present "A Guide to the AP European History Exam" on page 11. Here you will become familiar with the basics of the exam. These include the exam's duration and number of questions; subject matter; historical time span; grading; multiple-choice section with hints, types, and samples; interpreting the essay questions; the document-based questions with hints, don'ts, and a sample of the thematic essay questions with the frequency of themes and hints. Knowing what to expect on test day will reduce any test anxiety you may have—allowing you to perform your best.

Part Two of the book consists of fifteen chapters of review of the major historical periods covered on the exam along with sample multiple-choice questions and answers and practice thematic essays.

Finally, Part Three includes two model AP exams with multiple-choice questions, thematic essays, and document-based questions with suggested answers.

> ## A SUGGESTED APPROACH FOR USING THIS BOOK
> 1. Peruse the Systematic Methods for Studying History section.
> 2. Study the Guide to the AP European History exam.
> 3. Study any or all of the review chapters and answer the sample and practice questions.
> 4. Take and score the model exams. Examine the questions you missed and look for any connections that can tell you what areas you need to concentrate on.
> 5. If you purchased the book/CD-ROM package take the exams on the CD for added practice.

To the Teacher

For use of the book as a classroom aid the various review chapters in this book can be used as year-long supplements to sum up or reinforce particular teaching units and homework assignments. The historical review section of each chapter will help your students to frame the big picture; the sample and practice essays and multiple-choice questions will reinforce the learning.

Part Two, the review section, can be used near the end of the year to pull the course work together and to prepare your students for the exam.

It's often helpful for students to study Part One at the beginning of the course to help them to study history and to give them an idea of what the exam will be like. Knowing what they will face is both a motivator and method of organizing the course's information.

To the Student

This book can be used independent of your course in European history or it can be used along with assigned materials to sum up, pull together, clarify, and review.

It's best to use it at the beginning of the year and to read Part One right away. That will help you to study better in and out of class, and it will give you an idea of what's ahead if you decide to take the AP exam. Review the appropriate chapters in Part Two right before you start each topic in class to "frame the picture" and to help fit everything into place in your mind. Or go to the appropriate chapter after studying that unit in class in order to pull it all together.

If you intend to use the book as review and practice for the exam, **don't wait until late April or May**. Instead of getting nervous and wasting energy on test anxiety, put time aside in late March or early April to study the review chapters and to do the sample questions on content you have already covered in class and in homework. Save the model exams for late April or early May, then use these exams and the ones on the CD-ROM to check your progress, and to keep practicing the skills that will earn you your 5 on test day.

Systematic Methods for Studying History

What follows are some time-tested methods for studying history. Although there is no substitute for being an involved student in a challenging history course, these suggestions will help you with homework, supplementary reading, and preparation for the AP European History exam.

How to Recognize the Logical Order of History Materials

Most history readings—especially texts—are organized logically:

Facts support a theme: The Magna Carta, the Puritan Revolution, and the personalities involved help trace the development of constitutional government in England.

Great events define an era: The French Revolution colored the political, social, cultural, and diplomatic life of Europe for over a hundred years after it happened.

Cause-effect relationships are ascertained: The outbreak of World War I in August 1914 was caused by long-term trends, such as nationalism and imperialism, that stretched back decades into the 19th century.

The influence of individuals on an age is identified: The totalitarian dictatorships of Hitler and Stalin impacted on the entire planet before and long after World War II.

In reading history materials, the object is to focus on this inherent logical order. This can be done by *pre-reading* and by *framing the big picture.*

How to Pre-Read

Before tackling the text itself, be sure to skim the chapter by reading each of the following *in order:*

✔ The chapter heading
✔ The introductory paragraph
✔ Focus questions at the beginning of the chapter
✔ Subheadings
✔ The concluding paragraph
✔ Review questions at chapter's end
✔ Bold print or italics within the text

It is better to concentrate on the reading at this point than to try to take notes.

How to "Frame the Big Picture"

During both the *pre-reading* and the *reading of the text,* pose the following questions as a natural way of keeping the mind's eye on the main story, on the *logical order* of the material:

✔ What is the theme of the chapter? (What is it about? What is the author trying to prove?)
✔ What are main events? (What happened and what caused it?)
✔ Who are the principal personalities? (Who did what, and why?)
✔ What are the important results? (New ideas? Significant changes? Power shifts?)

Remember: "Don't lose the forest for the trees."

HOW TO READ THE TEXT

Once you have *pre-read* the material and *framed the big picture,* you are ready to attack the text itself. Difficult material deserves a "straight read" before you try to highlight, underline, or take notes; most readings allow you to do both simultaneously as long as you have *pre-read.*

If You Own the Book

HIGHLIGHTING OR UNDERLINING

Advantages: easy, quick, neat; has visual appeal; the text itself provides an instant condensation.

Disadvantage: too much highlighting/or underlining defeats the purpose.

MARGINAL NOTES

Advantage: making notes in the margin of the book requires a synthesis that is itself a learning tool.

Disadvantages: time-consuming; often illegible, messy, or incomplete.

Note: using both highlighting and marginal notes together can work very well.

If You Don't Own the Book

Notetaking and outlining on separate paper are traditional and effective methods of condensing and synthesizing a reading. Notetaking has the advantage of requiring critical thought for the condensation, the disadvantage of often being jumbled and confusing.

Sample Reading with Underlining, Accompanying Notes, Brief Outline

Underlined Passage

Early 19th-Century <u>industrialization</u> in England depended upon <u>steam</u> engines made of iron and fueled by coal. Steam-powered <u>textile mills</u> created a <u>factory economy</u> and a new <u>working class</u>. Steam-powered railway <u>trains</u> moved people and products speedily over great distances, <u>concentrating</u> <u>populations</u> into expanded cities and linking the sources of raw materials with the centers of manufacturing. Functional <u>new architectural designs</u>—using structural steel— reflected the practical needs of the new society. <u>Class conflict</u>, brought on by disparities of wealth, extremes of poverty, and the unexpected difficulties of industrialization, raged throughout most of the century.

Notes

Industrialization, 19th-Century England

Coal-fueled, iron steam engines powered textile mills = factory economy + new working class.

Speedy steam-powered railroads = expanded cities; links raw materials + factories.

New steel architecture; class conflict because of income differences + effects of industrialization.

Brief Outline

19th-Century Industrialization in England

I. Steam power, the essential element

   A. Iron engines fueled by coal
   B. Textile factories, new working class
   C. RRs move masses: people, products

II. Effects of industrialization

   A. Expanded cities
   B. New architecture
   C. Class conflict: disparities of wealth

> ### SUMMARY FOR HOW TO READ HISTORY MATERIAL
> 1. *Pre-read:* Skim the chapter *heading, first and last paragraphs, subheadings.*
> 2. *Focus* on the logical order of the reading—*themes, events, cause-effect relationships, personalities*—by *framing the big picture.*
>
>   What is the chapter's theme?
>   What are the main events, causes, personalities, results?
>
> 3. *Read* the text; highlight or take notes; outline.
> 4. Be able to answer the questions you posed while *framing the big picture* and any *review questions* in the text.

How to Connect Events by Using Chronology

A consistent problem in studying history is the failure to appreciate that significant trends are often concurrent, that influential people are sometimes contemporaries. For instance, the Reformation and the Age of Exploration shared the 16th century, and the personification of absolutism, Louis XIV, reigned while the greatest scientist of the Enlightenment, Isaac Newton, formulated his theories of gravitation.

An excellent method for *connecting* events, trends, and personalities of history is to *identify their century.* History is not a series of separate strands but rather a fabric of causes, effects, and interwoven influences.

15th CENTURY The Renaissance; the fall of Constantinople to the Ottoman Turks; the voyages of Portuguese explorers and Columbus. Contemporaries: Leonardo da Vinci, Sulieman the Magnificent, Gutenberg, Henry the Navigator.

16th CENTURY The Reformation and Catholic and Counter-Reformations; the Age of Exploration; the growth of national monarchies. Contemporaries: Luther, Henry VIII, Loyola, Holy Roman Emperor Charles V, Copernicus, Elizabeth I, Phillip II.

17th CENTURY The Age of Colonization; the Commercial Revolution and the rise of capitalism; the rise of modern science; the Thirty Years' War; the Age of Absolutism and the rise of constitutionalism. Contemporaries: Descartes, Galileo, Newton, the Stuart kings and Cromwell, Grotius, Locke, Mazarin, the Romanovs, Louis XIV.

18th CENTURY The growth of capitalism; the Age of Enlightenment and of Reason; the Age of Benevolent Despotism and of Revolution. Contemporaries: Adam Smith, Voltaire, Rousseau, Frederick the Great, Mary Wollstonecraft, Maria Theresa, Catherine the Great, Louis XVI, George III, Robespierre, George Washington.

19th CENTURY The Age of Napoleon; the Age of Metternich; the Age of Romanticism; the Age of Nationalism and Unification; the Age of "ISMs"; the Age of Imperialism; the Age of Progress. Contemporaries: Talleyrand, Metternich, Chartism, Women's Suffrage, Wordsworth, Goethe, Bismarck, Cavour, Marx, Darwin, Cecil Rhodes, Teddy Roosevelt, Gregor Mendel, Louis Pasteur.

20th CENTURY The Age of Violence; the Age of Technology; the Nuclear Age; the Age of Information; the Age of Anxiety; the Age of Totalitarianism; the Cold War; the European Union; the Age of Democracy. Contemporaries: Kaiser Wilhelm, Clemenceau, Lenin, Wilson, Stalin, Hitler, Gandhi, Churchill, Freud, Einstein, Franklin Roosevelt, Hirohito, Mao, Adenauer, De Gaulle, Thatcher, Gorbacher, Reagan, Yeltsin, Walesa, Havel.

TIP

When studying a historical event, personality, or trend:

1. Determine its century (or centuries).
2. Make up an open-ended chart of the centuries, and make it a habit to place events, people, and trends in the appropriate time frame.

A Guide to the AP European History Exam

Time Allowed for Each Part of the Exam

The exam lasts a total of 3 hours and 5 minutes.

1. *55 minutes* will be allowed for *80 multiple-choice* questions.

2. *130 minutes* will be allotted for the entire *free-response* section.

3. *15 minutes* will be allowed for a mandatory reading period to analyze the *document-based question* (DBQ) documents and to consider choices of thematic essays.

4. *45 minutes* will be allowed to answer the DBQ.

5. *70 minutes* will be allotted to answer two thematic essays (*5 minutes* planning and *30 minutes* writing recommended for each of the thematic essays).

Themes

Political-diplomatic history of Europe: The nation-state; nationalism; political parties; ideologies; revolution and reform; political rights; colonialism and imperialism; diplomacy and war (30–40 percent of questions).

Economic-social history of Europe: Social classes; cultural values; industrialization; urbanization; demography; family and gender; economic systems; commerce and markets; life-styles; race and ethnicity (30–40 percent of questions).

Cultural-intellectual history of Europe: Religion; science and technology; literature and art; intellectual developments; political, social, and economic thought; secularization, education; cultural developments (20–30 percent of questions).

TIP

The importance of the roles of women in history is of significant importance because it relates to both economic-social and cultural-intellectual aspects of historical study, and therefore there are often exam questions related to this topic.

Time Span

The history of Europe from the Renaissance (1450) to contemporary times.

Multiple-Choice Questions: One half of the questions pertain to the period from the Renaissance to the French Revolution and Napoleon (1450–1815); one half pertain to the period from 1815 to the present.

Free-Response Questions: The two essays will be on subjects of significance during this period; the document-based question (DBQ) will draw on evidence pertaining to this period.

No questions in either the multiple-choice or free-response sections use pre-Renaissance information.

Scoring the Exam

The AP European History exam is composed of two sections, an 80-question multiple-choice portion with 55 minutes for completion, an essay section in which you must answer the assigned DBQ, and two free-response questions (FRQs) that you select from two groups of three questions. You will be given 130 minutes to read and interpret the documents and finish all three essays.

The multiple-choice test is scored with one point given for each correct answer. *There is no penalty for guessing as of May 2011*, so you should answer every question on the exam.

Each essay is given a score from 0 to 9 as will be detailed later in this section and throughout the sample essays seen in the book.

To attain your final AP score, the following method should be used:

AP European History Exam Composite Score Conversion Chart

Score Range	AP Score
119–180	5
100–118	4
71–99	3
60–70	2
0–59	1

Multiple-Choice Score × 1.125 = _____

+

DBQ Score × 4.5 = _____

+

FRQ 1 Score × 2.75 = _____

+

FRQ 2 Score × 2.75 = _____

Total of all above scores is composite score = _____

SCORES

5 extremely well qualified, is accepted by most colleges for either course credit or placement into a higher level section.

4 well qualified, is accepted by many colleges.

3 qualified, is accepted by some colleges.

2 possibly qualified, is rarely accepted for either credit or placement.

1 no recommendation, is not accepted anywhere.

Some colleges require additional documentation about course work.

You may choose to suppress a score on the AP exam once it has been reported to you. You may also cancel the test within a certain time after you have taken it but before the score has been reported.

Multiple-Choice Questions

The multiple-choice section consists of eighty questions, each followed by five answer choices. You have 55 minutes to complete this section. Questions will be on the social, political, economic, artistic, intellectual, and cultural history of Europe from 1450–2000 in roughly equal numbers.

Generally, you must answer close to 50 percent of the multiple-choice questions correctly and perform in the middle of the pack on your free-response section to attain a score of 3 ("qualified").

HINTS FOR TACKLING MULTIPLE-CHOICE QUESTIONS

1. Answer all questions. There is no penalty for incorrect answers.
2. The more incorrect answers you eliminate, the better the odds for guessing.
3. Be methodical. Even on questions you are sure of, put a line through the letters of the incorrect answers as they are eliminated. Circle the number of any question you are unsure of so you can return to it if you have the time.
4. Go with your intuition. Your first choice is usually correct, so change an answer only if you are absolutely certain.
5. Underline the key idea in each question.
6. Try reading the answer choices from E back to A.

Types of Multiple-Choice Questions

✔ identification
✔ analysis
✔ quotation
✔ interpretation of a picture, art object, cartoon, or photo
✔ map study
✔ graph or chart

SAMPLES OF IDENTIFICATION QUESTIONS

Of the multiple-choice questions, 35 to 40 percent tend to be *identification*.

Identification requires very specific information to link things like an idea with a thinker; a style with an artist; a dogma with a religion or ideology; a social, economic, cultural, or political environment with a geographic location, or a development with an era.

1. Machiavelli's *The Prince* (1513) was primarily

   (A) a secular handbook on modern statecraft
   (B) a guide to courtly etiquette
   (C) a scathing critique of the New Monarchies
   (D) a glorification of the independent city-states of Renaissance Italy
   (E) a pious testament to the secular role of the Popes

2. The belief that only a small portion of humanity has been elected, since the beginning of time, for eternal salvation was fundamental to

   (A) Lutheranism
   (B) Roman Catholicism
   (C) Calvinism
   (D) all Protestant sects
   (E) the Society of Jesus

3. Which best describes the 18th-century *philosophes?*

   (A) They used their satiric skills to support the *ancien régime.*
   (B) They believed in the primacy of emotion in human affairs.
   (C) They argued for social improvement based on piety and prayer.
   (D) They believed in the inevitability of human progress based upon natural law.
   (E) They rejected empirical science as incompatible with Deism.

4. Which describes the political situation in Germany in 1800, prior to Napoleon's conquests?

   (A) Thirty-nine separate and independent states
   (B) Over 300 independent political entities
   (C) A unified empire of all the German-speaking peoples in Europe
   (D) A confederation of the Northern German states
   (E) Part of the Hapsburg Empire

Answers

1. A   **2.** C   **3.** D   **4.** B

Comments

Identification questions are answerable primarily if you know the information. Analysis is applicable in eliminating inappropriate choices, but very specific information is required to zero in on the one correct answer.

If you don't have the requisite information and elimination through analysis is not possible, make your best guess.

Question 1 is the "purest" form of identification in that it requires knowledge of the significance and context of *The Prince*. Choices B, C, and E can be eliminated only if you know the basic subject matter of the book, that Castiglione wrote the classic on etiquette, that the New Monarchies supported Machiavelli's ideas. Choice D is incorrect because Machiavelli's reason for writing the book was to correct the political chaos that had been caused by disunity in the Italy of his day.

Question 2 also demands very specific information, but it is easier because the concept of the Elect or the Saints is central to Calvinism's distinguishing belief in predestination.

Question 3 allows more analysis than the previous two. Since the philosophes were critics of society before the French Revolution and the ancien régime was the existing form of government, choice A can be eliminated. Since the concept of the primacy of emotion is part of the Romantic movement that followed the French Revolution, choice B is out. Most of the philosophes were Deists, so choice C is inaccurate. Choice E is wrong because Deism is an outgrowth of the findings of empirical or natural science.

Question 4 allows some of the answers to be eliminated by applying some general understandings of German history. Choice C is easily eliminated because there has never been "a unified empire" of all the German-speaking peoples in Europe. Choice E is out because, even at its height in the early 16th century, the Hapsburg Empire did not include all of Germany. Since the North German Confederation was a creation of Bismarck just prior to the unification of Germany in the latter third of the 19th century, choice D can be eliminated. Choices A and B are left. You would have to know that Napoleon tended to consolidate independent states after his conquests in both Italy and Germany to pick choice B as the correct answer.

SAMPLE ANALYSIS QUESTIONS

Twenty to twenty-five percent of the multiple-choice questions tend to be *analysis*.

Analysis lends itself to working out the answer with more general understandings or less specific information by considering cause and effect relationships or sorting out the chronology.

1. Which of the following did NOT contribute to bringing about the Industrial Revolution?

    (A) The supremacy of Parliament after 1688, which favored the interests of large landowners
    (B) The improvement of food production, which occurred after the enclosure movement
    (C) The shift of the rural population to cities and towns
    (D) The widespread employment of the internal combustion engine
    (E) The use of steam power

2. Which best describes the nature of German military tactics in 1940?

    (A) Use of highly mobile armored forces with air support
    (B) Establishment of "impregnable" fortresses on the borders
    (C) Use of mazes of trenches to consolidate military gains
    (D) Massed infantry attacks across a broad front
    (E) Use of "terror weapons" such as V-2 rockets

3. A major result of the Treaty of Utrecht of 1713 was

    (A) that French became the "universal tongue" in Europe
    (B) the restoration of the "balance of power" on the continent
    (C) an end to the Wars of Revolution
    (D) the ascension of Louis XIV to the French throne
    (E) an end to absolutism in France

Answers

1. D   **2.**   A   **3.**   B

Comments

Analysis questions let you eliminate some answers if you can figure out that one thing could not cause another because it came later in time. Knowing the general time frame of events and developments helps immeasurably.

It is worth the trouble and time to try to figure out the answer to this type of question.

Question 1 is a classic cause-effect problem. Beware of "not." If you can determine the sequence of events, you can eliminate certain choices. Since the Enclosure Acts were passed by a Parliament that represented the interests of the rich landowners, and since they led to the migration to cities of small farmers displaced by the fencing off of common pasture lands, a labor force was created. This cause-effect relationship eliminates choices A, B, and C as factors that did not contribute to the Industrial Revolution. Even if you did not know that the use of steam power to pump water seepage from mines, to run textile mills, and to move transport was a crucial factor in industrialization, you could eliminate it if you considered the time frame of the other choice. The internal combustion engine is a late 19th century invention; the Industrial Revolution occurred from 1780 to 1830.

Question 2 can be answered by determining the general time frame of each tactic. If you did not know that the infamous *Blitzkrieg* or "lightning war" was the German tactic employing fast armor and air support that was used to defeat France during the spring of 1940, you could still use the process of elimination. Choices C and D were tactics of the "war of attrition" during the First World War. Choice E was used by the Germans near the end of World War II as a desperation measure. Choice B was a World War I tactic that was employed by the victors, the French, and would not have been used by the losers, the Germans. Winners tend to play the game the way they won; losers change the rules.

Question 3 can be answered primarily by determining time sequence. Choice C is out because the Wars of Revolution happened after the French Revolution began in 1789. Choice E is out because absolutism ended in France because of the French Revolution. Choice D is out because Louis was king during the wars that ended with the Treaty of Utrecht. He took the throne in 1647. Choice A can be eliminated because the Treaty of Utrecht was not a significant factor in the spread of French culture throughout Europe. This is a great example of choosing the *most correct* answer, which is clearly choice B as the restoration of the balance of European power was much more clearly the result of the Treaty of Utrecht than the possible furthering of a trend that was already in place.

SAMPLE QUOTATION QUESTION

Quotation analysis, like most analysis questions, can be done with less specific information than identification requires. Again chronology and cause-effect help in the process of elimination.

About 10 percent of the multiple-choice questions tend to be *quotation* analysis.

> "Not only was he accused of imprisoning and torturing or murdering his enemies, but he set into place the whole apparatus of totalitarian repression. He denied basic human rights in pushing forward his policy of industrialization, and the human cost can be measured in the deaths of tens of millions of his own countrymen. His detractors also accuse him of governing according to a 'cult of personality.'"

The individual referred to is

(A) Napoleon
(B) Lenin
(C) Hitler
(D) Stalin
(E) Tojo

Answer and Comments

(D) Choice A is incorrect because totalitarianism is an invention of the 20th century and because Napoleon neither effected industrialization nor killed millions of his countrymen. Choice B is out because Lenin did not rule long enough to do this and because the description does not seem to fit his character. Choice C is out because although Hitler murdered 12 million people as part of his racist policies, they were not all his countrymen. Choices D and E would seem to fit. The key phrase was his *own* countrymen. Tojo is responsible for tens of millions of deaths, most of which were Chinese and Korean deaths.

Chronology was the prime sorter here. A specific bit of information was the last piece of the puzzle.

SAMPLE INTERPRETATION QUESTION

Less than 10 percent of the multiple-choice questions are this type.

Interpretation can involve identifying the artist, style, subject, or period of a work of art; it may require interpretation of a cartoon, photo, or picture.

What innovation in painting was developed by Renaissance artists?

(A) The use of color
(B) The use of religious themes
(C) The illusion of depth
(D) The use of symbolism
(E) The use of abstract geometric figures

Answer and Comments

(C) Perspective, or the illusion of depth, was a technical innovation of the Renaissance painters. Religious themes and symbolism were used by the medievals; color was used even by the ancients. Abstract art belongs to the 20th century.

SAMPLE MAP INTERPRETATION QUESTION

Map interpretation questions require very general map skills and less general information to work out. They are worth the time and trouble to examine.

Less than 10 percent of the multiple-choice questions are map interpretations.

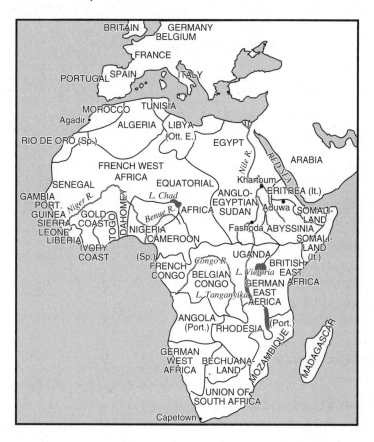

The map above represents Africa in what year?

(A) 1880
(B) 1914
(C) 1939
(D) 1946
(E) 1975

Answer and Comments

(B) Go for the obviously incorrect choices first. Choice E is out because the map does not show most of the nations of contemporary Africa. Choices D and C are incorrect because the Italian and German colonies would certainly have been lost after the defeats in World War II, and the German colonies were seized after World War I. That leaves choice A, which is wrong because Africa was terra incognita before the start of imperialism in 1880, and choice B, which is correct because it marks the highwater period of imperialism.

SAMPLE CHART QUESTION

Less than 10 percent of the multiple-choice questions are of this type.

Graphs and charts frequently provide all the information necessary in order to answer the question correctly. Graphs are diagrams representing successive changes; charts are information sheets that employ tables or graphs.

Population of Cities in Thousands

Year	Cities				
	London	Paris	Antwerp	Berlin	Moscow
1800	960	600	60	170	250
1850	2,700	1,400	90	500	360
1900	6,500	3,700	280	2,700	1,000

Which would be the most likely explanation for the population rise between 1800 and 1900 in the cities included on the chart above?

(A) Malthusian "unbridled lust"
(B) Foreign immigration
(C) Population shift from other cities
(D) Increase in the average life span
(E) Industrialization

Answer and Comments

(E) The clue to the correct answer is in the early, nearly sevenfold increase of the population of London. Since the Industrial Revolution coincided with a mass movement from the countryside to the cities that also may have been caused by the enclosure movement, and since both began in Britain then caught on later in the rest of Europe, the answer is choice E, industrialization.

Free-Response Section

This section requires you to write three essays total: one document-based question (DBQ), and two free-response questions (FRQs). You must respond to the only DBQ prompt presented, but you will be able to choose each FRQ question from a group of three essay prompts.

You will be given a total of 2 hours and 10 minutes to plan and write all three essays. This time will be further broken down by the test proctor into 15 minutes to read the questions and documents and make notes on them, and 115 minutes to write all three essays. It is recommended that you take 45 minutes to write the DBQ response and 35 minutes for each FRQ response.

Free-Response Section Scoring

All essays on the exam are scored on a scale of 1–9. There is a rubric that is used for all DBQ questions, and separate rubrics are developed by the readers of the exam for each FRQ question that vary according to the question. In general, a score of

0–2 is an inferior essay, a score of 3–4 is an adequate essay, a score of 5–6 is an average essay, and a score of 7–8 is above average, while a score of 9 is reserved for only the most superior essays.

Interpreting the Essay Questions

In both the thematic essay and the document-based question (DBQ), it is necessary to understand the way in which the answer is to be presented. In order to do this, you must interpret the *key term or terms* in the question.

EXAMPLES OF KEY TERMS

1. *Defend or refute* (argue for or against a specific statement by framing an essay that uses *factual support*)

   Sample:

   "World War II was the inevitable result of a failure of the democracies to confront aggression by totalitarian dictatorships."

   Defend or refute this with factual evidence from the diplomatic history of the 1930s.

2. *Analyze* (examine in detail; determine relationships; explain)

   Sample:

   Analyze the ways in which the Protestant Reformation fostered both the growth of capitalism and the rise of modern science.

3. *Evaluate* (judge the worth of; discuss advantages and disadvantages, pluses and minuses)

   Sample:

   Evaluate both the domestic policies and the foreign involvements of the government of France during the reign of Louis XIV.

4. *To what extent and in what ways* (how and how much?)

   Sample:

   "*To what extent and in what ways* did Napoleon carry out the ideals of the French Revolution?"

5. *Assess the validity* (judge the value of; determine the truth)

   Sample:

   "The religious wars of the 16th and 17th centuries were more the result of the territorial ambitions of rival states and the economic interests of competing factions than of doctrinal differences."

   Assess the validity of this statement.

6. *Contrast and compare* (show differences and examine for similarities)

   Sample:

   "*Contrast and compare* the art and architecture of the Renaissance with that of the Romantic period and explain how each reflected the prevailing culture."

7. *Explain* (offer the meaning, the cause, the reason for; make clear; detail)

   Sample:

   "*Explain* how the theories of Copernicus, Galileo, Kepler, and Newton impacted the religious beliefs and intellectual trends of the 17th and 18th centuries."

8. Discuss (consider various points of view; write about; examine)

   Sample:

   "Discuss the accomplishments of the various governments in France during the French Revolution."

9. Describe (tell about; offer an account or a word picture)

   Sample:

   "Describe the life-style of noble women in Italy during the Italian Renaissance. Refer to family life, political status, and economic conditions."

Additional sample and practice free-response questions will appear in the review chapters and in the sample exams.

The Document-Based Essay Question (DBQ)

The DBQ is designed to test your ability to analyze documentary materials and use that analysis to support a thesis proposed by the prompt. Each DBQ question is followed by a short historical background that you should read. The way the scoring works most years, *the DBQ, if properly done, can often get more than one half of the points needed to attain a score of "3" on the exam.* This section is based upon a skill that can be developed by using documents and the author's points of view in those documents to prove a historical point. Thus, this skill is worth practicing.

The first key to success on the DBQ is to understand how the question is scored. The readers all must use a rigid rubric for grading the DBQ that, if understood, can be used to your advantage. An outline of that rubric follows.

DBQ Rubric

Basic Core

Score one point if accomplished	**Basic Core:** If any one of the following tasks is not performed, *the essay cannot get a score higher than 6.* The basic core points are objective like a checklist with one point for each.

1. Provides an appropriate, explicitly stated thesis that directly addresses all parts of the question—**thesis may not simply restate the question**.

2. Discusses a majority of the documents individually and specifically.

3. Demonstrates understanding of the basic meaning of a majority of the documents (may misinterpret no more than one).

4. Supports the thesis with appropriate interpretations of a majority of the documents.

5. Analyzes point of view or bias in at least three documents.

6. Analyzes documents by explicitly organizing them in at least three appropriate groups.

Sum of Scores Above:	***Only* if all six of the above criteria are met**, then the writer may attain a score of 7–9 if the writer can accomplish the expanded core elements. The more thoroughly the writer completes any of the following elements, the higher the additional score will be.

Expanded Core

Expanded Core: If all core requirements are met, the writer may score points in any of the criteria below. *Very thorough application of any element below can score multiple points.* A **maximum** of 3 points may be awarded on the expanded core area. Scoring here is more subjective, and this section is not a checklist and to be awarded points writers must clearly accomplish any of the additional scoring criteria:

- The thesis is clear, analytical, and comprehensive.

- The essay uses all or almost all documents.

- Addresses all parts of the question thoroughly.

- Uses documents persuasively as evidence.

- Shows understanding of nuances in the documents.

- Analyzes point of view or bias in at least four documents cited in the essay.

- Analyzes the documents in additional ways, or groupings.

- Brings in relevant "outside" historical content.

Total sum of core plus any expanded points	If core score was 6, then add any expanded points to the core to get a final score from 0–9.

If you can write an essay in 45 minutes that completes all of these elements, then you will be very successful on the DBQ.

Rules for Writing the DBQ

There are a few rules to writing a successful DBQ. If these rules are followed, then the essay will be at the top of the scoring scale.

✔ **Answer the question.** It is amazing how many students do not directly answer the question, but go off on some tangent. Remember to check that the thesis addresses all parts of the question before proving the thesis.

✔ **Read the documents** and write comments on them, including letters to indicate to what group each belongs. If groups are positive or negative reactions, use ±.

✔ **Create an outline** and check that you will prove the thesis with it.

✔ **Group the documents** to show they are understood and can be analyzed. There will usually be some way to group the documents to show profession, nationality, class, or some other factor that affects the outlook of the document's author.

✔ **Integrate the use of the documents** smoothly into the overall reasoning of the essay, and do not make it a laundry list of documents and points of view. It is important not to accept all documents at face value but to analyze them for *validity*, *origin*, and *purpose* of the author. Use the documents to answer the question and to show understanding and the ability to aptly use them as evidence.

✔ **Stay within the time frame** of the question. The question will usually give a specific time frame—do not use anachronistic information.

✔ Write an essay with good structure that **follows grammatical conventions**. Use the past tense, avoid clichés and terms like "the people," "history has taught us," "thing," "stuff," and oversimplistic generalizations such as good or bad, and always refer to authors and other historical figures by their last names or royal titles.

✔ **Read and use the source citations**. The information given in those citations is critical to demonstrating point of view.

✔ The key to writing a successful DBQ response is to do a good job presenting **point of view**. Remember that the reader will generally attribute persuasive document use, as well as expanded point of view use, to the writer who uses point of view well and often. An essay can receive more than one expanded core point just for doing an excellent job on point of view. In reference to the DBQ, point of view is best described as not just saying what an author wrote, but *why* the author wrote it. The focus is on *why* the author would choose to write in the tone chosen, or choose the specific words that were used.

Apart from not directly answering the question asked, not demonstrating clear point of view for the documents is the most common error that students make. If many points of view of many authors is shown, then your DBQ response will likely be a success.

Sample DBQ

TIME:
15 MINUTES TO READ AND MARK DOCUMENTS.
45 MINUTES TO WRITE ESSAY.

Directions: The following question is based upon documents 1–12. (These documents may have been edited in order to engage the student.)

The DBQ is designed to test your ability to read and interpret documents. Show your mastery of this skill by analyzing the content and the <u>point of view and validity of the source's author</u>. Answer the question fully by utilizing your analysis of the documents and the time period discussed to support a well-constructed essay.

1. Analyze the various responses and reactions to the changes brought on by the advances in methods of production in Great Britain from the 1770s through the 1880s and how those reactions changed over time.

   Historical Background: James Watt's 1765 condensing chamber steam engine, combined with the spread of the concept of the division of labor, allowed the British to develop their production methods far beyond those which the world had ever seen. Before the Industrial Revolution, most people lived rurally, and cities were centers of commerce, but production was accomplished throughout the countryside. Cities like Manchester had population booms. Lifestyles and the concept of class changed drastically. The structure of the family and the morés of society went through significant changes.

Document 1

Source: P. Bairoch International Industrialization Levels from 1750 to 1980 as published in the *Journal of European History* fall of 1982.

Industrialization Levels in Great Britain from 1750 to 1913

Year	Level per capita with 100 being equal to 1900 production
1750	10
1800	16
1830	25
1860	64
1880	87
1900	100
1913	115

Document 2

Source: Philosopher and economist, Adam Smith, *An Inquiry into the Nature and Causes of the Wealth of Nations*, 1776.

I have seen a small manufactory where ten men only were employed, and where some of them consequently performed two or three distinct operations. Those ten persons could make among them upwards of forty-eight thousand pins in a day. Each person might be considered as making four thousand eight hundred pins in a day. But if they had all wrought separately and independently, they certainly could not each of them have made twenty, perhaps not one pin in a day. That is a consequence of a proper division and combination of their different operations.

Document 3

Source: Letter from the Cloth Merchants of Leeds, England, advocating for the introduction of steam powered looms, 1791.

In the manufacture of Woollens, the Scribbling Mill, the spinning frame, and the fly shuttle, have reduced manual labor nearly one third, and each of them at its first introduction carried an alarm to the work people, yet each has contributed to advance the wages and to increase the trade, so that if an attempt was now made to deprive us of the use of them, there is no doubt, but every person engaged in the business, would exert himself to defend them.

Document 4

Source: Richard Guest, *Compendious History of the Cotton Manufacture* (Manchester 1823), pp. 44–48.

It is a curious circumstance, that, when the Cotton Manufacture was in its infancy, all the operations were completed under the roof of the weaver's cottage. At the present time, all the operations are again performed in a single building. Those vast brick edifices in the vicinity of all the great manufacturing towns which strike the attention and excite the curiosity of the traveler, now perform labors which formerly employed whole villages.

Document 5

Source: Fanny Kemble, British Actress, Description of her first ride on a railroad, 1830.

You can't imagine how strange it was to be traveling on thus, without any visible means of progress other than magical machine. When I closed my eyes, this sensation of flying was quite delightful and strange beyond description; yet strange as it was, I had a sense of security and not the slightest fear.

Document 6

Source: Andrew Ure, Glasgow professor, *The Philosophy of the Manufacturers*, 1835

This island is pre-eminent among civilized nations for the prodigious development of its factory wealth, and has been therefore long viewed with a jealous admiration by foreign powers. This very pre-eminence, however, has been contemplated in a very different light by many influential members of our own community, and has been even denounced by them as the certain origin of innumerable evils to the people, and of revolutionary convulsions to the state. I believe such allegations and fears will prove to be groundless.

Document 7

Source: *The People's Petition*, a petition circulated and sent to Parliament, 1838

With all the elements of national prosperity, and with every disposition and capacity to take advantage of them, we find ourselves overwhelmed with public and private suffering. Required as we are, universally, to support and obey the laws, nature and reason entitle us to demand, that in the making of the laws, the universal voice shall be implicitly listened to.

WE DEMAND UNIVERSAL SUFFRAGE.

The suffrage to be exempt from the corruption of the wealthy, and the violence of the powerful, must be secret.

Document 8

Source: Patience Kershaw, age 17, Halifax, testimony to Parliament, 1842

I go to pit at 5 o'clock in the morning and come out at 5 in the evening; I get my breakfast, porridge and milk, first; I take my dinner with me, a cake, and eat it as I go; I do not stop or rest at any time for the purpose, I get nothing else until I get home, and then have potatoes and meat, not every day meat.

Document 9

Source: Philosopher and economist Karl Marx, *The Communist Manifesto*, 1848

The bourgeois sees his wife a mere instrument of production. He hears that the instruments of production are to be exploited in common, and, naturally, can come to no other conclusion that the lot of being common to all will likewise fall to the women.

He has not even a suspicion that the real point aimed at is to do away with the status of women as mere instruments of production.

Document 10

Source: British Illustration, 1860s.

Document 11

Source: Harriet Robinson's autobiography after she married well, *Lowell Mill Girls,* 1883

One of the first strikes that ever took place in this country was in Lowell in 1836. One of the girls stood on a pump and gave vent to the feelings of her companions in a neat speech, declaring that it was their duty to resist all attempts at cutting down the wages. It is hardly necessary to say that, so far as practical results are concerned, this strike did no good. The girls were soon tired of holding out, and they went back to their work at the reduced rate of wages.

Document 12

Source: Thomas Escott, *England: Her People, Polity, and Pursuits*, 1885

Before the eventful year 1832, most of the places under Government were in the hands of the great families. The Reform Bill admitted an entirely new element into political life; a host of applicants for Parliamentary position at once came forward, and as a consequence the social citadel was carried by persons who had nothing to do with the purely aristocratic section which had hitherto been paramount.

COMMENTS ON THE DBQ

This type of question is common for the DBQ because it asks you to describe the *reactions* and *responses* to some event or movement and how they changed over time. There are two tasks to this question. The first task is to identify the *reactions* and *responses* of Europeans to the rise of the Industrial Revolution. The second task is to illustrate how those *reactions* and *responses* changed over time.

The first task is accomplished by reading the documents, analyzing the documents and making notes on them, grouping them, and using them to illustrate how Europeans reacted and responded to the new methods of production that were emblematic of the Industrial Revolution.

The second task is made easier because the documents are presented in chronological order. You can choose to have separate paragraphs, illustrating how the reactions and responses changed over time, or to illustrate how responses and reactions changed over time within each paragraph about a separate group of documents.

Do not forget to *demonstrate point of view* for many of the documents, which will further help to illustrate the reactions and possibly responses of Europeans to the onset of the Industrial Revolution.

Grouping documents is critical to success, and there are many ways to group the documents presented in this DBQ. Possible groupings include those who viewed the Industrial Revolution in a positive light, those who viewed the Industrial Revolution in a negative light, the bourgeois bosses and their proponents, workers, and those who observed society, such as historians and artists.

It is best to create a short outline. The structure that is easiest to write quickly includes a thesis that addresses both parts of the question and includes all of the groups you intend to use. Each group identified should have a separate paragraph, with a possible paragraph on change over time, followed by a concluding paragraph.

TIP

Before writing your essay, glance at the documents and their authors, and check the question to be certain that your thesis and your essay address all parts of the question.

DBQ Sample Response

The evolution in the ways that goods were produced brought profound changes, first to Great Britain, and then to the rest of the world, during the Industrial Revolution, which increased Great Britain's production capabilities (document 1). Reactions and responses to these changes evolved as the era developed and can be understood through the eyes of those who observed society such as historians and artists (documents 2, 12, 9, 6, 4, 10), the bourgeois bosses and their proponents (documents 3, 6, 5), and the workers (documents 8, 11, 7).

Historians and others who commented on society changed their views on the means of production as these means evolved. Adam Smith, the father of economics, was very excited by the increases in productive capacity brought on by the introduction of the division of labor (document 2). As the first British student of economic conditions, he was naturally impressed by the gains made in that field. Richard Guest also thought the changes made when cottage industry was moved to the factory were notable (document 4). Andrew Ure must have been a proponent of manufacturers even though he was a university professor because he was denouncing the critics of the factories in 1835 just after the Reform Bill of 1832 was passed (document 6). Karl Marx, the ultimate critic of capitalism, points out how this system of economy, and thus of production, exploits women by its very nature (document 9). He was likely to over-exaggerate the flaws of a system of which he was calling for the downfall. As the Industrial Revolution progressed, observers started to extol the virtues of the factory system again as can be seen in the drawing showing people's acknowledgement of the impressive nature of new machinery (document 10). By the 1880s, historians like Escott were assessing the changes in the political climate (document 12). It appears that those who observed these changes professionally were at first in favor, then turned against these changes, and finally came to accept and study these changes.

One group that seemed to be universally in favor of the changes in production was the bourgeois bosses and their proponents. As time progressed, the bosses felt their power grow and demanded more control of their workers and their property. The Leeds wool manufacturers argued that their new methods of production were helping everyone in society, although they did note the fears of the workers (document 3). They were attempting to sway opinion in their direction to allow them to create steam powered wool looms, so their facts were suspect due to their motives to increase output and thus profit. Professor Ure, a likely apologist for the bourgeoisie to the title of his book, defends the changes in production methods (document 6). Fanny Kemble appears very supportive of the largest change in producing transportation with her ringing endorsement of the railroad (document 5). As an actress who played mostly for bourgeois audiences, she was supporting the class who supported her living. By 1844, employers could get away with draconian rules that made working conditions difficult for workers (document 10). The community of business men continually favored changes in the modes of production over time.

Those who worked or who had worked in the factories seemed to think of the changes brought on by the Industrial Revolution in negative terms despite the fact that these changes had nearly doubled their standard of living by 1850. The People's Charter of 1838 demanded more rights for workers, such as voting, in order to help them address the ills of the factory system (document 7). This charter became the basis for the worker's chartist movement that eventually did enlarge the franchise. A teen mine worker testified to parliament about the difficulty of her life in the mines (document 8). She may have embellished a bit due to the public spectacle of the parliamentary investigation, but it is likely that she had a meager existence. The rules of the factory in document 10 also support the view of the workers that their lives were difficult. The autobiography of a former worker explaining a strike may have been motivated by the fact that she married out of her class and wanted to do something to better the lot of those with whom she used to work (document 11). Workers continued to look negatively at the changes brought on by the Industrial Revolution across the century.

The responses and reactions of the people living in Great Britain from 1770 through 1880 to the changes in production seem to be based upon their station in life with social observers changing their views to suit the times, employers being in favor of the changes, and workers being against them.

COMMENTS ON THE SAMPLE ANSWER TO THE DBQ

This is a top notch answer that would receive a **score of 8 or 9**. This essay demonstrates insightful use of documents to prove a cogent *thesis that fully addresses all parts of the question.*

This essay should certainly meet all of the core requirements because it has a thesis that makes sense, demonstrates proper use of all documents to support the thesis, analyzes point of view in more than three documents, and creates at least three groups of documents.

A sample scored rubric for this essay is on page 32. Notice that some expanded core categories have an X. That is where the essay meets the requirements; note that one point is **not** awarded for each mark.

The first key to success on the DBQ is to understand how the question is scored. The readers all must use a rigid rubric for grading the DBQ that, if understood, can be used to your advantage. An outline of that rubric is on the following page.

The essay receives expanded core points for demonstrating point of view in at least eight documents, has a clear, analytical, and comprehensive thesis, uses all of the documents, brings in relevant outside information such as the chartist movement, demonstrates an insightful and complete analysis of the documents, and uses the documents persuasively. The essay, however, does not have additional groupings. Because of that one missing element, the essay may not receive a 9, but if the reader believes that the essay excelled in other areas such as point of view, then the scorer can give it a 9, which seems most likely in this case.

The most important characteristic of this response is the creative use of point of view to demonstrate command of the skill of using primary sources. The use of point of view in document 5 was creative and historically supportable. The essay also had some panache without using clichés, which may set it apart from other essays the graders read.

For more information on scoring DBQ essays, turn to "DBQ Rubric" on page 23.

DBQ Rubric for Sample Essay

Basic Core

Score one point if accomplished	**Basic Core:** If any one of the following tasks is not performed, *the essay cannot get a score higher than 6.* The basic core points are objective like a checklist with one point for each.
1	1. Provides an appropriate, explicitly stated thesis that directly addresses all parts of the question—**thesis may not simply restate the question**.
1	2. Discusses a majority of the documents individually and specifically.
1	3. Demonstrates understanding of the basic meaning of a majority of the documents (may misinterpret no more than one).
1	4. Supports the thesis with appropriate interpretations of a majority of the documents.
1	5. Analyzes point of view or bias in at least three documents.
1	6. Analyzes documents by explicitly organizing them in at least three appropriate groups.
Sum of Scores Above: 6	*Only* **if all six of the above criteria are met**, then the writer may attain a score of 7–9 if the writer can accomplish the expanded core elements. The more thoroughly the writer completes any of the following elements, the higher the additional score will be.

Expanded Core

	Expanded Core: If all core requirements are met, the writer may score points in any of the criteria below. *Very thorough application of any element below can score multiple points.* A **maximum** of 3 points may be awarded on the expanded core area. Scoring here is more subjective, and this section is not a checklist and to be awarded points writers must clearly accomplish any of the additional scoring criteria:
X	• The thesis is clear, analytical, and comprehensive.
X	• The essay uses all or almost all documents.
X	• Addresses all parts of the question thoroughly.
X	• Uses documents persuasively as evidence.
X	• Shows understanding of nuances in the documents.
X	• Analyzes point of view or bias in at least four documents cited in the essay.
X	• Analyzes the documents in additional ways, or groupings.
X	• Brings in relevant "outside" historical content.
Total sum of expanded points plus core 6 + 3 = 9.	All six core points were awarded and all three expanded core points were awarded as well.

Thematic Essay Question

The thematic essay part of the free-response section requires you to answer two interpretive questions that measure both knowledge and analytical skills. They are designed to test your understanding of the events and trends of the political-diplomatic, economic-social, and cultural-intellectual history of Europe from 1450 to contemporary times. Like any essay question, they are open to subjective interpretation both in answering and in evaluating the answer. It helps to be a good writer, to interpret the question accurately, to design an approach, to marshal relevant data, to present it all clearly. The essays require a broader and deeper understanding of the history than the multiple-choice section does, but they can be a showpiece for a good grasp of the subject.

HINTS FOR ANSWERING THE THEMATIC ESSAY QUESTIONS

1. Read all the choices before deciding on which two to do.
2. Underline each task in each question and count the tasks. Try to take on the question in each group that has the fewest tasks that can be fully answered.
3. Your primary consideration should be *how much you know about the specific subject*. This may seem obvious, but it is easy to pass over a question if you are confused about what it asks. Read. Reread those questions that encompass areas you have focused on in class or in your studies.
4. Interpret the *key terms*. (See pages 21–22.)
5. Make your choice by *mentally framing* the argument of your essay. (The "argument" is the point of view, the proof, the statement, the thesis, the core of your essay, and you should follow your intuitions since they flow from what you know most about.)
6. Read the question again and *jot down anything* that comes to mind.
7. Organize your essay by *outlining* your argument. Don't fret over format; you are the only one who is going to see or use the outline.
8. *Gather facts* to support your argument. (If you are not certain of a fact—a date, an event, a cause, a person—*don't use it*.)
9. *Check for consistency.* What seems like supporting evidence may actually contradict your assertions.
10. Be certain the thesis addresses all parts of the question and that evidence is strong enough to support that thesis before beginning to write.
11. Now, you are ready to write. Make a *clear statement of the intent* of your argument in the introduction, a *clear summary* of your argument in the conclusion.
12. *Reread! Rewrite!* Delete. Add. "Substance takes precedence over neatness." Don't be afraid to cross out words, sentences, whole paragraphs, whole pages.

How to Write an Essay

It is a lot easier than you think . . . if you pick the right question, interpret the terms correctly, and follow a few simple procedures. The tricks to picking the right question and interpreting its terms are given in the preceding section.

What then are these "simple" procedures?

THE ESSENCE OF YOUR ESSAY IS THE BODY

It is here that you do your job of showing "to what extent and in what ways," or of "assessing the validity," or of "contrasting and comparing," or of "explaining," and so on. The introduction simply points out the direction your argument will take. The conclusion simply summarizes your argument. What you have to do is write a clear, convincing argument in your essay. (Remember, an "argument," as used here, is whatever you write to answer the question.)

The Simple Procedures

✔ First, ask yourself what the question wants to know.
✔ Second, ask yourself what you know about it.
✔ Third, ask yourself how you put it into words.

SAMPLE QUESTION

To what extent and in what ways did Napoleon carry out the ideals of the French Revolution?

First, what does the question want to know?

"How and how much did Napoleon, an autocrat, fulfill the democratic aims of the Revolution?"

Second, ask yourself what you know about it?

Napoleon was a dictator and an emperor and both are generally undemocratic roles.

He made domestic reforms in the law, education, and government that furthered democracy. He carried the ideals of the Revolution—"liberty, equality, fraternity"—to other countries during his conquests. He had personal reasons for trying to change the "old order."

Third, how should you put it into words?

Write about the historical irony: one of history's "bad guys"—a dictator, conqueror, and vainglorious emperor—actually helped the experiment in democracy, called the French Revolution, get put into practice.

There are two mainstream ways to structure this essay. You could write a thesis paragraph, then one paragraph about the extent to which Napoleon carried out the ideals of the French Revolution and another about how he carried them out across Europe, or there could be a thesis, then one paragraph about each major ideal: liberty, equality, brotherhood, and "Enlightenment ideals" in general. Another advanced method could be to trace Napoleon's narrative as those ideals were carried out chronologically and/or geographically evaluating Napoleon's progress along the way with a strong thesis either at the start or the end, but preferably *the thesis will be stated at BOTH the beginning and end of every FRQ essay.*

Use the *Simple Procedures* to plan the body of every essay.
Use the *Hints for Answering the Thematic Essay Questions* to do the actual writing.

How Will the College Board Score the Free-Response Question?

As Sun Tzu stated in *The Art of War*, "If you know your enemy and you know yourself, you cannot be defeated in one hundred battles." In the case of test preparation, the test and its graders are your "enemy," and understanding the rubrics for the DBQ and the FRQ will help you defeat them. A sample rubric for the sample FRQ is seen below:

9–8 POINTS

- ✔ Thesis explicitly identifies **both** the extent to which and in what ways Napoleon carried out the ideals of the French Revolution. Thesis does not need to be in the opening paragraph.
- ✔ Organization is clear, consistently followed, and effective in support of the argument.
  - May devote individual paragraphs to an examination of the extent and manner in which Napoleon carried out the ideals of the French Revolution.
  - Must identify individual ideals of the French Revolution (liberty, equality, and brotherhood, among any other Enlightenment ideals that may also be presented) and consider the extent to which and how each of the ideals of the French Revolution were carried out by Napoleon; does not have to present both categories for each ideal.
- ✔ Essay is well balanced; the extent to which and in what ways Napoleon carried out the ideals of the French Revolution are analyzed at some length. Essay covers the rise, reign, and fall of Napoleon to some extent.
- ✔ Major assertions in the essay are supported thoroughly and consistently by relevant evidence.
- ✔ Evidence of the spread of these ideals may prove more specific or concrete.
- ✔ May contain errors that do not detract from the argument.

7–6 POINTS

- ✔ Thesis explicitly identifies **both** the extent to which and in what ways Napoleon carried out the ideals of the French Revolution, but may not be developed fully.
- ✔ Organization is clear and effective in support of the argument but may introduce evidence that is not pertinent to the task.

✔ Essay covers all major topics suggested by the prompt but may analyze an aspect of Napoleon's rule, ideal of the French Revolution, or the extent to which Napoleon carried out that ideal in greater depth rather than in a balanced manner.

✔ Major assertions in the essay are supported by relevant evidence.

✔ May contain an error that detracts from the argument.

5–4 POINTS

✔ Thesis identifies **both** the extent to which and in what ways Napoleon carried out the ideals of the French Revolution but without any development; thesis may address only part of the question effectively; thesis may be a simple, single-sentence statement.

✔ Organization is clear but may not be consistently followed; essay may veer off task chronologically or thematically or both.

✔ Essay may not complete all tasks:
  • May discuss only the extent to which OR what ways Napoleon spread the ideals of the French Revolution.
  • May discuss only two or fewer ideals of the French Revolution.
  • May focus only on one nation.
  • May be primarily descriptive rather than analytical.

✔ Essay offers some relevant evidence.

✔ May contain errors that detract from the argument.

3–2 POINTS

✔ Thesis may simply paraphrase the prompt OR identify Napoleon or the ideals of the French Revolution without analyzing the extent to which he carried them out or the methods he employed to that end.

✔ Organization is unclear and ineffective; essay may focus on the personal attributes of Napoleon rather than analyzing the extent to which he carried out the ideals of the French Revolution or the methods he employed to that end.

✔ Essay shows serious imbalance; discussion of the ways and extent to which Napoleon carried out the ideals of the French Revolution is superficial; much of the information may be significantly out of the time period or geography of the question.

✔ Offers minimal OR confused evidence.

✔ May contain several errors that detract from the argument.

1–0 POINTS

✔ Thesis is erroneous OR irrelevant OR absent.

✔ No effective organization is evident.

✔ Discussion of the ways and extent to which Napoleon carried out the ideals of the French Revolution is generic.

✔ Provides little or no relevant supporting evidence.

✔ May contain numerous errors that detract from the argument.

PART TWO

REVIEW SECTION

The Italian Renaissance, The Northern Renaissance (1450–1550)

Key Terms/People

- Renaissance
- quattrocento
- city-states
- pagan
- The Medici Family
- Leonardo da Vinci
- Michelangelo Buonarroti
- Petrarch
- Boccaccio
- Baldassare Catiglione

- Niccolo Machiavelli
- Desiderius Erasmus
- Thomas More
- Johann Gutenberg
- Albrecht Dürer
- Elizabethan Age
- Laura Cereta
- secularism
- humanism
- individualism

Overview

While the *Renaissance* was a period of artistic, cultural, and intellectual revival, the term "Renaissance," a rebirth, can be misleading. It implies that the 15th and 16th centuries marked a distinct awakening for Europeans from the "darkness" of the Middle Ages. Actually, the medieval period gave rise to the basic institutions of Europe, its laws, languages, and economics. The elite culture that developed during the *quattrocento* (Italian for 15th century) in the city-states of the Italian peninsula, though, not only borrowed from the ancient cultures of Greece and Rome but also expressed a new conception of humankind—individualism—through innovative art and literature. It was in these independent domains, governed by a merchant class, despots, or republicans, that pure secularism (a belief that life was more than a preparation for the hereafter) first appeared in the modern world.

Humanism (a literary movement that was truly modern in that a class of non-clerical writers concerned themselves with secular issues) rose in Italy in the 14th and 15th centuries and found a special affinity with classical Greek and Roman culture. In Northern Europe, the "pagan" humanism of the Italian Renaissance was rejected in favor of a blend of religion and classical literature. Christian humanists, such as Erasmus and Thomas More, tried to recapture the moral force of early Christianity by studying the Greek and Hebrew texts of the Bible and the writings of the Church Fathers.

Whether or not the Renaissance marks the beginning of the modern age, it provided a conception of the role and destiny of humankind vastly different from that of the Middle Ages, and its artistic achievements influenced the culture of all of Europe.

Since the Renaissance is defined less by specific events than by individual accomplishments and ideas, the following review focuses on significant personalities, achievements, and concepts. First, though, a few words about the setting for one of the most creative periods in all of human history.

The Italian Renaissance

The Italian City-States

By the 15th century, certain Northern Italian towns—which had been trade centers of the Roman Empire—had expanded into independent city-states that ruled wide areas of the surrounding countryside.

"Geography is destiny" proved true for the Italians of the 14th and 15th centuries. Fragmented as a nation since the fall of Rome, a battleground for the more unified peoples of Europe, they took advantage of their proximity to the sea and applied the energy that springs from being always at the focus of crisis to establish a seagoing trade with the peoples in the eastern Mediterranean. They became the "middlemen" of Europe.

THE MAJOR CITY-STATES

Republic of Florence (considered the cultural center of the Italian Renaissance; often compared to ancient Athens for its utter brilliance over a brief period)

- ✔ Republic of Genoa
- ✔ Duchy of Milan
- ✔ Rome, the Papal states
- ✔ Naples, Kingdom of the Two Sicilies
- ✔ Venice, Venetian Republic

Venice, Genoa, and Pisa (in the Republic of Florence) used their strategic locations on the Mediterranean to control the European trade with the Middle East and Asia; Florence, and, to a lesser extent, Rome, Naples, and Milan thrived as manufacturing and market centers. Bankers from all of these prosperous cities made profitable loans to the popes and to the monarchs of Europe and financed successful commercial ventures.

The economic power of these city-states, combined with Rome as the center of Catholic power, made Italy a center of culture and luxury in Western Europe during the 14th and 15th centuries. As a major cog in trade routes between Europe and Asia, Italian city-states helped to spread ideas from different cultures around the world throughout Europe. The city-states shared Arab mathematics and technology, as well as Asian ideas and products, to the continent. The presence of ideas from many cultures and the revival of ancient Greek and Roman ideas, which revived a sense of Italian pride in their past, all contributed to creating a prosperous merchant-centered society that fostered the age of the Renaissance.

This powerful middle class of merchants and bankers controlled the governments of the city-states and served as patrons to the artistic geniuses of the times. Their new-found wealth encouraged appreciation of earthly pleasures and diminished dedication to the pious traditions of the Middle Ages. It was not that most were irreligious, but rather that accidents of history and geography presented them with great wealth, far beyond any expectations of the subsistence feudal economy that had ruled Europe for a thousand years. Money is meant to be spent. It just so happened that the more they spent on the beautiful handiwork of the skilled artisans in their cities, the more beautiful things were made for the buying. Beauty for its own sake, and art for art's sake, values lost to Europeans with the end of the ancient world, replaced the medieval notion that art not dedicated to God is irreverent. To these people, the world could be changed without the help of God. "Money is power" was never more true. Secularism was born. The rich nurtured it; the lower classes copied it.

The Medici Family

This was the most famous dynasty of those merchants and bankers who used their vast wealth both to govern the city-states and to patronize illustrious creators in the arts.

Giovanni de' Medici (d. 1429): Merchant and banker of Florence, founder of the dynasty. He could be considered one of the world's first modern people, an ultimate adapter who ignored the church's prohibitions of lending for interest to provide the necessary funds for a changing world economy. Although his son and great-grandson were the ones who brought glory to the family name by spending the fortune that he established, his originality is reflected in his deeds rather than his ideas, and he is one of the people of Europe whose restless genius molded the modern world.

Cosimo de' Medici (1389–1464): Son of Giovanni who used the family fortune to fill the vacuum of power created by the lack of a national monarchy. Allied with other powerful families of Florence, he became unofficial ruler of the republic.

Lorenzo the Magnificent (1449–1492): Cosimo's grandson, not only the republic's ruler but a lavish patron of the arts. He personified the Renaissance attitude of living life rather than waiting for its fulfillment after death. His genius was his recognition and support of the creative talent in his city; his luck was to be surrounded by geniuses.

The Medici family ruled the Grand Duchy of Tuscany, of which Florence was the principal city, well into the 18th century. Two popes, many cardinals, and two queens of France belonged to the family.

Individualism, A New Conception of Humankind

"Man is the measure of all things." A sense of human power replaced religious awe. Pleasure and accomplishment superseded the medieval dedication to the cloistered life of the clergy. Instead of the disdain for the concerns of this world that the piety of the Middle Ages had fostered, people now valued involvement, a life of activity.

Virtu: Literally, "the quality of being a man"; possible for a woman to express, but expected among aggressive males, the "movers and shakers" of the day; whatever a person's pursuit—in learning, the arts, or even in war—it meant living up to one's highest potential and excelling in all endeavors. The Renaissance man was an all-around man, as comfortable with the pen or the brush as with the sword; lover, poet, painter, conversationalist.

THE ARTS AS AN EXPRESSION OF INDIVIDUALISM

Before the Renaissance, the Church was the greatest patron of the arts. Painters and sculptors labored anonymously to fill the churches and cathedrals of the Middle Ages with figures of the saints that lacked the proportions and animation of real human forms or faces. During the Renaissance, although the church remained a major patron of the arts, the new commercial class and the governments of the city-states also supported the arts. Even though the art was religious in nature, the forms were anatomically proportional, the faces filled with emotion, and the artists reveled in their individuality of style.

Architecture adapted Greco-Roman symmetry, classical columns, arch, and dome. Architects such as *Filippo Brunelleschi* (1377–1446) and *Leon Battista Alberti* (1404–1472) studied ancient Roman buildings and used their principles of design to build cathedrals.

Sculpture was freestanding, not designed to fit in niches of churches, and showed nude subjects in the Greek tradition in both religious and mythological representations. *Lorenzo Ghiberti* (1378–1455) sculpted a set of bronze doors for the Florentine baptistry with not only crowds of human figures but the illusion of depth.

Painting was primarily religious in theme but radically different from medieval art because of the invention of oil paints and because of the illusion of three dimensions created by precise variation of size (perspective). All art was less symbolic, more representational, depicting real people in recognizable settings and glorifying the beauty of the corporeal world. *Giotto* (1267–1337) painted on walls in Florentine buildings and created the illusions of depth and movement. *Massaccio* (1401–1428) used light and shadow, nude figures, and the illusion of perspective. *Sandro Botticelli* (1444–1510) painted themes from classical mythology such as his *Birth of Venus*. *Raphael* (1483–1520) is considered one of the greatest painters of any era; his portraits and Madonnas epitomize the Renaissance style.

The Greatest of the Great

Leonardo da Vinci (1452–1519): personification of the "Renaissance man." Painter, sculptor, architect, engineer, writer, scientist—the versatility of his genius marks the last time that a single human could command virtually all the realms of knowledge and create masterworks in several areas of competence. His *Mona Lisa* and his *Last Supper* rival any of the world's great paintings for the perfection of their execution and for their sheer beauty.

Michelangelo Buonarroti (1475–1564): Primarily a sculptor whose *Pieta*, Mary mourning the limp body of Christ across her lap, is often considered the most perfect marble carving. His awesome statues of *Moses* and *David* are unrivaled masterpieces that reflect religiosity and real human emotion. His paintings on the *Sistine Chapel* in Rome, over which he labored for four years, portray biblical and allegorical figures with power, grace, and human clarity. He glorified God by depicting the beauty of his earthly creations.

Humanism

This was a literary movement distinct from the writing of the late Middle Ages in both its subject matter (it dealt with issues of politics and personal concern outside the realm of religion) and in its practitioners (laypeople who considered writing a profession rather than a pursuit of the clergy). They drew on antiquity, which ironically had been preserved by monks doing the laborious copying of ancient manuscripts by hand. They wrote in Italian rather than Latin, and thereby created the first European vernacular literature. The works of the great poet *Dante* (1265–1321), especially the *Divine Comedy*, and the speech patterns of Florence became the standard form of modern Italian.

Petrarch (1304–1374): Considered the first "modern" writer, he wrote sonnets in Italian, other works in Latin, and he used writing to consider the ebb and flow of his life and the human condition itself.

Boccaccio (1313–1375): A contemporary of Petrarch and like him a Florentine, his most famous work is the *Decameron,* entertaining tales that reflected upon the human condition.

Leonardo Bruni (1370–1444): A chancellor of the Republic of Florence in the late 14th century, he wrote perhaps the first modern history, an account of the development of Florence, using narrative, drawing on authentic sources, and introducing new historical periods.

Baldassare Castiglione (1478–1529): Offered a manual for the manners of the modern gentleman, *The Book of the Courtier:* A gentleman is trained for polite company, poised and well dressed, skilled in arms and sports, capable of making music and conversation, a reader of the classics, a social mixer who is good humored, lighthearted, and considerate of others' feelings. It was a civilized anti-dote to the crude social habits of the day in which even the wellborn spit on the floor, wiped noses on sleeves, ate without utensils, shrieked, and sulked. Prosperity had bred civility.

Niccolò Machiavelli (1469–1527): *The Prince* is the first political science work, an observation of how governments actually rule without moral judgment or exhortation. It is one of the most maligned and misinterpreted books of modern times, called "cynical and ruthless," the "handbook of dictators," and the origin of the concept "The end justifies the means." Machiavelli discovered that the successful governments of his times—whether Italian city-states or national monarchies—acted in their own political interests, making war or keeping the peace, true to their word or deceitful, benevolent or brutal when it was useful. Religion had virtually ceased to influence the process of governing as the rise of the nation-state became the ultimate goal, and *The Prince* (1513) offers keen insights. It was meant as a guide to the survival of the separate and independent city-states of Italy, which were vulnerable to the predatory powers in the north.

Laura Cereta (1469–1499): A well-known humanist and early feminist, she probably taught moral philosophy at University of Padua, a center of Renaissance learning. Her 1488 *Epistolae familiars* (Familiar Letters) were widely criticized for her criticism of 15th-century gender bias. When told by a man that intelligent women were unattractive, she retorted that so were unintelligent men.

The Northern Renaissance

The Northern Renaissance was the spread of Renaissance ideals from Italy to the rest of Northern Europe, including modern-day Germany, England, Switzerland, France, Belgium, and Holland. This period saw the emergence of market economies in England and the Netherlands, bringing prosperity and artistic renewal to Northern Europe. The Northern Renaissance differed from the Italian Renaissance in that the Italian Renaissance was much more secular whereas religion was emphasized in the north. Social reform through Christian values and an emphasis on reforming all of society through better Christian living were the hallmarks of the Northern Renaissance. Pietism, encompassing more arduous religious devotion of the laity, emerged as an aspect of this line of reasoning.

Christian Humanism also emerged as the thinkers and writers in the north adopted a Renaissance curiosity for knowledge, but based their research on the Hebrew and Greek texts of the bible while the Italians had applied their new zeal for knowledge to earlier pagan texts of ancient Greece and Rome. The Northern Renaissance originated in part because northern students went to Italy to study, and then came back with new ideas and ideals. The thirst for knowledge and new artistic and engineering techniques of the Italian Renaissance were transferred to northwestern Europe, leading to a Renaissance that was strongest in the Germanic areas and the Low Countries (Holland and Belgium).

GERMANY

On the eve of the Reformation, at the turn of the 16th century, Germany was at the heart of European progress. Politically diverse (the German-speaking world included most of central Europe, Switzerland, and parts of the Netherlands), its economy thrived anyway. Towns sprouted, grew, traded. Banking expanded: the Fuggers and other German families controlled more capital than the Italian bankers and all other Europeans combined.

Science and Technology

The **printing press** was popularized by *Johann Gutenberg* (ca.1400–1468), but Johann Faust and Peter Schoffer also used it around the same time as Gutenberg. It was actually invented in China, but Gutenberg was the first one to make *interchangeable moveable type* from lead molds. The introduction of the printing press had a massive impact on society because it became easier to spread ideas, propaganda, and education. Books became cheaper so more people read, which caused a reading revolution in society as reading became an individualized activity, rather than one person reading to a group aloud. It also allowed the bible to be printed in many vernacular languages for the laity to read for themselves, which would have a significant social impact. This also helped lead to the advent of the Reformation as many in Europe did not need the Catholic priest to be God's intermediary and religion became much more individualized.

Regiomontanus (Johann Muller, 1436–1476) and *Nicholas of Cusa* (1401–1464) laid the foundations for modern mathematics and science in the 15th century.

Martin Behaim (1459–1507) and *Johannes Schoner* (1477–1547) developed the era's most accurate maps. *Copernicus* (1473–1543) upset the time-honored *geocentric view* (that heavenly bodies revolved around the earth) of astronomy with calculations that offered proof of a *heliocentric* (sun-centered) system. This view contested the Aristotelian view that had been adopted as the official Roman Catholic view of the solar system. This contradiction is a major milestone in the creation of a divide between religion and science that began during the period of the Renaissance and continued as a theme throughout European history, helping to mark the Renaissance as the start of the modern era.

The notion that humankind could understand and control nature evolved from the work of these Germans.

Mysticism

This involved the belief that an individual, alone, unaided by church or sacraments, could commune with God. The mystics—such as *Meister Eckhart* (1260–1328) and *Thomas à Kempis* (1380–1471), author of the inspirational *Imitation of Christ*—pursued religious depth rather than rebellion. They stayed true to the Church, but sought to offer, to the few faithful who could understand, a substance that transcended traditional religiosity.

Gerard Groote (1340–1384), a Dutch lay preacher, organized the *Brothers of the Common Life* in the late 14th century, a religious organization that stressed personal virtues of Christianity rather than doctrine. Its movement of *modern devotion* preached Christ-like love, tolerance, and humility.

Both mysticism and the basic religious devotion of many laypeople contrasted, ominously, with the worldliness and smugness of the clergy.

Desiderius Erasmus (1456–1536), "The Christian Gentleman" personified Christian humanism in his pholosophic stances known as the Philosophy of Christ. A man of letters, he disdained the Middle Ages, ignored hard philosophy, admired antiquity, and wrote on humanist issues in purified Latin. The ultimate moderate, he championed gradual reform, ridiculed hypocrisy among the powerful, distrusted the fickle opinions of common people, and abhorred violence. He satirized the worldliness of the clergy and was critical of the Catholic emphasis on saints in *The Praise of Folly*; he offered a model of practical Christian behavior in *Handbook of a Christian Knight*; he wrote new Greek and Latin editions of the Bible. A confidant of kings and a critic of church abuses, he aimed at gentle reform of the Church from within. He was the most famous and influential intellectual of his times, and he used his writings and his example to preach peace, reason, tolerance, and loving reform. It is possible that had Martin Luther not pushed for radical reform in the early 1600s, the *Erasmian spirit* might have corrected the abuses of the Church while maintaining its structure.

This is a *hypothesis contrary to fact*. Since it did not indeed happen, there is no way we can know what would have followed if it had.

Artists

Albrecht Dürer (1471–1528) was one of the master artists of the era. His self-portraits and woodblock prints, such as *The Four Horsemen of the Apocalypse*, are still revered today. He was a mathematician who was painting landscapes and self-portraits at age thirteen. *Peter Brueghel the Elder* (1520–1569) focused on lives of ordinary people and painted and made prints that depicted them at work and play, which challenged the notion of the Italian Renaissance that art should be focused only on religious and aristocratic subjects.

ENGLAND

The Renaissance here coincided with, and was fostered by, the reign of *Elizabeth I* (1558–1603). An era of intense nationalism, produced by the resolution of dynastic rivalries and religious turmoil, it gave birth to perhaps the greatest vernacular literature of all time. The dramatist *Christopher Marlowe* (1564–1593), the poet *Edmund Spenser* (1552–1599), and the scientist *Francis Bacon* (1561–1626) helped form modern English during the *Elizabethan Age*. The greatest writer in English—maybe in any language—*William Shakespeare* (1564–1616) reflected the influence of the dramatists of the ancient world and also the writers of the Italian Renaissance. He single-handedly set the standard for the English language.

During the reign of Elizabeth's father, *Henry VIII* (1491–1547), a contemporary of Erasmus, *Sir Thomas More* (1478–1535), had fostered the Erasmian spirit in his *Utopia,* a book that criticized the correctible abuses of various institutions and that offered the blueprint for a perfect society. A devout Roman Catholic, he was beheaded for not supporting the king against the Pope during the English Reformation.

FRANCE

After the *Hundred Years War* (1337–1453), the monarchy in France was strengthened by a renewal of commerce, which expanded and enriched the middle class. France was also realizing a wave of nationalism during the Renaissance era, possibly in part as a reaction to the Hundred Years War. Government was centralized because the nobility had been weakened by a century of warfare and the bourgeoisie provided an ample source of revenue for the royal treasury. Through the late 15th and early 16th centuries, a succession of strong kings—*Louis XI, Charles VIII, Louis XII*—reduced the power of the nobility, firmed up the structure of the modern nation-state, and brought the middle class into government as advisors. *Francis I* (1515–1547) not only inherited a strong monarchy but extended its power by establishing a taille (a direct head tax on all land and property). During his reign and that of his successor, *Henry II* (1547–1559), the Renaissance took hold in France.

Rabelais (1494–1553), a priest and a classicist, attacked the failings of French society and the Church in his *Gargantua and Pantagruel* while advocating rational reform.

Montaigne (1533–1592) invented the format of the essay, which is derived from the French term, *essais,* meaning to test. His *Essays* preached open-mindedness and rational skepticism and offered an urbane, modern view of life.

SPAIN

Locked into Catholic orthodoxy by centuries of warfare against the Moslems (Moors), who had conquered much of the Iberian peninsula, the Spanish reached the height of their expansion in the 16th century through exploration and overseas colonization. Xenophobia and rigidity diluted the impact of Renaissance individualism and humanism. In 1492 (when Aragon and Castille united to form modern Spain), the Jews and Moslems, the nation's educated middle class, were expelled. *Miguel de Cervantes* (1547–1616) satirized his society's anachronistic glorification of chivalry and medieval institutions in one of the world's greatest novels, *Don Quixote.*

The century from 1550 to 1650 marks the "Golden Age" of Spanish culture. *Lope de Vega* wrote hundreds of dramas; *Bartolomé Estaban Murillo, Doménikos El Greco* (1541–1614), and *Diego Velázquez* (1599–1660) painted magnificent pictures on religious themes; and the Jesuit *Francisco Suárez* wrote widely admired works on philosophy and law.

LOW COUNTRIES

There were many societal and artistic achievements made in the Low Countries, which became a center of banking and commerce. This wealthier society placed greater importance on knowledge and art, and thus produced some magnificent artists.

Jan van Eyck or *Johannes de Eyck* (c.1385–1441) was a Dutch painter of the 15th century known as one of the great masters. He was known for his excellent, and often higly symbolic, oil paintings with meticulous detail that focused on either religious or secular themes.

Rembrandt van Rijn (1606–1669) was a Dutch master. He is generally considered one of the greatest painters and printmakers. His use of chiaroscuro (dark and light) was powerful and manifested in his many self-portraits and paintings of stormy naval scenes. He died very poor, as did many Northern Renaissance painters.

Hieronymus Bosch (c. 1450–1516) was a Dutch painter of the era who used complex symbolism and explored themes of sin and moral failing. His complex, imaginative, and prevalent use of symbolic figures and obscure iconography was undeniably original and may have been an inspiration for the surrealist movement of the early 20th century.

Peter Brueghel the Elder (1520–1569) (see page 46).

Albrecht Dürer (1471–1528) (see page 46).

Renaissance Views on Women and Minorities

The Renaissance was a period of loss of status for upper class and merchant women. The protections on their property and bodies that had been strong during the medieval era were rescinded. Whereas the penalty for rape in the medieval era was castration, the penalty in the 15th century was a fine payable to the father or husband, whosever property had been damaged. Women were banned from many guilds, preventing them from inheriting their husbands' businesses. Few women were allowed into institutions of higher learning, and women were not taken seriously as powerful minds. This makes women like Laura Cereta, Isabella d'Este, and Catherine de Medici even more impressive. Cereta was a prototype feminist and lecturer at the most advanced university of the day in Padua. Isabella d'Este created a court at Mantua that became a center of arts and learning in her day. Catherine de Medici was a power broker, queen, and regent of France as well as the mother of Louis XIII. The status of ordinary peasant women was not affected by the Renaissance.

This was also a time of renewed faith in many ways. Those who found that they disagreed with the Church (the Roman Catholic Church), which was the only official religion in Western Europe at the time, were often persecuted. These religious conflicts became more and more widespread in the 16th century. This era also saw the beginnings of racial bias of African servants, who were simultaneously seen as exotic symbols of wealth and prestige and evil because their dark skin was religiously commonly believed to symbolize evil. Consequently, immigrants from Africa were not afforded access to the higher levels of society.

RENAISSANCE POINTS TO REMEMBER

✔ It was focused on three ideals: humanism, secularism, and individualism.

✔ It occurred primarily in cities because contact with other cultures happened there first.

✔ Secularism became more pervasive in the cities and art, but the Renaissance *did not* abandon interest in religion; in fact, the greatest patron of the arts continued to be the Church.

✔ Intellectually there was a focus on this world rather than the afterlife, and on description of the world and universe rather than a prescription to religious dogma.

✔ The use of the vernacular in literature revolutionized literature and helped national identities solidify.

✔ New intellectual ideals gained focus, especially human experience, manners, politics, and so on; these new subjects were known as "the humane letters," from whence the term "humanism" is derived.

✔ For the first time, artists of all types, from painters to authors, became wealthy; it was the birth of new professions that catered to wealthy patrons.

✔ The ideal of a "Renaissance Man" emerged in the writings of Castiglione and Alberti as someone who is virtuous in every way and has many talents, such as the abilities to sing, compose poetry, dance, and combat.

✔ Remember that the Renaissance was not a rebirth in law, government, or economic production; in most ways Europe was still medieval.

✔ There was some difference in the way that the Renaissance was perceived in northern and southern Europe.

• Southern Europe was wealthier due to increasing trade with the Arabs and the Byzantines, providing the luxury to spend on arts, learning, and public projects.

• Northern Europe focused more on practical learning, science, and technology. This is one reason why the Reformation began there—that and its distance from Rome, where the wealth and power of the Church was so prevalent. Northern Europeans created many institutions of higher learning, while the Italians and Spanish focused on art and religion, respectively. The North used the precepts of the Renaissance spirit of the individual, and took it in a religious direction to mysticism. This belief holds that the individual soul can commune with God all by itself without the Church, other people, or sacraments.

The Renaissance Characters

A brief description of the people whose ideas began the modern era follows.

The Masters of the Arts

At first, the Renaissance was mostly an artistic movement, which brought significant changes to Renaissance society.

Giotto (1266–1336) Florence Painter	Very influential pre-Renaissance painter and a friend of Dante. His work is notable for its use of realistic scenes from nature.
Brunelleschi (1377–1446) Florence Architect	Created *Il Duomo*, the first Italian freestanding dome since antiquity. He is credited with introducing perspective to Renaissance artists.
Donatello (1386–1466) Florence Sculptor	His bronze *David* was the first freestanding bronze statue of a human created in Europe since antiquity.
Masaccio (1410–1428) Florence Painter	Often called "The Father of Modern Art," his *Expulsion* and *Holy Trinity* mark the advance from Medieval to Renaissance painting due to the use of anatomy and perspective.
Giovanni Bellini (1430–1516) Venice Painter	A leading painter of the Venetian School, he was the master of Giorgione and Titian. He is known chiefly for his altarpieces and his madonnas.
Botticelli (1444–1510) Florence Painter	Most famous for his *Birth of Venus*, he assisted on decorating the Sistine Chapel. He was also a follower of Savonarola.
Ghirlandiao (1449–1494) Florence Painter	Founder of a school of painting, he was the teacher of Michelangelo.
Leonardo da Vinci (1452–1519) Florence Painter, sculptor, architect, engineer, and scientist	Painter of *The Last Supper*, *Mona Lisa*, and many other masterpieces, he was an engineer who designed flying machines and tanks. He was a rival of Michelangelo; his patrons were Lorenzo the Magnificent and Lodovico Sforza.
Michelangelo Buonarroti (1474–1564) Painter, sculptor, architect, and poet	Famous for painting the ceiling of the Sistine Chapel for Pope Julius II. His great sculptures included the *Pieta*, *David*, and *Moses*. He was the greatest sculptor of hands and was part of the trinity of great 15th-century artists including Leonardo da Vinci and Raphael.
Raphael Sanzio (1483–1520) Urbino, Italy Painter	Chief architect of St. Peter's Basilica in Rome and master of frescoes such as *The School of Athens*, he is noted for his madonnas. He was part of the trinity of great 15th-century artists including Leonardo da Vinci and Michelangelo.
Artemesia Gentileschi (1590–1642) Italian Painter	Her father was also a painter whose patrons included King Charles I of England. She is especially noted for her "Judith" paintings.

Masters of Letters

Dante (1265–1321) Florence	Author of *The Divine Comedy* (about an imaginary journey through Hell, Purgatory, and Heaven), in which he helped define the *vernacular* of what is now Italian.
Petrarch (1304–1374) Italian	He was the first great *humanist* thinker and a scholar of Latin. His major works were *Triumphs* and *On the Solitary Life*. He is known as the "Father of Humanism."
Boccaccio (1313–1375) Italian	Friend of Petrarch and a major contributor to the development of classic Italian prose. His *Decameron* is a classic bawdy tale of love in all of its forms.
Leonardo Bruni (1369–1444) Italian humanist	His history of Florence is noted for a new sense of the need for authentic sources in examining history. He translated Plutarch, Demosthenes, Aristotle, and Plato from Greek into Latin.
Thomas à Kempis (1380–1471) German ecclesiastic and writer	An early religious purist who wrote *Imitation of Christ*, in which mysticism holds that the individual soul can commune directly with God in perfect solitude, without sacraments, people, or Church.
Lorenzo Valla (1406–1457) Italian humanist	A leading Renaissance humanist most famous for "On Pleasure," his piece about the Epicureans.
Pico della Mirandola (1463–1494) Italian humanist	Leading humanist of the Italian Renaissance and author of "Oration on the Dignity of Man."
Erasmus of Rotterdam (1466–1536) Catholic author and scholar	His new Greek and Latin translations of the New Testament led him to write *The Praise of Folly* and *Handbook of a Christian Knight*. He was an enemy of Luther and a friend of Thomas More. He wanted reform within the Catholic Church and was a leader in Renaissance learning in Northern Europe.
Niccolò Machiavelli (1469–1527) Florence	*The Prince,* his application for employment with Lorenzo Medici, became the most important work on political science for centuries.
Baldassare Castiglione (1478–1529) Milan and Urbino	Author of *The Book of the Courtier*, the first book of etiquette for nobles.
Thomas More (1478–1535) England	Author of *Utopia*, he opposed Henry VIII's break from the Catholic Church even though he was the lord chancellor of England. He was beheaded for his principles.
Rabelais (1494–1553) France	This priest attacked the failings of the Church in *Gargantua* and *Pantagruel*.

These writers shared new ideas and focused on writing in vernacular languages, which made pieces accessible to their fellow countrymen.

Benvenuto Cellini (1500–1571) Florence Sculptor, goldsmith, and author	His *Autobiography*, an excellent record of life in Renaissance Italy, shows why he was the prime exemplar of "virtu." He worked under Michelangelo and under the patronage of Clement VII.
Montaigne (1533–1592) France	Invented the essay, which is derived from the French word for test.
Miguel de Cervantes (1547–1616) Spain	Satirized the chivalry of the Spanish court and the medieval institutions of the state in his *Don Quixote*.

Leaders of Religion

These leaders saw to the needs of the Renaissance flock.

Nicholas of Cusa (1401–1464) Rhineland (Germany) Churchman	Roman Catholic prelate and philosopher who focused on mystical philosophy. He anticipated Copernicus by his belief in the earth's rotation and revolution around the sun.
Pope Nicholas V (r.1447–1455) Italian	A great patron of art and literature.
Pope Innocent VIII (r.1484–1492) Italian	A busy guy, he declared Henry VII to be the lawful King of England and appointed Torquemada as the Grand Inquisitor of Spain.
Pope Alexander VI (r.1492–1503) Spanish	He bribed his way to the papacy. His kids were Cesare Borgia and Lucretia Borgia who hung around the Vatican and were granted land. He was a great patron of the arts (especially of Bramante, Michelangelo, and Raphael) and ordered the execution of Savonarola. He purportedly said, "God has given us the papacy. Now let us enjoy it!"
Pope Julius II (r.1503–1513) Italian	He decided to rebuild St. Peter's Basilica, and patronized Raphael, Michelangelo, Bramante, and others.
Pope Leo X (r.1513–1521) Italian	He was the second son of Lorenzo the Magnificent and the most opulent pope, who ate from gold plates and threw them away. He failed to realize the importance of the Reformation and issued the bull excommunicating Luther.
Girolamo Savonarola (1452–1498) Ferrara, Italy Dominican monk and church reformer	His vehement sermons about the corruption of secular life, the ruling class, and the worldliness of the clergy led Romans to revolt. He began the "Bonfires of the Vanities" (in which Botticelli threw his paintings to be burned) and drove Piero Medici from power in Florence. After becoming the virtual dictator of the city, he preached for a crusade for the establishment of an ideal Christian state. Denounced by Pope Alexander VI, he lost power in Florence to the aristocrats and was ultimately captured by them. He was tried for sedition and heresy and then tortured, hanged, and burned.

Scientific Minds

Regiomontanus (1436–1476) Germany Mathematician and scientist	An influential thinker, he laid the foundation for mathematical conception of the universe. His real name was Johann Muller.
Nicholas Copernicus (1473–1543) Poland Scientist	He revived the idea of a heliocentric (sun-centered) solar system from the ancients in his *On the Revolutions of the Celestial Spheres*.
Gutenberg (1398–1468) German	He is often credited as the first to produce books with moveable lead type circa 1450.

These were the first great scientists.

Political Leaders

Giovanni de Medici (1360–1429) Florence	A merchant who became wealthy, he was a supporter of smaller guilds and common people, became virtual ruler of Florence between 1421 and 1429, and began a banking dynasty.
Cosimo de Medici (1389–1464) Florence	He was the son of Giovanni, a banker, patron of the arts, and "father of his country."
Lorenzo de Medici aka "The Magnificent" (1449–1492) Florence	Major patron of the arts, father of a pope, and general proponent of his family. He is alleged to have been an immoral and tyrannical ruler.
Cesare Borgia (1475–1507) Originally Spanish	The son of Pope Alexander VI, he conquered much of central Italy including Urbino and acted with cruelty and treachery. He was Machiavelli's ideal "Prince."
Isabelle d'Este (1474–1539) Marchioness of Mantua	Married to Giovanni Gonzaga, she was an outstanding diplomat and patron of learning. She turned Mantua into the center of learning and thought.

These are the people who controlled the masses during the Renaissance and the age of absolutism.

Sample Essay Question

The sample thematic essay questions presented in this chapter are types found on the AP exam.

SAMPLE QUESTION

"The secular humanism of the Italian Renaissance reflected the modern world while the Christian humanism of the Northern Renaissance compromised between medievalism and modernity."

Defend or refute this statement.

Comments on the Sample Question

Follow the "Simple Procedures" for writing an essay. (See page 34.)

First, *What does the question want to know?* The best way to approach a question like this—laden with terms and concepts—is to identify each of them, and, then and only then, determine whether the statement can be more easily defended or refuted.

What was the Italian Renaissance? Did it occur before or after the Northern Renaissance? Did one influence the other? What did they have in common? How did they differ?

What is "secular humanism"? How did it draw on ideas from the ancient world while adapting them to the unique historical circumstances of 15th century Italy?

What is "Christian humanism"? How was it influenced by secular humanism and by Christian tradition?

What is meant by "medievalism" and "modernity"? Do the attitudes expressed in secular humanism come closer to the attitudes of our world than those of Christian humanism? Is an idea that "reflects" a future development one of its causes?

Second, *What do you know about it?* Once you have answers to these questions, the choice of whether to defend or refute the statement is actually made for you. If the secular humanism of the Italian Renaissance is significantly different from the Christian humanism of the North, you can measure which more closely reflected the world that followed and then you can build a strong case for defense or refutation of the statement.

Third, *How would you put it into words?* Remember, since history rarely offers "either/or" simplicities, sometimes the best approach to a *defend or refute* question is to argue both sides. Be careful, though, not to make your essay a circle of contradictions. State your defenses and refutations clearly, and let your evidence point to the sophistication of your understanding.

Rubric for Sample Answer

Before you read the sample answer, examine the rubric. What will the reader be looking for when he or she grades this essay? A sample rubric, shaded to show the reader's evaluation, is seen below:

9–8 POINTS

- ✔ Thesis explicitly identifies **both** the extent to which the secular humanism of the Italian Renaissance reflected the modern world, whereas the Christian humanism of the Northern Renaissance compromised between medievalism and modernity to *either* defend or refute the statement. Thesis does not need to be in the opening paragraph.
- ✔ Organization is clear, consistently followed, and effective in support of the argument.
  - May devote individual paragraphs to how the Italian Renaissance reflected the modern world, whereas the Christian humanism of the Northern Renaissance compromised between medievalism and modernity.
  - Must identify specific details of how modernity and secular humanism was or was not reflected in the Italian Renaissance, such as ideals of individual excellence, pursuit of knowledge, and perfection, and how the Christian humanism was or was not observed in the Northern Renaissance works of masters.
- ✔ Essay is well balanced; the ways in which monarchs used the arts and the sciences to enhance state power are analyzed at some length. Essay either refutes or defends the statement clearly for both the Italian and Northern Renaissances.
- ✔ Major assertions in the essay are supported thoroughly and consistently by relevant evidence.
- ✔ Evidence of the defense or rebuttal may prove more specific or concrete.
- ✔ May contain errors that do not detract from the argument.

7–6 POINTS

- ✔ Thesis explicitly defends or refutes **both** the extent to which the Italian Renaissance reflected the modern world and how the Christian humanism of the Northern Renaissance compromised between medievalism and modernity, but may not be developed fully.
- ✔ Organization is clear and effective in support of the argument but may introduce evidence that is not pertinent to the task.
- ✔ Essay covers all major topics suggested by the prompt but may analyze an aspect of the Italian Renaissance, the Northern Renaissance, or how the quote applies to either in terms of validity in greater depth rather than in a balanced manner.
- ✔ Major assertions in the essay are supported by relevant evidence.
- ✔ May contain an error that detracts from the argument.

5–4 POINTS

✔ Thesis identifies **both** the extent to which the Italian Renaissance reflected the modern world and how the Christian humanism of the Northern Renaissance compromised between medievalism and modernity but without any development; thesis may address only part of the question effectively; thesis may be a simple, single-sentence statement.

✔ Organization is clear but may not be consistently followed; essay may veer off task chronologically or thematically or both.

✔ Essay may not complete all tasks:
  • May defend or refute only the extent to which the Italian Renaissance reflected the modern world OR how the Christian humanism of the Northern Renaissance compromised between medievalism and modernity.
  • May discuss only one or two ways in which the Italian Renaissance reflected the modern world and/or how the Christian humanism of the Northern Renaissance compromised between medievalism and modernity.
  • May focus only on one aspect of Christian humanism or secular humanism.
  • May be primarily descriptive rather than analytical.

✔ Essay offers some relevant evidence.

✔ May contain errors that detract from the argument.

3–2 POINTS

✔ Thesis may simply paraphrase the prompt or identify the extent to which the Italian Renaissance reflected the modern world and/or how the Christian humanism of the Northern Renaissance compromised between medievalism and modernity without analyzing enough to refute or defend the statement in a meaningful way.

✔ Organization is unclear and ineffective; essay may focus on the specific attributes of the Italian and Northern Renaissances rather than analyzing to refute or defend.

✔ Essay shows serious imbalance; discussion of the extent to which the Italian Renaissance reflected the modern world and/or how the Christian humanism of the Northern Renaissance compromised between medievalism and modernity is superficial; much of the information may be significantly out of the time period or geography of the question.

✔ Offers minimal or confused evidence.

✔ May contain several errors that detract from the argument.

1–0 POINTS

✔ Thesis is erroneous or irrelevant or absent.

✔ No effective organization is evident.

✔ Discussion of the extent to which the Italian Renaissance reflected the modern world and/or how the Christian humanism of the Northern Renaissance compromised between medievalism and modernity is generic.

✔ Provides little or no relevant supporting evidence.

✔ May contain numerous errors that detract from the argument.

Sample Answer

A defense of the statement would be both expected and easy. History—or at least the teaching of it—is full of convenient generalizations. "The Italian Renaissance was pagan in tone"; "the Northern Renaissance was religious." The trouble with the terms "secular humanism" and "Christian humanism" is that there was no absolute distinction between the religiosity of the Italian and Northern Renaissance because the men of both were Christians by birth, belief, and practice.

What is meant by "reflected the modern world"? That attitudes, interests, and activities were similar to those in our times or a cause for them?

It is tempting to assume that our secular age had its start in the literary movement, humanism, that began in Renaissance Italy and departed from the literature of the Middle Ages in that it dealt with issues other than law, philosophy, and theology. True, nonclerical writers such as Castiglione and Machiavelli wrote about social manners or politics without arguing their cases from a theological base, but the cultured Italian courtiers and ruthless princes prayed regularly and considered themselves men of God.

The glorification of the culture of the ancients by the so-called "pagan humanism" of the Italians (a term that was probably derisively applied by the self-righteously pious Northern Europeans) did not cancel out their Christianity. "Secularism" in the modern world applies, not necessarily to atheism or a disbelief in religion, but rather to a network of attitudes, interests, and activities that do not include religion. A modern secular person would consider the Renaissance men very religious.

What caused the growth of secularism? The Italian humanists may have been the first to write in the vernacular and about nonreligious issues—politics and the human condition—but secularism in our world grew from our reliance on the findings of science rather than on the mysteries of religion. The rise of science took place in Northern Europe in the 16th and 17th centuries.

The Northern humanists did much more than use Hebrew and Greek versions of the Bible or the writings of the Church Fathers like St. Augustine to revitalize tradition-bound Christianity. If Erasmus was the "Christian gentleman" who tried to reform the church from within, he also championed social reform. Gerard Groote also stressed individualism by arguing for personal virtue over reliance on religious dogma. The approaches of these "Christian humanists" were far removed from the traditionalism of the medieval world.

In France, the writings of Montaigne reflected skepticism, a very modern attitude, and those of Rabelais criticized the existing social structure. In England, Thomas More wrote of a utopian society more modern than medieval, and the great Shakespeare captured the human condition in his dramas. All these men would undoubtedly have counted themselves as religious Christians.

The humanism of the Northern Renaissance included writers who were concerned with religious issues but in radically new dimensions from that of the authority-bound religiosity of the Middle Ages. Many Northern humanists wrote of very earthy issues and with very secular outlooks. To call the work of the "Christian humanists" a compromise between medievalism and modernity is to dilute the potency of their very modern individualism and secularism. To classify the Italian humanists as "pagan" or "secular" is to diminish their commitment to Christianity. It is imperative in history as in human affairs not to allow generalization to degenerate into stereotyping.

EVALUATE THE SAMPLE ANSWER

Now go back and look at the rubric. It is clear that this essay fulfills all of the requirements for a score of 8 or 9 on the rubric. The essay answers all parts of the question thoroughly with concrete evidence at length with a well-balanced essay. The extra concrete support gets this essay a score of 9.

RATER'S COMMENTS ON THE SAMPLE ANSWER

9—Extremely well qualified

This essay is a very mature and nuanced essay and could only be crafted in the time allotted by one who mastered the subject. It is a good example of what will stick out to a reader, and it clearly answers the question with strong specific supporting evidence. This is an expertly crafted essay that challenges the generalizations of the period and addresses the vocabulary of the question cogently. It uses numerous references to figures of the time and their ideas to support the thesis. Remember that taking the harder path on a FRQ can be very rewarding. The reader will reward the intellectual approach of the writer in distinguishing between generalization and fact. Most importantly, this essay makes a thesis that the proposed statement is too general and supports it very well with appropriate references. This essay might have also challenged the meaning of medievalism and modernity.

Practice Essay Questions

The questions that follow are samples of the various types of thematic essay questions that appear on the AP exam. The review chapters in this section (Part Two) will have samples of the major types of thematic essays: defend or refute, analyze, evaluate, to what extent and in what ways, assess the validity, contrast and compare, explain.

Generic Essay Scoring Rubric

9–8 POINTS

- ✔ Thesis explicitly addresses **all parts of the question**. Thesis does not need to be in the opening paragraph.

✔ Organization is clear, consistently followed, and effective in support of the argument.

- May devote individual paragraphs to an examination of each part of the question.
- Must identify major terms associated with the question and put them into context for the question; does not have to present every detail for every part.

✔ Essay is well balanced; issues are analyzed at some length. Essay covers all chronological requirements of the question to some extent.

✔ Major assertions in the essay are supported thoroughly and consistently by relevant evidence.

✔ Evidence may prove more specific or concrete.

✔ May contain errors that do not detract from the argument.

7–6 POINTS

✔ Thesis explicitly identifies **all parts of the question**, but may not be developed fully.

✔ Organization is clear and effective in support of the argument but may introduce evidence that is not pertinent to the task.

✔ Essay covers all major topics suggested by the prompt but may analyze an aspect in greater depth rather than in a balanced manner.

✔ Major assertions in the essay are supported by relevant evidence.

✔ May contain an error that detracts from the argument.

5–4 POINTS

✔ Thesis identifies **all parts of the question**, but without any development; thesis may address only part of the question effectively; thesis may be a simple, single-sentence statement.

✔ Organization is clear but may not be consistently followed; essay may veer off task chronologically or thematically or both.

✔ Essay may not complete all tasks:

- May discuss only …
- May focus only on …
- May be primarily descriptive rather than analytical.

✔ Essay offers some relevant evidence.

✔ May contain errors that detract from the argument.

3–2 POINTS

✔ Thesis may simply paraphrase the prompt OR identify the parts of the question without analyzing.

✔ Organization is unclear and ineffective; essay may focus on personal or national attributes rather than analyzing.

✔ Essay shows serious imbalance; discussion is superficial; much of the information may be significantly out of the time period or geography of the question.
✔ Offers minimal OR confused evidence.
✔ May contain several errors that detract from the argument.

1–0 POINTS

✔ Thesis is erroneous OR irrelevant OR absent.
✔ No effective organization is evident.
✔ Discussion is generic.
✔ Provides little or no relevant supporting evidence.
✔ May contain numerous errors that detract from the argument.

QUESTION 1

To what extent and in what ways did the Italian Renaissance result from Italy's geographic advantage in the world trade of the 15th century?

COMMENTS ON QUESTION 1

"Geography is destiny." So it is said. And the strategic location of Italy, a peninsula jutting into the Mediterranean, gave it advantages in the world trade of the 15th century. "How and how much" are the questions to answer here. The clues are inherent in the geography. With what parts of the world did the Europeans carry on trade at this time? Why did Italy have an advantage? What were the rewards of that advantage? How were those rewards instrumental in fostering the greatest brief period of creativity in history?

QUESTION 2

"Although the term 'Renaissance' is misleading, the modern world began with Renaissance secularism and individualism." *Assess the validity* of this statement.

COMMENTS ON QUESTION 2

This question is about judging the truth or validity of the given statement. This question can be answered by taking either side. The more conventional way would be to argue that individualism and secularism as they relate to industrialization and the emergence of capitalism and democracy support the generalization. This must be supported with citations from writers and thinkers of the Renaissance and Enlightenment who are more modern. An Ayn Rand citation would be a nice topper. The other side argues that terms like "modernity" and "Renaissance" are not valid terms in this context and that citing any era as being caused by another is a dubious argument. Either way, the question requires careful thought and planning to answer.

QUESTION 3

Explain why Machiavelli's *The Prince* is both one of the most misinterpreted books of modern times and the first modern treatise in political science.

COMMENTS ON QUESTION 3

"Explain" offers no choice. You must "make clear," "detail," and "offer meanings, causes, reasons for." The essence of the book is in the phrase "The welfare of the state justifies everything . . . ." Is this equivalent to arguing that the end justifies the means? What was Machiavelli's purpose in writing the book? How did his methods of observation and his arguments make it the "first modern treatise in political science"? This essay must also address why and how *The Prince* has been misinterpreted. Would medieval philosophers have considered the same issues? If so, what would their arguments be based upon?

QUESTION 4

Contrast and Compare the Italian and the Northern Renaissance.

COMMENTS ON QUESTION 4

"Show differences"; "examine similarities." In showing the differences, consider how each began, which influenced which, how their emphases differed, how they interpreted common concepts differently, how they expressed their differences. How did the art and literature of each differ? How did the personalities vary—who was the "ideal Renaissance man" in Italy, in Northern Europe? What were the accomplishments of each?

In examining similarities, consider common concepts such as "individualism" and "secularism"; look for similarities in their religious commitments, in their artistic and literary techniques and themes, in their approaches to defining human life.

QUESTION 5

Analyze how the Northern Renaissance gave rise to two diverse trends: *religious mysticism and revival* and *science and technology.*

COMMENTS ON QUESTION 5

In this case, *analyze* means primarily to "determine the relationships" between the Northern Renaissance and two glaringly different approaches to the human condition: religion and science. How did the study of ancient texts—specifically Hebrew and Greek versions of the Bible and the writings of the early Church Fathers—revitalize religious devotion? How did the concept of "individualism" encourage the very personal religious experience of mysticism? How did "individualism" and "skepticism" give rise to modern science?

Why did the revival of religion and the growth of mysticism occur primarily in Northern Europe? Was Italian religious devotion centered on the arts? Did the papacy have less sway in the North?

Why did Northern Europe give birth to modern science? Was the desire to understand and control nature the Northern counterpart to Italian virtu or richness of the human spirit? Was it a tradition that began with the mathematician Regiomontanus and evolved into the Copernican formula for a heliocentric universe?

Practice Multiple-Choice Questions

(These represent the different types of questions that appear on the AP exam.)

1. The Renaissance marks the beginning of the modern era in large part due to the development of all of the following EXCEPT

    (A) the foundations of capitalism were laid at this time
    (B) individualism emerged as a trend
    (C) trade with the New World began a trend of global trade
    (D) scientific thought emerged with an emphasis on the scientific method
    (E) northern Europe began to dominate southern Europe

2. "Geography is destiny" proved true for the Italians of the 14th and 15th centuries for all of the following reasons EXCEPT

    (A) their proximity to the Mediterranean
    (B) their establishment of overland trade with Asia
    (C) their role as the "middlemen" of Europe
    (D) their ability to adapt to victimization by more united peoples
    (E) their seagoing trade with the eastern Mediterranean

3. Which of these city-states is said to have been the cultural center of the Renaissance and has been compared to ancient Athens for its burst of creativity over a relatively short time span?

    (A) Venice
    (B) Milan
    (C) Rome
    (D) Genoa
    (E) Florence

4. The powerful middle class that developed in the independent city-states of Renaissance Italy was involved in all of the following EXCEPT

   (A) making profitable loans to popes and monarchs
   (B) financing commercial ventures
   (C) patronizing the arts
   (D) encouraging manorialism
   (E) controlling the governments of the city-states

5. Which dynasty of merchants, bankers, and despots of Florence used its wealth to patronize the great creative artists of the day?

   (A) Petrarch
   (B) Bellini
   (C) Medici
   (D) Sforza
   (E) Condottieri

6. Which of these concepts was NOT valued by Renaissance thinkers?

   (A) Humans as the measure of all things
   (B) The cloistered life
   (C) The ideas of ancient Greece
   (D) Pursuit of excellence
   (E) Living up to one's potential

7. For the majority of women in Europe during the period, the Renaissance

   (A) had very little impact
   (B) improved the material conditions of their life
   (C) worsened their status
   (D) allowed them access to education for the first time
   (E) improved their status in society

8. Michelangelo's *David* displays which thematic innovation of Renaissance artists?

   (A) The depiction of religious personages
   (B) Accurate human anatomy
   (C) The use of marble as a material
   (D) The portrayal of enigmatic expressions
   (E) The depiction of classical costumes

9. The sculpture of the Renaissance differed from that of the Middle Ages in all the following ways EXCEPT

    (A) the forms were anatomically proportional
    (B) the faces expressed emotion
    (C) the figures expressed animation
    (D) the artists prided themselves on the individuality of style
    (E) the subject matter was nonreligious

10. The social group that most often supported the centralizing efforts of the "new monarchs" was the

    (A) peasantry
    (B) nobility
    (C) bourgeoisie
    (D) urban workers
    (E) clergy

11. The so-called pagan humanism of the Italian Renaissance differed from the so-called Christian humanism of the Northern Renaissance primarily because

    (A) the art of the Italian Renaissance depicted only classical themes
    (B) the literature of the Northern Renaissance drew upon the Hebrew and Greek texts of the Bible and the writings of the Church Fathers
    (C) Italian Renaissance writers were often antireligious
    (D) The merchant-princes who ruled the Italian city-states resisted the influence of the Church in civic affairs
    (E) The Northern churches were the biggest patrons of the arts

12. Which of the following was NOT an important development of the Northern Renaissance?

    (A) The use of the first movable-type printing press in Europe
    (B) The formulation of the heliocentric view
    (C) The establishment of a brilliant English vernacular literature
    (D) Mysticism's assertion that an individual could commune directly with God, unaided by the Church
    (E) The invention of the banking system

13. The "Prince of Humanists," who attempted through satiric writings to reform the Roman Catholic Church while remaining loyal to it was

    (A) Sir Thomas More
    (B) Erasmus
    (C) Luther
    (D) Cervantes
    (E) Rabelais

"It was a literary movement that reflected a new way of looking at the human condition. The writers were laymen, not clergy, who examined secular issues such as politics and the emotional life of the individual. While they drew on the themes of the ancient classics and often wrote in classical Latin and Greek, they also laid the foundations for modern language and literature by writing in their mother tongues."

14. The literary movement described above is

 (A) secularism
 (B) individualism
 (C) classicism
 (D) humanism
 (E) *virtu*

15. Italian balance-of-power diplomacy

 (A) was designed to prevent a single Italian state from dominating the peninsula
 (B) successfully prevented foreign domination of Italy
 (C) was primarily concerned with controlling the papacy
 (D) was critical to the economic success of Italy
 (E) was only focused on internal affairs and did not include international alliances

Answers and Answer Explanations

1.	E	**6.**	B	**11.**	B
2.	B	**7.**	A	**12.**	E
3.	E	**8.**	B	**13.**	B
4.	D	**9.**	E	**14.**	D
5.	C	**10.**	C	**15.**	A

1. **(E)** Northern Europe did not dominate southern Europe until the decline of Spain in the 17th century.

2. **(B)** Analysis demonstrates that all the other choices support the idea.

3. **(E)** This is identification. If you did not know that Florence was the "center of the Renaissance," it would be difficult to work it out.

4. **(D)** Manorialism was a feature of feudalism, and the shift in power from the feudal nobility to the middle class eventually ended it because money took precedence over land.

5. **(C)** This is mostly an identify question in that the test taker must know that the Medici family dominated Florence.

6. **(B)** The cloistered life was the dedication to piety, solitude, chastity, and poverty of the medieval monk.

7. **(A)** Ordinary women were powerless peasants with no political or economic status or power before the Renaissance and after. The Renaissance was also a time of declining status for women of noble, artisan, and merchant families, but they were far from ordinary women.

8. **(B)** Accurate and proportionate representations of anatomy was a Renaissance "innovation" reintroduced from classical sculpture.

9. **(E)** The people of the Renaissance were devout Roman Catholics and that dedication to faith is reflected in their art.

10. **(C)** The bourgeoisie was most supportive of the centralization of central power. In places like England, land was traded to them for their support, but either way, a strong government was good for business. Nobility and the peasantry were most often against the increase in royal authority because they respectively lost power and freedom.

11. **(B)** The key term in the question is "so-called." It demonstrates the limitations of the terms "pagan" and "Christian."

12. **(E)** Banking developed in Europe in Italy among the "merchant princes" who sought to invest their surplus capital by lending, for profit, to the popes and monarchs.

13. **(B)** "Prince of Humanists" is the giveaway. In his day, Erasmus was one of the most famous people in Christendom.

14. **(D)** Humanism was primarily a development of the secular writers of the period who looked at human life from another perspective than that of the medieval clerics. It involved "classicism," a study of ancient writings; it encouraged individualism, the glorification of individual experience and value; it resulted in secularism, the consideration of nonreligious issues. Virtu was a quality of extreme individualism.

15. **(A)** The original purpose of balance-of-power diplomacy was to prevent any one city-state from dominating the peninsula, allowing all to flourish.

CHAPTER 2

Protestant Reformation, Catholic and Counter-Reformations, Wars of Religion (1517–1648)

Key Terms/People

- Reformation
- Johann Tetzel
- Pope Leo X
- Indulgences
- Martin Luther
- The Diet of Worms
- The Peasant's War
- The Diet of Speyer

- League of Schmalkalden
- Pope Paul III
- John Calvin
- Statute of the Six Articles
- Ignatius of Loyola
- Jesuits
- Index of Prohibited Books
- The Thirty Years' War

Overview

Historians generally agree that the Protestant Reformation marks the beginning of modern Europe and that it influenced the development of Western civilization. What began as an attempt to reform the Roman Catholic Church was co-opted by political forces and resulted in the destruction of the religious unity of Western Europe and in the subjection of Europeans to bitter wars of religion.

Protestantism was adopted by the growing nation-states of the north as they were about to replace Italy and Spain as leaders of modern Europe. It inherited and adapted the concept of *individuality* from the Renaissance, and it influenced monumental developments in Western civilization: nationalism, capitalism, democracy, science.

The Catholic and Counter Reformations were responses of the Roman Catholic Church to both the criticisms of the reformers and the spread of Protestantism. The Council of Trent redefined the doctrines of the Church; the Jesuits propagated them; the Inquisition enforced orthodoxy. The Inquisition in Spain was designed to encourage a sense of national unity based on Catholicism. The Moslem Moors and the Jews—the educated groups in Spanish society—were either driven into exile or forcibly converted. The Inquisition was later adapted in Spain and in Spanish territories to combat Protestantism, and it was imported to Italy for the same purpose. Protestantism, though, dominated most of Northern Europe, and the continent suffered devastating disruptions during the wars of the 16th and 17th centuries.

Causes of the Reformation

1. Corruption of the Roman Catholic Church during the Renaissance; sale of church offices (simony); nepotism; sale of indulgences; decline of morality among the clergy

2. Impact of Renaissance *humanism,* which questioned Church traditions
   Humanist "glorification of humanity" contradicted the Church's emphasis on salvation.
   Prosperity brought the "virtue of poverty" into disrepute and the Church lost the "spirit" of Christ's message and was out of touch with the mass of believers.

3. Declining prestige of the papacy
   Babylonian Captivity of the Church in the 14th century when popes, subservient to the French king, took up residence in Avignon and lost prestige in the rest of Christendom.
   The *Great Schism* beginning in 1378, when French and anti-French cardinals elected two popes—one of whom lived in Rome, the other in Avignon—and lasting over forty years.
   Moral decline of the Renaissance popes bred cynicism.
   Papal involvement in secular politics fostered contempt.

4. Influence of religious reformers, such as Wycliffe and Huss
   Stressed personal communion with God
   Diminished the importance of the sacraments.
   Weakened the influence of the clergy.

5. Resentment of secular rulers over the power of the popes and clergy
   Monarchs of growing nation-states resisted papal supremacy over national churches. There was also resentment over vast landholding of the Church within national boundaries.

6. Resistance to the power of Charles V
   The princes of the Germanic lands resented the new Holy Roman Emperor, Charles V (r. 1519–1558), who at age nineteen took the throne along with his vast Hapsburg holdings and proclaimed at his coronation, "the empire from of old has had not many masters, but one, and it is our intention to be that master." The Holy Roman Emperor had been more of a symbolic title, and his desire to make it more actual caused resistance to the power of Charles V. Protestantism helped the princes do just that.

7. Invention of the printing press, allowing dissenters to spread their ideas throughout Europe and making the Bible available to the common people.

Chronological Overview of Events, Personalities, Ideas

1517

Johann Tetzel (1465?–1519), a wandering friar, was authorized by *Pope Leo X* to sell *indulgences* (which guaranteed the remission of sins), the proceeds of which would be used to rebuild St. Peter's Church in Rome and to provide funds to local dioceses.

Martin Luther (1483–1546), a Roman Catholic priest, Augustinian monk, and theologian at the University of Wittenburg in Germany, condemned these sales as impious expediencies. Tormented by obsessions of his own damnation, despite a life dedicated to holy service, he came to believe that the traditional means of attaining salvation (*Good works*, such as the sacraments, prayer, and fasting) were inadequate. He nailed his *95 Theses* to the door of the Wittenburg church (his day's equivalent of calling a press conference), listing the points of his opposition to the indulgences and inviting debate.

1519–1520

When an appeal to Pope Leo X (r. 1513–1521) for reform of this abuse went unanswered, Luther began to formulate the tenets of his beliefs, ideas that he had been mulling over for nearly a decade.

Tenets of Lutheranism as published in a series of tracts:

1. *Salvation by faith alone:* Good works (the sacraments and such) cannot guarantee salvation but rather are an outward manifestation of the faith that a loving God will grant that salvation. This concept was inspired by Luther's reading, many years earlier, of a passage from Romans I; 17; in which St. Paul says "the just shall live by faith. . . ."

2. *The Bible is the ultimate authority:* Neither the Pope nor church councils can define Christian doctrine; every believer should read and interpret the Bible, and the faithful will be divinely guided.

3. *The grace of God brings absolution:* Neither indulgences nor confession can bring forgiveness of sins; the individual is freed of sin only by the Grace of God; pilgrimages, veneration of saints, fasts, and worship of relics are useless.

4. *Baptism and communion are the only valid sacraments:* The Roman Catholic Church regarded seven sacraments (baptism; confirmation; eucharist or communion; matrimony; penance; extreme unction, last rites, or annointing of the sick; holy orders) as outward signs of inner grace. Luther rejected all but

baptism and communion. Luther also rejected the Roman Catholic doctrine of *Transubstantiation* (the belief that while the bread and wine of the Mass maintain their appearance, they are transformed into the Body and Blood of Christ). In its place he offered the doctrine of *Consubstantiation* (the doctrine that the transformation of the bread and wine was not literal but that God was somehow actually present in more than a symbolic way).

5. *The clergy is not superior to the laity:* Marriage is permitted; Christianity is a "priesthood of all believers"; monasticism should be abolished.

6. *The church should be subordinate to the state:* In all matters other than the theological—the appointment of church officials, the matter of taxing church lands, the organization of the church—the state is supreme. This appealed to the monarchs and to the German princes who resented papal authority and who coveted the vast landholdings and wealth of the Roman Catholic Church. It would have ramifications for Lutheranism in Germany well into the 20th century.

1520

Luther burned a *papal bull*, an official proclamation that demanded his recantation, and he was excommunicated by *Pope Leo X.* Holy Roman Emperor *Charles V* (r. 1519–1558), instead of arresting Luther and suppressing Lutheranism, which had a growing appeal in Germany and Scandinavia, honored a political debt to Frederick the Wise, Elector of Saxony, by refusing to outlaw Luther without a hearing.

1521

Luther was called to the Rhineland in Germany to appear before *The Diet of Worms*, a tribunal of the Holy Roman Empire with the power to outlaw—to condemn to be burned at the stake. Confronted by the sharpest theological debaters of the Roman Catholic Church, Luther contended that only the Bible or reason would convince him. "I neither can nor will I recant anything, since it is neither right nor safe to act against conscience."

The empire outlawed him. Brought to safety in Wittenberg by Frederick the Wise, he organized his reformed church and translated the Bible into the vernacular, profoundly influencing the development of the modern German language.

1520s

Lutheranism spread. Preoccupied with wars against the Ottoman Turks and the French, Charles V, Holy Roman Emperor, was unable to suppress the growth of Protestantism in Northern Europe. In addition to Northern Germany, Denmark and its province of Norway, Sweden and its holdings in Finland, and the Eastern Baltic all embraced Lutheranism.

1522

A league of Lutheran knights, under the leadership of *Franz von Sickengen*, converted to Lutheranism, attacked the Catholic princes of the Rhineland, was suppressed, but encouraged most of the Northern German princes to convert. One motive was the financial gain brought by confiscating Roman Catholic lands.

1524–1526

Luther's theological dissent inspired a variety of radical religious sects to form and to demand social reform based on the early Christian model. Demanding abolition of manorialism—the economic and social order of medieval feudalism—German peasants used force against the landowners, and Germany was wracked by the *Peasant's War*. Luther was appalled by these extremists and others who he believed took his ideas too far, such as the Anabaptists who preached adult total-immersion baptism, and the Millennarians, who expected the imminent return of Christ. He condemned the revolutionaries as "filthy swine" and encouraged the princes to exterminate them.

The radical revolt influenced Luther to demand that his followers obey constituted authority and that, while they read the Bible themselves, they leave its interpretation to knowledgeable ministers. His social and economic conservatism helped check the spread of Lutheranism in Southern Germany and elsewhere in Europe.

1529

The Diet of Speyer refused to recognize the right of the German princes to determine the religion of their subjects.

1531

The *League of Schmalkalden* was formed by newly Protestant princes to defend themselves against the emperor. Charles appealed to the Pope to call a church council that could compromise with the Lutherans and regain their allegiance to the Roman Catholic Church. The Pope, fearing the papacy's loss of power, refused and lost all opportunity to reunite Western Christendom.

1530s

The Reformation spread beyond Germany.

1531

In *Switzerland, Huldreich Zwingli* (1484–1531), who established Protestantism in Switzerland, was killed in a nationwide religious civil war. Although his followers accepted most of Luther's reforms, they argued that God's presence during communion is only symbolic.

The Peace of Cappel allowed each Swiss canton to determine its own religion.

1534

Pope Paul III (r. 1534–1549) assumed office as the first of the "reform popes."

1534

In *England;* Parliament passed the *Act of Supremacy,* which made *Henry VIII* (r. 1509–1547) and his successors the heads of the Anglican Church and its clergy. In 1521, when Luther was banned by the empire, Henry had been awarded the title "Defender of the Faith" by the Pope for his tract "Defense of the Seven Sacraments." By 1529, Parliament, partly because of Henry's influence, declared the English Church independent of Rome, cutting off revenues to the papacy. Henry, eager to divorce *Catherine of Aragon* in order to marry *Anne Boleyn,* had been denied an annulment for political reasons (Catherine was the aunt of Charles V, Holy Roman Emperor). Henry appointed *Thomas Cranmer* as Archbishop of Canterbury in 1533, was granted a divorce by him, and was excommunicated by the Pope.

1534–1539

The English Parliament abolished Roman Catholic monasteries, confiscated their lands, and redistributed them to nobles and gentry who supported the newly formed Anglican church.

1536

In *Switzerland; John Calvin* (1509–1564) published his *Institutes of the Christian Religion* in the Swiss city of Basel. Like Zwingli, he accepted most of Luther's ideas but differed on the role of the state in church affairs.

1. *Predestination:* Calvin argued (from an idea of St. Augustine) that since God knows even before birth whether a person is saved or damned, there is nothing anyone can do to win salvation. *The Elect* or *Saints* are a select few saved only by God's love from corrupt humanity and given indications of their status by *conversion* (a mystical encounter with God) or by material prosperity. The latter gave rise to the *Puritan* or *Protestant Ethic,* an incentive to avoid poverty as a sign of damnation, and served to justify the rise of capitalism.
2. *Church government:* Calvin replaced the Catholic hierarchy with a democratic system whereby each individual congregation elected its minister and governed its policies. He disagreed with Luther's claim that the church should be subordinate to the state, and argued that it should actually be a moral force in the affairs of secular government. This stand encouraged *theocracy,* whereby Calvinism became the official religion and intolerant of dissent not only in parts of Switzerland but later in England and the Massachusetts Bay Colony in North America.

1539

In *England,* Parliament approved the *Statute of the Six Articles.*

1. The seven sacraments were upheld.
2. Catholic theology was maintained against the tenets of both Lutheranism and Calvinism.
3. The authority of the monarch replaced the authority of the Pope.

Despite attempts by *Mary Tudor* (Henry's daughter by Catherine) to reinstitute Catholicism and the *Puritan Revolution* of the following century, the Six Articles helped define the Anglican Church through modern times.

1540s

Calvinism spread.

1541

Calvin set up a model theocracy in the Swiss city of Geneva.

The Scottish Calvinists *(Presbyterians)* established a national church.

The French Calvinists *(Huguenots)* made dramatic gains but were brutally suppressed by the Catholic majority.

The English Calvinists (Puritans and Pilgrims—a separatist minority) failed in their revolution in the 1600s but established a colony in New England.

1540s

The Catholic and Counter-Reformations began.

1540

Ignatius Loyola (1491–1556) established the *Jesuits (Society of Jesus)*, a holy order that was organized in a military fashion, requiring of its members blind obedience and absolute faith.

The Jesuits swore to suppress Protestantism:

1. They served as advisors to Catholic kings.
2. They suppressed heresy through the Inquisition (clerical courts that tried and convicted religious dissenters who were subject to deportation, torture, or death).
3. They established schools in Catholic nations to indoctrinate the young.
4. They sent missionaries to far corners of the earth to convert "the heathen."

The Society of Jesus became the militant arm of the Catholic and Counter-Reformations.

1542

The Jesuits were given control of the Spanish and Italian *Inquisitions*. Perhaps tens of thousands were executed on even the suspicion of heresy.

The *Index of Prohibited Books* was instituted in Catholic countries to keep heretical reading material out of the hands of the faithful.

1545–1563

The Council of Trent responded to the challenge of Protestanism by defining Catholic dogma. Its main pronouncements:

1. Salvation is by both *good works* (such as the veneration of saints and fasts) and *faith.*
2. The seven sacraments are valid, and transubstantiation was reaffirmed.
3. The sources of religious authority are the Bible, the traditions of the Church, and the writings of the Church Fathers. Individuals cannot interpret the Bible without the guidance of the Church, and the only valid version of the Bible is the Vulgate, St. Jerome's Latin translation.
4. Monasticism, with celibacy of the clergy, and the existence of purgatory were reaffirmed.

   Attempts were made to reform abuses: the principle of indulgences was upheld while its abuses were corrected; bishops were given greater power over clergy in their dioceses; and seminaries were established in each diocese for the training of priests.

1555

The Peace of Augsburg, after over two decades of religious strife, allowed the German princes to choose the religion of their subjects, although the choice was limited to either Lutheranism or Catholicism. *Cuius regio, eius religio*—"whose the region, his the religion."

RESULTS OF THE PROTESTANT REFORMATION

1. Northern Europe (Scandinavia, England, much of Germany, parts of France, Switzerland, Scotland) adopted Protestantism.
2. The unity of Western Christianity was shattered.
3. Religious wars broke out in Europe for well over a century.
4. The Protestant spirit of individualism encouraged democracy, science, and capitalism.
5. Protestantism, specifically Lutheranism, justified nationalism by making the church subordinate to the state in all but theological matters.

THE THIRTY YEARS' WAR (1618–1648)

1. The first continent-wide war in modern history, fought mostly in Germany, it involved the major European powers.
2. It was the culmination of the religious wars of the 16th century between Catholics and Protestants.
3. Politically, German princes sought autonomy from the Holy Roman Empire; France sought to limit the power of the Hapsburgs who sought to extend Hapsburg power in Germany; Sweden and Denmark hoped to strengthen their hold over the Baltic region.

THE FOUR PHASES OF THE WAR

1. *The Bohemian Phase (1618–1625):* The Czechs, also called Bohemians, who, together with the Slovaks, formed the modern nation of Czechoslovakia after World War I, were largely Calvinist. Fearful that their Catholic king, *Mat-*

thias, would deny their religious preferences, they *defenestrated* (used the old custom of registering dissent by throwing officials out a window) his representatives and installed, as king, a Calvinist, *Frederick V from the Palatinate.* After Matthias's death, *Ferdinand II* became Holy Roman Emperor and King of Bohemia. Supported by troops of the Spanish Hapsburgs, he defeated the Bohemians at the *Battle of White Mountain* in 1620, gave away the lands of the Protestant nobles, and enabled the Spanish to consolidate power along the Rhine River.

2. *The Danish Phase (1625–1630): Christian IV of Denmark* (r. 1588–1648), a Lutheran, entered the war to bolster the weakened Protestant position in Germany and to annex German lands for his son.

   Holy Roman Emperor Ferdinand II (r. 1619–1637) countered by commissioning Albert of Wallenstein to raise a mercenary army, which pillaged and plundered Germany and defeated the Danes in 1626. In 1629, the emperor issued The *Edict of Restitution*, which restored all the Catholic states in Germany that had been secularized before the Peace of Augsburg (1555). When Wallenstein disapproved, Ferdinand dismissed him.

3. *The Swedish Phase (1625–1630): Cardinal Richelieu*, Roman Catholic regent of France, was concerned with the gains made by the Hapsburg emperor in Germany. He offered subsidies to encourage the capable Swedish king *Gustavus Adolphus* (r. 1611–1632) to enter the war.

   Adolphus, a Lutheran, was eager to help the Protestant cause. After decisive victories over the Hapsburg forces, Adolphus was killed; Wallenstein was assassinated for contemplating disloyalty to the emperor, and the Protestant states of Germany made a separate peace with the emperor.

   The Peace of Prague revoke the Edict of Restitution. The Swedes were defeated, but Richelieu was determined to undermine Hapsburg power in Germany.

4. *The French-International Phase (1635–1648):* France, Holland, and Savoy entered the war in 1635 on the Swedish side. Spain continued to support the Austrian Hapsburgs. After a series of victories and reversals on both sides, *Henri Turenne*, a French general, defeated the Spanish at Rocroi, and in 1644 peace talks began in Westphalia in Germany.

The Peace of Westphalia, 1648

1. The Peace of Augsburg was reinstated *(cuius regio, eius religio),* but Calvinism was added as acceptable for Germany.
2. The Edict of Restitution was revoked, guaranteeing the possession of former Church states to their Protestant holders.
3. Switzerland and Holland were made independent states, freed from the Hapsburg dominions.
4. France, Sweden, and Brandenburg (the future Prussia) received various territories.
5. The German princes were made sovereign rulers, severely limiting the power of the Holy Roman Emperor and the influence of the Austrian and Spanish Hapsburgs. With over three hundred separate rulers in Germany, national unification was delayed until well into the 19th century.

Effects of the Thirty Years' War

1. Germany was devastated, its population reduced in some parts by well over a third. Once a cultural and political leader in Europe, it stagnated, postponing its entrance as a sovereign, united nation for more than two centuries and complicating its relations with the rest of the world into the 20th century.
2. The age of religious wars ended; the modern age of sovereign states began in Europe, and *"Balance of Power"* politics prevailed in Europe, whereby nation-states and dynasties went to war to prevent any one power from dominating the continent.
3. The Hapsburgs were weakened. The Austrian monarchy lost most of its influence over Germany, ending the possibility of a Europe united under the family. Hapsburg Spain was left a second-rate power.
4. The Catholic and Counter Reformations were slowed; Protestantism was safely established in its European strongholds.
5. The Holy Roman Empire ceased to be a viable political structure and the Germanic states would not be unified again until 1871.
6. Calvinism gained acceptance throughout Protestant Europe.
7. Anabaptists were persecuted and disappeared as a religion.

Women and Minorities During the Reformation

Women received mixed blessings from this era. Women did rise in status as Luther and the Protestants preached that there was merit in all work in the eyes of the Eternal including the household work of women. Also ministers were allowed to marry, which raised the status of the women who married them considerably from their position as adulteresses. On the other hand, there was still considerable misogyny evident in this society, which led to the witch trials that were also prevalent at this time. Mostly women were accused of practicing witchcraft and many were burned at the stake after tortured confessions or without evidence.

This was an age in which minority religion was finding its power, but it was also an era of zealotry. Practitioners of many religions were intolerant of those who practiced other faiths, and this resulted in the many religious wars of the era and the extermination of the Anabaptists. Those of African descent were enslaved and mistreated in larger numbers both in Europe and in the colonies, where the native inhabitants were also enslaved and mistreated. Tens of millions of Native Americans were killed and enslaved as Spain and other European powers became rich from the natural bounty of those lands. Slavery and genocide of the non-Europeans is part of the legacy of this age.

The Baroque Period of Art

The graphic arts began to flourish and become more awe-inspiring; thus, Baroque art was born. The general intent of the *Baroque* period was to create a unity where all forms of art in a single expressive purpose could converge toward a single aim—to engage the viewer physically and emotionally. The term "Baroque" derives from a Portuguese word jewelers used to denote an irregularity in a misshapen or irregular pearl. Baroque therefore literally meant imperfect, grotesque, or absurd. The Baroque era began in the late 1500s in Italy and ended in some areas around the early 1800s. The term also refers to the 17th century as a whole and is sometimes used as a general term indicating eccentric or fanciful modes of paintings, architecture, sculpture, dress, or behavior in any period. Baroque art spread throughout Western civilization and could be found in Latin America, the English colonies, and Northern Europe. Never had the Western world known such active international exchange in the intellectual field. The internationalism was not checked by differences in religious belief. For example, Rubens, a Flemish painter, worked in Italy, France, Spain, and England. He was considered a "European" painter, whereas Jacques-Louis David, a Neoclassical French painter, worked in France for most of his life.

Baroque art was an instrument of the *Counter Reformation*, which took place from 1545 to 1563. The Catholic Church was losing its followers in rapid numbers due to the rise of Protestantism, so it created the *Council of Trent* to set about renovating the Catholic Church itself. The society at this time was generally illiterate. Knowing this, the Catholic Church decided to bring back the wayward Catholics through Art. Baroque artists frequently capitalized on the immediacy of these emotional reactions, and "spiritual" art became an art of sensation. Its effect was not to elevate the spirit but to stagger and overpower the senses.

Baroque art was larger than life, escaping boundaries and overpowering the viewer. Some examples of Baroque painters and their defining characteristics include *Rubens'* (1577–1640) fleshy nudes, *Gentileschi's* (1593–1652) paintings of dramatic tension and suffering, *Rembrandt's* (1606–1669) innovative portraits and use of light, *Caravaggio's* (1571–1610) contrast of light and dark, and *Vermeer's* (1632–1675) clear domestic scenes. Beyond the realm of the two-dimensional, Bernini (1598–1650) was the greatest sculptor of the era. In the musical world, *Bach* (1685–1750) was the ultimate Baroque composer. Others include *Monteverdi* (1547–1643) who wrote the first opera *Orfeo, Vivaldi* (1678–1741) who composed *The Four Seasons*, and *Handel* (1685–1759) whose *Messiah* has become a classic.

Eventually, the Baroque style led to the *Rococo Style* of art, characterized by elegance, pleasantness, and frivolity. It greatly contrasted the emotional grandeur of the Baroque.

Many Faiths Chart

This chart may be helpful in remembering the differences among the many new Christian faiths that emerged from the Protestant Reformation.

The Many Faiths of the Protestant Reformation

	Catholic	Anglican	Luther	Calvin	Zwingli	Knox	Anabaptists
Leadership	Pope and religious hierarchy	King and religious hierarchy		Ministerial government divinely ordained			No head
Sacraments	Seven	Began with communion, baptism, and penance; then became just communion and baptism	Communion, baptism, Absolution	Communion, baptism	Communion, baptism	Communion, baptism	Lord's Supper, adult baptism
Clergy	Priests: Only clergy may interpret scripture	Married priests	Ministers and priesthood of all believers	Ministers, elders, deacons, people	Ministers	Ministers	Ministers including women
How is salvation achieved?	Faith and works	Faith and works	Faith: When one is justified one is forgiven; therefore, one can repent fully and do good works. Good works come from justification.	Faith: Good works may or may not be evidence of justification but wealth is.	Faith: Justification is God's endorsement of the morals of the individual.	Faith	Faith

	Pope is the Catholic leader of sovereigns.	The sovereign controls the church.	Religious choices are up to the individual who owes obedience to lawful ruler.	Religious organization dominates the state, and in fact IS the state, example: Geneva.	Religion controls the state.	Separation of church and state
Role of state						
Where	Italy, parts of Germany, Ireland, Poland, and France	England	Parts of Germany Sweden, Norway, and Denmark	Holland, France, and Geneva, Switzerland	Scotland; Zurich, Switzerland	Switzerland
Eucharist	Transubstantiation		Consubstantiation	Eucharist is just a symbol, not a divine action	Eucharist is a memorial, not a sacrifice	
Other	Indulgences, purgatory Abuses: simony, nepotism, pluralism, absenteeism			Predestination "Protestant ethic and the spirit of capitalism"—Max Weber "The elect."	Focused on rebuilding the community not the individual.	

Sample Essay Question

The sample and practice thematic essay questions presented in this chapter are types found on the AP European History Exam, and they require knowledge of causes, effects, personalities, ideas, and events.

SAMPLE QUESTION

Luther did not ask new questions, but offered new answers to old questions. What were these questions? What were Luther's answers and how did they contradict Roman Catholic answers?

Comments on the Sample Question

Follow the "Simple Procedures" for writing an essay. (See page 34.)

First, *What does the question want to know?* List the questions, Luther's answers, and the Roman Catholic Church's answers. Assess the answers for similarities and contradictions.

Second, *What do you know about it?* You need to know that the basic questions are: How is salvation achieved? What are the sacraments? Where does religious authority reside? What is the Church? What kind of miracle occurs during mass? The different answers to these questions must be examined for Luther and for the Roman Catholic Church.

Third, *How would you put it into words?* This essay lends itself to easy paragraphs for each of the questions of faith examined. If you write a thesis explaining that Luther's different answers to basic questions of religion led him to challenge the Roman Catholic Church, and then explains each question in its own paragraph, the structure will be strong. You should examine how these different answers were appealing enough to Luther and Northern Europe to cause the Protestant Reformation.

Rubric for Sample Answer

Before you read the sample answer, examine the rubric. What will the reader be looking for when he/she grades this essay? A sample rubric, shaded to show the reader's evaluation is seen below:

9–8 POINTS

- ✔ Thesis explicitly identifies the questions, Luther's new answers to them, and proposes to examine how they contradicted those of the Roman Catholic Church. Thesis does not need to be in the opening paragraph.
- ✔ Organization is clear, consistently followed, and effective in support of the argument.

- May devote individual paragraphs to an examination of each of the questions covering the extent to which Luther's answers contradicted the Church. May also devote paragraphs to questions, Luther's answers, and Church answers.
- Must identify the four questions How is salvation achieved? Where does Church authority reside? What is the Church? What are the Sacraments? and consider the extent to which and how each of the new answers Luther gave did or did not contradict the Church; does not have to present both categories for each question.

✔ Essay is well balanced; it identifies the questions, Luther's new answers to them, and examines how they contradicted those of the Roman Catholic Church, which are all analyzed at some length. Essay covers the chronology of Luther's schism with the Church to some extent and may mention Tetzel, indulgences, 95 Theses, Diet of Worms, and so on.

✔ Major assertions in the essay are supported thoroughly and consistently by relevant evidence.

✔ Evidence of the spread of these ideals may prove more specific or concrete.

✔ May contain errors that do not detract from the argument.

7–6 POINTS

✔ Thesis identifies the questions, Luther's new answers to them, and proposes to examine how they contradicted those of the Roman Catholic Church, but may not be developed fully.

✔ Organization is clear and effective in support of the argument but may introduce evidence that is not pertinent to the task.

✔ Essay covers all major topics suggested by the prompt but may analyze an aspect of the questions, Luther's new answers to them, and the examination of how they contradicted those of the Roman Catholic Church in greater depth rather than in a balanced manner.

✔ Major assertions in the essay are supported by relevant evidence.

✔ May contain an error that detracts from the argument.

5–4 POINTS

✔ Thesis identifies the questions, Luther's new answers to them, and proposes to examine how they contradicted those of the Roman Catholic Church but without any development; thesis may address only part of the question effectively; thesis may be a simple, single-sentence statement.

✔ Organization is clear but may not be consistently followed; essay may veer off task chronologically or thematically or both.

✔ Essay may not complete all tasks:
  - May discuss only the questions and Luther's new answers, or how Luther contradicted the Church.
  - May discuss only two or three of the questions and answers.
  - May focus only on the Church or Luther.
  - May be primarily descriptive rather than analytical.

✔ Essay offers some relevant evidence.

✔ May contain errors that detract from the argument.

3–2 POINTS

✔ Thesis may simply paraphrase the prompt OR identify the questions or the answers without analyzing the extent to which Luther contradicted the Church.

✔ Organization is unclear and ineffective; essay may focus on the personal attributes of Luther rather than analyzing the questions, Luther's new answers to them, and proposes to examine how they contradicted those of the Roman Catholic Church.

✔ Essay shows serious imbalance; discussion of the questions, Luther's new answers to them, and proposes to examine how they contradicted those of the Roman Catholic Church is superficial; much of the information may be significantly out of the time period or geography of the question.

✔ Offers minimal OR confused evidence.

✔ May contain several errors that detract from the argument.

1–0 POINTS

✔ Thesis is erroneous OR irrelevant OR absent.

✔ No effective organization is evident.

✔ Discussion of the questions, Luther's new answers to them, and proposes to examine how they contradicted those of the Roman Catholic Church is generic.

✔ Provides little or no relevant supporting evidence.

✔ May contain numerous errors that detract from the argument.

Sample Answer

In a time when faith and the Church were the central institutions of society, most people were concerned with salvation. Martin Luther's concern for his own salvation and that of others caused him to come to different conclusions than the Roman Catholic Church on the questions: How is salvation achieved? What are the sacraments? Where does religious authority reside? What is the church? What kind of miracle occurs during mass? Luther's well-reasoned answers to these age-old questions contradicted the Church. His answers along with the increase in general knowledge and curiosity of the Renaissance and political pressures brought on a revolution in the practice of Christianity.

The Roman Catholic Church had always taught that salvation was achieved through both faith in the Holy Trinity and good works. Luther, who had contradicted his father in becoming a member of the clergy (thus breaking the commandment to honor thy father), came to the conclusion that eternal salvation could come through faith alone. He believed that unwavering faith would lead one to a life of good work and was enough to achieve salvation. The Church taught that good works, such as donating to the Church or buying indulgences, could achieve salvation for a person. Luther's moral opposition to the practice of indulgences and John Tetzel's sale of them to his students prompted Luther to write his 95 Theses.

Another point that Luther contradicted the Church on was the question of what were the holy sacraments. Luther believed in baptism, the sacrament of the altar, and absolution as being the only acts that were truly sacraments while there are four other Roman Catholic ones according to Luther: confirmation, anointing of the sick, Holy Orders, and matrimony. Luther radically dismissed matrimony as having a less visible link to the Holy Spirit.

The third disagreement between Luther and the Church revolved around where religious authority rests. Luther stated that all religious authority came from the bible, whereas Catholicism taught that religious authority comes from the bible and papal/religious decrees. Luther stated in his debates with Eyck that unless someone would show him a place in the bible that justified papal decrees, he would believe that all religious authority resides in the bible. This contradiction was a major justification for many other Protestant sects which developed shortly after Lutheranism.

The fourth contradiction Luther made with Roman Catholicism was about the definition of the Church. Catholicism teaches that the buildings and the clergy define the Church. Luther defined his church as the community of Christian believers. This community was another important innovation that led many to embrace new forms of Protestantism.

The fifth and final contradiction was the difference between *transubstantiation* and *consubstantiation*. Roman Catholicism taught *transubstantiation,* the act during the Eucharist when the bread and wine become the *actual* body of Christ, while Luther taught *consubstantiation,* in which the bread and wine became the *spirit* of Christ.

Before Luther shared his revolutionary new answers to these important questions of Christian faith, there was a monopoly on religious power in Western Europe. After Martin Luther gained political support of the German princes including Frederick the elector of Saxony, the Roman Catholic Church was no longer *the* Church, but a church among many on the continent.

EVALUATE THE SAMPLE ANSWER

Now go back and look at the rubric. It is clear that this essay fulfills all of the requirements for a score of 8 or 9 on the rubric. The essay answers all parts of the question thoroughly with concrete evidence at length with a well-balanced essay. The extra concrete support gets this essay a score of 9.

RATER'S COMMENTS ON THE SAMPLE ANSWER

9—Extremely Well Qualified

This is an answer that could certainly have been written in the time allotted, and it answered all parts of a multifaceted question. This essay explained the significance of the conflicts of thought between Luther and the Roman Catholic Church, as well as how these conflicts led to the splintering of the Church in Western Europe. The indignation of Luther with the sale of indulgences is noted, but not emphasized unduly. The essay also does not write about the Protestant Reformation as solely a religious movement, but gives credit to the political and social factors that also played roles in ushering it in.

The essay structure was logical and allowed for a quick clear progress through a question that requires many tasks. The tasks included stating the questions, answering them for both Luther and Roman Catholicism, and analyzing the conflicts on those questions and the long-term results of those conflicts. The introduction and conclusion of this essay are particularly strong, hitting the reader hard at both the start and end to make an impact.

Although this is a very strong essay, it did not cover any other Protestant faiths or leaders, and could have benefitted from showing the pent-up religious questioning that Luther unleashed. Although it was not required for this essay, some readers may feel more confident giving higher marks to essays that show more historical perspective.

Practice Essay Questions

The questions that follow are samples of the various types of thematic essay questions that appear on the exam. The review chapters in this section (Part Two) will have samples of the major types of thematic essays: defend or refute, analyze, evaluate, to what extent and in what ways, assess the validity, contrast and compare, explain. (See pages 21–22 for a detailed explanation of each type and an example of each.) Check over the **generic rubric** (see pages 58–60) before you begin any of these essays and use that rubric to score your essay if you write one.

QUESTION 1

"Calvin's doctrines were a radical departure from those of both the Roman Catholic Church and Lutheranism." Evaluate this statement.

COMMENTS ON QUESTION 1

This question leaves some room for choice. In evaluating the statement, you may choose to compare the doctrines on *salvation* of each of these Christian sects. In his stand against the indulgences, Luther departed from Roman Catholic doctrine and from Church tradition. Calvin argued still another view. The question could be approached through this issue alone.

Another way to attack the question would be through the differing relations of each of these sects to the issues of religion and the state and of church government. A clear contrast can be shown among the three.

QUESTION 2

"The Reformation was caused by long-term political, social, and economic developments." Discuss this statement.

COMMENTS ON QUESTION 2

The "discuss" essay is, by nature, less focused than other essay tasks. Like the others, it requires that you take a stand on the statement; unlike the others, it does not narrow the possible approaches. Choices bring opportunities and dangers. *This type requires strict organization.*

In this particular question, the crucial term is "caused." Any great historical event is brought about by multiple and complex developments. These are the *long-term causes.* For instance, corruption among Church officials and the influence of Renaissance ideas are long-term causes of the Reformation. But people—personalities—are often at the center of immediate causation. *Immediate causes* are actions that precipitate great events. Tetzel's sale of indulgences provoked Luther to issue his *95 Theses.*

QUESTION 3

"The Catholic and Counter Reformations attempted not only to reform the Church but also to suppress heresy." Defend or refute this statement.

COMMENTS ON QUESTION 3

In a "Defend or refute" essay, it is still possible to present a mixed argument—partly for, partly against. After all, there are few human endeavors that do not encompass the whole range of moral possibility. However, it is always best to choose one side of the fence unless you can support both sides thoroughly, which is a lot more work. In this case, there is ample evidence for both sides so picking a side would be the easier essay to write in the time allotted.

To "reform" implies a noble goal for a noble institution; to "suppress" implies the application of power for the denial of freedom. The point to remember with this question is not to make moral judgments but rather to consider the varying roles of individuals and organizations during the Catholic response to Protestantism.

QUESTION 4

"The Protestant emphasis on one's personal relationship with God was a logical outgrowth of the Renaissance." Assess the validity of this statement.

COMMENTS ON QUESTION 4

A reminder: To "assess validity" is to determine whether a statement is true, false, or partly both. The pivotal concept in this statement is "logical outgrowth." Consider its implications before choosing an approach. Does it mean a necessary effect? Or the result of one influence among many?

In order to answer this, you must be familiar with the Renaissance ideas that emphasized individuality as well as how they differed with notions of the preceding age (the medieval period). These ideas must then be linked as influences for various Protestant theological or social concepts that differed from Roman Catholic views.

This is a tough question! It would be easy to fall into the trap of oversimplifying by jumping to conclusions based on a superficial knowledge of complex ideas and doctrines.

QUESTION 5

"Protestantism spread with the growth of nationalism." Discuss this statement.

COMMENTS ON QUESTION 5

This question exposes the link between political and spiritual power in the world. Religion has influenced politics throughout the ages and continues to do so today. In the case of the Protestant Reformation, it is clear that without political support, Luther would have been no more successful in allowing personal religious freedoms than was Jan Huss before him.

The key to answering this question is an understanding of the changed attitudes and political relationships in the 16th century and of the way Protestantism fostered nationalism.

Practice Multiple-Choice Questions

Refer to Part One, A Guide to the AP European History Exam, for advice on taking the multiple-choice section of the exam. The practice questions that follow are representative of the various types that appear on the AP Exam.

1. All of the following can be considered a long-term cause of the
   Protestant Reformation EXCEPT

   (A) the declining prestige of the papacy
   (B) the German mystics who emphasized individual communion
   with God
   (C) the activities of the Jesuits
   (D) the humanist accusation that the Church was losing the substance
   of Christ's message
   (E) the corruption of the Roman Catholic Church during the Renaissance

2. "Salvation by faith and by faith alone" is a major tenet first adopted by

   (A) Calvinism
   (B) Lutheranism
   (C) Catholicism
   (D) Anglicanism
   (E) Anabaptism

3. In his *On Christian Liberty*, Luther used the term "freedom" to mean

   (A) freedom from poverty
   (B) political liberty
   (C) freedom from the Roman Catholic Church
   (D) freedom from any type of servile situation
   (E) freedom from taxes

4. Luther's political conservatism is revealed in which of the following?

   (A) His preference for political order over social justice
   (B) His willing acceptance of the support of the German princes
   (C) His condemnation of the Peasants' War
   (D) His support for the extermination of the Munster Commune
   (E) All of these

5. Which of the following was NOT a reason for the rapid spread of Lutheranism in the 1520s and 1530s?

   (A) The rise of dissenting sects
   (B) The conversion of the princes of Northern Germany
   (C) Charles V's involvement in foreign wars
   (D) The failure of the Pope to call a church council
   (E) Popular resentment in Germany against Rome

6. Calvin differed from Luther by stressing which theological doctrine?

   (A) The right of the clergy to marry
   (B) The Bible as the ultimate authority for Christian doctrine
   (C) The concept of predestination
   (D) The effect of "good works" in winning personal salvation
   (E) The rejection of all but two of the sacraments

7. Charles V's vast empire was

   (A) a well-knit political entity
   (B) a diverse collection of states, each with its own local laws but subject to the imperial constitution
   (C) held together by the powerful imperial bureaucracy
   (D) held together only by the person of the emperor
   (E) limited to holdings in Europe

8. "Poverty, considered a virtue by the Catholic Church, became shameful to the Calvinists. The middle class found in Calvinism a justification for the pursuit of wealth."

   This passage implies that Calvinism may have been a powerful influence in the development of which of the following?

   (A) Communism
   (B) Capitalism
   (C) Nationalism
   (D) Democracy
   (E) Science

9. Which of the following was NOT a goal of the Catholic and Counter-Reformations?

   (A) The conversion of the populations of southern Europe
   (B) The reform of abuses within the Roman Catholic Church
   (C) The confirmation of the Church's basic dogma
   (D) The stemming of the spread of Protestantism
   (E) The suppression of heresy

10. Which of the following accurately depicts a doctrine defined by the Council of Trent?

    (A) Salvation is attained by "good works" alone.
    (B) The ultimate authority for Christian doctrine is the Bible, Church traditions, and the writings of the Church Fathers.
    (C) Monasticism and clerical celibacy are forbidden.
    (D) Only Holy Communion and Baptism, of the seven sacraments, are necessary to the attainment of salvation.
    (E) The Church is subordinate to the state in all but theological matters.

11. "Like an army, it was ruled by a general who was responsible directly to the pope. Its holy soldiers practiced blind obedience, maintained absolute faith, and willingly suffered extreme hardship." This passage best describes

    (A) the Inquisition
    (B) the Diet of Worms
    (C) the Society of Jesus
    (D) the Index of Prohibited Books
    (E) the papacy

12. The Jesuits

    (A) became involved in the education of Catholic children
    (B) served as advisors to Catholic kings
    (C) rooted out heresy through press censorship
    (D) converted "heathens" through missionary work
    (E) All of these

An Eyewitness Account of the Saint Bartholomew's Day Massacre by François Dubois. From the Musée Des Beaux-Arts, Lausanne, Switzerland. The Granger Collection, New York. (0009687)

13. The above picture depicts which two groups engaged in battle?

    (A) The French Huguenots and Catholics
    (B) French and Austrian Soldiers
    (C) Catholics and Anabaptists
    (D) Lutherans and Catholics
    (E) Peasants and nobles

14. Protestant values, sometimes differing from one sect to another, helped in the development of which of the following?

    (A) Capitalism, nationalism, monasticism
    (B) Science, capitalism, nationalism
    (C) The conciliar movement, science, democracy
    (D) Nationalism, individualism, clerical celibacy
    (E) Science, nationalism, monasticism

15. The Thirty Years' War

    (A) was a religious struggle between Catholics and Protestants
    (B) was an attempt by the princes of Germany to diminish the influence of the Holy Roman Empire
    (C) was an attempt by France to limit Hapsburg power
    (D) involved most of the major states of Europe
    (E) All of these

Answers and Answer Explanations

1.	C	6.	C	11.	C
2.	B	7.	B	12.	E
3.	C	8.	B	13.	A
4.	E	9.	A	14.	B
5.	A	10.	B	15.	E

1. **(C)** The Jesuits did not receive a papal charter until 1540; the Reformation began in 1517.

2. **(B)** This is the crux of Luther's theological divergence from indulgences and "good works."

3. **(C)** Luther was only in favor of freedom from the Roman Catholic Church and the papacy. When the peasants used his writings to justify their revolt against the German princes, Luther corrected them by publishing *Against the Murderous Thieving Hordes of Peasants*. He was concerned with salvation and not the temporal world.

4. **(E)** A religious radical, Luther still prized social stability above social justice.

5. **(A)** The dissenting sects competed for converts with the Lutherans. The conversion to Lutheranism of the German princes led to the conversion of their populations. Charles's wars against the French and the Turks prevented him from using force to suppress the Lutherans. Various popes' concerns over losing power to the church councils postponed a reforming council that might have checked or accommodated Protestantism.

6. **(C)** Calvin borrowed the concept of predestination from St. Augustine, who argued that God, being omniscient, knew before their births who would be saved and who would be damned. Calvin regarded both faith and good works as signs of salvation rather than means for attaining it.

7. **(B)** The empire of Charles V was a loosely organized collection of states that was not well-knit to the point that he split the empire between his son and brother when he died. He lacked an imperial bureaucracy that could handle the empire, which is why the German kingdoms were in revolt for the better part of his rule.

8. **(B)** This is the so-called Protestant Ethic, which developed from the Calvinist tenet that material prosperity is a good indication that an individual is one of the "elect."

9. **(A)** They were already strongholds of Catholicism.

10. **(B)** This statement of dogma countered Luther's assertion of "salvation by faith alone" and Calvin's concept of predestination.

11. **(C)** The Jesuits (Society of Jesus), organized by Ignatius Loyola, were an arm of the Catholic and Counter Reformations.

12.   **(E)** The Jesuits used various methods to root out heresy, to maintain orthodoxy in Catholic nations, and to spread the faith.

13.   **(A)** The St. Bartholomew's Day Massacre was between French Catholics and Huguenots.

14.   **(B)** Science was fostered by the Protestant spirit of inquiry. Capitalism benefited from the Puritan work ethic, which saw material success as indicative of being one of the "elect." Nationalism was fostered by Luther's assertion that the church is subordinate to the state in all but theological matters.

15.   **(E)** These complex rivalries culminated in the Thirty Years' War (1618–1648), which devastated Germany, weakened the Hapsburgs, and brought the religious conflicts of the previous hundred years to a bloody climax.

CHAPTER 3

The Growth of European Nation-States in the 1500s and 1600s

Key Terms/People

- Prince Henry the Navigator
- Diaz
- da Gama
- Cabral
- Christopher Columbus
- Cortés
- Pizzaro
- Suleiman the Magnificent
- Ivan the Terrible
- Peter the Great
- Hohenzollern
- Frederick William
- Absolutism
- Francis I
- Concordat of Bologna
- Henry II
- Edict of Toleration
- Catherine de Medici
- Massacre of St. Bartholomew's Day
- Henry IV
- Edict of Nantes
- Duke of Sully
- Cardinal Richelieu
- Louis XIV
- Mazarin
- Wars of Frondes
- divine right theory of rule
- Jean Baptiste Colbert
- Henry VII
- War of the Roses
- Henry VIII
- Mary Tudor
- Elizabeth I
- The Thirty-Nine Articles
- Sir Francis Drake
- The Stuart Kings
- The Stuart Restoration
- Tories
- Whigs
- The Glorious Revolution
- John Locke

Overview

Centralization of governments led to the rise of powerful nation-states and concomitant European exploration of the globe and regional wars on the continent. Spain, following the Portuguese lead, explored the Atlantic and soon surpassed its Iberian neighbor in colonies, wealth, and military power. Gold and silver from the

New World helped shift the balance of power from the Mediterranean basin to the Atlantic coast of Europe. The wealth from mines in the Spanish colonies created a financial and commercial center in the Netherlands, brought about rampant inflation in Europe, and eventually led to the decline of Spain as a major power.

Feudalism died gradually. The Hundred Years' War (1337–1453), which devastated France and exhausted its nobility, indirectly led to a strong monarchy. Peace encouraged commerce, which gave rise to a taxable middle class that could support a national army independent of the nobility. From the midddle of the 15th century to the second decade of the 16th, the monarchs of France centralized the state, recruited bourgeois administrators into government, and strengthened the army. Through most of the 16th century, the foreign adventures of two strong kings and the upheaval caused by the Reformation weakened the monarchy. Under the intelligent guidance of Cardinal Richelieu (1585–1642), prime minster to Louis XIII (r. 1601–1643), the central government brought peace, prosperity, and stability to the realm during the first half of the 17th century. The Golden Age of France was during the reign of the Sun King, Louis XIV (r. 1643–1715), whose absolutist monarchy dominated all classes in Europe's wealthiest and most populous country, upset the balance of power on the continent, and claimed the "divine right" of rule.

The strong government that developed in France contrasted with the constitutional system that evolved in England. The powers of the English kings had been checked by the nobility as far back as the 13th century, with the Magna Carta. The Tudors took the English throne in the 15th century as a compromise among the claimants who battled over it in the War of the Roses. Having only a tenuous hereditary right to the monarchy, they were forced to work through Parliament, which gradually represented a greater and greater portion of English society and therefore avoided the class distinctions that divided France. The Reformation had its effects on English government: The independence of the Anglican Church from the papacy strengthened the monarchy and Parliament; the Puritan Revolution established the supremacy of Parliament over the king and nurtured the tradition of constitutionalism.

A strong tradition of absolutism developed in Eastern Europe especially in the rising states of Russia, Prussia, and Austria. Social reform was sporadic and largely ineffectual and serfdom was widespread in the region. The baroque style of architecture was favored by the absolute monarchs of these states as a manifestation of their power and glory.

Exploration and Colonization: 1400s to 1600s

The Portuguese, from the middle to the end of the 15th century, supported by their able leader, *Prince Henry the Navigator* (1394–1460), explored the South Atlantic. Expeditions led by *Diaz*, *da Gama* (ca. 1469–1524), and *Cabral* (1467–1520) explored the coast of Africa and eventually established trading posts in India.

Spurred by missionary zeal, personal gain, and national pride, and aided by the development of the magnetic compass, the astrolabe, and more seaworthy craft, explorers from several states on the Atlantic set out on their journeys of discovery.

Christopher Columbus (1451–1506), seeking a direct route to Asia for the Spanish crown, discovered the Western Hemisphere, and despite opening the "New World," laid the foundations for Europeans' oppression and exploitation of native peoples. *Ferdinand Magellan* (1480–1521) circumnavigated the globe for Spain, and *Cortés* (1485–1547) and *Pizarro* (1475–1541), respectively, conquered the great American empires of the Aztecs and Incas. Gold and silver flowed from the New World mines into the coffers of the Spanish monarchs and to the merchants and manufacturers of the Netherlands. These explorers opened up trade routes for new products on three continents that would bring large profits to Europeans for centuries to come. This exchange of valuable goods and resources from each continent was known as the *Columbian Exchange*. This trade brought European manufactured goods and alcohol to Africa and the Americas and products such as lumber, fur, gold, sugar, potatoes, and corn to Europe.

Chafing under the oppressive rule of the Spanish Catholic *King Philip II* (r. 1556–1598), the prosperous Low Countries whose leaders were Calvinist, revolted against the Spanish from 1556–1587. The bitter and bloody conflict led to the division of the Low Countries into the Spanish Netherlands in the south (which eventually became Belgium) and the United Provinces of the Netherlands in the north (eventually Holland). The defeat in 1588 of the attempt of Philip II's armada to invade England, an ally of the Netherlands, marked the beginning of the decline of Spain's hegemony in Western Europe.

The *Thirty Years' War* (1618–1648) began as a religious conflict, evolved into a national struggle for dominance of Central Europe, and led to the destruction of vast areas in Germany and the decline of the regional hegemony of the Holy Roman Empire. The Austrian Hapsburgs confronted the powerful Muslim Ottoman Turks in an attempt to expand their control of Eastern Europe. The 1683 attack on Austria by the forces of *Suleiman the Magnificient* was beaten back, and the Austrians eventually gained control of Bohemia, Hungary, and Transylvania.

Russia and Western Europe experienced radically different paths of development until the 18th century. For centuries, the princes of Moscow had been retainers of the Mongol conquerors, and the czars were able to use their influence with the Mongols to consolidate their power over the Russian people and to establish the hereditary role of czar. *Ivan the Terrible* (r. 1547–1584) was an autocratic expansionist who limited the power of the nobles (boyars), expanded the realm, and solidified the role of czar. A *Time of Troubles* ensued after his death, marked by civil war and the lack of an heir. The Romanov dynasty was established by the nobles in 1613, and the family ruled with an iron hand, reinstituting serfdom and gaining virtual control over the Russian Orthodox Christian Church.

Peter the Great (r. 1696–1725) expanded the power of the state and of the czars by establishing a powerful standing army, a civil service, and an educational system to train technicians in the skills developed by western science and technology. He imposed economic burdens, western ideas, and social restrictions on the peasants to further his power, erected the planned city of St. Petersburg on the Baltic, and built magnificent, ornate baroque palaces, churches, and public buildings to glorify his reign. Russia became one of the major powers of Europe during this period.

Brandenburg, an electorate of the Holy Roman Empire, was able to gain a degree of independence as a result of the weakening of the Hapsburg rule during the Thirty Years' War. The *Hohenzollern, Frederick William* (r. 1713–1740), solidified autocratic rule over Brandenburg, Prussia, and the Rhine territories with a strong army and an efficient bureaucracy, and with a policy of weakening the nobles (Junkers) and suppressing the peasants. The Junkers served as elite officers in the army and absolutist rule was established in Prussia.

The Development of Absolutism in France

Francis I (r. 1515–1547), a Valois rival of Holy Roman Emperor Charles V, battled unsuccessfully to weaken the Hapsburgs as Europe's most powerful family but managed to consolidate absolutism in France by instituting the taille (a direct tax on land and property). With the *Concordat of Bologna,* he granted the Pope the right to collect *annates* (the first year's revenue from Church offices) in return for the power to nominate high officials in the French church, effectively nationalizing the church in France and increasing the power of the monarchy.

Opposed to any reform of the Church that might weaken his influence over it, he and his successor, *Henry II* (r. 1547–1559), actively persecuted the *Huguenots* (French Calvinists). Continued persecution under *Francis II* and *Charles IX* provoked civil war, which was halted by an *edict of toleration* issued by *Catherine de Medici,* mother of, and regent for, Charles IX.

The *Massacre of St. Bartholomew's Day* renewed the brutal civil war when Catholic mobs slaughtered Huguenot leaders who had gathered in Paris to celebrate a royal wedding. Although the Huguenots were never more than 10 percent of the French population, they wielded great influence since they came from the nobility and the bourgeoisie.

Persecution, civil war, and dynastic rivalry left *Henry of Navarre,* a Huguenot, as the only legitimate claimant to the French throne, and he ascended, after an expedient conversion to Catholicism, as *Henry IV* (r. 1589–1610). He issued the *Edict of Nantes,* a remarkable expression of religious tolerance that guaranteed civil and religious freedom to the Huguenot minority. His finance minister, the *Duke of Sully,* reformed the tax collection system to make it more equitable and efficient, improved transportation, stimulated trade and industry, and fostered prosperity. All of this led to an increase in the prestige and power of the monarchy.

After the death of Henry IV, the government suffered from corruption and mismanagement during the regency of *Louis XIII.* In 1624, Louis appointed *Cardinal Richelieu* as prime minister, a post he held from 1624 to 1642. It was not uncommon in this religious era for churchmen to serve as advisors to the monarchs of Europe. Richelieu centralized the government further by encouraging the commerce and industry that increased the tax base, by strengthening the military, and by instituting the *intendant system,* in which bourgeois officials, answerable only to the king, supervised the provinces and diminished the power of the nobility.

Richelieu's domestic polices strengthened absolutism in France and prepared the way for its supreme embodiment in the *Sun King, Louis XIV*.

Louis XIV (r. 1643–1715) was four when he ascended the throne of France. His mother was his regent, and she chose *Italian Cardinal Mazarin* (1602–1661) as prime minister. Like Richelieu, Mazarin was a capable administrator, and he protected Louis's claim to the throne during the tumultuous *Wars of the Fronde*, which reached their height from 1650 to 1652. The *Frondeurs* were nobles who sought to limit the powers of the monarch and to decentralize the government in order to extend their own influence. With the support of the bourgeoisie and the peasants, who had little to gain in a return to the feudal order, Mazarin was able to subdue the *Frondeurs* and their ally, Spain.

When Mazarin died in 1661, Louis declared himself as his own prime minister. *L'Etat, c'est moi* ("I am the state") became the credo of this most absolutist monarch during the age of absolutism. *Bishop Jacques Bossuet* (1607–1704) provided the philosophical justification for the *divine right theory of rule* by claiming that Louis—like any absolutist monarch—was placed on the throne by God, and therefore owed his authority to no person or group.

According to feudal tradition, French society was divided into three *Estates*, made up of the various classes. The *First Estate* was the clergy; the *Second Estate*, the nobility; these comprised, respectively, 1 percent and 3 to 4 percent of the population. The *Third Estate* included the great bulk of the population: the bourgeoisie or middle classes, the *artisans* and *urban workers*, and the *peasants*. Since France was, as were all European nations at this time, predominantly *agrarian*, 90 percent of its population lived on farms in the countryside. Louis XIV reigned over the Golden Age of French culture and influence: With a population of 17 million (about 20 percent of Europe's total), France was the strongest nation on the continent.

Its industry and agriculture surpassed that of any other European country. *Jean Baptiste Colbert* (1619–1683), "The Father of French Mercantilism," revitalized trade as Louis's finance minister by abolishing internal tariffs and creating a free trade zone in most of France. He stimulated industry by subsidizing vital manufacturing and by building up the military. He hoped to make France self-sufficient by building a large fleet that would rival that of the English and Dutch and enable the French to acquire an overseas empire. Since even France could not afford both a powerful army and navy, Louis opted for the army; the end result was the global supremacy of the British.

France developed Europe's first modern army. Artillery—usually supplied by civilian private contractors—was made a part of the army. The government—instead of officers—recruited, trained, equipped, and garrisoned troops. A chain of command was established, and the army was increased from 100,000 to 400,000, the largest in Europe.

War was an instrument of Louis's foreign policy. For two thirds of his reign, France was at war.

The War of the Devolution (1667–1668): France's unsuccessful attempt to seize the Spanish Netherlands (Belgium) as part of a feudal claim.

Invasion of the Dutch Rhineland (1672–1678): Revenge for the Dutch role in defeating France in the War of Devolution and an attempt to seek France's "natural boundary in the west," the Rhine River. Largely unsuccessful.

Seizure of Luxembourg and attempt to annex Alsace-Lorraine (1681–1697): Although France retained Luxembourg, most of Louis's ambitions were frustrated by The League of Augsburg, an alliance of Holland, Spain, the Holy Roman Emperor, and England.

The War of the Spanish Succession (1702–1714): Louis threatened to upset the Balance of Power (the theory that no single state should be predominant on the continent) in Europe by laying claim to the Spanish throne for his grandson. The Grand Alliance, which included the major states of western Europe, fought to prevent this union of the French and Spanish thrones.

The Treaty of Utrecht (1713–1714): Restored the balance of power by allowing Philip V, Louis's grandson, to remain on the Spanish throne so long as France and Spain were never ruled by the same monarch. It also awarded to the victors various European and overseas possessions of the Spanish Empire.

France enjoyed a Golden Age of culture and cultural influence during Louis XIV's reign:

French became the "universal tongue," spoken by diplomats and in the royal courts of all Europe.

Louis patronized artists and especially writers such as *Corneille, Racine* (1639–1699), *Molière* (1622–1673), *de Sévigné, de Saint-Simon* (1607–1693), *La Fontaine, De La Rochefoucauld* (1621–1695).

French literature and style—in dress, furniture, architecture—became standards by which all Europeans measured their sophistication.

Although his reign solidified central government and marked the high point of absolutism in France, his many wars exhausted the treasury. This left the bourgeoisie and the peasantry with an enormous tax burden since the clergy and nobility were exempted from most taxes. His personal extravagances aggravated the situation: The Royal Palace at *Versailles* cost over $2 billion in 2007 dollars to build, and added to that was the money spent on his elaborate entertainments for the "captive nobility" at court. (He defanged the nobles by making participation in court life a social requirement.) He suppressed religious dissent, outlawing *Jansenism,* a form of Catholic Calvinism, revoking the *Edict of Nantes,* which had guaranteed toleration for the Huguenots, and making Catholicism mandatory.

The central government that developed in France from the era of the religious wars to Louis's reign was efficient: The power of the nobles was weakened; tax collection was systematized; royal edicts were enforced; the bourgeoisie was given a role in administration. The economic system was successful: Agriculture and trade were stimulated. The seeds for revolution were sown in the national debt that had to be paid off by the Third Estate, which bore many responsibilities and enjoyed few privileges.

The Development of Constitutionalism in England

Henry VII (r. 1485–1509), the first of the *Tudor* monarchs, established a strong central government even though many regarded the family as usurpers invited to the throne as an expedient compromise to end the *War of the Roses*. By regulating trade and internal commerce through monopolies, charters, and licenses, Henry raised revenues from the prosperous middle class. This money enabled him to finance a standing army and keep the nobility in check. The *Court of the Star Chamber* administered central justice and further subdued rebellious nobles. Since the Tudors were beholden to Parliament for inviting them to the throne, Henry and his successors, including his son *Henry VIII* (r. 1509–1547), consulted Parliament on significant issues.

Unlike his father, who was levelheaded and tightfisted, Henry VIII was an impetuous, extravagant, passionate man whose temper, ambitions, and appetites were legendary. The need to maintain legitimacy by having a male heir led Henry VIII to make those decisions, with Parliament's support, that led to the *English Reformation*. (See page 47.)

Edward VI (r. 1547–1553) assumed the throne upon the death of his father, Henry VIII, and since he was only ten and of fragile health, the government was run by a regent, the *Duke of Somerset*. A devout Calvinist, Somerset imposed his religion on the people, and, as a result, was ousted in 1550. Under another regent, the basic tenets of the Anglican Reformation were restated, and the *Anglican Book of Common Prayer* was made the basis for all church services.

Mary Tudor (r. 1553–1558), who was Henry VIII's daughter by his first wife, the Catholic Catherine of Aragon, became queen when Edward died at the age of sixteen. Unpopular, not only because she was Roman Catholic but because she was married to *Philip II* of Spain, she had to suppress a rebellion against her rule and her marriage alliance with Spain. *Bloody Mary* earned her name when she burned hundreds of Protestants at the stake for dissenting against her attempt to reinstitute Catholicism in England. When she died, she was succeeded by her half sister, *Elizabeth,* Henry's daughter by his second wife, Anne Boleyn.

Elizabeth I (r. 1558–1603), last and greatest of the Tudor monarchs, reigned when the population of England and Wales was between 3 and 4 million, while that of France was over 16 million and that of Spain nearly 9 million. Enriched by its conquests and colonies in the New World, Spain was the predominant power of Europe; its geographic destiny determined by its island nature, England was at the fringe of the religious upheaval and political change on the continent. Its church was independent from Rome but closer to Latin theology than any other Protestant sect. Its government balanced power between the monarchy and Parliament. Its wealth came from rich arable land and an energetic populace that excelled in commerce and trade. Its social system was unique: a *gentry,* lesser nobles whose original wealth came from ownership of land, expanded by entering the world of commerce and by intermarrying with the middle class. There were no glaring distinctions between the upper and middle classes as there were on the continent, and the interests of nobles, gentry, and bourgeoisie were represented in Parliament.

Since the Tudors had been invited to the throne of England to settle the rival claims of the Houses of York and Lancaster during the War of the Roses, Elizabeth, her charismatic father, and her capable grandfather had lived under the shadow of "dynastic pretender." The child of Anne Boleyn, whose marriage to Henry was scandalous if not outright illegal, The *Virgin Queen* (a euphemism for her never marrying, considering her notorious love affairs) had to prove her mettle in the face of the prejudices against her line, her parentage, and her gender. Her natural intelligence had been honed by substantial education; her powerful personality had been toughened by living as a family "outcast" at her father's, her half brother's, and her half sister's court. Adored by her people and feared by her enemies—at home and abroad—she reigned for nearly a half-century as one of Europe's greatest monarchs and one of the world's greatest women.

The Elizabethan Age

Religion

Upon assuming the throne, Elizabeth repealed Mary's pro-Catholic legislation and reinstated the Acts of Supremacy and Uniformity that established the English Reformation during her father's reign.

The Thirty-Nine Articles (1563) followed Protestant doctrine and was vague enough to accommodate most of the English except the *Puritans* (English Calvinists). They believed that the *liturgy* (prescribed ritual) and the *hierarchy* (the order of rank within the organization) needed "purification" from Catholic influence. Militant Puritans challenged royal authority, and while they were suppressed for the time, they grew stronger during the reigns of Elizabeth's successors and would influence the development of constitutionalism.

Diplomacy

When the Netherlands, a Hapsburg possession that had adopted Protestantism, revolted against Spanish rule, Elizabeth entered into an alliance with the Dutch in 1577 for fear that Holland would provide a base from which Spain could invade England. Both England and Holland sent *privateers* (pirates commissioned by the state) to prey on the treasure ships from the Spanish colonies in the new world. Outraged, *Philip II,* Spanish king and Holy Roman Emperor, conspired with English Catholics to overthrow Elizabeth and put her cousin, the Catholic Mary Stuart, queen of the Scots, on the throne. In 1587, Elizabeth ordered the execution of Mary for treason, and Philip declared war on England. The *La Felicima Armada*, or "great and most fortunate fleet," of 132 heavily armed warships loaded with troops, was defeated in 1588 by the superior naval tactics of the smaller, more maneuverable English fleet led by *Sir Francis Drake* (1540–1596). The superior navigational skills and military tactics of the English sailors were critical to their success as severe storms also sank many Spanish ships. The failure of the Spanish Armada marks the beginning of the fall of Spanish naval dominance and the rise of British naval dominance.

Culture

This was the Golden Age of English literature—the era of Shakespeare, Spenser, Donne, Marlowe, Francis Bacon—when a brilliant national literature was developed that instilled pride in the uniqueness of English culture.

The Stuart Kings and Parliament
(1603–1688)

James I (r. 1603–1625), king of Scotland and son of Mary Queen of Scots, took the throne upon Elizabeth's death since she had no direct heirs. A believer in the divine right of kings, he failed to understand the importance of Parliament in governing England. A conference at *Hampton Court*, 1604, failed to reconcile the Puritans, who opposed Anglican hierarchy, with the church of England. The *Gunpowder Plot*, 1605, was uncovered before disgruntled Catholics, led by Guy Fawkes and objecting to James's enforcement of laws that required participation in Anglican services, could blow up the king and Parliament. The years 1610 to 1611 saw the session of Parliament enmeshed in the issue of Parliament's role in financing government.

The *"Addled" Parliament* met in 1614 and was so-called by James because it spent its entire session arguing that taxes could be levied only with its consent and that rule was by king and Parliament in conjunction. Dissolving Parliament, James tried to rule without it until England's involvement in the Thirty Years' War necessitated his reconvening it. After a rancorous session in which Parliament criticized James's foreign policy, in 1621 Parliament passed the *Great Protestation*, claiming free speech and authority in conducting governmental affairs. James dissolved the body and arrested its leaders.

Charles I (r. 1625–1649) was, like his father, devoted to the divine right theory and woefully inept at dealing with Parliament. Embroiled in wars on the continent, he called for Parliament to vote funds, which it refused to do until he signed the *Petition of Right* in 1628: Parliament alone can levy taxes; martial law cannot be declared in peacetime; soldiers may not be quartered in private homes; imprisonment requires a specific charge. The Bishops' War of 1639–1640, after Archbishop Laud persecuted Puritans and tried to force Anglican worship upon the Presbyterian Scots, led Charles to reconvene Parliament in order to pay indemnities upon defeat of his forces.

The *Long Parliament* (1640–1660) demanded, in return for paying for Charles's defeat, that he impeach his top advisers; allow Parliament to meet every three years without his summons, and promise not to dissolve Parliament without its consent. When Charles attempted, in early 1642, to arrest opposition members, Parliament seized control of the army. Charles gathered his forces, and the *English Civil War* (1642–1649) began.

The Course of the War

The middle class, the merchants, the major cities, and a small segment of the nobility supported Parliament and were called *Roundheads*. The Anglican clergy, the majority of the nobility, and the peasants backed the king and were referred to as *Royalists* or *Cavaliers*.

1643

The Roundheads allied with Presbyterian Scotland, promising to impose Presbyterianism on England in exchange for military assistance. Charles called on Irish Catholics for help.

1644

Oliver Cromwell (1599–1658), a Puritan leader of Parliament, led his *New Model Army* of Puritans against the Cavaliers at *Marston Moor* and defeated them decisively.

1645

Charles surrendered to the Scots.

1647

The Scots turned Charles over to Parliament, which was led by Cromwell's *Independents,* who favored religious toleration. The Scots turned about and allied with Charles, who promised that he would impose Presbyterianism on the English.

1648

Cromwell defeated the Scots at the *Battle of Preston* and helped purge the Presbyterians from Parliament, thereby creating the *Rump Parliament,* which voted to behead Charles for treason.

1649

With the death of Charles, England became a republic, the *Commonwealth,* and Cromwell and his army wielded the power. In suppressing Irish supporters of the crown, the Puritans committed terrible atrocities and imposed injustices that would acerbate the *"Irish Question"* for centuries.

1653–1660

Cromwell was designated *Lord Protector* by a puppet Parliament and ruled with the support of Parliament until his death in 1658. His son Richard, a far less capable ruler, was deposed in 1660, and *Charles II* (r. 1661–1685) was proclaimed king.

The Stuart Restoration (1660–1688)

The *Cavalier Parliament* (1660–1679) marked the development of the Tory and Whig parties. The *Tories,* made up of the nobles, the gentry, and the Anglicans, were conservatives who supported the monarchy over Parliament and who wanted Anglicanism to be the state religion. The *Whigs,* mainly middle class and Puritan, favored Parliament and religious toleration. Since the Tories prevailed in the Cavalier Parliament, Anglicanism was restored by a series of laws that forbade dissenters to worship publically, required government officials and military personnel to practice Anglicanism, and discriminated against other sects.

The *Whig Parliament,* elected in 1679, was suspicious of Charles II's absolutist and pro-Catholic tendencies, and enacted the *Habeas Corpus Act,* which limited royal power by

- ✔ Enabling judges to demand that prisoners be in court
- ✔ Requiring just cause for continued imprisonment
- ✔ Providing for speedy trials
- ✔ Forbidding *double jeopardy* (being charged for a crime that one had already been acquitted of)

The Glorious Revolution

James II (r. 1685–1688) was unpopular the moment he took the throne. A devout Roman Catholic, he appointed Catholic ministers to important posts and gave the appearance of trying to impose Catholicism upon the English. In 1688, important nobles invited *William of Orange,* a Hollander, and the wife of James's oldest child, Mary, to take the English throne. When *William and Mary* (r. 1688–1704) arrived in England, James fled to exile in France, and the new monarchs accepted from Parliament, as a condition of their reign, the *Declaration of Rights* (enacted into law as the *Bill of Rights* in 1689). The *Habeas Corpus Act,* the *Petition of Right,* and the Bill of Right are all part of the *English Constitution.*

THE DECLARATION OF RIGHTS

1. Only Parliament can impose taxes.
2. Laws can be made only with the consent of Parliament.
3. A standing army can be maintained only through the consent of Parliament.
4. The people have the right of petition.
5. Parliament has the right of free speech.
6. The people have the right to bear arms.
7. People have the right to due process, trial by peers, and reasonable bail.
8. Parliament is to be freely elected and dissolved only by its own consent.

The *Glorious Revolution* was actually the culmination of an evolutionary process over centuries which, through historical accident, outright conflict, and painstaking design, increased the power of Parliament over the monarchy. In the centuries that followed, monarchs in England came to reign while Parliament came to rule. Although Parliament, at the time of the Glorious Revolution, served the interests of the wellborn or the wealthy, it came to represent "the people" as government came to be viewed as existing and functioning according to *John Locke's* Enlightenment concept of *"consent of the governed."* The English and those who inherited their political traditions would guarantee individual rights and would create modern democracy.

Women During the Age of Absolutism

There were a few powerful female monarchs such as Elizabeth I and Catherine II who showed by example how powerful a woman could be. When Elizabeth I led her troops into battle during the Spanish Armada, her speech was a rousing testament to what a woman can accomplish. Catherine overthrew her husband and ushered in the most enlightened era Russia had yet witnessed. The common woman, however, saw no increases in her freedom or importance before the law.

A Guide to Monarchs and Their Families

Many students throughout the years have had trouble keeping their rulers straight. This chart of national monarchical history is intended to help you with that task.

Rulers that are shaded mean STOP and memorize their names and know why they are important; these people will very likely be on the AP test.

Rulers in bold mean PAUSE and be familiar with who these people are; they may be on the test and rate some attention.

Rulers in regular text mean KEEP GOING. Sure, one might be on the test every ten years as a distracter in one of the last multiple-choice questions, but that is a chance we are willing to take. These names are included mainly for continuity's sake, but most professors do not know who they are and you don't need to either.

Insofar as dates go, keep a ballpark figure of when people reigned, lived, and so on, but memorizing the exact dates is frustrating and not necessary.

Austria

In 1276, Rudolf I of Hapsburg became the Duke of Austria; this might be significant, but the test does not start until 1450, so we will begin with Maximilian, the first Hapsburg Holy Roman Emperor. On the right is the ruler's given name. The next category is the Anglicized version of the name. Important advisors are listed below the king/queen.

Name	Reign	Notes
Maximilian I	**(r. 1493–1519)**	
Charles V	(r. 1519–1556)	Divided up the Hapsburg lands.
Ferdinand I	(r. 1556–1564)	
Maximilian II	(r. 1564–1576)	
Rudolf II	(r. 1576–1612)	
Matthias	(r. 1612–1619)	
Ferdinand II	(r. 1619–1637)	Started 30 Years War.
Ferdinand III	(r. 1637–1657)	
Leopold I	(r. 1658–1705)	
Joseph I	(r. 1705–1711)	
Charles VI	**(r. 1711–1740)**	**Pragmatic Sanction**
Maria Theresa	(r. 1740–1780)	
Joseph II	**(r. 1780–1790)**	
Leopold II	(r. 1790–1792)	
Francis I	(r. 1792–1835)	Declared Emperor of Austria in 1806.
Metternich	Foreign Minister	Congress System
Ferdinand I	(r. 1835–1848)	
Francis Joseph I	**(r. 1848–1916)**	
Charles I	(r. 1916–1918)	

Great Britain

The first nation in which the King agreed that his power was limited was also the first country to have the legislative branch execute the monarch legally. By the 16th century, the English monarchy was as much about negotiating between powerful parties and religious factions, as it was about pomp and circumstance.

Name	Reign	Notes
Henry VII	**(r. 1485–1509)**	**Tudor**
Henry VIII	(r. 1509–1547)	Tudor
Edward VI	**(r. 1547–1553)**	**Tudor**
Mary I	**(r. 1553–1558)**	**Tudor, "Bloody Mary"**
Elizabeth I	(r. 1558–1603)	Tudor, "The Virgin Queen"
James I	**(r. 1603–1625)**	**Stuart (James VI of Scotland)**
Charles I	(r. 1625–1649)	Stuart (Civil War 1642–1649)
Oliver Cromwell	(r. 1649–1658)	"Lord Protector" (dictator)
Richard Cromwell	(r. 1658–1660)	
Charles II	(r. 1660–1685)	Stuart
James II	(r. 1685–1688)	Stuart
Mary II and William III	(r. 1689–1702)	Mary Stuart, William of Orange, (Glorious Revolution)
Anne	(r. 1702–1714)	Stuart
George I	**(r. 1714–1727)**	**Hanoverian**
George II	(r.1727–1760)	Hanoverian
George III	(r. 1760–1820)	Hanoverian
George IV	(r. 1820–1830)	Hanoverian
William IV	(r. 1830–1837)	Hanoverian
Victoria	(r. 1837–1901)	Saxe-Coburg-Gotha (William IV's niece)
Edward VII	(r. 1901–1910)	Saxe-Coburg-Gotha
George V	(r. 1910–1936)	Windsor
Edward VIII	**(r. 1936)**	**Windsor (abdicated to marry divorcee)**
George VI	(r. 1936–1952)	Windsor
Elizabeth II	**(r. 1952–)**	**Windsor**

France

The model of absolutism under Louis XIV, this nation was once ruled by Louis XIV's grandfather who converted three times and in the final conversion before taking the throne declared that "Paris is worth a mass."

Name	Reign	Notes
Charles VII	**(r. 1422–1461)**	**Valois**
Louis XI	**(r. 1461–1483)**	**Valois, "Spider King"**
Charles VIII	(r. 1483–1498)	Valois
Louis XII	(r. 1498–1515)	Valois-Orléans, "Father of the People"
Francis I	(r. 1515–1547)	Valois-Angoulême
Henry II	(r. 1547–1559)	Valois-Angoulême
Francis II	(r. 1559–1560)	Valois-Angoulême
Charles IX	(r. 1560–1574)	Valois-Angoulême
Henry III	**(r. 1574–1589)**	**Valois-Angoulême**
Henry IV of Navarre	(r. 1589–1610)	Bourbon
Louis XIII Cardinal Richelieu	**(r. 1610–1643)**	**Bourbon** Chief Minister
Louis XIV	(r. 1643–1715)	Bourbon, "The Sun King"
Louis XV René de Maupeou	(r. 1715–1774)	Bourbon Chancellor
Louis XVI	(r. 1774–1792)	Bourbon (executed)
Louis XVII	(r. 1793–1795)	Bourbon (jailed throughout "reign")

Legislatures
  National Assembly
  Legislative Assembly
  National Convention
	(1789–1795)
	(1789–1791)
	(1791–1792)
	(1792–1795)
		The First Republic
		
		Committee on Public Safety (1793–1794)

Directory (Directoire)	(1795–1799)	The First Republic
Napoléon Bonaparte	(r. 1799–1815)	Bonaparte (First Consul until **1804**)
Louis XVIII	**(r. 1814–1824)**	**Bourbon (monarchy restored)**
Charles X	(r. 1824–1830)	Bourbon
Louis Philippe **François Guizot**	**(r. 1830–1848)**	**Bourbon-Orléans, "Citizen King"** **Chief Minister**
Louis Napoléon	(r. 1848–1852)	Second Republic (President)
Napoléon III (Louis Napoléon)	(r. 1852–1870)	Second Empire (Emperor)

Germany

Germany was formed in 1871 as a combination of many different German states, kingdoms, cities, pots, pans, sausages, and so on that was dominated by the ruler of Prussia, Wilhelm (William) I Hohenzollern. He, in turn, traced his lineage from the Electors of Brandenburg, an area on the other side of Germany. The Hohenzollern lineage is outlined here.

Name	Reign	Notes
Frederick William	(r.1640–1688)	"The Great Elector"
Frederick I	**(r. 1688–1713)**	**Crowned King of Prussia in 1701**
Fredrick Wilhelm I	(r. 1713–1740)	"The Soldier's King"
Fredrick II	(r. 1740–1786)	"Frederick the Great"
Fredrick Wilhelm II	(r. 1786–1797)	
Fredrick Wilhelm III	(r. 1797–1840)	
Fredrick Wilhelm IV	(r. 1840–1861)	
William I	**(r. 1861–1888)**	**Kaiser of the Second Reich**
Otto von Bismark		Chancellor
Fredrick III	(r. 1888)	
William II	(r. 1888–1918)	Kaiser during World War I

Russia

Though there were princes of Muscovy before Ivan III, he is the one who is credited with forming the modern nation of Russia and, more importantly for us, the earliest king the test makers would consider putting on the test.

Name	Reign	Notes
Ivan III	(r. 1440–1505)	"Ivan the Great"
Vasily III	(r. 1505–1533)	
Ivan IV	(r. 1533–1584)	"Ivan the Terrible"
Theodore I	(r. 1584–1598)	
Disputed Line of Succession	(r. 1598–1613)	"Time of Troubles"
Michael	**(r. 1613–1645)**	**Romanov**
Alexis I	(r. 1645–1676)	Romanov
Theodore III	(r. 1676–1682)	Romanov
Ivan V	(r. 1682–1689)	Romanov
Peter I	(r. 1682–1725)	Romanov, "Peter the Great"
Catherine I	(r. 1725–1727)	Romanov
Peter II	(r. 1727–1730)	Romanov
Anna	(r. 1730–1740)	Romanov
Ivan VI	(r. 1740–1741)	Romanov
Elizabeth	(r. 1741–1762)	Romanov
Peter III	(r. 1762)	Romanov
Catherine II	(r. 1762–1796)	Romanov, "Catherine the Great"
Paul I	(r. 1796–1801)	Romanov
Alexander I	**(r. 1801–1825)**	**Romanov**
Nicholas I	(r. 1825–1855)	Romanov
Alexander II	**(r. 1855–1881)**	**Romanov (reformer)**
Alexander III	(r. 1881–1894)	Romanov

Nicholas II
  Sergei Witte
  Peter Stolypin
	(r. 1894–1917)	**Romanov**
		Minister of Finance
		Chief Minister

Spain

Ferdinand and Isabella were the first kings of a unified Spain; hence, we start with them. Each "ruled" their own kingdom, although after 1506, Ferdinand became the regent of Castile as well.

Name	Reign	Notes
Ferdinand	(r. 1474–1516)	King of Aragon (joint rule)
Isabella	(r. 1474–1504)	Queen of Castile (joint rule)
Joanna and Philip I	(r. 1504–1506)	Rulers of Castile
Ferdinand	(r. 1506–1516)	Regent of Castile, King of Aragon
Charles I	(r. 1516–1556)	Hapsburg (Charles V of Austria)
Philip II	(r. 1556–1598)	Hapsburg
Philip III	(r. 1598–1621)	Hapsburg
Philip IV	(r. 1621–1665)	Hapsburg
Charles II	(r. 1665–1700)	Hapsburg
Philip V	**(r. 1700–1746)**	**Bourbon (great grandson of Philip IV)**
Ferdinand VI	(r. 1746–1759)	Bourbon
Charles III	(r. 1759–1788)	Bourbon
Charles IV	(r. 1788–1808)	Bourbon
Ferdinand VII	(r. 1808)	Bourbon
Joseph Bonaparte	(r. 1808–1813)	Bonaparte
Ferdinand VII	(r. 1813–1833)	Bourbon (restored)
Isabella II	(r. 1833–1868)	Bourbon
Francisco Serrano y Domínguez	(r. 1869–1870)	Elected regent
Amadeus	(r. 1870–1873)	Elected regent
Estanislao Figueras	(r. 1873)	First Republic (President)
Francisco Pi y Margall	(r. 1873)	First Republic (President)
Nicolás Salmerón y Alonso	(r. 1873)	First Republic (President)
Emilio Castelar y Ripoll	(r. 1873–1874)	First Republic (Prime Minister)
Alfonso XII	(r. 1874–1885)	Bourbon (King)
Alfonso XIII	(r. 1886–1931)	Bourbon (King)
Niceta Alcalá Zamora	(r. 1931–1936)	Second Republic (President)
Manuel Azaña	(r. 1936–1939)	Second Republic (President)
Francisco Franco	**(r. 1939–1975)**	**Nationalist Government (Chief of State)**
Juan Carlos I	(r. 1975–)	Bourbon (constitutional monarch)

Sample Essay Question

The sample thematic essay question and the practice essays presented in this chapter are types found on the AP exam, and they require knowledge of causes, effects, personalities, ideas, and events.

SAMPLE QUESTION

Machiavelli suggested that a ruler should behave both like a fox and a lion, and be both loved and feared. Analyze the policies of THREE of the following monarchs, indicating the degree to which they followed Machiavelli's advice, and how their application of that advice affected their rule.

Elizabeth I of England
Henry IV of France
Peter the Great of Russia
Louis XIII
Frederick William I
Charles I of England
Charles V

Comments on the Sample Question

Follow the "Simple Procedures" for writing an essay. (See page 34.)

First, *What does the question want to know?* Which rulers would Machiavelli have praised or criticized and why? Is it better to write about those he would have praised, criticized, or both?

Second, *What do you know about it?* Define Machiavellian principles and ideas and decide which monarchs would be good to use. Use the rulers that support the argument the best through facts. Machiavelli wanted strong rulers who knew when to take advice and when to give orders. He admired those who seemed virtuous but would do anything for the best of the nation. Machiavelli said to never make the people hate the ruler or take their religion, land, or women. He also distrusted mercenaries. One of the most important tasks here is to choose which rulers to examine. The people chosen will determine the structure of the essay.

Third, *How would you put it into words?* This essay lends itself to easy paragraphs for each of the rulers examined. If you write a thesis explaining that different rulers followed Machiavelli's advice to different degrees but those who followed it most closely were most successful, and then use one paragraph for each monarch discussed, the essay will be logically ordered.

Rubric for Sample Answer

Before you read the sample answer, examine the rubric. What will the reader be looking for when he/she grades this essay? A sample rubric, shaded to show the reader's evaluation is seen below:

9–8 POINTS

✔ Thesis explicitly identifies **both** the extent to which the chosen rulers followed Machiavelli's advice and how their rule was affected by their adherence to those principles or lack thereof. Thesis does not need to be in the opening paragraph.

✔ Organization is clear, consistently followed, and effective in support of the argument.

- May devote individual paragraphs to an examination of the extent to which specific rulers followed Machiavelli's advice and to an examination of how their rule was affected by their adherence to those principles or lack thereof. May also devote one paragraph to each chosen ruler and evaluate within that paragraph.

- Must identify pieces of Machiavellian advice (strong rulers who know when to take advice and when to give orders; seem virtuous but do anything for the best of the nation; never make the people hate the ruler or take their religion, land, or women; distrust mercenaries; take on the religion and customs of those they conquer; live among those they conquer). Must also consider the extent to which each chosen ruler followed that advice and how their rule was affected by their adherence to those principles or lack thereof; does not have to present both categories for each monarch.

✔ Essay is well balanced; the extent to which the chosen rulers followed Machiavelli's advice and how their rule was affected by their adherence to those principles or lack thereof are analyzed at some length. Essay covers the importance of Machiavellian ideas to ruling.

✔ Major assertions in the essay are supported thoroughly and consistently by relevant evidence.

✔ Evidence may prove more specific or concrete.

✔ May contain errors that do not detract from the argument.

7–6 POINTS

✔ Thesis explicitly identifies both the extent to which the chosen rulers followed Machiavelli's advice and how their rule was affected by their adherence to those principles or lack thereof, but may not be developed fully.

✔ Organization is clear and effective in support of the argument but may introduce evidence that is not pertinent to the task.

✔ Essay covers all major topics suggested by the prompt but may analyze a ruler, an aspect of Machiavelli's advice, or the extent to which a particular ruler followed his advice in greater depth rather than in a balanced manner.

✔ Major assertions in the essay are supported by relevant evidence.
✔ May contain an error that detracts from the argument.

5–4 POINTS

✔ Thesis identifies **both** the extent to which the chosen rulers followed Machiavelli's advice and how their rule was affected by their adherence to those principles or lack thereof, but without any development; thesis may address only part of the question effectively; thesis may be a simple, single-sentence statement.

✔ Organization is clear but may not be consistently followed; essay may veer off task chronologically or thematically or both.

✔ Essay may not complete all tasks:
- May discuss only the extent to which the chosen rulers followed Machiavelli's advice OR how their rule was affected by their adherence to those principles or lack thereof.
- May discuss only two or fewer rulers.
- May focus only on one or two of Machiavelli's pieces of advice.
- May be primarily descriptive rather than analytical.

✔ Essay offers some relevant evidence.

✔ May contain errors that detract from the argument

3–2 POINTS

✔ Thesis may simply paraphrase the prompt OR explain the extent to which the chosen rulers followed Machiavelli's advice without analyzing how their rule was affected by their adherence to those principles or lack thereof.

✔ Organization is unclear and ineffective; essay may focus on the personal attributes of rulers rather than analyzing how their rule was affected by their adherence to those principles or lack thereof.

✔ Essay shows serious imbalance; discussion of the extent to which the chosen rulers followed Machiavelli's advice and how their rule was affected by their adherence to those principles or lack thereof, is superficial; much of the information may be significantly out of the time period or geography of the question.

✔ Offers minimal OR confused evidence.

✔ May contain several errors that detract from the argument.

1–0 POINTS

✔ Thesis is erroneous OR irrelevant OR absent.

✔ No effective organization is evident.

✔ Discussion of the extent to which the chosen rulers followed Machiavelli's advice and how their rule was affected by their adherence to those principles or lack thereof is generic.

✔ Provides little or no relevant supporting evidence.

✔ May contain numerous errors that detract from the argument.

Sample Answer

Machiavelli's *The Prince* revolutionized political thought or at least outlined a revolution in political thought that was occurring at the time in the actions of the "new monarchs," such as Henry VII and Louis XI, in governing with the best interests of the state as the only measure of the goodness of any action. His little treatise, sent to the Medici family in hopes of regaining favor, outlined how a ruler should act in order to rule effectively. Elizabeth I followed his advice very well, as did Henry IV of Navarre, but Charles V, the Holy Roman Emperor, could have learned quite a deal from Machiavelli's advice.

Elizabeth I was both loved and feared, but never hated. She won the loyalty of the middle class by giving them a degree of religious freedom and freeing their business interests from government intervention, both things Machiavelli suggests. Machiavelli would have praised her reliance on English troops during the Spanish Armada and her use of her status of possible marriage as a weapon of diplomacy. Her use of tactics he would have approved won her people supremacy in trade and naval power and won her the eternal admiration of her nation as one of its greatest monarchs.

Henry IV of Navarre was a great example of using religion in the way that Machiavelli suggested, to get the support of the people. He used the differences between religions of the day to secure support for himself as a possible leader of the country. He then converted to Catholicism in order to rule, but preserved his alliances with his Huguenot roots. He used these tactics to begin the Bourbon dynasty in France, and men such as Cardinal Richelieu and Louis XIV into efficient means of controlling the state and influencing international politics further sharpened the tactics.

Charles V did not follow the advice of Machiavelli; his vast realm was in revolt for much of his reign and had to be divided by his heirs. Charles V did not go to live in the Germanic lands when he bribed his way into the title of Holy Roman Emperor at age nineteen and declared that he would exert more control in the region at his coronation. He fought religious wars, and the Germans hated him.

Elizabeth and Henry were good Machiavellian rulers, and Charles V helped Spain decline because he was not.

EVALUATE THE SAMPLE ANSWER

Now go back and look at the rubric. It is clear that this essay looks like a 6 or 7 on the rubric. The essay answers all parts of the question with concrete evidence but the essay focuses on one monarch and misses some major possible points. In this case, the lack of detail warrants a 6.

RATER'S COMMENTS ON THE SAMPLE ANSWER

6—Well Qualified

This essay has a very good thesis but deteriorates as it goes on. The thesis shows an understanding of the question and makes the reader believe that a complete answer will follow. What does follow is a strong examination of Elizabeth I, a partial examination of Henry IV, and a paltry examination of Charles V, with a nod toward a conclusion. This essay does answer the question, but just barely. The main strength of this essay is in its structure and thesis.

Weaknesses: If the paragraphs about the second two monarchs had included more support for why they were and were not good examples of Machiavellian rulers then the essay would have been much stronger. There are so many details about Henry of Navarre and the War of the Three Henrys and the way he began the consolidation of royal French power so typified by his grandson, Louis XIV, which should have been utilized. Likewise, the political blunders of Charles V are not few, and many more could be cited here.

Practice Essay Questions

These questions are samples of the various types of thematic essays on the exam. (See pages 21–22 for a detailed explanation of each type.) Check over the **generic rubric** (see pages 58–60) before you begin any of these essays and use that rubric to score your essay if you write one.

QUESTION 1

Contrast and compare the development of the nation-state in France and in England from the early 16th to the end of the 17th centuries.

COMMENTS ON QUESTION 1

This is a very general question on a very complex development. The *contrast* is glaring in that during this period the French developed *absolutism* to its pinnacle and that England continued the evolution of *constitutionalism*. "Who did what, when, and how" is a convenient formula for tracing the separate developments. Be careful not to get lost in detail. The large scope of the question requires a big-picture perspective.

The comparison of the development of these two very different styles of government is more difficult. "To compare" is to measure for similarities and differences. Were there similarities? Did the monarchs of these two diverse nations have similar traits of personality, similar methods for consolidating power? Were there similar obstacles to overcome, such as the vested interests of the nobility or the need for revenue? Despite the differences between absolutism and constitutionalism, were there common goals—consolidation, centralization of authority, and modernization?

QUESTION 2

Analyze the development of absolutism in France (1500–1715).

COMMENTS ON QUESTION 2

This is another question whose scope is very broad. Here you must "examine in detail" as well as "determine relationships." Examine the roles of the early Valois monarchs in centralizing authority, considering the religious wars of the 16th century and the role of Henry IV in restoring national order and royal esteem, examining the profound accomplishments of Richelieu (one of Hollywood's favorite villains), then touring the reign of Louis XIV.

QUESTION 3

To what extent and in what ways did the Puritan Revolution contribute to the supremacy of Parliament in 1689?

COMMENTS ON QUESTION 3

This is a difficult question because it requires that you demonstrate how and how much a complex set of events contributed to a complex development. An effective approach would be to divide the bigger issue into smaller questions: What was the Puritan Revolution? How did it increase the power of Parliament? How did the Restoration affect Parliament's role? How was the monarchy weakened by the Puritan Revolution? How and why did the Glorious Revolution occur?

QUESTION 4

"The Tudors brought England into the modern world." *Assess the validity of this statement.*

COMMENTS ON QUESTION 4

To "determine the truth or value" of this assertion, you must clarify what is meant by "the modern world," examine the Tudor reign—specifically Henry VII, Henry VIII, and Elizabeth I—and demonstrate whether or not the Tudors accomplished a transformation. Be careful about dismissing Henry VIII because of "bad press." Despite his glaring personal failings—abused wives and gluttony outstanding among them—he strengthened the monarchy and intitated the English Reformation. Elizabeth may be famous for standing up to the superpower of her day—Spain—but the Golden Age of English culture was also during her reign.

QUESTION 5

Explain how the Glorious Revolution of 1688 established constitutional government in England.

COMMENTS ON QUESTION 5

While this requires specific knowledge of events, laws, and effects, your answer should make clear how the abdication of James II, the invitation to the throne for William and Mary, and the conditions set for this by Parliament laid the foundation for a modern democratic state. How was Parliament's power solidified? How did the Bill of Rights establish a rule of law? How did the supremacy of Parliament and these basic rights limit the monarchy?

QUESTION 6

Describe the process of exploration, discovery, and colonization in the 1400s and 1500s among the European states bordering the Atlantic.

COMMENTS ON QUESTION 6

The best approach to this question would involve a chronological account beginning with the Portuguese and Spanish, contrasting their routes of exploration and their modes of colonization, and then outlining the roles of the other Western European states involved in the issue. The question is broad in scope, but needs specific factual references to illustrate the main points.

QUESTION 7

Contrast and compare the development of absolutism in 17th century Prussia and Russia.

COMMENTS ON QUESTION 7

Contrast (show differences), *compare* (show similarities) in the development of centralized monarchy under the Hohenzollerns of Prussia and the Romanovs of Russia. Compare methods; contrast unique historical backgrounds of the two nations. The Romanovs were able to go from the servants of the Mongol invaders to the monarchs of the largest nation geographically the world had ever seen. Every single non-noble person was their personal servant in waiting. The autocratic power that was developed by the Romanovs pales when compared to the hodgepodge of territory that the Hohenzollerns held together through alliances and the cooperation of the nobility. The Romanovs were tsars of all Russia, and the Hohenzollerns were the first among other equal nobles until the nobility were co-opted into the military by the Soldier King, Frederick William.

QUESTION 8

Explain how Spain became Europe's richest and most powerful nation-state during the 16th century and then fell into an equally dramatic decline during the 17th century.

COMMENTS ON QUESTION 8

Spain's ascendancy is attributable to the same broad factors as is its decline: a crusading zeal to explore, conquer, and colonize; a religious mission to suppress heresy and convert the nonbeliever; the acquisition of gold and silver in lieu of a vibrant commercial and manufacturing economy; the emmigration of the most entrepreneurial Spaniards.

Practice Multiple-Choice Questions

(These represent the different types of questions that appear on the AP exam.)

1. The end of the Hundred Years' War encouraged the growth of centralized government in France for all of the following reasons EXCEPT

   (A) the nobility had been weakened by the war
   (B) the monarchy had led the fight against the English
   (C) the revival of commerce increased the taxable revenues of the bourgeoisie
   (D) nobles were recruited to serve as government administrators
   (E) the king was able to keep a strong standing army

2. Francis I further consolidated centralized power by levying the taille, a tax on

   (A) all land and property
   (B) on peasant crops
   (C) on the Gallic Church's income
   (D) on the landholdings of the nobility
   (E) on imports

3. When Henry IV remarked, "Paris is well worth a Mass," he was referring to

   (A) his prayers for the fall of the city during his siege of it
   (B) his expected visit during the Easter season
   (C) his conversion to Catholicism to gain popular favor
   (D) his conversion to Calvinism to gain support of the Huguenots
   (E) his visit with the Pope to gain absolution

4. The Edict of Nantes, issued by Henry IV in 1598, was one of the most significant acts of his reign because of all the following reasons EXCEPT

   (A) it was one of the first governmental guarantees of religious freedom in Europe
   (B) it granted Huguenots civil and political equality with Catholics
   (C) it continued the bitter civil war between Catholic and Protestant
   (D) it brought peace to France
   (E) it granted Huguenots political control of many towns in France

5. Probably the most important step Cardinal Richelieu took to strengthen centralized government and an absolutist monarchy in France was

   (A) to involve France in the Thirty Years' War
   (B) to institute the intendant system to oversee the provinces
   (C) to levy taxes on the clergy and nobility
   (D) to suppress the musketeers
   (E) to ban private duels within the realm

6. When Louis XIV said "L'état, c'est moi," he was referring to

   (A) his role as an enlightened despot with the peoples' best interests in mind
   (B) his assumption of the role of his own prime minister upon the death of Mazarin
   (C) his title as French Sovereign
   (D) his resistance to the *Frondeurs*
   (E) his belief in the divine right of kings

Peter I. Mezzotint by John Sartain after Benjamin West. The Granger Collection, New York. (0012251)

7. The depiction of Peter I of Russia above, a rare surviving piece from the time critical of the tsar, is specifically criticizing

(A) the beard tax that Peter imposed on all men
(B) the dress of the boyars at the time
(C) the dentistry of Peter I who would extract teeth from subjects
(D) the relationship between Peter I and the clergy
(E) The Western styles of Peter I

8. Why, if during the reign of Louis French was the "universal language" and French styles were the measure of good taste, was the French army called the Huns of the 17th century?

   (A) It relied primarily on cavalry tactics.
   (B) It recruited troops from the Russian steppes.
   (C) Large, modern, and aggressive, it upset the continent's balance of power.
   (D) Its top commanders—Turenne, Vauban, and Conde—had trained under Attila.
   (E) It was the first European army to include integral artillery.

9. During the 16th and 17th centuries, while France developed absolutism, the English monarchy was checked by

   (A) a strong peasantry
   (B) a few powerful and independent noble families
   (C) a Bill of Rights guaranteeing individual freedoms
   (D) the Anglican Church
   (E) a strong Parliament

10. That England developed a constitutional government can be explained by all of the following EXCEPT

    (A) the English kings rejected the divine right theory
    (B) the Tudor monarchs, lacking a legitimate claim to the throne, had to cooperate with Parliament
    (C) the English gentry blurred the sharp class distinctions between the nobility and middle classes that existed elsewhere in Europe
    (D) revolution strengthened the role of Parliament
    (E) a tradition of individual rights served as a basis for constitutionalism

11. That the Anglican Church broke from Rome before altering Roman Catholic dogma indicates that

    (A) Henry started the English Reformation because he couldn't get a divorce sanctioned by the Pope
    (B) Henry's lust for Anne Boleyn motivated him to reject his devout Catholicism
    (C) because Henry was eager to have a male heir, he urged Parliament to pass the Act of Supremacy
    (D) Thomas Cranmer issued the divorce that precipitated the Reformation in return for his appointment as Archbishop of Canterbury
    (E) many factors, including resentment of papal abuses, contributed to the English Reformation

12. All of the following were significant accomplishments of the English during the reign of Elizabeth I EXCEPT

    (A) the Thirty-Nine Articles completed the English Reformation
    (B) her foreign policy encouraged the independence of the Netherlands, a commercial and colonial rival of Spain
    (C) she weakened the power of Spain, bastion of Catholic orthodoxy
    (D) she satisfied the Puritans who had criticized the Anglican liturgy as too close to Catholicism
    (E) she encouraged nationalism and the development of a unique culture

13. Probably the most significant long-term result of the Puritan Revolution (1643–1660) was

    (A) the restoration of the Stuarts to the throne
    (B) the issuance of the Petition of Right
    (C) the increased authority of Parliament
    (D) the vindication of the divine right of the monarchy
    (E) the recognition of Calvinism as England's official religion

14. Which of the following was NOT a provision of the Declaration of Rights, 1689?

    (A) Only Parliament can levy taxes.
    (B) The king may maintain a standing army without the consent of Parliament.
    (C) All laws must be made with the consent of Parliament.
    (D) The right of trial by jury is guaranteed.
    (E) Due process of law is guaranteed.

15. William and Mary's ascension to the English throne in 1689

    (A) restricted the right of Parliament to raise taxes
    (B) nullified the Declaration of Rights
    (C) was founded on the divine-right theory
    (D) indicated the supremacy of Parliament
    (E) restored the Tudor dynasty

16. The free flow of plants and animals, as well as trade goods, between Europe and the Americas is referred to by historians as

    (A) transcontinental adoption
    (B) food migration
    (C) international assimilation
    (D) Columbian interaction
    (E) Columbian exchange

17. Which was a result of the Thirty Years' War?

    (A) Germany replaced Austria as the predominant power in Central
        Europe.
    (B) The Hapsburg reign ended in Austria.
    (C) Germany was economically devastated and its population decimated.
    (D) The French lost all influence over German affairs.
    (E) Sweden was victorious in all phases of the conflict.

18. Serfdom was consolidated during the 1500s and 1600s in which of the
    following countries?

    (A) England and France
    (B) Russia and France
    (C) Prussia and the Netherlands
    (D) Austria and Spain
    (E) Russia and Prussia

Answers and Answer Explanations

1.	D	7.	A	13.	C
2.	A	8.	C	14.	B
3.	C	9.	E	15.	D
4.	C	10.	A	16.	E
5.	B	11.	E	17.	C
6.	E	12.	D	18.	E

1.   **(D)** This is an analytical question. The growth of centralized government occurred with the weakening of the nobility and the institutions of feudalism.

2.   **(A)** This is analysis. If you did not know that the taille was a direct tax on land and property, it helps to know that the clergy and nobility were exempt from all taxes.

3.   **(C)** Henry IV converted from Calvinism—the Huguenots were French Calvinists—in order to placate the fears of the French majority of Catholics.

4.   **(C)** The Edict provided rights for the Huguenot minority and so ended the bitter civil war.

5.   **(B)** This is analytical. Choice C is out because only the French Revolution ended the exemption of these two estates; choice D is frivolous; choice E was true but not significant in itself; choice A was costly to the realm.

6.   **(E)** When Louis said "I am the state," he was proclaiming his belief in the divine right theory.

7.   **(A)** Peter the Great was a complete autocrat as were all of the tsars. He censored the press and punished those who criticized him, such as Alexander Radishchev, whose *Journey from St. Petersburg to Moscow* got him exiled to Siberia even though he was a noble.

8.   **(C)** Europe's largest standing army, it ravaged the countrysides of the lands it attacked and earned the epithet "Huns," referring to the Asiatic invaders who were the scourge of Europe near the end of the Roman Empire.

9.   **(E)** Constitutionalism developed because of the struggle between the monarchy and Parliament for control of the English government, and the Bill of Rights was signed in 1689.

10.   **(A)** This is an analytical question in that an examination of the first choice reveals that it makes little sense in explaining the development of constitutional government.

11.   **(E)** The simplistic interpretation of Henry's personal motivations as the prime cause for the English Reformation ignores other important factors.

12.   **(D)** The Puritans continued to oppose Anglican liturgy and dogma, and this opposition was a precipitating factor for the Puritan Revolution.

13. **(C)** This is analytical in that the Stuarts were on the throne for only a few decades after the restoration, the Petition of Right was issued well before the Revolution, the theory was disgraced in England, and while Calvinism was tolerated, it was not the official religion.

14. **(B)** All of the other answers give rights to the parliament and the people while choice B grants rights to the monarch, which is antithetical to a Bill of Rights.

15. **(D)** Parliament invited William and Mary, whose acceptence of the Bill of Rights established Parliament's dominance of the governing process.

16. **(E)** The exchange of goods native to each of the continents has been termed the Columbian Exchange in honor of Columbus, who opened trade between Europe and the Americas.

17. **(C)** This confused conflict had many losers, no clear winners. France gained an influence in Germany after the treaty; Sweden fell into decline as a result of its involvement; Hapsburg Austria was frustrated in its aim to unite Germany; Germany, the battleground, was devastated and fell behind Western Europe for two centuries.

18. **(E)** Serfdom was abolished in Western European states during or even before this period; the unique political situation in Eastern Europe led to its re-establishment there.

CHAPTER 4

The 18th Century: The Expansion of Europe and the Enlightenment

Key Terms/People

- open-field system
- enclosure movement
- Mercantilism
- Adam Smith
- Francis Bacon
- René Descartes
- *Discourse on Method*
- Nicolaus Copernicus
- Galileo Galilei
- Isaac Newton
- Johannes Kepler
- deism
- scientific revolution
- The Enlightenment
- Madame Geoffrin
- Voltaire
- Jean Jacques Rousseau
- Baron de Montesquieu
- Denis Diderot
- Francois Quesnay
- Fall of Constantinople
- Mary Wollstonecraft

Overview

An agricultural revolution took place during the later years of the 17th century and through the 18th century. The traditional "open field" system, an utterly inefficient method of agricultural production, was replaced by "enclosure," and despite the social cost, productivity increased dramatically. New foods and a disappearance of the plague fostered rapid population growth. An Atlantic economy, built on trade between Europe—primarily England, France, and Holland—and the Americas benefited both Europe and the colonies, economically and socially. A series of conflicts over imperial possessions broke out among the leading European competitors during the 18th century, culminating in the French and Indian War in North America (The Seven Years' War on the continent) and the American Revolution.

The impact of science on the modern world is immeasurable. If the "Greeks had said it all" two thousand years earlier, the Renaissance Europeans rediscovered, evaluated, and elaborated or contradicted the ideas of Aristotle, Ptolemy, and other thinkers. Observation took precedence over tradition. To find out how many teeth a horse had, medieval academics scoured ancient texts to appeal to authority; modern thinkers opened the horse's mouth.

The 16th and 17th centuries saw the fruition of Renaissance individualism in religion and thought. Luther and the Protestants questioned the traditions of the Church and rebelled; Copernicus, Galileo, and Newton subjected the theories of Aristotle and Ptolemy to the inductive method and redefined the natural world. The habit of skepticism, which the Renaissance introduced and the Reformation strengthened, was science's driving force.

This skepticism gave rise to rationalism, the concept that human reason could uncover the natural laws that govern the universe and humankind itself. Inspired by the revolutionary theories of 16th- and 17th-century astronomy and physics, European thinkers ceased to be swayed by medieval superstition, by a belief in miracles, by a blind acceptance of tradition. Rationalism gave rise to the 18th-century Enlightenment, whose philosophers argued that if humans could discover the immutable laws of the universe through the light of reason, human progress was inevitable. Critics of the status quo, they commented on the political, economic, and social ills of society and offered designs for the betterment of humanity. Their optimism and impatience aroused the forces for change and contributed to the French Revolution.

The Expansion of Europe

The *open field system*, used during the Middle Ages, divided the arable land available to a farming community into narrow strips, which were designated to the individual families of the community. Due to a lack of chemical fertilizers and ignorance about nitrogen-fixing crops, a large portion of the community's land lay fallow.

The *enclosure movement* in England, during the late 17th and the 18th centuries, fenced off the open fields to enable large landowners to employ crop rotation. By planting nitrogen-fixing crops, such as beans and certain grasses, in soil that had been used for other crops, the soil remained fertile and little land lay fallow. Many small or inefficient farmers were displaced to the towns and cities, but ultimately, food production rose dramatically.

A greater variety of foods and the introduction of foods from the New World, specifically the potato, improved general nutrition and contributed, along with the disappearance of the plague, to a dramatic increase in population. Better sanitation, introduction of quarantine methods, and the elimination of the black rat, whose fleas carried the plague microorganisms, eliminated the plague. Except for the development of the smallpox vaccine in the late 18th century, the crude and often dangerous medical practices of the day contributed little to the health and longevity of the people.

Mercantilism was a system developed by various European states to guarantee a favorable balance of trade with other European nations or with their American colonies. By creating an imbalance of exports over imports, the difference was made up in gold or silver payments, a policy pursued to get precious metals from trading partners to pay for the costs of maintaining standing armies and government bureaucracies. Competition for colonies and for hegemony on the continent culminated in the Seven Years' War (1756–1763) fought by England and its allies against France. It resulted in the loss of France's North American possessions and in the growing independence of the British North American colonies.

Mercantilism was largely discredited by the economic liberalism of *Adam Smith* who argued that free competition, limited government regulation, and individual self-interest expressed through a supply and demand market system would foster economic growth.

The Enlightenment's Roots in the Development of Science

The Philosophers of Modern Science

Francis Bacon (1561–1626) was an English thinker who advocated the *inductive* or *experimental method:* observation of natural phenomena; accumulating data; experimenting to refine the data; drawing conclusions; formulating principles that are subject to continuing observation and experimentation.

René Descartes (1596–1650) was a French philosopher whose *Discourse on Method* (1637) argued that everything that is not validated by observation should be doubted, but that his own existence is proven by the proposition that "I think, therefore I am" *(cogito ergo sum).* God exists, he argued, because a perfect being would have existence as part of its nature. *Cartesian Dualism* divided all existence into the spiritual and the material—the former can be examined only through deductive reasoning; the latter is subject to the experimental method. His goal to reconcile religion with science was shortcircuited by the very method of skepticism that subsequent philosophers inherited from his writings.

The Revolutionary Thinkers of Science

Nicolaus Copernicus (1473–1543), a Polish astronomer, upset the comfortable assumptions of the *geocentric* (earth-centered) universe of *Ptolemy* (the 2nd century A.D. Egyptian) with his *heliocentric* (sun-centered) conception of the universe. Although his work, *Concerning the Revolutions of the Heavenly Bodies*, was not published until after his death, his theories were proven by *Johannes Kepler* (1571–1630), a German who plotted the elliptic orbits of the planets, thereby predicting their movements, and by the great *Galileo Galilei* (1564–1642) whose telescopic observations validated Copernican theory and whose spirited advocacy earned him condemnation by the Inquisition. The Copernican heliocentric view seemed to contradict the primacy of humanity in God's creation and therefore to deny the teachings of the Church. Supported in Protestant Northern Europe, where the Reformation had questioned all orthodoxy, the theory and the scientific method that had formulated it symbolized Europe's new intellectual freedom. When the Roman Catholic Church tried to suppress the Copernican revolution by banning writings and by trying the charismatic Galileo, it earned a lasting reputation for rigidity. It took nearly 350 years for the papacy to exonerate Galileo.

If Copernicus shook the medieval conception of Christianity to its foundations, the work of *Isaac Newton* (1642–1727) not only tested the notion of God's intervention in human affairs but established the ascendancy of science in the modern world. Newton, an Englishman, demonstrated that *natural laws* of motion—gravitation—account for the movement of heavenly bodies and earthly objects. Since these laws are unchangeable and predictable, God's active participation is not needed to explain the operations of the forces of nature, a repudiation of medieval belief.

Deism—God as a kind of cosmic clockmaker who created a perfect universe that he does not have to intervene in—grew out of Newton's natural law theories. *Rationalism*—the conviction that the laws of nature are fathomable by human reason and that humanity is perfectable—was an assumption and a goal of the Enlightenment.

The *scientific revolution* of the 16th and 17th centuries redefined astronomy and physics. Less dramatic but still significant advances took place in *mathematics,* especially with the development of probability and calculus, in *medicine* through advances in surgery, anatomy, drug therapy, and with the discovery of microorganisms, and with the establishment of *learned societies*, dedicated to the advance of science, such as the *French Academy of Sciences* and the *Royal Society of London.*

The development of science transformed the intellectual life of Europe by convincing people that human reason could understand the secrets of the universe and transform life without the help of organized religion. The 18th century marked the end of the *Age of Religion*, which had governed European thought for over a millennium. Skepticism and rationalism—offshoots of the development of science—encouraged the growth of secularism. These modes of thought guided the Enlightenment and defined modern life.

The Enlightenment

An Englishman, Newton, inspired the Enlightenment; a group of Frenchmen, the philosophes, shaped it. Newton's work in astronomy and physics convinced European thinkers that human reason, unaided by the tenets and rituals of religion, could uncover the immutable laws of nature. The philosophes, who were actually literary figures more than academic philosphers, argued that once the natural laws that governed nature and human existence were discovered, society could be organized in accordance with them and progress was inevitable. Leaders of French culture, which dominated Europe, they lauded Newton, borrowed from Locke, and flooded Europe with radically optimistic notions about how people should live and govern themselves, ideas that were to shake the old order to pieces and build in its place the democratic, humanistic Western World.

If Newton's theories served as the inspiration for the natural law philosophy of the Enlightenment, *John Locke's* political writings translated the natural law assumption into a conception of government. Locke (1632–1704), an Englishman, provided a philosophical apology for the supremacy of Parliament during the Glorious Revolution with his *Two Treatises on Civil Government:*

> In the *state of nature*, before governments existed, humans lacked protection. Although governments, once institututed, replace individual action with the rule of law, they rest upon the *consent of the governed.* The *social contract*—the agreement between a fair government and responsible individuals—is not unconditional. If government oversteps its role in protecting the life, liberty, and property of its citizens, the people have the right to abolish and replace it.

These conceptions of the *consent of the governed,* the *social contract,* and the *right of revolution* spearheaded the philosophes' criticism of the absolutist ancien régime or old order.

The *Philosophes*

Voltaire (1694–1778) personified the Age of Reason. Born *François Marie Arouet* in Paris at the height of Louis XIV's reign, he lived until two years after the American Declaration of Independence. Although he was more writer than philosopher—poet, essayist, dramatist, satirist—his genius for social criticism helped inflame desire for change and set the stage for the Age of Revolution. He preached against injustice and bigotry and for human rights and science. *"Ecrasez l'infame"* ("Crush the infamous") was his rallying cry against rigid religion, governmental abuse, and vestiges of medievalism. Imprisoned briefly in the Bastille, he visited England, lived in the court of *Frederick the Great, Enlightened Despot* of Prussia, and earned an international reputation. Like most of the Enlightenment thinkers, he was raised as a Christian but came to reject organized religion as corrupt in its leadership and remote from the urgent message of Jesus. He was a staunch advocate of *Deism,* the theological offshoot of natural law theory. As a Deist, he believed that prayer and miracles violated the perfect natural order God had created and that the world's evils are caused by man's straying from the natural law. The social reform that he called for fit the Deist notion that human reason alone could uncover the natural law and guide humans to comply with it.

Jean Jacques Rousseau (1712–1778) is considered a philosophe, a man of the Enlightenment, but he is more accurately the founder of the Romantic movement. After the excesses of the French Revolution, the Enlightenment's emphasis on the *rule of reason* gave way to a glorification of emotion. Despising—intellectually and personally—the rigid and inequitable class structure of the ancien régime, he developed the idea of the *noble savage:* that civilization corrupted humankind and that life in the *state of nature* was purer, freer, more virtuous. The goal of the individual, he argued in his many writings, was to attain full expression of natural instincts by stripping away the artificial restraints of society and returning as far as possible to nature. The goal of a people was to achieve self-determination, a clarion call to the nationalism that the French Revolution awakened all over Europe. In *The Social Contract,* he said, "Man is born free, but everywhere he is in chains," meaning that property, when regarded as more important than people, causes social injustice. The *general will,* a kind of consensus of the majority, he thought should control a nation. This was intended to support a democratic view of government, but because it does not recognize minority viewpoints and since it has no clear way to show itself, it could be used to rationalize extreme nationalism and repression. Whatever the flaws in his philosophy, Rousseau is considered one the most influential thinkers of his day. His distrust of *civilization* and its institutions led him to criticize rigid educational practices and the strict discipline of children. In his treatise *Emile,* he argued that children have to be understood as individuals and that they need caring from their teachers as well as from their parents. He and other *Enlightenment* critics helped to change the educational and child-rearing practices of 18th-century Europe.

Baron de Montesquieu (1689–1755) in his work, *Spirit of the Laws,* argued that the powers of government—legislative, executive, and judicial—must be separated in order to avoid depotism. When these functions are divided among various groups or individuals, each *checks and balances* the powers of the others. His theories served as a blueprint for the governmental structure outlined in the U.S. Constitution.

Denis Diderot (1713–1784) published the writings and popularized the ideas of many of the philosophes in his *Encyclopedia,* a collection of political and social critiques rather than a compilation of facts.

Francois Quesnay (1694–1774) led the *physiocrats* whose motto was laissez-faire and who believed that government should remove all restraints to free trade—such as tariffs—so that the natural laws of economics were free to operate for the good of society.

Adam Smith (1727–1790), an Englishman, refined and expanded the laissez-faire philosophy of the *physiocrats* in his *Wealth of Nations.* Published in 1776, the year of the Declaration of Independence, it is the book that defined capitalism. In it, he stated: the economy is governed by natural laws, such as *supply and demand;* in a free economy, competition will induce producers to manufacture most efficiently in order to sell higher-quality, lower-cost goods than competitors; government regulation only interferes with this natural self-governing operation.

Women and Minorities During the Enlightenment

This era saw the emergence of feminist ideas for the first time in earnest. Women like Mary Wollstonecraft and Madame Geoffrin made it clear to society that women could do what men could do mentally. The first women graduated from many European universities, and intellectuals discussed the idea that women should be equal before the law openly. The Enlightenment ideals of natural rights and just laws made people reexamine their preconceived notions of gender roles, and women's rights made some grudging progress.

The same ideals that made men question how they treated women had them examine how they treated slaves and the peoples of other nations too. Reform came slowly, with England outlawing slavery in all British holdings first, with France and the United States eventually following suit. Religious intolerance also was reduced, leading to more social harmony.

Great Thinkers of the Scientific Revolution and Enlightenment

This chart is designed to help you study for ideas that may be tested on specific items or used as evidence in essays about the era.

Who	When	Where	What
Copernicus	1473–1534	Poland/East Prussia	He was responsible for spreading the heliocentric (sun-centered) theory of the solar system throughout Europe. His *On the Revolutions of the Heavenly Spheres* was published posthumously.
Leeuwenhoek	1632–1723	Netherlands	He invented and used microscopes to create a basis for modern biological science; his drawings of blood corpuscles, sperm, and bacteria began the science of microbiology.
Montaigne	1533–1592	France	He was a skeptic and inventor of the essay. He stated that he knew nothing decades before Descartes wrote, "Cogito ergo sum."
Francis Bacon	1561–1626	England	He is often cited as the codifier of the inductive method. He believed "Knowledge is power," and it should be put to practical use.
Rene Descartes	1596–1650	France	He was an ardent advocate for the deductive method. His *Discourse on Method* defined two kinds of matter: thinking substance (everything within the mind), and extended substance (the objective world or everything outside the mind). This division of reality is known as Cartesian dualism. He invented analytical geometry and wrote the immortal line, "Cogito ergo sum" (I think; therefore I am).
Tycho Brahe	1546–1601	Denmark	This eccentric astronomer collected vast amounts of data and hired a mathematically gifted assistant named Johannes Kepler.
Johannes Kepler	1571–1630	Germany	Brahe's assistant. He discovered three laws of planetary motion that helped Newton later understand gravity, and proved that the orbits of planets are ellipses.

Who	When	Where	What
Galileo	1571–1642	Italy	Perhaps the best example of the Enlightenment emerging from the Renaissance, Galileo was a master of many sciences and tried to know everything he could. His astronomical observations of the moons of Jupiter proved that the Earth was not the center of the universe, getting him in trouble with the Church. His experiments with inertia proved that objects of different weights fall at the same rate.
Vesalius	1543	Belgium	His anatomical drawings based on his dissection of corpses were the first detailed anatomical maps of the human body.
William Harvey	1628	England	He was the author of *On the Movement of the Heart and Blood*, which explained the circulation of the blood through arteries and veins.
Isaac Newton	1642–1727	England	He synthesized Kepler's and Galileo's ideas together in his *Laws of Motion*. His definition of physics defined what scientists knew about the universe until Einstein conceived of relativity. He developed calculus to measure and predict curves and trajectories. Newton also explained the laws of universal gravitation. He said he "stood on the shoulders of giants," in deference to Galileo.
Leibnitz	1646–1716	German	He invented calculus simultaneously with Newton.
Charles-Louis de Secondat, Baron de La Brède et de **Montesquieu**	1689–1755	France	His *The Spirit of the Laws* revolutionized thinking on how people should be ruled by proposing checks and balances. His ideas provided much of the foundation for the American Constitution. His *Persian Letters* also gave Europeans a look at themselves from the perspective of foreigners for the first time, promoting Europeans to begin to ask if they had a Eurocentric view of the world.
François-Marie Arouet **Voltaire**	1694–1788	France	This man is symbolic of the Age of Reason. He was an ardent opponent of any censorship, bigotry of any type, and any form of organized religion as part of his aversion to censorship. His masterpieces included *Candide*, in which he criticized the flaws of his society, and was consequently imprisoned for his writings more than once. He was an advisor to Frederick the Great and had a torrid affair with Madame d'Chatalet, who translated Newton's *Principia Mathematica* into French.
Marie Thérèse Rodet **Geoffrin**	1699–1777	France	Madame Geoffrin ran the most celebrated salon in Paris. It was attended by the greatest minds of the era including Montesquieu and Fontenelle, her tutors. Other attendees included Jefferson, Franklin, d'Holbach, Lespinasse, Diderot, d'Alembert, and Adam Smith.

Who	When	Where	What
Dennis **Diderot**	1713–1784	France	He was the co-editor of the *Encyclopedia* who had to beg money from Catherine II of Russia.
Jean le Rond **D'Alembert**	1717–1783	France	Co-editor of the *Encyclopedia*
Paul-Henri Thiry, Baron d'Holbach	1723–1789	France/ Germany	This contributor to the Encyclopedia was an ardent atheist. He ran his own salon in France for thirty years. His *System of Nature* was threatening to many of the social elites such as the Church, but helped popularize the idea of naturalism.
Adam Smith	1723–1790	Scotland	In his treatise on the economic workings of England during the 18th century, *An Inquiry Into the Nature and Causes of the Wealth of Nations*, he invented the science of economics which he called "political philosophy." He argued that government should stay out of business, promoted *laissez-faire*, and disputed the prevailing economic theory of the day, *mercantilism*.
Marquis de **Condorcet**, Marie Jean Antoine Nicolas de Caritat	1743–1794	France	His *Sketch of the Progress of the Human Mind* was an argument for constitutionalism and women's rights as the next logical step in the progress of civilization.
Mary Wollstonecraft	1759–1797	England	She was a British writer and early feminist, and disputed Edmund Burke's sexist and conservative writings with *A Vindication of the Rights of Men*, followed by her more famous work, *A Vindication of the Rights of Women*. She also argued against the sexism of Rousseau in correspondence the two of them shared. Her daughter was Mary Shelley, author of *Frankenstein*.

The Evolution of Political Thought *or* Hobbes, Locke, and Rousseau

The chart on the next page is designed to compare the ideas of the great political thinkers of the 16th, 17th, and 18th centuries.

	Thomas Hobbes (1588–1679) English	John Locke (1632–1704) English	Jean-Jacques Rousseau (1712–1778) French
State of nature: What is life like for the uncivilized?	"Life is nasty, brutish and short." Hobbes believed that, in a state of nature, might makes right, and that we agree to be governed to protect us from living in a state of nature.	People are born a blank slate and made good or evil by their environment. People are created equal not in ability but in rights. All people have the rights to life, liberty, and property.	People are inherently unequal in ability, but this inequality only matters for the corrupted civilized man who deviated from the nobility of savagery.
Natural law: Defines what the basic human rights are in all societies.	The natural law that Hobbes focuses on is survival. He states that, in nature, every being is so concerned with survival that any idea of rights includes only what one can physically protect.	All humans are endowed at creation with rights to life, liberty, and property. These are the basic rights that all people have.	Rousseau describes the state of nature as noble. We only deviate from natural law, in which the needs of each individual are met by the group, due to the corrupting force of civilization.
Social contract	People give up some of their rights in order to gain some protection from the government.	People give up some of their rights in order to gain some protection from the government, but if the government does not do its job, the people must change it.	The social contract is between the people, not the people and the government. Each person gives up all rights to the "General Will" which then incorporates every individual through the legislature.
Role of the state	The state prevents people from taking each other's property and killing each other.	The state protects a person's right to life, freedom, and property.	The state enacts the General Will of the people as expressed through the legislature.
Property	Seen as a limited resource that people compete for.	Ownership of property is among everyone's natural rights.	Property is one of the worst inventions of society, used to manipulate the masses.
Religion	Believes that the state must have only one religion for unity.	Believes in religious toleration by the state.	Abhors organized religion, especially Christianity, but does not reject God.
Favored form of government	Absolute monarchy	Any representative government: constitutional monarchy, democracy, or republic	Complete consensus based on dictatorship of the General Will.
What was his essential question?	How can society prevent chaos and violence?	How can government protect the citizen and his/her possessions?	How can society combat inequality?

Enlightened Despotism

The ideal Enlightened Despot was a ruler who aimed for the advancement of society by fostering education, aiding the economy, and promoting social justice. Since Voltaire and most of the philosophers, and certainly most of Europe's monarchs, believed that the mass of people were incapable of self-government, Enlightened Despots stayed in power while promoting the good of their people.

In the 17th century, *Russia* and *Prussia* rose as powerful states, challenging Poland, the ancient *Hapsburg state of Austria*, and the declining empire of the Ottomans. In Prussia and, ironically, in Russia—whose culture often lagged decades, even centuries, behind that of the West—Enlightened Despotism held sway during important periods of the 18th century. Such rule helped slow the decline of Austria, whose monarchs still held the title of Holy Roman Emperor. In Western Europe, Enlightened Despotism manifested itself in Sweden, Spain, and Portugal, but it shone most brilliantly in the East.

Prussia

"Prussia was an army before it was a nation," it has been said, because its origin was as an outpost of the Holy Roman Empire and its *Hohenzollern* rulers cultivated a superbly trained and well-equipped army drawn from all areas of their domain. Local loyalties were transferred to the army, which then served as the focal point for Prussian nationalism. *Frederick William* (r. 1640–1688) and his son and grandson, *Frederick I* (r. 1688–1713) and *Frederick William I* (r. 1713–1740), centralized the government and encouraged industry in order to support the state's relatively large standing army. Their Enlightened Despotism reached fruition during the rule of Frederick I's grandson, *Frederick II* or *Frederick the Great* (r. 1740–1786). "First servant of the state," as he called himself, Frederick the Great was a military genius who made Prussia a major power in Europe, an urbane and educated man who patronized the great Voltaire, a domestic reformer who improved education, codified laws, fostered industry, invited immigration, and extended religious toleration. Twenty years after he died, his modernized and expanded nation was subdued by Napoleon, and the army—led by officers recruited from the Junkers (landowning aristocrats)—remained as the only viable institution to lead Prussia's resurgence in the mid-19th century and to define German nationalism well into the 20th.

Russia

Russia became a state in the 15th century when the *Duchy of Muscovy*, under *Ivan the Great* (r. 1462–1505) overcame subjugation by the Central Asian *Tartars*. After the *Fall of Constantinople* to the Ottoman Turks in 1453, Russia became not only the inheritor of Byzantine culture and the center of the Orthodox Church, but an empire with Moscow as "the third Rome" and a czar (Caesar) on the throne. Under *Basil (Vasily) III* (r. 1505–1533) and the much maligned but very capable *Ivan the Terrible* (1533–1584), expansion and consolidation of the new empire continued—with reverses, however. In order to get troops, the empire gave aristocractic landowners, the *Boyars,* control over their peasants, who gradually fell into *serfdom,* a condition of being bound to the land that had ended in virtually all of Western Europe. The Boyars influenced government policy through a council, the *Duma,* and, a theme common in most nations with a monarchy, there was a continuing battle for supremacy between a strong central government and a powerful aristocracy.

Peter the Great (r. 1689–1725), a Romanov and a contemporary of Louis XIV of France, gained vast territories to the Baltic Sea in the north, to the Black Sea in the south, and to the Far East. Probably his greatest contribution was the *Westernization of Russia.* Although he could not be considered an Enlightened Despot, he recruited hundreds of Western artisans, built a new capital on the Gulf of Finland, *St. Petersburg,* his "window to the West," reformed the government bureaucracy and the Russian Orthodox Church, reorganized and equipped the army with modern weapons, and encouraged commerce and industry.

Catherine the Great (r. 1762–1796), a German who succeeded to the throne after the murder of her husband, *Tsar Peter III* (r. 1762), was a patron of many of the French philosophes and considered herself an Enlightened Despot. When a rebellion of the Cossacks, the Pugachev Rebellion, gained some ground with the peasantry, Catherine at first tried to dismiss the rebellion; later she took it much more seriously and ended her enlightened reforms. She did continue Peter the Great's work of territorial expansion by annexing both Polish and Ottoman land.

Austria

In Austria, during the 18th century, *Maria Theresa* (r. 1740–1780) and her son, *Joseph II* (r. 1780–1790), qualify as genuine Enlightened Despots. The *Hapsburg Dynasty* had been weakened by the time Maria Theresa inherited the throne under a cloud of counterclaims, and she was determined to strengthen the realm by centralizing the government, promoting commerce, and limiting the power of the nobles. Joseph furthered his mother's reforms by guaranteeing freedom of the press and of religion, reforming the judicial system toward greater equality for all classes, making German the official language for the empire's many ethnic minorities in order to foster centralization, and especially *abolishing serfdom.*

Sample Essay Question

The sample and practice thematic essay questions presented in this chapter are types found on the AP exam and they require a knowledge of causes, effects, personalities, ideas, and events.

SAMPLE QUESTION

Analyze the relationship between the Newtonian Revolution and the Enlightenment.

Comments on the Sample Question

Follow the "Simple Procedures" for writing an essay. (See page 34.)

First, *What does the question want to know?* The wording of the question implies a direct relationship between Newton's discoveries and the philosophical underpinnings of the Enlightenment.

Second, *What do you know about it?* The task is twofold: Determine the relationship; examine it in detail.

Third, *How would you put it into words?* You have to clarify the issues. What was the Newtonian Revolution? How did its discoveries influence ideas beyond the realm of the physical sciences? Who were the proponents of these ideas? How did the ideas and personalities set the tone for the so-called Age of Reason?

Rubric for Sample Answer

Before you read the sample answer, examine the rubric. What will the reader be looking for when he or she grades this essay? A sample rubric, shaded to show the reader's evaluation, is seen below:

9–8 POINTS

- ✔ Thesis explicitly identifies **both** the Newtonian Revolution and the Enlightenment AND analyzes their relationship. Thesis does not need to be in the opening paragraph.
- ✔ Organization is clear, consistently followed, and effective in support of the argument.
  - • May devote individual paragraphs to an examination of the Newtonian Revolution, the Enlightenment, and their relationship.
  - • Must identify individual hallmarks of the Newtonian Revolution and the Enlightenment (Newtonians discovered and publicized the natural laws that governed the universe, whereas the Enlightenment attempted to apply logic and science to the understanding and betterment of the human condition) and consider their relationship.
- ✔ Essay is well balanced; the Enlightenment and the Newtonian Revolution and their relationship are analyzed at some length. Essay covers the content from Newton to 1815.
- ✔ Major assertions in the essay are supported thoroughly and consistently by relevant evidence.
- ✔ Evidence of this relationship may prove more specific or concrete.
- ✔ May contain errors that do not detract from the argument.

7–6 POINTS

- ✔ Thesis explicitly identifies **both** the Newtonian Revolution and the Enlightenment AND analyzes their relationship, but may not be developed fully.
- ✔ Organization is clear and effective in support of the argument but may introduce evidence that is not pertinent to the task.

✔ Essay covers all major topics suggested by the prompt but may analyze an aspect of the Newtonian Revolution, the Enlightenment, or the analysis of their interaction, rather than in a balanced manner.

✔ Major assertions in the essay are supported by relevant evidence.

✔ May contain an error that detracts from the argument.

5–4 POINTS

✔ Thesis identifies both the Newtonian Revolution and the Enlightenment AND analyzes their relationship, but without any development; thesis may address only part of the question effectively; thesis may be a simple, single-sentence statement.

✔ Organization is clear but may not be consistently followed; essay may veer off task chronologically or thematically or both.

✔ Essay may not complete all tasks:
  • May discuss only the Enlightenment or the Newtonian Revolution with some analysis.
  • May discuss only one or two aspects of the Enlightenment or the New-tonian Revolution.
  • May focus only on one interaction between the Enlightenment and the Newtonian Revolution.
  • May be primarily descriptive rather than analytical.

✔ Essay offers some relevant evidence.

✔ May contain errors that detract from the argument.

3–2 POINTS

✔ Thesis may simply paraphrase the prompt OR identify the Newtonian Revolution and the Enlightenment without analyzing their relationship.

✔ Organization is unclear and ineffective; essay may focus on the characters of the Newtonian Revolution and/or the Enlightenment rather than analyzing the way one affected the other.

✔ Essay shows serious imbalance; discussion of the Newtonian Revolution and the Enlightenment and their interaction is superficial; much of the information may be significantly out of the time period or geography of the question.

✔ Offers minimal OR confused evidence.

✔ May contain several errors that detract from the argument.

1–0 POINTS

✔ Thesis is erroneous OR irrelevant OR absent.

✔ No effective organization is evident.

✔ Discussion of the Newtonian Revolution and the Enlightenment and their interaction is generic.

✔ Provides little or no relevant supporting evidence.

✔ May contain numerous errors that detract from the argument.

Sample Answer

Copernicus's heliocentric universe had shaken conventional religion's smug assumptions of humanity's importance as much if not more than the Reformation had upset orthodoxy. Since the earth was no longer the center of all creation, perhaps humankind was not the focus of God's attention. To 16th-century Europe, this idea was immeasurably more traumatic than the landing of space aliens of superior intelligence would be to late 20th-century earthlings. Copernicus turned the easy biases of an age upside down. Newton's discoveries, published a century and half after the death of Copernicus, established the intellectual foundations for an age: the Enlightenment.

Newton demonstrated that unchangeable natural laws governed the motion of all bodies in the universe—from the movement of the stars to the rotation of the earth to the motion of physical things on the earth's surface. Gravity and all the other natural laws were not only unchangeable, but they were predictable.

A deeply religious man who believed he would be remembered to history because of his biblical studies, Newton had no conception that his findings would lead other thinkers to discount the need for God to explain the functioning of the universe and would argue that God never intervened in a universe that he had created to function according to perfect and precise laws. *Deism,* the resulting epistemology, was the religious persuasion of many of the thinkers of the Enlightenment.

Commentators on Newton's findings insisted that if natural law governs the motions of physical objects, it also controls the functioning of human society. Once human intellect could uncover these laws, it could design a world in harmony with them. Progress was the faith of this Age of Reason. What these natural laws were and how human society should be designed in accordance with them was open to interpretation. That was the role of philosophes, mostly French writers and social commentators who were more literary men than academic philosophers.

Newton's laws of physics and astronomy served as models for a rational universe whose mysteries were discoverable by human reason, whose natural laws would make this "the best of all possible worlds."

EVALUATE THE SAMPLE ANSWER

Now go back and look at the rubric. It is clear that this essay looks like a 4 or 5 on the rubric. The essay has a weak thesis that may be relatively tangential. The imbalance favors the Newtonian Revolution and includes a narrative. In this case, the essay warrants a 5.

RATER'S COMMENTS ON THE SAMPLE ANSWER

5—Qualified

This essay has a weak thesis that seems too tangential to the task. The first paragraphs spend so much time on Newton that the reader is unclear as to where the essay is going. The essay doesn't mention the Enlightenment in a meaningful way until the third paragraph. There are few supporting details. The organization of this essay is suspect. However, this essay clearly does accomplish its task of analyzing a relationship between the Newtonian revolution and the Age of Reason. The sentence about Newton's revelation of deism becoming the epistemology of the Enlightenment is the crux of the issue, and it alone deserves merit. The problem with this essay is the lack of supporting detail from the Enlightenment figures to make the case, but the conclusion is strong.

Practice Essay Questions

The questions that follow are samples of the various types of thematic essays that appear on the AP exam. (See pages 21–22 for a detailed explanation of each type.) Check over the **generic rubric** (see pages 58–60) before you begin any of these essays and use that rubric to score your essay if you write one.

QUESTION 1

Contrast and compare the contributions to the development of modern science of Bacon and Descartes with those of Copernicus and Galileo.

COMMENTS ON QUESTION 1

"Show the differences; examine similarities." This task appears to be straightforward since, as the question implies, the roles of Bacon and Descartes in the rise of modern science are similar, and they contrast with those of Copernicus and Galileo. Bacon and Descartes are "philosophers of science" whose writings helped establish the methodology of science: skepticism, observation, generalization, experimentation. Copernicus and Galileo, on the other hand, were "genuine" scientists whose theories or experimentation furthered the store of scientific knowledge. Additionally, both Galileo and Copernicus worked in the science of astronomy, and Newton claimed that he owed his accomplishments to the foundational work of Galileo.

The tricky part of this question is to apply the "contrast and comparison" rule to Bacon and Descartes, then to Copernicus and Galileo as well as to the two pairs. Did Bacon's writings contribute differently than Descartes's to the "scientific mind"? Were Copernicus's methods and findings different from those of Galileo?

QUESTION 2

"Newton inspired the Enlightenment, Locke provided the blueprint; the philosophes shaped it." *Assess the validity* of this statement.

COMMENTS ON QUESTION 2

The goal here is to "determine the truth" of this statement by ascertaining how Newtonian physics and astronomy gave rise to "natural law" theory, how Locke applied that theory to the relations between the individual and government, then how the philosophes used Newtonian "natural law" and Lockian political theory to shape the Age of Reason.

Be careful to define "natural law," to spell out Locke's applications of it in his theory of government, to characterize the Enlightenment that dominated the intellectual life of 18th-century Europe, and to show how important philosophes—Voltaire, Montesquieu, Rousseau, Quesnay—influenced the movement.

QUESTION 3

Contrast and compare Locke and Rousseau's concept of the social contract.

COMMENTS ON QUESTION 3

The chart on the evolution of political power from this chapter can help to develop an outline for this essay. Locke, who lived before the Enlightenment, influenced Rousseau. Rousseau, who dominated the Enlightenment's push for social reform, has been called more of a Romantic than a philosophe insofar as he departed from Locke's political theory. The way to "show differences" would be first to "examine similarities" in their concepts of the state of nature and the social contract, then, to show how Locke's ideas influenced Rousseau's, and finally to examine how Rousseau departed from Locke. Although this question is straightforward, it requires a thorough understanding of the abstract theories involved.

QUESTION 4

"The Enlightened Despots were more despotic than enlightened." *Defend or refute* this statement.

COMMENTS ON QUESTION 4

According to the democratic biases of our age, an Enlightened Despot is a contradiction in terms. For the world of the 18th century, mired in the excesses of anachronistic absolutism, the "Enlightened Despots" were products of the Age of Reason. They were monarchs who maintained a firm hold on the reins of power but who made decisions "for the good of the masses," whom they did not trust to be self-governing.

This requires specific references and evaluations of the various monarchs who claimed to be—or are labeled by history as—Enlightened Despots. Who are some? Frederick the Great of Prussia? Peter the Great and Catherine the Great of Russia? Maria Theresa and Joseph II of Austria? Make reference to three or four. Measure their reigns for genuine reform: Did the reforms change the life of the people? Did they last? Decide whether to defend or refute.

QUESTION 5

To what extent and in what ways is Deism a logical offshoot of the theory of "natural law?"

COMMENTS ON QUESTION 5

How and how much did the concept of natural laws give rise to the "religion of the Enlightenment"? The key term in the question is "logical offshoot." The task is to demonstrate how Deism—the belief in God's nonintervention in a perfectly created universe—follows logically from the concept of a universe guided by unchangeable natural laws. The question does not require a logician's reasoning; it requires that you trace the historical development of Deism from the applications of Newtonian natural law. How did Voltaire, for instance, use natural law and the concept of the Prime Mover to argue against traditional Christianity? Why would he have argued against prayer and miracles?

QUESTION 6

Explain how the replacement of the open field system by the enclosure movement increased agricultural productivity in 18th-century Europe.

COMMENTS ON QUESTION 6

The enclosure movement should be explained as the most important and least known revolution in European history. Describe the open field system and the concept of common lands, focusing on the limitations on land improvement and fallow lands. Explain how the enclosure movement made land improvement, such as irrigation, crop rotation, and fertilization, more practical and widespread. The best essays will also examine how the enclosure movement led to the putting out system that increased domestic production and disturbed the order of society by moving many farming families from their lands, causing them to find new means of employment.

QUESTION 7

Why did the population of Europe increase dramatically in the 1700s?

COMMENTS ON QUESTION 7

Explain the roles of food production, new foods, and the disappearance of the plague; emphasize that the medical practices of the day played little part in the increase.

Practice Multiple-Choice Questions

(These are representative of the types of questions found on the AP exam.)

1. Which was NOT a significant factor in the development of science during the 15th and 16th centuries?

   (A) The Renaissance
   (B) Scientific writings of the ancient Greeks
   (C) The Protestant Reformation
   (D) The Roman Catholic emphasis on an appeal to authority in intellectual matters
   (E) The experiences of direct observation

2. The primary purpose of Fontenelle's *Conversations on the Plurality of Worlds* (1686) was to

   (A) popularize the findings of the Scientific Revolution
   (B) attack French absolutism
   (C) adapt scientific thought to Christian doctrine
   (D) counteract the influence of the Enlightenment
   (E) dispute the claims of Copernicus and Galileo

3. The Copernican Revolution was so named because

   (A) it reconciled the Ptolemaic conception of the universe with observation
   (B) it eliminated Ptolemy's cumbersome mathematics
   (C) it upset the comfortable assumptions of humanity's central place in the universe
   (D) it was suppressed by the Inquisition
   (E) its elegant simplicity reflected godliness

4. The most important reason absolute monarchs like Catherine II and Frederick II attempted reform was

   (A) because they believed in the Enlightenment
   (B) to strengthen their states
   (C) to improve the lot of their serfs
   (D) to gain the respect of the philosophes
   (E) because they wanted to show off their power to other monarchs

5. In his *Principia Mathematica,* 1687, Isaac Newton demonstrated all EXCEPT

   (A) that gravity and centripetal and centrifugal forces account for the motion of heavenly bodies
   (B) that gravity and centripetal and centrifugal forces move earthly objects
   (C) that the natural laws that govern these forces allow the prediction of all natural movement
   (D) that the natural laws explain how the universe is held together
   (E) that God created the universe but does not intervene in it

6. The famous phrase "Cogito ergo sum," "I think, therefore I am," was the logical foundation upon which the systematic doubt of 17th-century thinker René Descartes built a proof of reality. His philosophy was significant because

   (A) it repudiated Christianity
   (B) it defined many of the significant issues of modern philosophy
   (C) it proved Deism
   (D) it established Cartesian duality as the basis for modern science
   (E) it relegated God to the role of Prime Mover

7. All of the following can be said of the 18th-century Enlightenment EXCEPT

   (A) the Newtonian Revolution of the previous century set it in motion
   (B) it was based on the belief that unchangeable natural laws governed human society as well as the physical universe
   (C) it supported the assumption that human reason could fathom the natural laws
   (D) it reflected acceptance of social inequities and injustice as inevitable effects of the natural law
   (E) it was optimistic and progress oriented

8. What has been called the "religion of the Enlightenment"?

   (A) Protestantism
   (B) Agnosticism
   (C) Atheism
   (D) Rationalism
   (E) Deism

Oil by Lemonnier of Madame Geoffrin (1699–1777) in her salon at Hotel de Rambouillet in Paris. The Granger Collection, New York. (0103701)

9. The painting above is a gathering of notable writers and thinkers in order to

   (A) plan a new constitution for their country
   (B) evaluate different paintings being exhibited
   (C) observe the latest fashions in clothing
   (D) redecorate the hotel
   (E) discuss important philosophical issues and points of knowledge

"When popes and priests define their dogmas and discipline their followers, corruption is the rule and abuse is the result. 'Crush the infamous thing!' The simple beauty of Christ's message has been lost in ignorance and encrusted with superstition."

10. The above speaker would probably adhere to the views of

   (A) Bishop Bossuet
   (B) Voltaire
   (C) Montesquieu
   (D) Baron Holbach
   (E) Diderot

11. Whose *Spirit of the Laws*, 1748, served as a basis for the American Constitution's "separation of powers"?

    (A) Montesquieu
    (B) Voltaire
    (C) Rousseau
    (D) Diderot
    (E) Quesnay

12. Rousseau can be called an advocate of democracy and an apologist for dictatorship because

    (A) many of his closest friends were of the nobility
    (B) he argued that property is the root of social evil
    (C) he introduced the concept of the "Noble Savage"
    (D) his vague concept of the general will could be misinterpreted
    (E) he believed that civilization corrupts people

13. The philosophes shared the following characteristics EXCEPT

    (A) most were Deists
    (B) most rejected organized religion
    (C) most believed that this was "the best of all possible worlds"
    (D) most sought to foster human progress according to the principles of natural law
    (E) most accepted the philosophical principles of John Locke

14. Which best characterized Enlightened Despotism?

    (A) The monarch is an educated person who exercises absolute authority solely as he sees fit.
    (B) The monarch encourages the spread of Deism and rationalism.
    (C) The monarch supports and fosters the growth of democracy.
    (D) The monarch rules with absolute authority for the good of the people.
    (E) The monarch believes in the people's ultimate right to, and capability for, self-rule.

15. Which of the following was generally not considered an Enlightened Despot?

    (A) Frederick the Great of Prussia
    (B) Peter the Great of Russia
    (C) Catherine the Great of Russia
    (D) Maria Theresa of Austria
    (E) Alexander the Great of Russia

Answers and Answer Explanations

1.	D	6.	B	11.	A
2.	A	7.	D	12.	D
3.	C	8.	E	13.	C
4.	B	9.	E	14.	D
5.	E	10.	B	15.	E

1. **(D)** The traditions of the Roman Catholic Church discouraged scholarly pursuits that relied on the inductive method of inquiry. Reverence for authority was a key to study.

2. **(A)** Fontenelle's book was meant to explain the ideas of the Copernican theory, and other popular ideas of the Scientific Revolution, to the masses. It was one of many in a genre of books that simplified the ideas of the great thinkers of the day for digestion. It may have been the *Brief History of Time* of its day.

3. **(C)** An earth-centered universe supported the medieval world's conception of the utter importance of humankind as expressed by biblical creation.

4. **(B)** The *most important* reason that the Enlightened Despots modernized their realms was because they believed that it would strengthen their states. This is particularly true of Frederick II and Catherine II.

5. **(E)** That God created but does not intervene in the universe is a precept of Deism, a religious view that was influenced by Newton's theories but not part of them. Newton was a biblical scholar who believed he would be remembered for this rather than his scientific work.

6. **(B)** A religious man in a religious age, Descartes hoped to provide a logical foundation for the existence of the supernatural while he stressed the importance of observation in studying the natural world.

7. **(D)** The philosophes argued for progress and social justice as reflective of the natural law.

8. **(E)** It was a philosophical offshoot of Newton's natural law explanation for the motions of the universe.

9. **(E)** The salons were meetings of the greatest minds of the Enlightenment era to discuss the issues of the day, and Madame Geoffrin's was perhaps the best example.

10. **(B)** Voltaire coined the phrase "Crush the infamous thing," referring primarily to bigotry.

11. **(A)** It is the most familiar concept of his complex political theory.

12. **(D)** He never defined "general will" clearly. If it is equivalent in a democracy to the majority what are the rights of the minority? In dictatorship, a despot can claim to be the embodiment of the general will.

13. **(C)** This concept was contrary to their belief in the perfectability of humanity.

14. **(D)** The monarch, who might rule by divine right, still has the obligation to do good for his people, who are incapable of self-rule.

15. **(E)** Tsar during the Napoleonic Wars and after, his reforms were short-lived and halfhearted.

The French Revolution, Napoleon, and the Congress of Vienna

Key Terms/People

- The Old Regime
- National Assembly
- Tennis Court Oath
- Declaration of the Rights of Man and the Citizen
- March on Versailles
- Declaration of Pillnitz
- Robespierre
- Marat
- Danton
- Bastille

- Old Regime/estate System
- Jacobins
- Girondins
- National Convention
- The Thermidorian Reaction
- Code Napoleon
- nepotism
- Battle of Leipzig
- Bourbons
- Congress of Vienna

Overview

In 1789, France had a population of about 25 million, a productive economy, rich farmlands, and a culture that dominated the continent. French was not only the language of diplomacy, but it was the tongue spoken in most of the courts of Europe. France was the center of the 18th-century Enlightenment. Despite its wealth and influence, its government was corrupt, inefficient, and in debt, its class structure archiac and unjust, its institutions encrusted with medieval traditionalism. Stoked by the ideals and illusions of the Enlightenment, smoldering class resentments erupted in revolution. The revolution began as a moderate attempt at reform, degenerated into radical bloodletting, then swung back to authoritarianism and a short flirtation with empire in search of order. Impelled by the ideals of "liberty, equality, fraternity" and by military power, the French Revolution became an international movement that overthrew the feudal structures of the Old Regime in France and shook the political and social order in all of Europe.

Napoleon defined an age, 1799 to 1815. A capable person in the right place at the right time becomes great. His genius for military success created in less than a decade a French empire that stretched across the continent. His gift for administration and reform implemented the ideals of the Revolution. Ambition, growing nationalism throughout Europe, and unexpected events led to his downfall. He lost the cream of his magnificent army in the wasteland of the Russian winter; he arrayed most of Europe against him when his victories in the field awakened nationalism in the rest of Europe. After his fall, the old order tried to restore itself at the Congress of Vienna. A balance of power maintained relative peace for a century, but Europe had entered the Age of "Isms," and powerful new social, economic, and political forces would define the Western World.

The French Revolution

The Old Regime

A class structure left over from the Middle Ages determined the political and social order of France:

The First Estate, the clergy, made up considerably less than one percent of the population, but the Roman Catholic Church of France (Gallican Church) owned twenty percent of the land. The clergy and the Church were exempt from taxes.

The Second Estate, the nobles, numbered between two and four percent of the population and also owned about twenty percent of the land. They were also exempt from taxes.

The Third Estate, the middle class, urban artisans, and peasants, made up over ninety-five percent of the population. Although France had developed a significant commercial or middle class, the bourgeoisie, the mass of the people were peasants who lived on the land.

The Third Estate, especially the peasantry, was subjected to a variety of oppressive taxes: taille, a land tax; tithe, a church tax equivalent to ten percent of annual income, income tax, poll tax, salt tax, and local duties paid to the feudal lord. Personal freedom was jeopardized by the lettre de cachet, by which the government could imprison anyone without charges or trial. The bourgeoisie was disenchanted by its lack of influence in a system that it disproportionately supported.

Burdened by debts run up by Louis XIV's (r. 1643–1715) wars and extravagances, by the corruption and inefficiency of the administration of his successors, and by France's support of the American Revolution, the government of *Louis XVI* (r. 1774–1792) attempted to tax the previously exempt clergy and nobility. A high court of France, the *Parlement of Paris*, ruled that new taxes could not be levied unless approved by the *Estates-General*, the legislative body equivalent to a parliament, which had not met in 175 years, representing the three estates mentioned above.

The First or Moderate Stage of the Revolution (1789–1792)

May 5, 1789: The Estates-General met in Versailles.

June 13, 1789: Supported by a few members of the First Estate, the Third Estate broke a voting deadlock in the Estates-General by declaring itself the *National Assembly.*

June 20, 1789: After being locked out of their meeting place by the king's troops, members of the National Assembly swore the *Tennis Court Oath* not to disband until they had written a new constitution for France.

July 14, 1789: After food riots in the cities, peasant rebellions in the countryside, and the inaction of Louis and his ministers, a Parisian mob stormed the *Bastille,* a fortress that symbolized royal injustice.

August 4, 1789: The Decrees of this date mark when the National Assembly *abolished feudalism and manorialism.*

August 26, 1789: Declaration of the Rights of Man and the Citizen was passed. Freedom of speech, thought, and religion were guaranteed; due process of law was guaranteed; taxes could be imposed only by consent of the governed; the right to rule was said to be not just the king's but the whole nation's.

August 1789–1790: The Great Fear swept through the countryside as the third estate rose up against the nobility and destroyed feudal records and noble residences. This movement lent strength to the movement to end feudalism.

September 1789: The National Assembly was also named the *Constituent Assembly* because it was drafting a constitution.

October 1789: A Paris mob, mostly of women, was incited by Jean Paul Marat to *march on Versailles* and force the king to relocate to the *Tuileries,* the royal residence in Paris. The assembly also went to Paris and was intimidated by the Parisians.

November 2, 1789: The assembly *seized Church and monastery lands* for revenue.

1790: The Civil Constitution of the Clergy was drafted. Convents and monasteries were abolished; all clergyman were to be paid by the state and elected by all citizens; the clergy was forbidden to accept the authority of the pope. Alienated by this decree, half of the priests of the Gallican Church refused to accept it.

1791: The National (Constituent) Assembly drafted a new constitution that instituted an *elected Legislative Assembly,* which made the king chief executive officer, largely responsible to the assembly; the latter established voting qualifications for male citizens.

June 21, 1791: The *Flight to Varennes* of the royal family, in order to raise a counterrevolutionary army, was stopped, and the king and queen became prisoners of the Parisian mobs.

August 1791: The *Declaration of Pillnitz* by the king of Austria threatened military action to restore order in France and encouraged the radical revolutionaries who wanted to overthrow the monarchy.

The Second or Radical Stage of the Revolution (1792–1795)

April 20, 1792: The *Legislative Assembly*, the legislature under the new constitution, *declared war on Austria* in response to an ultimatum. The *"Wars of the Revolution"* began.

July 25, 1792: The commander of a Prussian army, about to invade France, issued the *Brunswick Manifesto*, threatening the people of Paris if harm came to the king. *Jacobin* (radical republican) leaders aroused the Paris mobs.

August 10, 1792: The *Tuileries were stormed* and the king was taken prisoner; the mobs slaughtered over a thousand priests, bourgeois, and aristocrats who opposed their program.

September 21, 1792: France was proclaimed a republic, the first.

1793: An appeal to nationalism inspired the French people to drive back their invaders, and the *First Coalition,* an alliance of Austria, England, Netherlands, Prussia, and Spain, was organized to combat the French advance.

The *Jacobins,* supported by the Paris mobs, and the *Girondists,* supported by the peasants in the rural areas, battled for control of the *National Convention,* which was the new assembly under the republic.

Maximilien Robespierre (1758–1794), leader of the Jacobins, pushed for the execution of the king—tried for treason—and both *Louis XVI* and his queen, *Marie Antoinette* (1755–1793) were guillotined in January 1793.

May 1793: Enragés—radical working-class leaders of Paris—seized and arrested Girondist members of the *National Convention* and left the Jacobins in control under the leadership of Robespierre.

Summer 1793: A dictatorial *Committee of Public Safety* launched the Reign of Terror. Over 20,000 people—nearly 75 percent of them working class and peasants—were executed from the summer of 1793 to that of 1794.

Late 1793: The *Republic of Virtue* was proclaimed by the Committee of Public Safety in an attempt to de-Christianize France; it largely alienated the Catholic majority of the nation.

1794: Both *Danton* (1759–1794) an original Jacobin, and Robespierre, leader of the Republic of Virtue, were executed by the National Convention when public opinion turned against the excesses of the Reign of Terror.

The Final or Reactionary Stage of the Revolution (1795–1799)

The *Thermidorian Reaction*, which took place during the month of *Thermidor* (August 18–September 16) on the new non-Christian calendar, returned the moderate bourgeois reformers to power.

1795–1799: The *Directory*, a five-member executive, was established by the National Convention to run the government. When a Paris mob threatened the new government, *Napoleon Bonaparte* (r. 1799–1815), a young general who by chance was in Paris at the time, put down the riot and was rewarded with the command of the French armies fighting the Austrians in Italy.

Women's Role in the Revolution

Women also played a major role in the French Revolution. In October of 1789, the Revolution was at a turning point. In the midst of a continuing shortage of bread, rumors of counterrevolution spread among the guards and royalty at Versailles. In response, many women and some men dressed as women in Paris gathered to march to Versailles to demand an accounting from the king. They marched 12 miles from Paris in the rain, where the women were joined by thousands of men. The next day the crowd became rowdy and eventually broke into the royal apartments, killing two of the king's bodyguards. To prevent further bloodshed, the king agreed to move his family back to Paris.

Women's participation was not confined to rioting and demonstrating. Women started to participate in meetings of political clubs, and a guarantee of women's rights became a topic of discussion during the revolution. In July of 1790, the Marquis de Condorcet published a newspaper article in support of full political rights for women, which increased the importance of the discussion. He argued that France's women should enjoy equal political rights with men. His ideas were supported by the publication of the *Vindication of the Rights of Women* by Mary Wollstonecraft in 1791.

Cause and Effect Chart for the French Revolution

If you can understand and retain the information in this chart then you are ready for any question that the AP exam will have about the French Revolution.

1. The Estates-General meet for the first time

Cause:

The French nation had seen famine and economic collapse. The Estates-General had not met in 175 years but was called to meet in order to raise taxes after the Parliament of Paris refused to do so. ·

Effect:

The meeting unified the nobility with the Third Estate and they took the Tennis Court Oath, promising not to leave until they had created a constitution for France.

2. Declaration of the Rights of Man

Cause:

The monarchy had consolidated power through the intendant system, and the failure of crops and the economy. These woes along with the ideas of the Enlightenment and the American Revolution led to the demand for a French constitution at the storming of the Bastille which helped to create it.

Effect:

The French Revolution began in earnest with the Great Fear and the path was cleared for the creation of the National Assembly.

3. The Great Fear

Cause:

The pent-up aggression of the Third Estate is unleashed as a reaction to the Declaration of the Rights of Man.

Effect:

A chasm developed between the nobility and the peasantry and factions formed in France about what the new government should look like and how it should act.

4. Formation of the National Assembly

Cause:

The disintegration of order in France and the Declaration led to the formation of the National Assembly, or Constituent Assembly, in order to make a constitution and rule the country.

Effect:

They created a constitution that allowed for election of a Legislative Assembly with the king at the helm. The king then tried to escape with his family.

5. Attempted escape of Louis XVI and family

Cause:

The revolutionary mood in France made them fear more for their lives than for their titles and possessions.

Effect:

This further cemented national sentiment against the royal family and was a factor in their later execution.

6. The Legislative Assembly declares war on Austria

Cause:

The Declaration of Pilnitz saw Austria try to intervene in French affairs by pursuing military action to protect the monarchy.

Effect:

The sans-culottes and the radicals came together with support building all over France against foreign invasion.

See #7 next page

7. Radicals and sans-culottes gain power

Cause:
The pendulum of change had been held to the right for so long that it swung far in the other direction. Pent-up aggression from the Third Estate led to the most demagogical leaders gaining power, Marat, Danton, and Robespierre.

Effect:
Revolutionary zeal swept the common people of France. Society was turned upside down and the Reign of Terror would eventually result.

8. The National Convention is formed

Cause:
The new constitution, which created the First Republic, called for a National Assembly to be formed.

Effect:
This body was very politically biased with the radical Jacobin Party in power. The modern-day terms for right and left for conservative and liberal come from the seating arrangement in this body.

9. The Jacobin Club gains prominence

Cause:
The radical mood of Paris and the overwhelming support of the poor and the peasants led the radical Jacobin Party to gain power. The powerful demagogues mentioned in box 7 and the French military needs also contributed.

Effect:
The revolution goes through a second stage that is more radical and sometimes known as the Reign of Terror.

10. Execution of King Louis XVI

Cause:
The radical turn of the revolution, the king's alliance with Austria, and his life of excess and poor national management led to his execution.

Effect:
The other nations of Europe condemned France, and the revolution becomes more radical as it becomes clear that no one who opposes the revolution is safe in France.

11. Committee of Public Safety oversees Reign of Terror

Cause:
The radical mood of Paris, the rise of radicals, and the execution of the king combine to lead the Third Estate to kill over 20,000, most of whom were in the Third Estate. Anyone associated with nobility was in danger, and many innocents were executed at the guillotine.

Effect:
Many abroad opposed the revolution, and the terror soon convinced many of the French that the revolution had gone too far.

12. End of the Reign of Terror and the rise of the Directory

Cause:
The leadership of the committee turned on each other and by 1794, Marat, Robespierre, and Danton were dead, the last two killed as enemies of the revolution. The radical phase ran its course and the people wanted stability.

Effect:
France was ruled by moderates, and many of the sans-culottes felt abandoned by the revolution.

13. Napoleon rises to power

Cause: There was definitely a power vacuum and the nation was looking for a strong leader to emerge, which Napoleon did in style. He was a brilliant general and a lesser noble who was not a part of the establishment, but who understood power very well.

Effect: Napoleon soon took over France and most of Europe. He instituted reforms of the law and instituted freedom of religion across the continent. He also unified Italy and Germany under French rule for the first time (in centuries for Italy). His legacy was a reorganization of European power that took place at the Congress of Vienna after his defeat.

Napoleon

In 1799, Napoleon, after spectacular victories against the Austrians and later against English armies in Egypt, overthrew the Directory in a coup d'état and formed a new government, the *Consulate*, made up of three consuls with Napoleon as head consul.

Napoleon's Domestic Reforms

Even as emperor, Napoleon Bonaparte was committed to many of the ideals of the French Revolution. Son of an impoverished minor aristocrat and a virtual foreigner—Corsica, the island of his birth, had been owned by Italy for centuries until its annexation by the French shortly before his birth—Napoleon reached the heights he did because the Revolution opened society to men of ability. His reforms assured the dissolution of the Old Regime by establishing egalitarianism in government, before the law, and in educational opportunity.

Napoleon signed *The Concordat of 1801* with the Pope whereby the papacy renounced claims over church property seized during the Revolution and was allowed to nominate bishops. In return, those priests who had resisted the Civil Constitutions of the clergy would replace those who had sworn an oath to the state. Since the pope gave up claim to church lands, those citizens who had acquired them pledged loyalty to Napoleon's government.

With the *Code Napoleon*, 1804, Napoleon replaced varied and inequitable medieval law with a uniform legal system. It was a model for codes of law in many European countries. In 1808, he instituted a *state-supported educational system* with rigorous standards and available to the masses.

He created a *merit system* to recruit and reward those in government, despite the fact that he practiced flagrant *nepotism* by placing his relatives on the thrones of nations he conquered.

He lowered the taxes on farmers, and guaranteed that the redistributed church lands remained in the hands of their new owners, who were mostly peasant farmers. This created an *independent peasantry* that would be the backbone of French democracy.

Napoleon's Conquests and Defeats

His aim was to unite Europe under France's leadership. In a decade, he was able to conquer vastly more territory and to influence the destinies of more nations than the Sun King, Louis XIV, had in his sixty and more years' reign. His very success convinced the peoples he conquered or battled that the future lay in national unity, and the force of nationalism led to his downfall and shaped the destiny of Europe well into the 20th century.

Italy: In 1797, his victories led to a Northern Italian Republic, the *Cisalpine*, and several satellites in Central and Southern Italy under French control. By 1809, he controlled virtually all of Italy, abolishing feudalism and reforming the social, political, and economic structures. He decided against *national* unity for the Italians, who had been divided into competing city-states and kingdoms during the Middle Ages, because unity might pose a threat to French dominance of the region.

Germany: After soundly defeating the two most powerful and influential German states—Austria and Prussia—Napoleon reorganized Germany. He consolidated many of the nearly 300 independent political entities (among these creations was the *Confederation of the Rhine*), and he abolished feudalism and carried out reforms. He awakened German nationalism.

The Continental System: Through a series of shifting alliances, the English had consistently opposed the upset of the European balance of power brought about by French victories on the continent. Unable to destroy British supremacy at sea and invade Britain, Napoleon decided to starve Britain out by closing the ports of the continent to British commerce. He coerced Russia, a temporary ally of the French, his defeated enemy Prussia, neutral Denmark and Portugal, and French satellite Spain all to adhere to the boycott.

Spain: When Napoleon tried to tighten his control over Spain by replacing the Spanish king with one of his own brothers, the Spanish people waged a costly *guerrilla war* that was aided by the British under one of their ablest commanders, the *Duke of Wellington* (1769–1852).

Russia: Napoleon *invaded Russia* in June of 1812, when the Russians withdrew from the Continental System which was preventing Russia from trading with Great Britain, causing Russian economic hardships. Napoleon brought more than 600,000 of his best soldiers and marched into Russia, only to be met by "scorched earth" tactics rather than pitched battle. The Russians destroyed all materials that could be foraged by Napoleon's army and only attacked in skirmishes at strategically advantageous points. Napoleon's army took Moscow, but due to the city being burned, stretched supply lines, and the oncoming winter, Napoleon's army retreated. He returned with approximately 22,000 soldiers. This decimated Napoleon's army and his image.

The Collapse of the Napoleonic Empire

Having lost 500,000 of his 600,000-man Grand Army, facing riots in Italy and a British invasion of Southern France by Wellington's army, Napoleon was defeated by the combined forces of Russia, Prussia, and Austria in October 1813 at the *Battle of Leipzig*, also known as the *Battle of Nations*.

Napoleon abdicated as emperor on April 4, 1814 after he had rejected the *Frankfurt Proposals* to keep him on the throne but to withdraw French troops from Germany and after allied armies entered Paris. The *Bourbons* were restored to the throne of France in the person of *Louis XVIII* (r. 1814–1824), and Napoleon was exiled to the island of *Elba* in the Mediterranean.

France surrendered all territory gained since the Wars of the Revolution had begun in 1792, and King Louis created a legislature that represented only the upper classes. The restoration, though, maintained most of Napoleon's reforms such as the Code Napoleon, the concordat with the Pope, and the abolition of feudalism.

The Congress of Vienna (September 1814–June 1815)

Representatives of the major powers of Europe, including France, met to redraw territorial lines and to restore, as far as was possible, the social and political order that existed before the Revolution and Napoleon. The *rule of legitimacy* was one primary goal: to return the "rightful" rulers of Europe to their thrones. A return to a balance of power that would guarantee peace was the other.

The august assemblage consisted of *Klemens Von Metternich* (1773–1859), chancellor *of Austria*; Viscount *Castlereagh* (1769–1822), foreign minister *of England*; *Czar Alexander of Russia* (r. 1801–1825); *Prince Hardenberg of Prussia*; and Foreign Minister *Tallyrand* (1754–1838) *of France*.

THE SETTLEMENT

To prevent future expansion, France was surrounded by a number of strong states—a newly united Holland and Belgium called the Kingdom of the Netherlands, a Prussian satellite area on the Rhine, and Austrian buffer states in Northern Italy.

In Germany, Napoleon's reorganization remained, and the 300 originally independent states were reduced to 39.

The Hapsburg Holy Roman Empire was not reestablished.

The Hundred Days began on March 1, 1815, when Napoleon managed to escape from his exile in Elba and made it to the south of France with a small honor guard of less than 100 men and marched, to popular acclaim, into Paris. He raised an army, defeated a Prussian army in Belgium on June 16, 1815, but was defeated by the Duke of Wellington and Prussian general, Gebhard von Blücher at *Waterloo*, in Belgium, on June 18. He was imprisoned on the island of *St. Helena* in the South Atlantic and died on May 5, 1821.

The Concert of Europe was an alliance, also known as the *Quadruple Alliance*, signed by England, Prussia, Russia, and Austria in November 1815. Its aim was to maintain the status quo that the Congress of Vienna had established, upholding the territorial boundaries and shoring up the monarchies of Europe against the spread of revolutionary ideas, such as *republicanism* (that the people should elect their rulers).

Even though the alliance did not last for long, the balance of power created by the Congress of Vienna prevented a general war for a hundred years.

Sample Essay Question

The sample thematic essay questions presented in this chapter are types found on the AP exam, and they require knowledge of causes, effects, personalities, ideas, and events.

SAMPLE QUESTION

Explain how, although he was an autocrat, Napoleon helped put into practice many of the ideals of the French Revolution.

Comments on the Sample Question

Follow the "Simple Procedures" for writing an essay. (See page 34.)

First, *What does the question want to know?* In this question, "to explain" requires that you make clear and detail how Napoleon could be an autocrat and still fulfill many of the promises of the French Revolution. This is not a choice question where you might take the opposite position.

Second, *What do you know about it?* An "autocrat" is a ruler with absolute power; Napoleon was first a dictator and then an emperor. The ideals of the Revolution can be summed up by the phrase "Liberty, equality, fraternity," and these ideals would appear to contradict Napoleon's roles.

Third, *How would you put it into words?* The task is to "make clear" and "detail" what the ideals of the Revolution were and how Napoleon's domestic and foreign policies helped realize them both in France and beyond its borders.

Rubric for Sample Answer

Before you read the sample answer, examine the rubric. What will the reader be looking for when he or she grades this essay? A sample rubric, shaded to show the reader's evaluation, is seen below:

9–8 POINTS

- ✔ Thesis explicitly identifies **both** how Napoleon put into practice the ideals of the French Revolution and how this was done through or in spite of his autocratic power throughout most of Europe. Thesis does not need to be in the opening paragraph.
- ✔ Organization is clear, consistently followed, and effective in support of the argument.
  - May devote individual paragraphs to an examination of Napoleon's autocracy and how Napoleon carried out the ideals of the French Revolution.
  - Must identify individual ideals of the French Revolution (liberty, equality, and brotherhood among any other Enlightenment ideals that may also be presented) and consider how each of the ideals of the French Revolution were put into practice by Napoleon, as well as explain how his autocratic rule affected putting the ideals of the French Revolution into practice.
- ✔ Essay is well balanced; the ways in which Napoleon put the ideals of the French Revolution into practice while explaining how his autocratic rule affected his putting the ideals of the French Revolution into practice are

> analyzed at some length. Essay covers the rise, reign, and fall of Napoleon to some extent.
> ✔ Major assertions in the essay are supported thoroughly and consistently by relevant evidence.
> ✔ Evidence of the spread of these ideals may prove more specific or concrete.
> ✔ May contain errors that do not detract from the argument.

7–8 POINTS

✔ Thesis explicitly identifies **both** how Napoleon put into practice the ideals of the French Revolution and how this was done through or in spite of his autocratic power throughout most of Europe, but may not be developed fully.

✔ Organization is clear and effective in support of the argument but may introduce evidence that is not pertinent to the task.

✔ Essay covers all major topics suggested by the prompt but may analyze an aspect of Napoleon's rule, an ideal of the French Revolution, and how this was done through or in spite of his autocratic power throughout most of Europe in greater depth rather than in a balanced manner.

✔ Major assertions in the essay are supported by relevant evidence.

✔ May contain an error that detracts from the argument.

5–4 POINTS

✔ Thesis identifies **both** how Napoleon put into practice the ideals of the French Revolution and how this was done through or in spite of his autocratic power throughout most of Europe, but without any development; thesis may address only part of the question effectively; thesis may be a simple, single-sentence statement.

✔ Organization is clear but may not be consistently followed; essay may veer off task chronologically or thematically or both.

✔ Essay may not complete all tasks:
  • May discuss only how Napoleon put the ideals of the French Revolution into practice or his autocratic rule.
  • May discuss only one or two ideals of the French Revolution.
  • May focus only on one nation.
  • May be primarily descriptive rather than analytical.

✔ Essay offers some relevant evidence.

✔ May contain several errors that detract from the argument.

3–2 POINTS

✔ Thesis may simply paraphrase the prompt OR identify Napoleon or the ideals of the French Revolution without analyzing how this was done through or in spite of his autocratic power throughout most of Europe.

✔ Organization is unclear and ineffective; essay may focus on the personal attributes .of Napoleon rather than analyzing how his autocratic power influenced his putting the ideals of the French Revolution into practice across Europe.

✔ Essay shows serious imbalance; discussion how Napoleon put the ideals of the French Revolution into practice or how his autocratic power influenced his putting the ideals of the French Revolution into practice across Europe is superficial; much of the information may be significantly out of the time period or geography of the question.

✔ Offers minimal OR confused evidence.

✔ May contain several errors that detract from the argument.

1–0 POINTS

✔ Thesis is erroneous OR irrelevant OR absent.

✔ No effective organization is evident.

✔ Discussion of how Napoleon put into practice the ideals of the French Revolution and how this was done through or in spite of his autocratic power throughout most of Europe is generic.

✔ Provides little or no relevant supporting evidence.

✔ May contain numerous errors that detract from the argument.

Sample Answer

Even an autocrat can be a reformer. Napoleon, with all the power of a modern state in his grasp, with all the trappings of an empire, could be considered "a son of the French Revolution." Maybe the ideals of the Enlightenment—"liberty" from cruel and arbitrary government; "equality" before the law and based on merit, "fraternity," a modern sense of the unity of a whole people—could have been imposed upon the old order only by a strong ruler.

Old habits die hard, and the first or moderate stage of the French Revolution may have drafted the Declaration of the Rights of Man and the Citizen, but it was not able to put its lofty goals into practice. The third or reactionary stage set the tone for Napoleon; the nation was weary of terror and turmoil and it welcomed order, even if imposed by a "strong man," such as Napoleon.

In the coup d'état of Brumaire, November of 1799, Napoleon returned from his ill-fated Egyptian campaign and overthrew the Directory. He formed the Consulate, making himself first consul among three, and within a month he had pushed through a new constitution, engineered a landslide of popular approval, and filled the legislature with his supporters. He was dictator of France, an autocrat with virtually absolute power. By 1804, his toady Senate had named him emperor.

Napoleon's motives for putting into practice many of the ideals of the Revolution are varied. Reform, not simply raw power, was an instrument for maintaining his position. By rewarding those who had supported him, he earned their loyalty; by improving the lot of whole segments of society, he won popularity. Not the least of his motives was to contribute to the sense of human progress that glowed in the Age of Enlightenment. He was probably more "enlightened despot" than "modern dictator."

Some of the ideals of the French Revolution are found in the Declaration of the Rights of Man, which was meant to apply to all people, not just the French.

It was proclaimed on August 26, 1789, to back up the Decrees of August 4, which ended feudalism and the privileges of manorialism. The declaration guaranteed freedom of religion and speech, due process of the law, and equality before the law—whatever one's origins. It also stated that sovereignty, the right to rule, was not the king's alone but rested with the whole nation.

If freedom of religion was one of the ideals of the Revolution, Napoleon's Concordat of 1801 satisfied the Catholic majority of France by revoking the Civil Constitution of the Clergy, which had allowed the state to unduly influence religious matters. If equality was another ideal, the Concordat also fostered this when the Pope renounced all claims to confiscated church lands, thereby creating independent landholders among the bourgeoisie and peasantry. When Napoleon lowered the old feudal taxes for the peasants, he guaranteed liberty from the old order by enabling them to prosper under the new, and thus created meaningful reform.

The Code Napoleon, 1804, replaced the mishmosh of medieval laws that favored the nobility with a uniform set of laws that applied to all French men and women equally. Napoleon's state support of education for all classes of citizens and his merit system in government, rewarding ability rather than birth, both furthered the goal of equality.

Napoleon spread the ideals of the Revolution to many of the nations of Europe through his conquests. In Italy and Germany, he abolished feudalism and manorialism and he reformed social, political, and economic institutions. His consolidation of the separate and often squabbling political entities in Italy and especially Germany offered a sense of national unity to these people: fraternity. The successes of his armies taught other peoples that national unity meant national power, and that sense of fraternity, ironically, led to Napoleon's defeat at their hands.

Despite his dictatorial tendencies, his imperial ambitions, his megalomania, Napoleon put into practice many of the ideals of the French Revolution. His legal, educational, and governmental reforms engendered equality. His peacemaking with the papacy encouraged a freer expression of religion, a powerful liberty, and strengthened independent landowners among the peasants and middle classes, a foundation for democracy. His conquests helped spread and put into practice the universal principles of the Declaration of the Rights of Man and the ideals of "liberty, equality, fraternity."

EVALUATE THE SAMPLE ANSWER

Now go back and look at the rubric. It is clear that this essay fulfills all of the requirements for a score of 8 or 9 on the rubric. The essay answers all parts of the question thoroughly with concrete evidence at length with a well-balanced essay. The sparser concrete support gets this essay a score of 8.

RATER'S COMMENTS ON THE SAMPLE ANSWER

8—Extremely well qualified

This is a clearly argued, factually supported, and well-written essay. Its introduction not only lays out the body of its argument, but it ties together the two significant developments of that period, the French Revolution and the rule of Napoleon. It makes specific factual references that are relevant, accurate, and concise. It explains how Napoleon became an autocrat, what the ideals of the French Revolution involved, what his motives may have been for including them in his domestic and foreign policies, and how he put them into practice. It sums up the argument in a lucid conclusion. It could have more flourish and better use of quotes.

Practice Essay Questions

The questions that follow are samples of the various types of thematic essays that appear on the AP exam. (See pages 21–22 for a detailed explanation of each type.) Check over the **generic rubric** (see pages 58–60) before you begin any of these essays and use that rubric to score your essay if you write one.

QUESTION 1

Contrast and compare the stages of the French Revolution.

COMMENTS ON QUESTION 1

The "contrast" part of this question is easy since the various stages of the Revolution have significant differences: the groups, personalities, and methods are glaringly different in each. The tough part of this question is to detail what they had in common, what their similarities were. Each had a form of government, a type of leadership, a constitution, a legislative body, goals. Sort them out and stress their similarities.

QUESTION 2

Analyze the way Louis XVI's attempt to raise taxes to pay off his government's debts precipitated the French Revolution.

COMMENTS ON QUESTION 2

To answer this question, you must apply all the meanings of the term "analyze." You must "determine the relationship" between Louis's attempt to raise taxes and the Revolution. The calling of the Estates General for the first time in over 150 years started the chain of events. You must "examine" the sequence of events "in detail." Class factionalism in the Estates General led to the creation of the National Assembly. And you must "explain" why this particular attempt to raise taxes was significantly different from previous attempts. Louis wanted to tax the First and Second Estates, which had been exempt since the Middle Ages.

QUESTION 3

"Napoleon's very successes in battle awakened the nationalistic forces that defeated him."
Assess the validity of this statement.

COMMENTS ON QUESTION 3

In this case "assess the validity" means to "determine the truth" of the statement. Almost inevitably, the statement itself is the easiest to argue for in "assess" questions. The strategy is simple: Show how his victories over specific states led to increased nationalism both there and back in France. Napoleon's installation of relatives and his weakening of the Hapsburg power, as well as his addiction to victories, should also be mentioned. Perhaps the most important factor to cite is that Napoleon united Germany and Italy for the most part, a feat that the Germans and Italians had failed to accomplish.

QUESTION 4

To what extent and in what ways did the Congress of Vienna restore the Old Order in Europe?

COMMENTS ON QUESTION 4

"How and how much" did the Congress restore the Old Order. What had the Old Order been? How had the Revolution and Napoleon changed it? What provisions of the Congress dealt with it? What was the overall result—immediately and in the long term?

QUESTION 5

"The accomplishments of the French Revolution were not worth the violence, instability, and war it led to." *Defend or refute* this statement.

COMMENTS ON QUESTION 5

Argue for or against or a little of each. What were the accomplishments—an end to the Old Regime, the spread of democratic ideals? What were the costs—the Terror, the Wars of the Revolution, the rise of Napoleon? Beware of simplistic moralizing. Great developments in human history are riddled with rights and wrongs on all sides.

Practice Multiple-Choice Questions

(These questions are representative of the various types that appear on the AP exam.)

1. The least important impact of the American Revolution on France was

    (A) providing young men with a taste of revolutionary action and ideals
    (B) providing a revolutionary role model
    (C) providing revenge against the hated English
    (D) increasing the financial burdens of the state
    (E) providing proof that a republic could be created and function

2. The immediate cause of the outbreak of revolution in 1789 was

    (A) grinding poverty among all classes of society
    (B) government oppression
    (C) the ideas of the philosophes
    (D) the insensitivity of Marie Antoinette
    (E) the government's financial crisis

3. Although the storming of the Bastille on July 14, 1789, is celebrated as the "start of the French Revolution," the first act of revolution may have been the resolve of the Third Estate to write a constitution. It is of

    (A) the first session of the Estates General
    (B) the swearing of the Tennis Court Oath
    (C) the storming of the Tuileries
    (D) the forming of the National Assembly
    (E) the public proclamation of the Declaration of the Rights of Man "Men are born and remain free and equal in rights."

4. What document supporting a new order of government has the above line as its first article?

    (A) The *Declaration of Independence*
    (B) The U.S. Constitution
    (C) *The Declaration of the Rights of Man and the Citizen*
    (D) Tom Paine's *Common Sense*
    (E) *What Is the Third Estate?*

5. Many historians divide the French Revolution into these three distinct stages:

    (A) "The Great Fear," "The Reign of Terror," and "The Directory"
    (B) The Monarchy, the Republic, the Empire
    (C) The radical, the moderate, and the reactionary stages
    (D) The moderate, the radical, and the reactionary stages
    (E) The storming of the Bastille, of the Tuileries, of the National Convention

6. Which of the following alienated the most French Catholic clerics and believers?

   (A) The provision of freedom of religion in the Declaration of the Rights of Man
   (B) The determination of the various revolutionary governments to collect taxes from the First Estate
   (C) The seizure of church lands
   (D) The Civil Constitution of the Clergy
   (E) The abolition of monasteries

7. Who were the *sans-culottes*, and what was their role in the revolution?

   (A) They were the bourgeois factory owners who supported the revolution financially.
   (B) They were the leaders of the revolution who ran the new government.
   (C) They were an underground political party who supported the monarchy.
   (D) They were the poor city dwellers who added zeal and brutality to the revolution.
   (E) They were scholars who created a new calendar for the republic.

8. By the standards of the 20th century, the slaughter of French citizens during the Reign of Terror was relatively small in number. It claimed approximately how many victims?

   (A) 4 million
   (B) 1 million
   (C) 400,000
   (D) 40,000
   (E) 4,000

9. All of the following are accurate EXCEPT

   (A) France had a nonrepresentative government before the French Revolution as well as afterward
   (B) the Revolution destroyed the vestiges of manorialism
   (C) the Revolution failed to end the legal inequities between the classes
   (D) the Revolution influenced French society to measure status by ability rather than birth
   (E) the ideals of the French Revolution spread throughout Europe

10. Which of the following policies of Napoleon was most often used to cast him in a negative role by his opponents?

    (A) The Concordat of 1801
    (B) His use of nepotism in government
    (C) His use of the merit system in government
    (D) His Code Napoleon
    (E) His restructuring of the educational system

11. Napoleon's purpose in instituting the Continental System was to

    (A) defeat England through economic war
    (B) consolidate the separate states of Germany
    (C) unify Italy
    (D) create a united Europe under the leadership of France
    (E) punish Russia for his ill-fated invasion

12. Napoleon helped make the French Revolution an international movement in the areas he conquered

    (A) by imposing a universal currency based on the French franc
    (B) by the brutal suppression of guerrilla resistance
    (C) by abolishing feudalism and manorialism
    (D) by encouraging French as the universal language
    (E) by placing his relatives on the thrones

13. The Congress of Vienna hoped to restore the European balance of power after the Wars of the Revolution and the Napoleonic Wars by

    (A) surrounding France with strong states
    (B) unifying all of Germany
    (C) reestablishing the Holy Roman Empire
    (D) unifying Italy
    (E) giving Russia the left bank of the Rhine

14. Who was the man whose ideas and aims dominated the Congress of Vienna and after whom the age of reaction is named?

    (A) Castlereagh
    (B) Metternich
    (C) Alexander I
    (D) Talleyrand
    (E) Hardenburg

French Revolution, 1789. Contemporary French engraving. The Granger Collection, New York. (0020896)

15. What period of the French Revolution is depicted in the image above?

    (A) The drought of 1888
    (B) The storming of the Bastille
    (C) The Directory
    (D) The Great Fear
    (E) The Great Panic

Answers and Answer Explanations

1.	B	6.	D	11.	A
2.	E	7.	D	12.	C
3.	B	8.	D	13.	A
4.	C	9.	C	14.	B
5.	D	10.	B	15.	D

1. **(B)** The American Revolution did not provide a good model of revolution for France because there were too many differences. One was a nation of recent immigrants, the other was the mother country with thousands of years of traditions.

2. **(E)** The convening of the Estates General in response to the financial crisis precipitated the Revolution.

3. **(B)** The Tennis Court Oath marks the beginning of the Moderate Stage, before the Paris mobs intervened.

4. **(C)** The quote is from *The Declaration of the Rights of Man and the Citizen* and supports the ideals of that document.

5. **(D)** This is the prevailing view of historians of the French Revolution.

6. **(D)** That the government would appoint Church officials, non-Catholics could vote for parish priests, and the clergy had to swear allegiance to the state angered many Catholics and at least half of the French clergy.

7. **(D)** The *sans-culottes* were poor city dwellers who gave their energy and service to spur on the revolution.

8. **(D)** 12 million died as a result of Nazi extermination methods in World War II; 30 million or more died from Stalinist repression in the U.S.S.R. Some authorities claim that as many as 170 million individuals perished during the 20th century as victims of state-sponsored murder.

9. **(C)** The Decrees of August 4, 1789, ended feudalism and abolished manorialism; the Code Napoleon established uniform codes of justice.

10. **(B)** By putting his relatives, mainly siblings, on the thrones of states of Europe he had conquered, he often inspired nationalistic uprisings.

11. **(A)** The Continental System proved a greater burden to many of his allies—including Russia that he invaded for its refusal to continue compliance—than to Britain.

12. **(C)** The Old Order—feudalism and manorialism—was dismantled by decree, inspiring a shift of power from the landowning aristocracy to the middle classes and promising all classes social and economic justice.

13. **(A)** A United Netherlands and an expanded Prussia (it received territory at the French border in Germany) were to serve this function. Austria was a secondary barrier.

14. **(B)** The *Age of Metternich*, 1815–1848, is marked by reactionary policies by nearly all the states of Europe to cleanse themselves of the stain of French Revolutionary idealism.

15. **(D)** The surrounding countryside makes the Great Fear the only viable choice for this scene of destruction.

Mercantilism and the Rise of Capitalism; The Industrial Revolution

Key Terms/People

- Commercial Revolution
- Capitalism
- Industrial Revolution
- Medieval Common Lands
- Industrial Proletariat
- Sadler Commission
- Child Labor Laws
- Jeremy Bentham

- utilitarianism
- Thomas Malthus
- David Ricardo
- Comte de Saint-Simon
- Karl Marx
- James Watt
- Adam Smith

Overview

From the end of the 15th century to the beginning of the 18th, the discovery of the New World and the opening of the Atlantic to exploration and colonization changed the economy of Europe. Mercantilism—medieval manorial self-sufficiency on a national scale—became the prevailing economic system of the growing nation-states. Inflation, brought about by the stores of gold and silver imported from the New World, led to an increase in trade and manufacture that encouraged the growth of early capitalism. As economic activity shifted from the Mediterranean to the Atlantic, the Italian city-states declined as trading middlemen between Europe and the Near and Far East. Portugal and Spain became the major powers of the 16th century; the Netherlands, France, and England of the 17th.

An Industrial Revolution—given birth by the growth of commerce, the development of capitalism, the introduction of improved technology, and the unique political climate in Britain during the 18th century—changed life in Western Europe in the 1800s more profoundly than the French Revolution had. The landowning aristocracy, which had its origins in the early Middle Ages and whose decline had begun with the growth of a commercial and professional middle class, lost more wealth and political power with the inception of a spectacularly wealthy capitalist class. The lives of the mass of Europeans shifted from the farm to the factory, from the predictable rhythms of a rural existence to the grinding and impersonal poverty of the industrial cities. Along with the capitalists, a new proletariat, or working class, was created, and a whole new set of social and economic doctrines sought to explain their rights and better their lives. Added to the "isms" that grew out of the French Revolution, such as republicanism, conservatism, and nationalism, were socialism and Marxism. By the last third of the 19th century—"The Age of Progress"—a technological revolution had altered the Western world and was to lead the way into the woes and wonders of the 20th century.

Mercantilism and the Rise of Capitalism

The Commercial Revolution

For over 150 years after Columbus "discovered" the Americas for the Europeans, thousands of tons of silver and nearly two hundred tons of gold came to Spain from the riches of the conquered Native Americans and from the mines established by the Spanish colonials. *Inflation*—"too much money chasing too few goods"—resulted because while the money supply had vastly increased, productivity had remained stable, giving money reduced purchasing power.

The *inflation-stimulated production*, though, because craftsmen, merchants, and manufacturers could get good prices for their products. The middle class, the bourgeoisie, acquired much of this wealth by trading and manufacturing, and their political influence and social status increased. Peasant farmers benefited when their surplus yields could be turned into *cash crops*. The nobility, whose income was based on feudal rents and fees, actually suffered a diminishing standard of living in this inflationary economy.

The Rise of Capitalism

"Capital" is another term for money used as an investment; instead of investing labor, an individual invests capital in some venture in order to make a profit. The bourgeoisie, having accumulated more money than was needed to maintain a decent standard of living in 17th- and 18th-century society, used money to make money. They invested in *chartered companies* that were given a monopoly of trading rights by the state within a certain area; in *joint-stock companies* (forerunners of modern corporations), which sold shares of stock publically in order to raise large amounts for various ventures, provided *limited liability* to the shareholders, and offered a profitable return for the original investment; and in the bourse, a kind of stock exchange. Profit made from investment enabled more investment. The expansion of money created prosperity, advanced science and technology, and supported the growth of the nation-state.

Mercantilism

The monarchs of the early modern period needed money to maintain the standing armies that would dominate the powerful nobles of the realm and protect the state against foreign enemies. The commercial revolution and the growth of capitalism enriched a sizable segment of the population; personal riches translated into good tax revenues.

Mercantilism prevailed in the 17th and well into the 18th century as an economic policy because it seemed to offer a way for the monarchs of Europe to consolidate their centralized authority.

THE THEORY

A nation's wealth is measured by the amount of precious metals it has accumulated *(bullionism)* rather than by its productivity.

A *favorable balance of trade*—exports exceed imports—is made up of gold and silver and therefore increases the store of precious metals.

Overseas colonies supply the *mother country* with essential raw materials for manufacture and trade.

Essential industries—manufacturing for the national defense or making a product unique to the nation and valuable in trade—were encouraged through subsidies and tax credits.

The goal of mercantilism is national economic self-sufficiency.

Overseas colonization (Old Imperialism) was encouraged by the policy of mercantilism. Spain and Portugal, following up on the momentum of their early explorations to Asia around the African continent and to the Americas across the Atlantic, monopolized colonization in the 16th century. By the 17th century, the balance had shifted to the Dutch, French, and English, whose internal disorders of the previous century had stabilized and whose inroads in Asia and North America overcame the supremacy of the Spanish and Portuguese. The English colonial empire far surpassed that of any other European nation because its colonies attracted proportionately more of its subjects for settlement and because a number of them became powerful independent states: the United States, India, Canada, Australia, and a number of other nations in Asia and Africa.

The Industrial Revolution

There never was an industrial "revolution"—a violent, drastic change. Industrialization has been a continuous and usually gradual process throughout human existence, from the use of the first stone tools to the development of high technology. The so-called *Industrial Revolution* was a period of rapid development, roughly between *1780 and 1830,* during which new forms of energy from coal and other fossil fuels powered machines rather than muscles, water, or wind. The advent of the steam engine allowed massive amounts of energy to be exerted by machinery, such as the spinning jenny, the waterframe, and power looms, that appeared in large factories where most workers began to work. This contrasted markedly with pre-industrial society wherein textiles were made in cottages from thread spun on wheels on human-powered looms.

It began in Britain in the second half of the 18th century; moved to France, Holland, Belgium, and the United States in the second decade of the 19th; to Germany, Austria, Italy in the middle of the 19th; to Eastern Europe and Russia at the end of the 19th; to parts of Asia and Africa well into the 20th; and it continues.

The Agricultural Revolution in England

After the Glorious Revolution of 1688, English landowning aristocrats dominated Parliament and passed the *Enclosure Acts,* which fenced off the *medieval common lands.*

RESULTS OF THE ENCLOSURE MOVEMENT

✔ Large landowners became prosperous; they invested in technology—machinery, breeding, improved planting methods. Crop yields and livestock production soared.

✔ Surplus production enabled agriculture to support a larger population in the cities.

✔ The population of Britain doubled during the 18th century.

✔ Small farmers who were displaced by the Enclosure movement moved to the cities and made up the growing force of factory workers (the *industrial proletariat*).

Technological Advances

Inventions of new machines and improvement of production processes throughout the 18th century made large-scale production possible in *textile manufacturing* and *coal mining*. The *steam engine* revolutionized transportation.

THE SCARCITY OF ENERGY

By the 18th century, most of England's forests were denuded and its supply of wood for fuel nearly depleted. *Coal,* plentiful, but traditionally shunned as a fuel because of its polluting effects, gradually replaced wood as both a fuel and for industrial processes. The early *steam engines*—such as Newcomen's clumsy contraption that employed a maze of rods and leather straps—converted heat from burning coal into motion and were employed as pumps in mines, and eventually they were used to drive textile machinery.

TEXTILES

The *fly shuttle* (John Kay, 1733) cut manpower needs on the looms in half.

The *spinning jenny* (James Hargreaves, 1764) mechanized the spinning wheel.

The *water frame* (Richard Arkwright, 1769) improved thread spinning.

Use of the *steam engine* (Arkwright, 1780s) powered the looms and required factory production of textiles.

The *cotton gin* (Eli Whitney, American, 1793) separated seed from raw cotton fiber and increased supply of the raw material.

COAL

Steam pump (Thomas Newcomen, 1702) rid coal mines of water seepage.

Condensing chamber steam engine (James Watt, 1763).

Plentiful coal boosted iron production and gave rise to *heavy industry* (the manufacture of machinery and materials used in production).

TRANSPORTATION

The *steamship* (Robert Fulton, American, 1807) and the *railroad steam engine* (George Stephenson, 1829) enhanced an already efficient system of river transportation that had been expanded in the 18th century by a network of canals. Together they opened new sources of raw materials and new markets for manufactured goods, and they made it possible to locate factories in population centers.

The railroad building boom from 1830–1850, brought about massive social and economic changes in the largely agrarian economy in England. The ease of transport encouraged rural workers to move to the cities; the lower costs of shipping goods in bulk fostered expanding markets.

OIL

By the end of the 19th century, the refinement of petroleum allowed its use as a fuel for the newly developed *internal combustion engines* that propelled automobiles, locomotives, and even ships, and for heating and industrial processes.

Results of the Industrial Revolution

The most significant result was the *increased production and availability of manufactured goods*. Material prosperity increased because there were cheaper high-quality goods and because increased consumption led to more jobs.

Factory workers lived in poverty on subsistence wages, in dismal tenements, entire families—including children from age five up—working fourteen hours a day under unsafe and unhealthy conditions for the first half of the 19th century. Crowded slums were worsened by the absence of services in cities that had expanded too rapidly. Although these living conditions did not differ much from those under which people had lived for centuries on farms, the concentration of the population made them more unhealthy. This visibility led thinkers to ponder the causes of poverty and prompted the institutions of society to push for its alleviation. The *Sadler Commission* in Great Britain helped initiate legislation to improve working conditions in factories.

EFFECTS ON CLASS AND GENDER

Two new classes developed as a result of the Industrial Revolution—*industrialists/ capitalists* and *factory workers*. The competitive nature of the markets led many of the factory owners to offer low wages for long hours, create poor and unsafe working conditions, and to employ child labor. The rigid discipline of factory work contrasted with the rural pace of the farm work most of the laborers had been accustomed to; and not until the mid-19th century did the standard of living improve for the average industrial worker.

Child labor laws were enacted after the first three decades of the 19th century to limit the number of hours children could be required to work, and a sexual division of labor emerged. Men became the main breadwinners while married women tended to stay home to raise the children. Jobs available to women were "dead-end" and poorly paid. The early attempts of workers to organize were met with hostility from industrialists, anti-union regulations from governments, and very limited success.

The rapid growth of cities during the Industrial Revolution necessitated urban reform to improve conditions that had existed for centuries: poor sanitation and other services, overcrowded housing, inadequate transportation. Influenced by *Jeremy Bentham* (1748–1832), whose philosophy of *utilitarianism* emphasized "the greatest good for the greatest number," city planners and urban reformers redesigned the many European cities and initiated a public health movement to improve urban life for all classes.

The standard of living improved for most Europeans from the middle of the 19th century and into the early 20th. Disparities in wealth between the classes led to conflict between the classes and encouraged the growth of political radicalism. Hierarchies of wealth and status existed among both the middle and working classes, and the relegation of women to menial jobs or to child-raising fostered a women's rights movement, the first wave of *feminism*, whose goals included gender equality in opportunity, legal rights, and voting.

Theories of Economics

Adam Smith (see page 134) can be considered the first modern economist. His *Wealth of Nations* has been called the "Bible of capitalism" and is the foundation for *classical* or laissez-faire economics, which opposed the regulations imposed by mercantilism by arguing that certain natural laws, such as *supply and demand,* govern an economy and should be free to operate. If people follow their own "enlightened self-interest," without the interference of government in the economy, this private initiative will result in benefits to all in society.

Thomas Malthus (1766–1834) was the first of the classical economists to try to explain why the mass of people did not benefit from the operation of the "natural laws" of economics. Poverty existed, he said, because the *population increased at a geometric rate while the food supply increased arithmetically.* He believed that poverty was a divine punishment for humankind's lust.

David Ricardo (1772–1823) introduced the *Iron Law of Wages:* the natural wage is that which maintains a worker's subsistence. When labor is in demand, though, the wage will increase, the worker will prosper, the size of families will increase, and the general population will grow. The result will be more workers competing for fewer jobs and inevitable starvation. Government attempts to change this, he contended, only lead to greater suffering.

Utopian Socialists rejected the *"dismal science"* of the classical economists and sought solutions to the plight of the masses. *Robert Owen* (1771–1858) was a Scottish textile manufacturer whose humane working conditions—shorter workday, decent housing, free education—served as a model for capitalists who wanted to make a profit without exploiting workers. The *Comte de Saint-Simon* (1760–1825) was one of the early French founders of *socialism.* He helped define the movement by advocating *public ownership of factories* and a professional managerial corps to run them, the *technocrats.* He coined the slogan, "From each according to his ability, to each according to his need," an idealistic but vague proposal for a *planned economy.*

Karl Marx (1818–1883) is in a class of his own. His *Communist Manifesto,* written with *Friedrich Engels* (1820–1895) during the Revolution of 1848, calls for radical solutions to the dilemma of mass poverty in the industrialized world. *Das Kapital,* the first volume of which was published in 1867, offers a complete analysis of capitalism.

MARX'S THEORIES

Hegelian dialectic (so named after the German philosopher Georg Hegel): In every historical period a prevailing ideal, *thesis,* conflicts with an opposing ideal, *antithesis,* and results in a new ideal, *synthesis.* This becomes the thesis of the next period and the process continues.

Dialectical materialism: Marx adapted the Hegelian dialectic to argue that society is a reflection of economics. History progresses from agrarian communalism, to slaveholding, to feudalism, to bourgeois commercialism, to capitalism, to socialism, and finally to *Communism* (a classless society in which the workers own the means of production and government is unnecessary).

Class Struggle: The *dominant class* in every society—slaveholders, feudal lords, capitalists—is a thesis with an antithesis—slaves, serfs, workers—that will overthrow the old order.

Inevitable Revolution: This is the result of the capitalists' increasing profits by lowering the workers' wages for labor to the point that the proletariat cannot afford to consume the products of manufacture *(surplus-value theory).* Economic depression occurs and lays hardship on the working class until it carries out a revolution. A *dictatorship of the proletariat* will establish a socialist government to wipe out capitalism.

Communism: The *"withering away of the state"* will follow, whereby private property will cease to exist and economic exploitation will stop, ending crime, vice, and injustice; democracy will prevail on local level; *Utopia* (a perfect society) will result.

The Technological Revolution

Around the last third of the 19th century, the applications of science to industry brought about a radical change in the way Europeans lived. *Mass production* lowered the cost of goods and made them available to the general public; consumer goods became part of the mass market. Smaller companies merged and consolidated until whole industries were dominated by *big business.* High wages in the cities caused a *population shift* from the countryside. Electricity and the internal combustion engine not only increased productivity but improved the quality of life.

Inventors of the Industrial Revolution

1708	**Jethro Tull's** mechanical **seed drill** makes cultivation in rows widespread because it was more efficient and allowed for easier weeding.
1712	**Thomas Newcomen** builds the first commercially successful **steam engine**. It kept deep coal mines clear of water. It was the first significant use of fossil fuels and marked the first major power source invented since wind, water, and animal were used.
1733	**John Kay** invents the **flying shuttle**, which improves weaving significantly.
1761	**James Brindle's Bridgewater Canal** is opened. Barges carried coal from Worsley to Manchester.
1765	**James Hargreaves** invented the **spinning jenny**, which automated spinning for the first time.
1769	**Arkwright's waterframe** allows much more efficient spinning of thread.
1775	**James Watt** created the first efficient **steam engine** *with a condensing chamber.*
1779	The first **steam-powered mill** uses **Crompton's** "mule," and Hargreaves' and Arkwright's machines, thus fully automating the weaving process.
1787	**Edmund Cartwright** builds a **power loom**.
1793	**Eli Whitney** develops the **cotton gin**, increasing the efficiency of cotton as a source of textiles.
1801	**Robert Trevithick** demonstrates his **steam locomotive**, the *Rocket*.
1807	**Robert Fulton** built the *Clermont,* the first successful **steamboat**.
1830	The Liverpool and Manchester Railway began the first regular commercial rail service.
1831	**Michael Faraday** discovers **electromagnetic current**, making possible generators and electric engines.
1834	**Charles Babbage** creates the **analytic engine**, the first *ancestor of the computer.*

1837   **Samuel F. B. Morse** develops the **telegraph** and Morse code.

1838   **Daguerre** perfected the Daguerrotype, an early form of **photography**.

1850   **Gasoline** was refined for the first time.

1851   **Singer** invented the first practical **sewing machine**.

1854   **Bessemer** invented the **steel converter**, which revolutionized the production of steel.

1858   First **transatlantic cable** is completed. Cathode rays are discovered.

1859   **Charles Darwin** writes *The Origin of Species*, and his theory of evolution revolutionizes our view of our place in the universe.

1867   **Alfred Nobel** created **dynamite**, the first high explosive that can be safely handled.

1885   **Benz** develops the first internal combustion **automobile**.

1889   The **Eiffel Tower** was created for the World Exposition.

1896   **Marconi** patented the wireless **telegraph.**

1901   **Marconi** transmitted the first transatlantic **radio** message (from Cape Cod).

Sample Essay Question

The sample thematic essay and the practice essays that follow are of types found on the AP exam, and they require knowledge of causes, effects, personalities, ideas, and events.

SAMPLE QUESTION

To what extent and in what ways was the light of Adam Smith's economic optimism dimmed by the "dismal science" of Thomas Malthus and David Ricardo?

Comments on the Sample Question

Follow the "Simple Procedures" for writing an essay. (See page 34.)

First, *What does the question want to know?* How and how much was Smith's "natural law" theory of the operation of an economy altered by the pessimistic views of Malthus and Ricardo? This is the crux of the question.

Second, *What do you know about it?* Smith was considered an Enlightenment philosopher, a theoretician for the inevitable human progress that age had projected. Malthus and Ricardo observed the mass misery that the Industrial Revolution and laissez-faire economics had created, and, while accepting Smith's basic theory, they sought explanations for its failure in practice.

Third, *How would you put it into words?* Show how and how much Malthus and Ricardo created the "dismal science" of economics while still accepting the basic principles of Smith's "natural law" economy.

Rubric for Sample Answer

Before you read the sample answer, examine the rubric. What will the reader be looking for when he or she grades this essay? A sample rubric, shaded to show the reader's evaluation, is seen below:

9–8 POINTS

- ✔ Thesis explicitly identifies **both** the extent to which and in what ways the "dismal science" of Malthus and Ricardo dimmed the economic optimism of Adam Smith. Thesis does not need to be in the opening paragraph.
- ✔ Organization is clear, consistently followed, and effective in support of the argument.
  - May devote individual paragraphs to an examination of the extent and manner in which the "dismal science," of Malthus and Ricardo dimmed the economic optimism of Adam Smith.
  - Must identify individual facets of Smith's optimism and the extent and manner of Malthus and Ricardo dimming that optimism (Smith's Perfect Liberty, self-curing high prices, and other market advances, as well as Malthus's projections for world starvation and Ricardo's Law of Iron Wages may also be presented) and consider the extent to which and how Smith's economic optimism was dimmed by Malthus and Ricardo.
- ✔ Essay is well balanced; the extent to which and in what ways the "dismal science" of Malthus and Ricardo dimmed the economic optimism of Adam Smith is analyzed at some length. Essay covers evolution of economic thought from Smith through Ricardo.
- ✔ Major assertions in the essay are supported thoroughly and consistently by relevant evidence.
- ✔ Evidence of facets of Smith's optimism and the extent and manner of Malthus and Ricardo dimming that optimism may prove more specific or concrete.
- ✔ May contain errors that do not detract from the argument.

7–6 POINTS

- ✔ Thesis explicitly identifies **both** the extent to which and in what ways the "dismal science" of **both** Mathus and Ricardo dimmed the economic optimism of Adam Smith is analyzed, but may not be developed fully.
- ✔ Organization is clear and effective in support of the argument but may introduce evidence that is not pertinent to the task.
- ✔ Essay covers all major topics suggested by the prompt but may analyze an aspect of **both** the extent to which and in what ways the "dismal science" of Malthus and Ricardo dimmed the economic optimism of Adam Smith in greater depth rather than in a balanced manner.
- ✔ Major assertions in the essay are supported by relevant evidence.
- ✔ May contain an error that detracts from the argument.

5–4 POINTS

✔ Thesis identifies **both** the extent to which and in what ways the "dismal science" of Malthus and Ricardo dimmed the economic optimism of Adam Smith but without any development; thesis may address only part of the question effectively; thesis may be a simple, single-sentence statement.

✔ Organization is clear but may not be consistently followed; essay may veer off task chronologically or thematically or both.

✔ Essay may not complete all tasks:
  • May discuss only the extent to which OR what ways the "dismal science" of Malthus and Ricardo dimmed the economic optimism of Adam Smith.
  • May discuss only one or two supports for Smith's optimism or Malthus and Ricardo's dimming of it.
  • May focus only on one economic theory.
  • May be primarily descriptive rather than analytical.

✔ Essay offers some relevant evidence.

✔ May contain errors that detract from the argument.

3–2 POINTS

✔ Thesis may simply paraphrase the prompt OR the extent to which OR in what ways the "dismal science" of Malthus and Ricardo dimmed the economic optimism of Adam Smith without analyzing the facts.

✔ Organization is unclear and ineffective; essay may focus on the personal attributes of the Economists rather than analyzing the extent to which their ideas dimmed the economic optimism of Adam Smith.

✔ Essay shows serious imbalance; discussion of the ways and extent to which the optimism of Adam Smith was dimmed by Malthus and Ricardo is superficial; much of the information may be significantly out of the time period or geography of the question.

✔ Offers minimal OR confused evidence.

✔ May contain several errors that detract from the argument.

1–0 POINTS

✔ Thesis is erroneous OR irrelevant OR absent.

✔ No effective organization is evident.

✔ Discussion of the extent to which and in what ways the "dismal science" of Malthus and Ricardo dimmed the economic optimism of Adam Smith is generic.

✔ Provides little or no relevant supporting evidence.

✔ May contain numerous errors that detract from the argument.

Sample Answer

In 1776, at the peak of the Enlightenment and during the heyday of governmental mercantilistic regulation of European economies, Adam Smith published his *Wealth of Nations*. Describing the small business economy of the British "nation of shopkeepers," Smith applied the prevailing natural law theory to the operation of economies. An individual's "enlightened self-interest," if left alone (borrowing the laissez-faire economics of the French physiocrats), will allow the operation of the natural laws of economics.

Whenever a government interferes with one of these laws, such as that of "supply and demand," it creates more problems than are solved. In a free and unregulated economy, each producer will try to lower the cost of production by using the most advanced technology, by making the best use of materials, and by using efficient labor. In that way, the product can be sold cheaper than a competitor's and the profit will be higher. Also, producers will turn out high-quality goods to try to surpass those of their competitors.

Smith's natural laws of economics fit the progressive, optimistic view of human society that saturated the thinking of the Age of Enlightenment. Following Isaac Newton's momentous discoveries that universal and unchangeable laws govern the planets and all earthly motion, Enlightenment philosophes sought "natural laws" to govern everything from political morality to economics.

By the time the Industrial Revolution had taken hold of the British economy—in the first two decades of the 19th century—Smith's laissez-faire economics had not delivered the general prosperity he had promised. Poverty blighted the new industrial cities of England and Scotland. Men, women, and young children labored long hours for subsistence wages at tedious, dangerous, unhealthy work. Poverty had been the rule among the rural population of small farmers, but it was now unavoidably visible in the crowded, dirty slums of the cities.

Malthus, a clergyman, argued that people were poor because the population had outrun food production. Food increased at an arithmetic rate while population increased at a geometric rate. He thought that war, famine, and disease were divine punishments for humankind's lust.

Ricardo offered a less cosmic but equally despairing view of why poverty is inevitable. His Iron Law of Wages stated that while workers are usually paid a subsistence wage (enough to keep them and their family alive), when labor is in great demand, the wages will exceed the "natural wage." Workers prosper; prosperity leads to bigger families; a larger population causes an overabundance of workers; wages drop; workers and their families starve.

During the Age of Reason, Smith's natural laws of economics promised general prosperity. He was reacting against the arbitrary regulation of economics by modern monarchs seduced by the bullionism of mercantilist theory, and he was following the optimistic assumptions of the Enlightenment. Observing the abuses of industrialization, Malthus and Ricardo tried to salvage classical economics by explaining how poverty could exist in an unregulated economy. Once they had offered their theories, they felt no obligation to alleviate the economic and social ills that they had pronounced unavoidable. That they left to the socialists and Marxists who would follow them.

EVALUATE THE SAMPLE ANSWER

Now go back and look at the rubric. It is clear that this essay looks like a 2 or 3 on the rubric. The essay has a weak thesis that may be completely tangential. The question is not fully answered at all, but there are enough facts to warrant a score of 3.

RATER'S COMMENTS ON THE SAMPLE ANSWER

3—Not qualified

This essay is included to show the reader what not to do. This essay simply goes off on tangents and does not answer the question. There is no discernable thesis in the essay until perhaps the end. This essay is well written and factual, but it does not cohesively create an answer to the question asked. To review, the question was to determine *to what extent* Smith's science was altered by Malthus and Ricardo, who, in contrast, have both been discredited as time has passed, while Smith's ideas live on as the framework of the modern economy. If anything, Adam Smith is more pertinent in 2009 than he was in 1776, and certainly more so than Malthus or Ricardo; this was not examined at all. This essay examined the ideas of all three men, but it did not draw conclusions about how the study of economics was changed by Malthus and Ricardo. Remember, do not just write everything you know about a subject, throwing nonsense against a wall to see what sticks, but rather create a cohesive answer with a strong thesis that answers the question.

Practice Essay Questions

The questions that follow are samples of the various types of thematic essays that appear on the AP exam. (See page 21–22 for a detailed explanation of each type.) Check over the **generic rubric** (see pages 58–60) before you begin any of these essays and use that rubric to score your essay if you write one.

QUESTION 1

Analyze the way the opening of the Atlantic sparked the rise of capitalism.

COMMENTS ON QUESTION 1

This question requires all the applications of analysis: examining in detail, determining relationships, explaining. A special emphasis should be on determining the relationships between the new intercontinental trade and the growth of capitalism. How could the Atlantic discoveries and colonization of the New World have encouraged the growth of capitalism in Europe? There were strong and complex relationships between the colonization of the New World and the growth of capitalism. New markets, new products such as vanilla and cocoa, new territory, and new opportunities spurred entrepreneurship seen in men like Cortez and Pizarro and those who accompanied them. Abundant resources from the New World, including precious metals, led to exploitation by merchants, giving them huge profits.

Along with the resulting creation of the first merchant class and the development of surplus wealth, capitalism developed through these methods. The essay could also focus on inflation caused by the gold flow into Europe, and the emigration of skilled entrepreneurial artisans and merchants to the New World. There is a lot of supporting evidence that can be used in this essay.

QUESTION 2

Explain why the monarchs of Europe favored mercantilism.

COMMENTS ON QUESTION 2

In this and any "explanation" essay, the task is to offer reasons for your answer. The monarchs of Europe, the question is saying, DID favor mercantilism.

Approach this first by considering what mercantilism was and what it accomplished, and then by examining how that would benefit the growing nation-states and their monarchs in the 15th and 16th centuries. It was mostly about self-sufficiency and power.

QUESTION 3

"It is no accident that the Industrial Revolution occurred in late 18th-century England." *Assess the validity* of this statement.

COMMENTS ON QUESTION 3

"To determine the truth" of this assertion, it is necessary to examine why fertile fields nurtured the development of industrialization in England from 1780 to 1830. You must identify the links in the causal chain: the supremacy of Parliament after 1688, the Enclosure movement, the Agricultural Revolution, the growth of towns, the improvement of technology and the abundance of coal.

QUESTION 4

"The Industrial Revolution diminished the quality of life of the common person in Europe." *Defend or refute* this statement.

COMMENTS ON QUESTION 4

Use facts to argue for or against. This essay question is very open-ended and the appropriate response is to write an essay that says both, depending upon what era the question is asked. It is clear that the quality of life for the average Briton was reduced from 1750 to 1850. However, the quality of life for the British and the entire world began to improve after 1850 and continues to do so today, mostly due to the wonders of industrialization. Therefore, the miserable labor and living conditions of the early 19th century, as well as the reforms of the later part of that century, and how living improved, each deserve a paragraph. A strong thesis needs to explain why the statement is both supported and refuted depending upon what vantage point one uses.

QUESTION 5

Explain how Marx's theories offer both a reason for, and a solution to, mass poverty in the industrialized world.

COMMENTS ON QUESTION 5

In order to "make clear" and "detail," you must understand Marx's critique of capitalism and his theory of revolution, the social, economic, and political environment of his day (mid-19th century), and the failure of classical economics to alleviate poverty. This is a *very tough* question. The core of the answer lies in Marx's theories: the dialectic, the class struggle, surplus-value theory, inevitable revolution, socialism, and Communism.

Practice Multiple-Choice Questions

(These questions are representative of the various types that appear on the AP exam.)

1. Mercantilism, the prevailing economic theory of 17th-century Europe, was based on all of the following ideas EXCEPT

   (A) that a nation's wealth was measured by its accumulation of precious metals
   (B) that a nation's wealth would be increased by a "favorable balance of trade"
   (C) that war was a natural state of affairs between nations
   (D) that a nation's accumulated gold and silver was needed to build a navy and to equip a standing army
   (E) that government should not regulate or interfere with the nation's economy

2. The difficulties faced by the continental economies in their efforts to compete with the English included all of the following EXCEPT the

   (A) low prices of English mass-produced goods
   (B) complexity and expense of the new technology
   (C) resistance of landowning elites
   (D) scarcity of human capital
   (E) instability caused by the Napoleonic wars

3. Encouraged by the mercantilist theory that stressed the need for overseas colonization to obtain the essential raw materials to provide economic self-sufficiency, these three European nations established colonial empires during the 17th century:

    (A) Portugal, Spain, Italy
    (B) Portugal, England, France
    (C) England, France, Prussia
    (D) England, France, Holland
    (E) Portugal, France, Holland

4. All of the following are results of the opening of the Atlantic to commerce with Europe during the 16th and 17th centuries EXCEPT

    (A) tons of precious metals from the New World came to Spain
    (B) the money supply expanded but productivity remained stable
    (C) inflation occurred
    (D) inflation encouraged productivity
    (E) the nobility increased its wealth

5. An immediate result of the commercial revolution that occurred with the increased productivity stimulated by the precious metals coming from the Americas was

    (A) the formation of an urban working class
    (B) a dramatic shift of population from the countryside to the cities
    (C) a drastic increase in the manorial fees due from the peasants
    (D) the rise of capitalism
    (E) the abolition of the bourse

6. All of the following are characteristics of the Industrial Revolution (1780–1830) EXCEPT

    (A) that it replaced hand manufacture with machine production
    (B) that it concentrated the working force in factories
    (C) that it was a period of dramatic advancement
    (D) that it took place first in France
    (E) that it transformed European society

A woodcut print of the Krupp steelworks in Essen, Germany. The Granger Collection, New York. (0002293)

7. The illustration above shows the industrialization of Germany, including the bucolic surrounding area, indicating that this piece belongs in which of the following artistic movements?

(A) Naturalism
(B) Romanticism
(C) Neo-classicism
(D) Impressionism
(E) Surrealism

8. Scholarly statistical studies of the condition of the English working class indicate that

(A) their standard of living improved from the beginning of industrialization
(B) improvement did not come until the period after 1830
(C) the standard of living for English workers deteriorated throughout the 19th century
(D) only skilled workers enjoyed improvements in their standard of living
(E) incidences of infanticide increased throughout the 19th century

9. More recent interpretations of the sexual division of labor argue that it occurred for all of the following reasons EXCEPT

(A) an effort by older people to help control the sexuality of working-class youth
(B) the conflict between child care and factory discipline
(C) the conscious efforts of women to escape the horrors of the factory system
(D) the difficulty of managing an urban household
(E) the belief that men needed to earn more to support a family left women with lower wages

10. The Industrial Revolution demonstrated significant advances in all of the following EXCEPT

(A) the uses of the internal combustion engine
(B) the mining of coal
(C) the powering of ships
(D) the development of railroads
(E) the manufacture of textiles

11. Both the French and Industrial Revolutions gave rise to a number of conflicting doctrines, or "isms." Which of the following was expounded and popularized decades after the others?

(A) Marxism
(B) Liberalism
(C) Radicalism
(D) Conservatism
(E) Socialism

12. Thomas Newcomen's pumping machine, invented in the early 1700s, was considered a radical innovation because

(A) it generated electricity
(B) it was powered by electricity
(C) it was powered by steam
(D) it used fine-kilned brick as a heat insulator
(E) it was the world's first perpetual motion machine

13. All of the following are features of Marxist theory EXCEPT

(A) Hegelian dialectic
(B) dialectical materialism
(C) the Class Struggle
(D) natural selection
(E) inevitable revolution

Population Estimates in the Millions

Selected Nations in Europe	1800	1900
ENGLAND	9	33
GERMANY	25	56
ITALY	17	34
FRANCE	27	39

14. The chart above provides population estimates for selected European countries in the years 1800 and 1900. Which of the following is the most valid interpretation of the statistics?

(A) The population doubled in each of the countries identified.
(B) The population of Italy and Germany doubled because of national unification.
(C) The population growth reflects the degree to which each of the nations industrialized.
(D) The population of England grew at a faster rate than any of the nations identified.
(E) Colonialism caused the indigenous population of England to increase fourfold.

15. Which of the following economists accepted Adam Smith's classical economics and tried to explain why his prediction of general prosperity under laissez-faire capitalism was not coming to fruition?

(A) Utopian Socialists
(B) Karl Marx
(C) Proudhon
(D) Robert Owen
(E) Thomas Malthus

Answers and Answer Explanations

1.	E	6.	D	11.	A
2.	A	7.	B	12.	C
3.	D	8.	B	13.	D
4.	E	9.	C	14.	D
5.	D	10.	A	15.	E

1. **(E)** Most mercantilist economies were "command economies," controlled by government regulation and incentives.

2. **(A)** Landowners were actually in favor of capitalism because it could help them make more money. The English were underpricing the competition, the machinery was complex, the engineers were not allowed to leave England so human capital was scarce, and the Napoleonic wars had the continental leaders focusing on things other than production.

3. **(D)** See question 2.

4. **(E)** The commercial middle class accumulated the wealth; the landed nobility maintained itself on feudal fees that rarely rose.

5. **(D)** Inflation made productivity profitable; surplus wealth encouraged investment in economic ventures.

6. **(D)** Britain, by a fortunate set of circumstances, gave birth to the Industrial Revolution.

7. **(B)** The portrayal of industry as polluting pristine nature is a hallmark of Romantic art of all genres.

8. **(B)** After the beginning of the 19th century, there were improvements in the standard of living so that by 1900 a person living in a city was likely to live longer than one in the country.

9. **(C)** The women did not leave to avoid the harsh realities of the factory; they were forced into lower paying worse jobs that were less stable.

10. **(A)** The internal combustion engine—both diesel and gasoline—was a late-19th-century invention.

11. **(A)** Marx expounded his theories after the Revolutions of 1848. The others were ideologies that flowed from the experience of the French Revolution and the Age of Metternich.

12. **(C)** Animal and human muscle, wind and water, provided power before that.

13. **(D)** "Natural selection" applies to Darwin's theory of evolution.

14. **(D)** The other answers are misinterpretations of the chart.

15. **(E)** The term "dismal science" comes from his dire predictions.

CHAPTER 7

The Growth and Suppression of Democracy from the Age of Metternich to the First World War (1815–1914)

Key Terms/People

- The Great Reform Bill
- Chartist Movement
- Revolutions of 1848
- William E. Gladstone
- Age of Metternich
- Louis Napoleon Bonaparte
- Crimean War
- Dreyfus Affair

- Burschenschafts
- Zollverein
- Frankfurt Assembly
- Carlsbad Decrees/Diet
- Prague Conference
- Compromise of 1867
- Pan-Slavic movement

Overview

The period from the fall of Napoleon in 1815 to the Revolutions of 1848 is called the Age of Metternich. Klemens von Metternich (1773–1859) personified the spirit of reaction that followed a quarter-century of revolution and war. Chancellor of Hapsburg Austria and one of the chief participants at the Congress of Vienna, he and others like him all over Europe designed a Continental balance of power that would keep the peace for a century (until the First World War) and imposed a reconstructed Old Order that would burst at the seams in 1848.

Metternich was a tall, handsome man whose charm worked equally well on his fellow diplomats and on the elegant ladies of Vienna. He was the prototype of *conservatism* as a leadership style for European ministers. He spoke five languages fluently, thought of himself as a European, not as a citizen of any single country, and once said "Europe has for a long time held for me the significance of a fatherland." Early in his career, Metternich linked himself to the Hapsburgs and became Austria's foreign minister, an office he held for the next thirty-nine years. Because of his immense influence on European politics, these years are often called the *Age of Metternich*. He felt liberals were imposing their views on society mostly due to the nationalist self-determination ideal of the liberals that threatened Austria so much due to its diverse geographical scope of power.

Two great nations, during the Age of Metternich, developed the bases for modern constitutional democracy: one—England—through a continuation of the unique and stabilizing evolutionary process that represented the interests in government of more and more of its populace, the other—France—through unstabilizing seesaw battles between reaction and radicalism. For both nations the processes continued through the 19th century and into the early 20th until they had established the foundations for modern welfare states.

Three nations that played important roles in the 19th and early 20th centuries—Germany, Austria, and Russia—suppressed the democratic urges of significant elements of their populations. In Germany, the move toward unification of the varied and independent states fell out of the hands of the constitutionalists and into those of Prussian militarists. In Austria, the Germanic Hapsburg rulers continued to suppress the move toward autonomy of the polyglot nationalities that made up the empire. In Russia, sporadic attempts at reform and modernization were consumed by the ruling class's obsession with "Autocracy, Orthodoxy, and Nationalism."

The Growth of Democracy

England

The ideals and promises of the French Revolution and a growing and poverty-stricken working class vibrated the stability of Europe's greatest emerging democracy. Parliament, after the end of the Napoleonic Wars in 1815, represented the interests of aristocrats and the wealthy. The Corn Laws of 1815 effectively raised prices at a time when Europe was war torn because importation of foreign grain was prohibited until the price rose above 80 shillings per quarter-ton, helping the land owners who ran Parliament. This resulted in many riots and political unrest as food prices rose for the poor. The Corn Laws were repealed in 1846 in large part due to the actions of the Anti-Corn Law League, who convinced Tory Prime Minister Robert Peel and some of his party members to do what was "right for Britain rather than their personal interests." Free import of grain was again allowed. By the 1820s, though, new and younger leaders of the *Tories* (the conservative party) implemented reforms such as restructuring the penal code, providing for a modern police force, allowing membership in labor unions, and granting Catholics basic civil rights.

By 1830, when abortive revolutions had broken out all over the continent, the *House of Commons,* the lower chamber of Parliament, had not been reapportioned since 1688. Many of the boroughs that had representatives no longer existed, while large and growing industrial cities had none at all. *The Great Reform Bill,* 1832, abolished the *rotten boroughs,* expanded the electorate, and empowered the industrial middle class.

The *Chartist movement,* representing demands by radical working-class activists, sought an array of reforms from 1838 into the late 1840s. It advocated universal male suffrage, a secret voting ballot, "one man, one vote" representation in Parliament, abolition of property qualifications for public office, and public education for all classes. Although its program failed during the decade of its existence, all of its features were eventually incorporated into English society.

When the discontent of the working class on the continent exploded during the *Revolutions of 1848,* the English proletariat was able to trust in its government's capacity to make gradual reforms.

In 1866, *Whig* (liberal party) prime minister *William E. Gladstone* (1807–1898) attempted to expand voter eligibility but was defeated. A new government under Tory (conservative) *Benjamin Disraeli* (1804–1881) turned the tables on the Whig reformers by getting the *Second Reform Bill,* 1867, through Parliament. It not only doubled the size of the electorate, but it gave the vote to many industrial workers. When Disraeli's party lost the general election in 1868—the head of the party that wins the most seats in a parliamentary election forms a government and becomes prime minister—Gladstone returned to power and enacted sweeping reforms. *Labor unions were legalized;* the *secret ballot* was introduced; *free public education* was offered to working-class children. The Third Reform Bill of 1885, largely granted universal male suffrage.

In the decade immediately before the start of World War I, Britain laid the foundations for its *social welfare state:* government institutions and laws that guarantee all citizens a decent standard of living. The right of unions to strike was put into law; government insurance was provided for those injured on the job; unemployment insurance and old-age pensions were enacted; and a compulsory school attendance law went into effect.

France

During the *Age of Metternich*—the period of reaction after the Congress of Vienna, 1815, that ended with the continent-wide Revolutions of 1848—France was ruled by Bourbon reactionaries and a "bourgeois" king whose watered down constitutions excluded the expanding proletariat from representation. After the upheavals of 1848, a self-styled emperor, a relative of Napoleon, was on the French throne.

When Bourbon *Louis XVIII* (r. 1814–1824), a brother of the guillotined Louis XVI, was restored to the throne in 1814, he issued a constitution but gave power to only a small class of landowners and rich bourgeois. Absolutist pretenses were continued with his successor and younger brother, *Charles X* (r. 1824–1830), whose repressive measures led to rioting in Paris in the summer of 1830, a year when abortive insurrections broke out all over Europe.

Charles's abdication caused a rift between radicals who wanted to establish a republic and bourgeoisie who wanted the stability of a monarchy. Through the intercession of the *Marquis de Lafayette,* hero of the American Revolution, *Louis Phillipe* (r. 1830–1848), an aristocrat, became the *"bourgeoisie king"* by agreeing to honor the Constitution of 1814. His reign empowered the bourgeoisie but left the proletariat unrepresented.

Rampant corruption in his government incited republican and socialist protests, which erupted in violence and led to his abdication in February 1848. The *Chamber of Deputies,* the lower house of the two-chamber French legislature that was created in 1814 by Louis XVIII's constitution, was pressured by Parisian mobs to *proclaim a republic* and to name a provisional goverment that would rule temporarily until a Constituent Assembly could be elected to draft a new constitution. When the provinces—the countryside outside the large cities—elected a largely conservative Constituent Assembly, conflicts between the government and socialist and radical workers erupted into bloody class battles on the streets of Paris by early summer 1848.

Frightened by the threat of a radical takeover, the Constituent Assembly brutally suppressed the riots, then established the *single-chambered Legislative Assembly* and *a strong president,* both to be elected by *universal male suffrage.*

Louis Napoleon Bonaparte (r. 1848–1870), Napoleon's nephew, was elected President of the *Second Republic.* (The First Republic had been established in 1792 during the French Revolution.) He dedicated his presidency to law and order, the eradication of socialism and radicalism, and the interests of the conservative classes—the Church, the army, property-owners, and business. Through a political ploy, he was able to discredit many members of the Legislative Assembly, win a landslide re-election, and proclaim himself in 1852 as Emperor *Napoleon III* of the *Second French Empire.* (His uncle, Napoleon Bonaparte, had crowned himself emperor in 1804.)

While the Second Empire was not an absolutist government, it was an autocracy. Napoleon III controlled finances and initiated legislation. He was immensely popular in the early years of his reign because of his internal improvements—highway, canal, and railroad construction—and because of his subsidies to industry and his stimulation of the economy. The bourgeoisie was grateful for the general prosperity; the proletariat was appreciative of employment and the right to organize unions. During the *Liberal Empire* (1860–1870), he eased censorship and granted amnesty to political prisoners.

Foreign affairs were his downfall. The *Crimean War* (1853–1856), in which the French and English went to war to prevent the Russians from establishing dominance over the Black Sea possessions of the Ottomans, was costly on all sides. The French backdown in the 1860s, when confronted by the United States over establishment of a *French satellite in Mexico,* humiliated France. The Franco-Prussian war, which helped unify Germany, was a disaster for the French and Napoleon III. The Germans crushed the French and laid siege to Paris, forcing a humiliating defeat upon the French that would contribute to the destabilization of Western Europe during the 20th century. The French defeat in this war ended the Second Empire and began the Third Republic. Controlled by monarchists and the bourgeoisie, the new National Assembly brutally suppressed a radical socialist countergovernment, the *Paris Commune.*

In 1875, the assembly voted to set up a *Chamber of Deputies,* elected by universal male suffrage, a *Senate,* indirectly elected, a ceremonial president, elected by the whole legislature, and a premier, directly responsible to the Chamber of Deputies. From the establishment of the Third Republic in 1871 to the beginning of World War I in 1914, *the French government fell dozens of times.* The governments were inherently unstable because there were so many political parties—in a *multiparty system* unlike the British or American two-party systems—that none could win a clear majority in the Legislative Assembly, and the coalitions fell apart during many a crisis.

The *Dreyfus Affair* (1894–1906), in which a Jewish Army captain was falsely accused of spying by antirepublican conservatives, was one instance of the political infighting that often paralyzed the government.

The multiparty system of France seemed to carry democracy to excess, but by the First World War France had universal male suffrage and had instituted a *social welfare system* similar to that in Britain.

Britain and France by the early part of the 20th century had evolved into two of the world's three most powerful democracies, the United States being the third. The *old liberalism* of laissez-faire government had been replaced by a *new liberalism* that supported the extension of suffrage and the improvement of living conditions for all citizens.

The Suppression of Democracy

Germany Through the Age of Metternich (1815–1848)

The Congress of Vienna had set up a *Germanic Confederation* of the thirty-nine independent German states that existed after the fall of Napoleon in order to deal with problems common to all. Radical student organizations, *Burschenschafts,* which were dedicated to the creation of a unified Germany that would be governed by constitutional principles, organized a national convention in 1817 and, in 1819, attempted the assassination of reactionary politicians. In 1819, Metternich issued the infamous *Carlsbad Decrees,* which were anti-subversive laws designed to get the liberals out of Austria, its press, and the universities. He had a state secret police and attempted to control what was published and what was discussed at universities. The *Carlsbad Diet* drove liberalism and nationalism underground.

Although the reactionary forces in Germany quickly put down the *Revolutions of 1830,* Prussia set up an economic union of seventeen German states, the *Zollverein,* which eliminated internal tariffs and set the tone for greater union.

The Age of Metternich ended in the revolutions of 1848. Every nation in Europe save the most advanced, England, and the least advanced, Russia, had revolutions. This year saw Metternich flee Austria during the continent-wide revolutions that proved what Mary Wollstonecraft had said in reference to the oppression of women: "The bow that is bent twice as far snaps back twice as hard." All of the revolutions ended in failure for the most part, with the status quo before the revolutions very close to their conclusions.

The Prussian king *Frederick William IV* (r. 1840–1861) reacted to the *Revolutions of 1848* by calling a nominal legislative assembly rather than using military force. In 1850, he granted a constitution that established a *House of Representatives* elected by universal male suffrage but controlled by the wealthiest classes.

The *Frankfurt Assembly,* an extralegal convention not to be confused with the king's Legislative Assembly, met from May 1848 to May 1849 and *established the nature of the future union of Germany.* Advocates of a *Greater Germany* wanted to include Austria and to have a Hapsburg emperor rule over the union. Supporters of a *Lesser Germany* wanted to exclude Austria and to have Prussia lead the union. The debate was resolved when Austria backed away from the proposed union. When the Frankfurt Assembly offered Frederick William the crown of a united Germany—Austria excluded—he declined by saying that he would accept it only from the German princes themselves.

The failure of the Frankfurt Assembly to implement its design for a democratic union (it had framed a kind of bill of rights) left the job of German unification to Prussian militarism and *Bismarck's policy of "Blood and Iron."* (German politics until World War I will be considered in a later chapter.)

Austria from the Age of Metternich to World War I (1815–1914)

The Revolutions of 1830 hardly touched the reactionary government of Austria under Metternich. However, the ethnic mix that made up the Austrian Empire—Germans, Hungarians, Slavs, Czechs, Italians, Serbs, Croats, and others—helped bring about revolution in 1848. When Paris erupted in rebellion in March of 1848, *Louis Kossuth,* a Hungarian nationalist, aroused separatist sentiment in the *Hungarian Diet* (a national assembly legal in the empire). Rioting broke out in Vienna. Prince Metternich, then chancellor, fled the country, and the Hungarians, the Czechs, and three Northern Italian provinces of the empire declared autonomy. The empire collapsed.

The *Prague Conference,* called by the Czechs in response to the all-German Frankfurt Conference, developed the notion of *Austroslavism,* by which the Slavic groups within the empire would remain part of the empire but also set up autonomous national governments. Before the idea could be adopted, a series of victories by Austrian armies restored Hapsburg authority over the various nationalities that had declared independence.

Franz Joseph (r. 1848–1916) replaced *Emperor Ferdinand I,* and conservative forces within the government centralized power and suppressed all opposition. The Revolutions of 1848 failed in Austria largely because the empire's ethnic minorities squabbled among themselves rather than make a united front against imperial forces.

The defeat of Austria in the Austro-Prussian War of 1866 (to be considered in a subsequent chapter) led to some governmental reform. The *Compromise of 1867* set up a constitutional government with limited suffrage, granted the Hungarians internal autonomy, and created a *dual monarchy,* the *Austro-Hungarian Empire.* Exclusion of the Slavic minorities from a voice in government encouraged the *Pan-Slavic movement* to seek independence for ethnic minorities. It was an important cause for World War I.

The Revolutions of 1848

France

Causes	Length of Time	Protagonists	Events	Results
The economic changes in England as well as the expansion of the franchise there led to social pressures in France. Political demonstration was outlawed so people held political banquets, which were outlawed. Also the oppression of Louis Napoleon and his repressive minister Guizot pushed the people to the breaking point due to censorship and restriction of freedoms when 52 demonstrators were killed by soldiers.	1847–1848	Louis Blanc, Pierre Proudhon, Louis Cavaignac, Alphonse de Lamartine, Napoleon III	Louis Philippe fled to England, and Guizot resigned as barricades emerged across Paris. The Second Republic was formed in 1848 based upon universal male suffrage. A class struggle ensued between rich and poor, rural and urban. The urban workers tried a Marxist experiment that failed.	Napoleon III reigned after winning elections in landslides. He dismissed the National Assembly and ruled with more power and control than Louis Philippe had ruled.

German States

Causes	Length of Time	Protagonists	Events	Results
The news of the revolutions in France spread throughout Europe, and the people of the 39 Germanic states began to demand rights.	February 1848–May 1848	The French leaders and the bourgeoisie of Germany, Richard Wagner	The people of Baden demanded the first German Bill of Rights in February of 1848. Soon a crowd threatened the palace in Berlin and after an incident in which demonstrators were killed, King William Frederick IV demonstrated support for the revolutionaries and promised to reorganize his government. King Ludwig abdicated in Bavaria, and Saxony also saw calls for reform.	The king still reigned and Bismarck would soon come to power with Wilhelm I and unite the western German states into modern Germany through almost dictatorial rule.

Hapsburg Empire

Causes	Length of Time	Protagonists	Events	Results
This multiethnic empire had been held together with force and Metternich's political machinations. In 1848, Europe was mostly France, Germany, Russia, and the Hapsburg Empire or former Hapsburg Empire. The empire was in decline and was not held together well. The different ethnic groups all attempted to gain autonomy in 1848 as the idea of nationalism seemed to sweep the continent. This was the year that *The Communist Manifesto* was published in German.	February 1848– August 1849	Many listed in other columns.	The empire burst asunder and Austria, with the help of arch-conservative Russian Tsar Nicholas I was able to reassemble a weakened empire.	The Hapsburg Empire was returned to its former state of a multiethnic empire of Croats, Slovaks, Germans, Austrians, Poles, Huns, Serbs, Ruthenians, Italians, and Czechs, but the central authority had been further weakened, and the empire would only last until 1918.

Hungary

Causes	Length of Time	Protagonists	Events	Results
Ethnic oppression by the Austrian Hapsburgs burst the Austrian Empire asunder in 1848. The Hungarian Parliament had been called in 1825 to address financial matters. A bloodless revolution occurred in March of 1848 led by a governor and a Prime Minister.		Louis Kossuth and Louis Bathyany	The Hungarians took advantage of the general revolutions throughout the Hapsburg Empire and got Austria to grant them autonomy. Once Austria beat down the other revolutions, the new emperor, Franz Josef I, decided to crush Hungary. With help from Russia, the Hungarians were defeated in a failed war for independence.	The Hapsburg Empire was returned to its former state of a multiethnic empire of Croats, Slovaks, Germans, Austrians, Poles, Huns, Serbs, Ruthenians, Italians, and Czechs. The Hungarians practiced passive resistance against the Hapsburgs.

Italian States

Causes	Length of Time	Protagonists	Events	Results
Giuseppe Mazzini and others began to write about Italian nationalism and the greatness of the Roman Empire. The citizens of Milan revolted in March and the revolutions spread throughout the peninsula.	March 1848–May 1849	Giuseppe Mazzini, Giuseppe Garibaldi	The revolutions resulted in Venetian and Roman republics. The Austrians marched through Piedmont and southward into Italy, conquering most of Italy by May of 1849.	Almost 1,000 people were killed by the Austrians as they regained power throughout the peninsula.

Poland

Causes	Length of Time	Protagonists	Events	Results
The Prussians armed Polish prisoners and encouraged them to return to Poland with Revolutionary and anti-Russian motives.	March 1848–June 1848	Jerzy Zdrada, Frederick William IV, Natalis Sulerzyski, and Seweryn Elżanowski	The Prussians supported a Polish revolution to weaken the Russians. The Poles did not trust the Prussians, but needed them. The Poles and Prussians ended up in armed conflict which the Prussians won.	The Poles learned that they could not bargain with the Germanic states to gain statehood. They focused on economic growth rather than political growth.

Russia from the End of the Napoleonic Wars to World War I (1815–1914)

Alexander I (r. 1801–1825) began his reign by extending the reforms of Catherine the Great, by modernizing the functioning of his government, and by offering greater freedom to Jews within his empire. Napoleon's invasion of Russia in 1812 turned this disposition about, until, by 1820, Alexander had ordered statewide censorship and the adherence of all his subjects to the Russian Orthodox Church.

When Alexander died, a confusion of succession—his two brothers, *Constantine* and *Nicholas,* were in line—led to the *Decembrist Revolt* in December 1825 of army officers in the capital of St. Petersburg. They supported the candidacy of Constantine, who they believed would modernize the nation and offer a constitution. *Nicholas I* (r. 1825–1855) attained the throne after crushing the revolt, and his reign continued Alexander's autocratic policies. He was creator of the infamous *Third Section,* the secret police who prevented the spread of revolutionary or Western ideas. "Orthodoxy, Autocracy, Nationality" was the rallying cry of his reaction. Intellectuals in Russia developed two opposing camps during this period: *Slavophiles,* who believed that Russian village (the mir) culture was superior to that of the West; and *Westernizers,* who wanted to extend the "genius of Russian culture" by industrializing and setting up a constitutional government.

Alexander II (r. 1855–1881) began his reign as a reformer and ended it as a conservative. His *Emancipation Proclamation* of 1861 *ended serfdom*—the medieval institution largely abolished in the rest of Europe—under which peasants were bound to the land and virtually owned by the aristocratic landowners. His murder at the hands of a militant faction of the *Narodniks,* a socialist group who wanted Russia to return to some mythical ideal of village life, increased repression under his successors, who turned to "Autocracy, Orthodoxy, and Nationalism."

By the 1890s, Russia had undertaken *industrialization* in order to remain a world power. At the beginning of World War I, 25 million of its population of 140 million were city dwellers, the *Trans-Siberian Railroad* linked European and Asiatic Russia, and the members of the growing proletariat were largely employed in state-owned factories that exploited and abused them.

(Political developments of the early 20th century are dealt with in a subsequent chapter.)

Sample Essay Question

The sample thematic essay question and the practice questions that follow are types found on the AP exam, and they require knowledge of causes, effects, personalities, ideas, and events.

SAMPLE QUESTION

"Adam Smith's enormous authority resides, in the end, in the same property that we discover in Marx: not in any ideology, but in an effort to see the bottom of things. In both cases their greatness rests on an unflinching confrontation with the human condition as they could best make out."

Assess the above quote. What ideas did both men draw upon in order to formulate their ideas? What were their conclusions and why were they so different?

Comments on the Sample Question

Follow the "Simple Procedures" for writing an essay. (See page 34.)

First, *What does the question want to know?* This multifaceted question has many tasks. It may be good to list the tasks first. Who were Smith and Marx? What were their ideas? How did they form them? Does the quote apply? Why or why not? What were their conclusions and why were they so different?

Second, *What do you know about it?* You need to know that these two men are the economic philosophers upon whom the economies of the 19th and 20th centuries were based, *capitalism* and *communism*. You also need to know that they both based their ideas upon what they observed and that the differences in what they concluded was due in large part to the different conditions that they observed, supporting the quote. While it is sometimes good to go against the direction that the test leads you in these situations by trying to disprove the quote, it is not recommended in this situation.

Third, *How would you put it into words?* One way to structure this essay is with a thesis paragraph, one paragraph on what Smith saw and read, one on what Marx saw and read, and one on why their conclusions were so different, followed by a concluding paragraph. It can also be done with a thesis, followed by one paragraph on the quote, one on both men's influences, and a third one on what their conclusions were and why those conclusions were so different, followed by a conclusion. That is the format used in the sample answer.

Rubric for Sample Answer

Before you read the sample answer, examine the rubric. What will the reader be looking for when he or she grades this essay? A sample rubric, shaded to show the reader's evaluation, is seen below:

9–8 POINTS

✔ Thesis explicitly assesses the quote and **both** examines the ideas each man drew upon to formulate their ideas and explains why their ideas were so different form each other. Thesis does not need to be in the opening paragraph.

✔ Organization is clear, consistently followed, and effective in support of the argument.

- May devote individual paragraphs to assessing the quote, what ideas each man utilized, and why their conclusions differed so greatly. May also devote one paragraph to each economic thinker and evaluate within that paragraph.
- Must identify the ideas that influenced each man and their conclusions (Smith was influenced by the Enlightenment, the Scientific Revolution, the government support of monopoly companies such as the Dutch East India Company, and the emergence of trusts and therefore decided that a system of perfect liberty could be devised that would provide for all of societies' wants as long as the government did not get involved to support specific companies or industries. Marx was influenced by Hegel, the horrors of the Industrial Revolution, and factory life of the 19th century, as well as the developing labor movement to conclude that capitalism had sown the seeds of its own defeat through a proletarian uprising leading to an enlightened revolution in an industrialized age.) Must also consider why each man drew such different conclusions.

✔ Essay is well balanced; assesses the quote and both examines the ideas each man drew upon to formulate their ideas and explains why their ideas were so different from each other. Both are analyzed at some length.

✔ Major assertions in the essay are supported thoroughly and consistently by relevant evidence.

✔ Evidence may prove more specific or concrete.

✔ May contain errors that do not detract from the argument.

7–6 POINTS

✔ Thesis explicitly assesses the quote and **both** examines the ideas each man drew upon to formulate their ideas and explains why their ideas were so different from each other, but may not be developed fully.

✔ Organization is clear and effective in support of the argument but may introduce evidence that is not pertinent to the task.

✔ Essay covers all major topics suggested by the prompt but may analyze Smith, Marx, the quote, or why their ideas differed in greater depth rather than in a balanced manner.

✔ Major assertions in the essay are supported by relevant evidence.

✔ May contain an error that detracts from the argument.

5–4 POINTS

✔ Thesis assesses the quote and **both** examines the ideas each man drew upon to formulate their ideas and explains why their ideas were so different from each other, but without any development; thesis may address only part of the question effectively; thesis may be a simple, single-sentence statement.

✔ Organization is clear but may not be consistently followed, essay may veer off task chronologically or thematically or both.

✔ Essay may not complete all tasks:
  • May discuss only the quote as it applies to each economist, or the ideas each man drew upon to formulate their ideas and explains why their ideas were so different from each other.
  • May discuss only one economist.
  • May focus only on one or more of the ways the economists agree or disagree.
  • May be primarily descriptive rather than analytical.

✔ Essay offers some relevant evidence.

✔ May contain errors that detract from the argument.

3–2 POINTS

✔ Thesis may simply paraphrase the prompt OR assesses the quote and examines the ideas each man drew upon to formulate their ideas OR explains why their ideas were so different from each other without analyzing why they drew different conclusions.

✔ Organization is unclear and ineffective; essay may focus on the personal attributes of each economist rather than analyzing how the quote applies to both of them and examines the idea each man drew upon to formulate their ideas and explains why their ideas were so different from each other.

✔ Essay shows serious imbalance; discussion of the quote examines the ideas each man drew upon to formulate their ideas and explains why their ideas were so different from each other but in a superficial way; much of the information may be significantly out of the time period or geography of the question.

✔ Offers minimal OR confused evidence.

✔ May contain several errors that detract from the argument.

1–0 POINTS

✔ Thesis is erroneous OR irrelevant OR absent.

✔ No effective organization is evident.

✔ Discussion of the quote examines the ideas each man drew upon to formulate their ideas and explains why their ideas were so different from each other in a generic fashion.

✔ Provides little or no relevant supporting evidence.

✔ May contain numerous errors that detract from the argument.

Sample Answer

Two of the men who have changed the world immensely are Adam Smith and Karl Marx. Both of these men were brilliant historians and philosophers due to their ability to synthesize the situations of their times, and both provided conclusions to help change society. Their conclusions differ greatly, due to the different times in which they lived, yet have both changed the world immensely.

Both Smith and Marx were products of their time. Much of the reason that Smith and Marx were so influential was that both men were looking to assess the conditions that really existed and to discover what needed to be done in order to improve these conditions. Because of this, the people of their contemporary societies could relate to their ideals and beliefs. Smith arose as a wealthy Scotsman during the prime of the Commercial Revolution. The processes of proto-industrialization and land enclosure were reaping fine rewards for the entrepreneurs of the day. Smith observed this at the same time as the system of mercantilism and joint-stock companies rose. The ideas he was confronted with were those of early English entrepreneurship and rising wealth. Smith was influenced by principles of fair competition that were becoming popular during his time. François Quesnay, who opposed mercantilism and supported laissez-faire economics, was a particularly strong influence to Smith. These observations and ideas, along with the fact that he lived in the wealthiest nation in the world, shaped his conclusions that an invisible hand of self-interest controlled prices and wages as well as what was produced very well as long as the government did not interfere.

Marx, on the other hand, lived long enough after Smith to see the developing system of capitalism rear the ugly head of industrialization. He was a student of the French socialists, whose writings were popular in his time, and he was also strongly influenced by social science. The exploitation of the proletariat worker, and the dirty trend of urbanization and industrialization, had led to the stratification of society and the gap between classes, which left Marx screaming for a revolution. In essence, Smith's and Marx's conclusions that capitalism was rapacious and would be replaced by a revolution of the abused working class who would grow were based upon what they observed and what they thought was the most efficient means of managing society, yet the varying historical perspectives and experiences of these men caused their conclusions to be so different.

The conclusions of Marx and Smith, while so different, both changed the world greatly. A major difference between the two men is that Smith saw self-interest as a positive thing, while Marx saw it as the downfall of society. Another major difference was that, due to history, Marx was more politically radical than Smith. While Smith institutionalized the idea of entrepreneurship, which had only been recently realized through the Protestant idea of work ethic to that point, he never dreamed his ideas of laissez-faire would be used to rebel against economic control and taxation, or be part of the causes of the American and French Revolutions. The first movements toward representative governments and political freedom also sprung from the ideas of laissez-faire. Smith gave the entrepreneur a voice in a time when international trade was growing and economies were developing. On the other hand, Marx fomented revolution in the name of the worker, justice, and efficiency.

Although both men came to vastly different conclusions, they transformed industrial and postindustrial society. In the end, Smith and Marx were both great thinkers, who based their ideas on what they saw around them, and due to their difference in experiences, their ideas clashed greatly. While currently, no part of the world uses Smith's style of capitalism, and no country uses Marxist communism, the ideas and worldviews of both men have been highly influential in the establishment of economic systems and social movements. They were both extremely successful at "getting to the bottom" of the societies that created them, and analyzing the human condition as best they could.

EVALUATE THE SAMPLE ANSWER

Now go back and look at the rubric. It is clear that this essay fulfills all of the requirements for a score of 8 or 9 on the rubric. The essay answers all parts of the question thoroughly with concrete evidence at length with a well-balanced essay. The minimal concrete support gets this essay a score of 8.

RATER'S COMMENTS ON THE SAMPLE ANSWER

8—Highly Qualified

This is a strong essay with a strong thesis. This essay answered all parts of the question with historic insight and support. It was well crafted and explored qualities of each man in many paragraphs rather than the simpler format of one paragraph per man, and a third about their differences and why. All topics were covered thoroughly and the explanation was strong.

The essay would have been stronger if it had mentioned Hegel, Proudhon, and other writers who had a strong influence on Marx. The eras of Enlightenment versus Romanticism could also have been examined.

Practice Essay Questions

The following are samples of the various types of thematic essays that appear on the AP exam. (See pages 21–22 for detailed explanations of each type.) Check over the **generic rubric** (see pages 58–60) before you begin any of these essays and use that rubric to score your essay if you write one.

QUESTION 1

To what extent and in what ways did the move toward unification in mid-19th-century Germany fall out of the hands of the constitutionalists and into the hands of the Prussian militarists?

COMMENTS ON QUESTION 1

There is little room for choice in this question, since it requires that you show "how and how much" of German unification was the result of a failure of the forces of democracy to take the lead, thereby leaving it to the militarists in Prussia. Refer to specifics in the breakdown of the leadership of constitutional forces, in the assumption of leadership by Prussia, and in the militaristic nature of Prussian leadership.

QUESTION 2

"Attempts at reform and modernization in 19th-century Russia were inevitably diluted by the habit of reaction." *Assess the validity* of this statement by offering factual evidence.

COMMENTS ON QUESTION 2

To "assess the validity" is to determine whether a statement is true, false, or partly both. The pivotal concept in this statement is "inevitably diluted." Does it mean that "the habit of reaction" canceled or weakened "reform and modernization"?

QUESTION 3

"Austria's suppression of Slavic autonomy within the empire created more dissolution than unity." *Defend or refute* this statement.

COMMENTS ON QUESTION 3

"Defend or refute" usually allows the presentation of a mixed argument. In this case—because of the crucial phrase "more dissolution than unity"—the argument must show that one or the other was true.

As is often the case, the question itself shows the direction of the best possible argument: that dissolution was the result of Austria's policy toward its Slavic minorities.

QUESTION 4

Evaluate the achievements of Napoleon III.

COMMENTS ON QUESTION 4

There is always room in an "evaluation" question since it requires "judging the worth" or comparing "pluses and minuses." The trick here is to give a balanced view. History's greatest villains appealed to *somebody* for *some reason*.

Napoleon III was immensely popular for a time and for specific achievements.

QUESTION 5

Contrast and compare the growth and suppression of democracy in 19th-century Europe.

COMMENTS ON QUESTION 5

This is a double effort: to "show differences" and to "examine similarities." Democracy did not grow easily in the states where it was ultimately successful nor did it flounder completely in those where it was suppressed. This is a broad question that requires more than a comparison of only two states.

Practice Multiple-Choice Questions

(These questions are representative of the types found on the AP exam.)

1. The period from the fall of Napoleon in 1815 to the Revolutions of 1848 is often referred to as the Age of Metternich for all the following reasons EXCEPT

    (A) the reactionary policies of Prince Metternich of Austria dominated continental politics
    (B) republicanism was suppressed and the nationalistic urges of most ethnic groups were denied
    (C) support of the Old Order was widespread among the political elite
    (D) the industrial middle class was increasingly denied representation in government
    (E) the liberal ideas of the French Revolution were suppressed

2. All of the following policies reflect the conservative nature of the British government from 1815–1825 EXCEPT

    (A) the Corn Laws
    (B) the Peterloo Massacre
    (C) the "Rotten Borough system"
    (D) the Six Acts of 1819
    (E) the establishment of a modern police force

3. Metternich and other diplomats were able to accomplish all of the following as a result of the Congress of Vienna (1814–1815) EXCEPT

    (A) Switzerland was recognized as a neutral nation
    (B) Metternich gained status internationally as a minister of Europe
    (C) the balance of power between nations and alliances was restored
    (D) Italy was unified under Sardinian leadership
    (E) the Netherlands were reunited with Belgium politically

4. Which would be the best description of the political situation in France from 1815 to the start of World War I?

    (A) A series of contrasting types of governments were established and removed.
    (B) There was a gradual but continual move toward reform and greater representation for all classes.
    (C) There was a disintegration of republicanism.
    (D) Imperialism replaced Bourbon despotism.
    (E) Ceaseless despotism was relieved by brief periods of revolution.

5. Elected by a landslide after the failed Revolution of 1848, he founded the Second French Empire:

   (A) Louis XVIII
   (B) Louis Philippe
   (C) Louis Napoleon
   (D) Louis Blanc
   (E) Louis Quatorze

6. The Revolutions of 1848

   (A) overthrew the governments of France, Germany, and Russia
   (B) erupted in England as well as on the continent
   (C) marked the decline of the political influence of the proletariat
   (D) gave rise to Communism and realpolitik
   (E) dissipated the nationalistic urges of the peoples of Eastern Europe

7. The original goal of the Frankfurt Assembly (1848–1849) was to

   (A) design and implement a constitutional government for a unified Germany
   (B) consolidate Germany under Austrian Hapsburg leadership
   (C) unify the northern states of Germany under Prussia
   (D) create a united Germany for Germans only
   (E) convince Prussia to unite Germany by force

8. Which is the best characterization of the status of reform in Russia from 1815 to 1914?

   (A) "Orthodoxy, Autocracy, Nationality" was the slogan of all.
   (B) Repeated attempts to Westernize and reform resulted in reaction.
   (C) Gradual democratization was effected by the "Westernized" intelligentsia.
   (D) A purge of all Western influences was effected by the "Slavophiles."
   (E) There was a total suppression of all attempts to reform and modernize.

9. All of the following represent a change in the democratic movement in Europe in the last three decades of the 19th century EXCEPT

   (A) liberals sought to limit government authority in social and economic affairs
   (B) suffrage had expanded to include most of the male population
   (C) liberals argued for government regulation of industry
   (D) governments became increasingly involved in alleviating poverty
   (E) industrial workers demanded a higher standard of living

10. Between the end of the Second Empire in 1871 and the start of World War I, France

    (A) had one stable government
    (B) had developed a two-party system
    (C) suffered a single-party dictatorship
    (D) had dozens of separate and unstable governments
    (E) was ruled by socialist radicals

11. All of the following are features of the social welfare systems that had developed in France and England before World War I EXCEPT

    (A) the right of workers to strike
    (B) government insurance for job injuries
    (C) old-age pensions
    (D) compulsory school attendance
    (E) universal suffrage

    "He is guilty! Damn that Jewish officer and his rabble-rousing novelist friend! Republicans and their spies will be the ruin of us. That cursed officer has become a symbol. Let him not blind us to the truth that we need a king. May he rot on Devil's Island."

12. To whom is the speaker referring?

    (A) Leon Gambetta
    (B) Marshal MacMahon
    (C) Alfred Dreyfus
    (D) Major Esterhazy
    (E) Georges Boulanger

13. The accused in the above passage was exonerated, partly through the efforts of Emile Zola, the writer. The conflict involved an attempt by a rival political faction to embarrass the government with trumped-up charges of espionage. Which faction was responsible for the false imprisonment of the man referred to above?

    (A) monarchists
    (B) liberals
    (C) republicans
    (D) radical workers
    (E) socialists

14. The man whose reestablishment of a French Empire brought in the mid-1800s temporary prosperity then ruinous defeat to the nation was

(A) Cavour
(B) Louis Napoleon
(C) Louis Kossuth
(D) Leon Gambetta
(E) Georges Boulanger

Troops storming a barricade in the Donesgasse in Frankfurt, Germany, on Sept. 18, 1848, contemporary German colored engraving. The Granger Collection, New York. (0009086)

15. The picture above depicts an uprising of the Revolution of 1848 which occurred in most of Europe with the exception of

(A) Russia and England because Russia was too backward and unindustrialized and England was too advanced politically, economically, and industrially
(B) Russia and England because both were controlled by a merciless government—the tsar in Russia and Parliament in England
(C) Russia and Austria because both were controlled by long-established monarchies and punished serfs harshly
(D) Austria and Switzerland because Austria was controlled by a long established monarchy and punished serfs harshly, and Switzerland was too isolated
(E) England and France because England had the most stable government and France had the least stable

Answers and Answer Explanations

1. D	6. D	11. E
2. E	7. A	12. C
3. D	8. B	13. A
4. A	9. A	14. B
5. C	10. D	15. A

1. **(D)** The wealth of the industrial middle class gave it leverage with the government.

2. **(E)** This was a reform since crime was on the rise in the rapidly expanded cities.

3. **(D)** Italy was not unified by the Congress of Vienna.

4. **(A)** Instability of individual governments and change of types of government prevailed.

5. **(C)** A nephew of the great and first Napoleon, he capitalized on his uncle's fame to get elected and to establish an empire.

6. **(D)** The failure of the revolutions inspired new methods of getting power for the "have-nots."

7. **(A)** The other issues came up during the conference and helped wreck the chances for a democratic Germany.

8. **(B)** For every step forward, a step back.

9. **(A)** This was the liberal program in the earlier part of the century. Abuses of industrialization changed it.

10. **(D)** The coalition governments often fell at the hint of a major crisis.

11. **(E)** Women did not get the vote until after World War I in Britain, after World War II in France.

12. **(C)** The infamous Dreyfus Case pitted supporters of a republican government against the conservative classes. Strong evidence indicates that Major Esterhazy was the guilty party who passed military secrets to the Germans.

13. **(A)** Although a court-martial never found him innocent, the president of France pardoned him and public opinion turned against the monarchists and other conservative factions.

14. **(B)** It is Louis Napoleon, also known as Napoleon III. Cavour was the unifier of Italy; Gambetta and Boulanger were French politicians; Louis Kossuth was the Hungarian nationalist hero.

15. **(A)** Russia and England were the only two major nations to escape revolution in 1848; England was the most advanced and Russia the least.

19th Century "-ISMs": Nationlism, Ideologies, and Culture

Key Terms/People

- Age of Nationalism
- Unification
- Otto von Bismarck
- Austro-Prussian War
- Franco-Prussian War
- Guiseppe Garibaldi
- Camillo di Cavour
- Victor Emmanuel II
- Liberalism
- Socialism
- Romanticism
- Realism
- Impressionism

Overview

The period following the French Revolution and the Napoleonic Wars, known as the *Age of Metternich* (see Chapter 7), saw the rise of powerful ideologies— "-isms"—some of which were legacies of the French Revolution, and some of which were responses to the political, economic, and social upheavals of the previous decades. *Nationalism* was the most promising and the most pernicious of these. It was the prime motive for the unification of Italy and of Germany; it was a force that redefined political boundaries and loyalties and that encouraged claims of national or racial superiority.

Liberalism, socialism, and romanticism profoundly influenced the politics, economics, and culture of the first half of the 19th century. *Realism* defined the literature of the later half of the century, *impressionism* brought the artist's personal visual experience to painting, and *Social Darwinism* and *positivism* provided scientific models for politics and the arts.

One decade, 1861 to 1871, saw the triumph of the large nation-state as Europe's primary political unit. Italy and Germany consolidated; Austria and Hungary formed autonomous but united states; Russia centralized government control.

The nation-state is founded upon a sense of nationalism: a common identity; a specific geographic area; a common language, history, destiny, culture, ethnicity, or religion. It is a consciousness of belonging and of the differences between one's own people and all others on this planet.

The French Revolution and Napoleon's successes inspired the drive to unity. Nationalism promised power, the mystical connection that the Romantic movement glorified, and autonomy from the remote leadership of amorphous multinational empires. France and England were the two most powerful nation-states before 1861; Italy became a united kingdom in 1861; Germany formed a new empire in 1871. War played the crucial role in both processes.

The idealism of the Revolutions of 1848 had failed to realize the nationalist aspirations of the Italians or the Germans. If the Italian and German peoples, separated into traditionally small independent states, were ready for unification, it still took the "power politics" (realpolitik) of two determined men to bring about unity. Camillo di Cavour, Sardinian prime minister, and Otto von Bismarck, Prussian chancellor, used the might and prestige of their states to bring smaller independent entities together to create the modern nation-states of Italy and Germany. After 1871, the balance of power in Europe was changed well into the 20th century.

The Age of Nationalism

Nationalism became more prevalent in Europe and around the world after 1848. The supremacy of the nation-state was gaining ground in organizing the political, social, economic, and cultural activities of a group. Ethnic identities were central to the development of nationalism, which should not be confused with patriotism, or the level of support for a nation-state.

Louis Napoleon was the nephew of *the Napoleon* (Napoleon I) who despite defeat, exile, and death was considered by the French to be one of their greatest leaders. Louis Napoleon was elected president of France by a landslide in 1848, largely because of his illustrious name. Between 1852, when he had proclaimed a Second Empire, and 1870, after France's ignominious defeat in the Franco-Prussian War, he had restored the economy, laid the foundations for democratic reforms, and renewed the national pride of the French people.

The Civil War (1861–1865) in the United States resulted in a more solid union and in a more powerful federal government.

After defeat at the hands of the French and English in *The Crimean War* (1853–1856), Russia modernized, industrialized, and initiated a program of limited reforms to solidify tsarist control over the multinational peoples of Russia's vast reaches.

Japan, in response to Western incursions in the 1850s and 1860s, developed a modern military, an industrial economy, and a centralized government under Emperor Mejii, whose ancestors had been figureheads.

The Unification of Italy

Italy Before Unification

THE SEPARATE STATES

The Kingdom of Naples (Two Sicilies) was made up of Sicily and the southern half of the Italian boot.

The *Papal states* were in the middle of the peninsula.

Lombardy-Venetia were industrialized provinces in the north, and they were ruled by Austria as were Tuscany, Lucca, Modena, and Parma.

The Kingdom of Sardinia (Piedmont-Sardinia), was made up of the island of Sardinia and the northwestern provinces of Nice, Savoy, and Piedmont.

Sardinia was a constitutional monarchy ruled by *Victor Emmanuel II* (r. 1849–1878), and it was the only independent state in Italy. In 1854, *Camillo di Cavour* (1810–1861) became prime minister of the parliament instituted during the Revolutions of 1848. He rejected the romantic nationalism of *Giuseppe Mazzini* (1805–1872), who had argued in his *Duties of Man* that the nation was a divine device and an extended family, and decided that Italy could be unified only through force and that Sardinia would have to lead the battle.

In order to gain the support of liberals throughout Italy, Cavour reformed the government of his state by weakening the influence of the papacy, by investing in public works such as railroads and harbor improvements, by abolishing internal tariffs, by encouraging the growth of industry, by emancipating the peasantry from the vestiges of manorialism, and by making the Sardinian government a model of progressive constitutionalism.

Cavour's "Power Politics"

After the Crimean War ended in 1856, Cavour, who had brought Sardinia into the war on the side of France, petitioned Emperor Napoleon III to support Sardinia in a projected war with Austria, which controlled many Italian provinces. At *Plombieres* in 1858, Cavour got Napoleon to agree to send a supporting army into Italy in the event that Sardinia could trick Austria into a war. Napoleon, who wanted to weaken the Austrians, was promised the French-speaking provinces of Nice and Savoy in return for allowing the Sardinians to annex Northern Italy.

In April 1859, *Austria declared war on Sardinia* and the French came to Cavour's aid. After a series of victories by the combined Sardinian-French forces, Napoleon suddenly pulled out of the war because of criticisms at home and threats from the Prussians. The Austrians were left with Venetia, and only Lombardy went to the Sardinians. Several of the northern duchies under Austrian domination declared independence and carried out plebiscites for union with Sardinia by 1860.

Giuseppe Garibaldi (1807–1882), an ardent nationalist, invaded Sicily in 1860 with the encouragement of Cavour. His thousand-man *Red Shirts* used popular support to defeat a Bourbon ruler's force that was ten times that number. Within months, Garibaldi had subdued Sicily and Naples. The *Two Sicilies* (Kingdom of Naples) joined Sardinia, and in *March 1861 the Kingdom of Italy was proclaimed* with Victor Emmanuel II on the throne.

Final Unification

By 1870, Venetia and the Papal states—despite opposition from the Pope—had been incorporated into the union. *Italia Irredenta* ("Italy unredeemed"—Italian areas still under Austrian control) remained unliberated, but Italy had been united and was a constitutional monarchy. Democracy was diluted by the small percentage of the male population that had suffrage and by the dominance, in Southern Italy, of the landowners.

The Unification of Germany

Germany Before Unification

In the two or so decades before German unification took place, the population, productivity, and wealth of the German states increased many times over. The *Zollverein* (customs union) had opened most of the states to a mutually advantageous trade, and Germany became a single economic unit. Prussia, with its booming industry, powerful army, militaristic Junkers (land-owning aristocrats), and expansionist ambitions led the states of Northern Germany and faced off against Austria. The Hapsburgs of Austria—rulers of a multinational empire held together by tradition and raw power and the prime influence among the divided states of Germany—had long feared a Germany united by the Hohenzollerns of Prussia. After the Frankfurt Assembly failed to unify the independent German states in 1848, though, the Prussian *Hohenzollern* kings determined to achieve it by force.

Bismarck's Realpolitik

When the Prussian Parliament refused to approve military expenditures in 1862, *King Wilhelm I* (r. 1861–1888) appointed Otto von Bismarck (1815–1898), a prominent and conservative Junker, as chancellor. He trampled the Parliament by collecting illegal taxes, ignoring its protests, enlarging the army, and, in the process, killing democracy in Prussia.

"Blood and Iron," he insisted, would unite Germany, and after involving Prussia in three wars, he achieved unification under Prussian leadership.

The War Against Denmark, 1864, allied Prussia, Austria, and the other German states in an *all-German war* against Denmark, which had hoped to annex the neighboring province of *Schleswig.* Denmark was quickly defeated, and, after some prodding by Bismarck, Prussia and Austria fell out over who should get what.

The *Austro-Prussian War (Seven Weeks' War),* 1866, broke out when the issues of the war with Denmark remained unresolved. Although the Austrians enlisted the help of most of the other German states, the superior arms, training, and leadership of the Prussian Army defeated them in seven weeks. Hoping to gain Austria's support in the inevitable struggle with France, which had become alarmed by Prussia's swift victories, Bismarck made the surrender terms lenient.

Bismarck established the *North German Confederation*—in 1867 to replace the *German Confederation*—that loose union that Napoleon had set up and that the Congress of Vienna had confirmed. Twenty-one states of North Germany were united under the leadership of the Prussian king, with a two-house legislature, the *Reichstag* or lower house to represent all the people and to be elected by universal male suffrage, and the *Bundesrat* or upper house to represent the princes.

The *Franco-Prussian War*, 1870, broke out after a dynastic dispute over the Spanish throne led to a flurry of diplomatic exchanges between Prussia and France. Bismarck deliberately altered the wording of the *Ems Dispatch*, an account of the German king's meeting with the French ambassador over the issue, and made the inflammatory revision public. Napoleon III, bowing to public opinion and bad advice, declared war on Prussia in July 1870. In less than four months, the Prussian army had defeated the French and taken the emperor prisoner. *The Treaty of Frankfurt*, May 1871, gave *Alsace-Lorraine* to Germany and imposed a punishing *indemnity*, both of which the French people were to resent for generations to come.

Unification

Four South German states—Baden, Bavaria, Hesse, and Württemberg—that did not belong to the North German Confederation joined after the flush of victory, and *the German Empire was born* in January 1871. The Prussian king became emperor or *kaiser*.

The Empire with Bismarck as Chancellor

Although the lower house of the imperial legislature, the *Reichstag*, was elected by universal male suffrage, it had little real power because the chancellor and his ministers were responsible to the kaiser rather than to the legislature. Democracy in Germany took a backseat to autocracy.

Bismarck's *Kulturkampf* (cultural conflicts) was his repression of the so-called subversive elements in the empire—Catholics and socialists. Reversing his original attacks on the *Catholic Center Party* by the late 1870s, he turned to the socialist "menace" represented by the growing *Social Democratic Party*. When his official measures backfired and the party grew even more popular, he pulled the rug out from under it by sponsoring a series of social reforms himself. Workmen's compensation, old-age pensions, and medical protection created one of the world's most advanced social welfare systems.

Bismarck's Fall

When *Wilhelm II* (r. 1888–1918) assumed the throne in 1888, he brought with him the archaic notion of *divine right* of rule and a deep resentment of Bismarck's personal power. In 1890, he *dismissed Bismarck* and up until his abdication at the close of World War I, 1918, he dominated his chancellors. Arrogant and limited, his ambitions and aggressiveness in the late 1800s and early 1900s upset the balance of power and drove Europe closer to world war.

Results of Nationalism

Nationalism became a very important force in world and European politics during the last half of the 19th century. That is why this chart is located here even though many of the people listed lived during the 20th century. National identities became increasingly important, and national autonomy for each ethnic group, in the form of national self-determination, became an ardent desire for many historically oppressed ethnic groups, just as it became an important justification for unification of Italy and Germany. The identity of a "we vs. them," discussed by Johan Gottfried Herder as part of his concept of the *volk* (folk of one nation), also explains much of the war and hardship of the 20th century. Many of the worst conflicts in the world today still focus on this concept of one nation or ethnic group being better than or having more right to an area than any other nation or group. Nationalism also led to more popularly elected governments because of nationalist revolutions and unifications.

Modern Leaders of Assorted European Countries or "Musical Chairs"

From the early 1800s, the parliamentary system began to come into vogue across the continent, though in a lurching manner. However, suffice it to say that the parliamentary system these countries adopted usually had several parties and coalition governments. Rarely would one party gain enough votes to form its own government, leading to the creation of coalition governments composed of several parties with different agendas. Party loyalties shifted frequently and without cause. When one party decided to withdraw from the government (perhaps because they did not like the colors with which the prime minister was decorating his house), new elections would have to be held. Thus, there are many changes in European leadership to keep track of.

Rulers in **bold** mean STOP and memorize their names and know why they are important; these people will very likely be on the AP test.

Rulers in *italics* mean PAUSE and be familiar with who these people are; they may be on the test and rate some attention.

Rulers in regular text mean KEEP GOING. Sure, one might be on the test every ten years as a distracter in one of the last multiple-choice questions, but that is a chance we are willing to take. These names are included mainly for continuity's sake, but most professors don't know who they are and you don't need to either.

Insofar as dates go, keep a ballpark figure of when people reigned, lived, and so on, but memorizing the exact dates is frustrating and not necessary.

France

The French change rulers as often as some people change clothes. The variety of rulers has been mostly unimportant, but a few French leaders after 1871 may indeed pop up on the exam.

Name	Duration in Office	Notes
Louis Adolphe Thiers	*1871–1873*	*Third Republic (President)*
Marie E. P. M. de MacMahon	1873–1879	Third Republic (President)
François P. J. Grévy	1879–1887	Third Republic (President)
Sadi Carnot	1887–1894	Third Republic (President)
Jean Casimir-Périer	1894–1895	Third Republic (President)
François Félix Faure	1895–1899	Third Republic (President)
Émile Loubet	1899–1906	Third Republic (President)
Clement Armand Fallières	1906–1913	Third Republic (President)
Raymond Poincaré	**1913–1920**	**Third Republic (President)**
Paul E. L. Deschanel	1920–1920	Third Republic (President)
Alexandre Millerand	1920–1924	Third Republic (President)
Gaston Doumergue	1924–1931	Third Republic (President)
Paul Doumer	1931–1932	Third Republic (President), assassinated
Albert Lebrun	1932–1940	Third Republic (President)
Henri Philippe Pétain	*1940–1944*	*Vichy Government (Chief of State)*
Charles de Gaulle	**1944–1946**	**Provisional Government (President)**
Félix Gouin	1946	Provisional Government (President)
Georges Bidaul	1946–1947	Provisional Government (President)
Vincent Auriol	1947–1954	Fourth Republic (President)
René Coty	1954–1959	Fourth Republic (President)
Charles de Gaulle	**1959–1969**	**Fifth Republic (President)**
Georges Pompidou	1969–1974	Fifth Republic (President)
Valéry Giscard d'Estaing	1974–1981	Fifth Republic (President)
François Mitterrand	1981–1995	Fifth Republic (President)
Jacques Chirac	**1995–2007**	**Fifth Republic (President)**
Nicolas Sarkozy	2007–	Fifth Republic (President)

Germany

The German nation came into existence in 1871 but did not gain a democratic rule until after World War I. This is a list of German chancellors and the governments they represented.

Name	Duration in Office	Notes
Friedrich Ebert	1919–1925	Weimar Republic
Paul von Hindenburg	1925–1934	Weimar Republic
Adolf Hitler	**1934–1945**	**Third Reich**
Karl Doenitz	1945	Third Reich
Konrad Adenauer	**1949–1963**	**West Germany**
Ludwig Erhard	1963–1966	West Germany
Kurt Georg Kiesinger	1966–1969	West Germany
Willy Brandt	**1969–1974**	**West Germany**
Helmut Schmidt	1974–1982	West Germany
Helmut Kohl	**1982–1990**	**West Germany**
Wilhelm Pieck	1949–1960	East Germany
Walter Ulbricht	1960–1973	East Germany
Willi Stoph	1973–1976	East Germany
Erich Honecker	*1976–1989*	*East Germany*
Egon Krenz	1989	East Germany
Manfred Gerlach	1989–1990	East Germany
Sabine Bergman-Pohl	1990	East Germany
Helmut Kohl	**1991–1998**	**Germany**
Gerhard Schröder	1998–2005	Germany
Angela Merkel	2005–	Germany

Great Britain

Though the cabinet system was begun under Charles II, the position of a prime minister answerable to Parliament did not really develop until Robert Walpole.

The British party system did not develop until the time of the American Revolution. The Torys were the conservative party while the Whigs were the more progressive party. Eventually these, respectively, evolved into the Conservative and Liberal Parties. The Liberal Party went on to become the Labour Party. During times of national emergencies (World War I, World War II, and the Falkland Islands War), the two parties would "overcome their differences" and form a coalition government, which usually broke apart once peace was in sight.

Listed below are all of the British prime ministers since Walpole.

Name	Duration in Office	Notes
Sir Robert Walpole	*1721–1742*	
Earl of Wilmington	1742–1743	
Henry Pelham	1743–1754	
Duke of Newcastle	1754–1756	
Duke of Devonshire	1756–1757	
Duke of Newcastle	1757–1762	
Earl of Bute	1762–1763	
George Grenville	*1763–1765*	
Marquess of Rockingham	*1765–1766*	
William Pitt the Elder	*1766–1768*	*(Earl of Chatham)*
Duke of Grafton	1768–1770	
Lord North	1770–1782	
Marquess of Rockingham	1782	
Earl of Shelburne	1782–1783	
Duke of Portland	1783	
William Pitt the Younger	*1783–1801*	*Tory*
Henry Addington	1801–1804	Tory (Later Viscount Sidmouth)
William Pitt the Younger	*1804–1806*	*Tory*
Baron Grenville	*1806–1807*	*Whig*
Duke of Portland	1807–1809	Tory
Spencer Perceval	1809–1812	Tory
Earl of Liverpool	1812–1827	Tory
George Canning	1827	Tory
Viscount Goderich	1827–1828	Tory (later Earl of Ripon)
Duke of Wellington	*1828–1830*	*Tory (Defeated Napoleon at Waterloo)*
Earl Grey	1830–1834	Whig
Viscount Melbourne	1834	Whig
Sir Robert Peel	*1834–1835*	*Tory*
Viscount Melbourne	1835–1841	Whig
Sir Robert Peel	*1841–1846*	*Conservative*
Lord John Russell	1846–1852	Whig (Later Earl of Russell)
Earl of Derby	1852	Conservative
Earl of Aberdeen Peelite	1852–1855	Conservative
Viscount Palmerston	*1855–1858*	*Liberal*
Earl of Derby	1858–1859	Conservative
Viscount Palmerson	*1859–1865*	*Liberal*
Earl of Russell	1865–1866	Liberal
Earl of Derby	1866–1868	Conservative
Benjamin Disraeli	**1868**	**Conservative**

Name	Duration in Office	Notes
William Gladstone	**1868–1874**	**Liberal**
Benjamin Disraeli	**1874–1880**	**Conservative**
William Gladstone	**1880–1885**	**Liberal**
Marquess of Salisbury	1885–1886	Conservative
William Gladstone	**1886**	**Liberal**
Marquess of Salisbury	1886–1892	Conservative
William Gladstone	**1892–1894**	**Liberal**
Earl of Rosebery	1894–1895	Liberal
Marquess of Salisbury	1895–1902	Conservative
Arthur Balfour	*1902–1905*	*Conservative*
Sir Henry Campbell-Bannerman	1905–1908	Liberal
Herbert Asquith	*1908–1916*	*Liberal*
David Lloyd George	**1916–1922**	**Coalition**
Andrew Bonar Law	1922–1923	Conservative
Stanley Baldwin	*1923–1924*	*Conservative*
Ramsay MacDonald	*1924*	*Labour*
Stanley Baldwin	*1924–1929*	*Conservative*
Ramsay MacDonald	*1929–1931*	*Labour*
Ramsay MacDonald	*1931–1935*	*National*
Stanley Baldwin	*1935–1937*	*National*
Neville Chamberlain	**1937–1940**	**National**
Winston Churchill	**1940–1945**	**Coalition**
Clement Attlee	**1945–1951**	**Labour**
Sir Winston Churchill	**1951–1955**	**Conservative**
Sir Anthony Eden	*1955–1957*	*Conservative*
Harold Macmillan	1957–1963	Conservative
Sir Alec Douglas-Home	1963–1964	Conservative
Harold Wilson	1964–1970	Conservative
Edward Heath	1970–1974	Conservative
Harold Wilson	1974–1976	Labour
James Callaghan	1976–1979	Labour
Margaret Thatcher	**1979–1990**	**Conservative**
John Major	1990–1997	Conservative
Tony Blair	*1997–2007*	*Labour*
Gordon Brown	*2007–*	*Labour*

Russia

This "democracy" was born out of the Revolution of 1905, and has seen a series of either ineffectual or oppressive rulers hold the top elected post in the nation since that time.

Name	Duration in Office	Notes
Prince Georgi Lvov	1917	Provisional Government
Alexander Kerensky	*1917*	*Provisional Government*
Vladimir Ilyich Lenin	**1917–1924**	**Union of Soviet Socialist Republics**
Joseph Stalin	**1924–1953**	**Union of Soviet Socialist Republics**
Georgi M. Malenkov	1953–1955	Union of Soviet Socialist Republics
Nikolai A. Bulganin	1955–1958	Union of Soviet Socialist Republics
Nikita S. Khrushchev	**1958–1964**	**Union of Soviet Socialist Republics**
Leonid I. Brezhnev	*1964–1982*	*Union of Soviet Socialist Republics*
Yuri V. Andropov	1982–1984	Union of Soviet Socialist Republics
Konstantin U. Chernenko	1984–1985	Union of Soviet Socialist Republics
Mikhail S. Gorbachev	**1985–1991**	**Union of Soviet Socialist Republics**
Boris Yeltsin	*1991–1999*	*President of Russian Republic*
Vladimir Putin	2000–2008	President of Russian Republic
Alexander Medvedev	2008–	President of Russian Republic

At this point you may have noticed that Austria has been omitted. There is a simple reason for this—after 1917 (and some would argue after 1848), the country ceased to be important to international politics.

Unification of Italy and Germany

Year	Italy	Germany
1848	• Revolutions throughout Europe erupted after the French Revolt. • They were quickly put down after an unsuccessful revolt. • Giuseppe Garibaldi fled to back Uruguay with other expatriates. • Victor Emmanuel ruled Piedmont Sardinia after the Austrians repressed the revolts.	• Frederick William IV refused to accept the crown of a united Germany "from the gutter" when the Frankfurt Assembly offered it to him. • The revolutions in Germany led to Frederick William IV reorganizing the government and promising to be more attuned to the people.
1852	• Count Camillo Benso di Cavour becomes Prime Minister of Piedmont Sardinia.	
1859	• The French saved Piedmont Sardinia from Austrian invasion. • The French then betrayed them in a separate peace, which infuriated many Italians. • Tuscany, Modena, Parma, and Romagna all voted to join Piedmont Sardinia.	
1860	• Giuseppe Garibaldi and his 1,000 *Red Shirts* invaded Sicily and started to move northward through the peninsula. • Garibaldi wanted to establish a republic, while Victor Emmanuel and Cavour wanted a monarchy. • Garibaldi was met with overwhelming support from the people who joined his forces. • Garibaldi met Cavour outside of the Papal States, and a deal was made to create a constitutional monarchy in Italy.	
1861	• All of Italy save Rome and Venice became part of a unified state with a parliament.	• Wilhelm I became the king of Prussia. • Named **Otto von Bismarck** his chief minister.
1864		• Prussia defeated Denmark in the battle of Schleswig-Holstein.
1861–1866		• Bismarck engaged in a constitutional struggle with the Prussian parliament. • He utilized his *gap strategy* to ensure monarchical privilege.
1866	• Venice joined Italy after Austria's defeat in the *Seven Weeks War*.	• Prussia defeated Austria in the *Seven Weeks War*. • Demonstrated that it is the most powerful Germanic military.

Year	Italy	Germany
1867		• Bismarck organized the Northern German Confederation of the 21 northern, mostly Protestant German states.
1870	• Rome was added to Italy when the French troops leave during the Franco-Prussian War. The entire Italian Peninsula was united into one nation for the first time since the fall of Rome.	• Bismarck manufactured a war with France as a means of uniting the German states against a common enemy. • The Franco-Prussian War was a rout in which the Parisians had to eat the animals in the zoo during a siege. • All of the German states unite behind Wilhelm I and Bismarck.
1871		• Wilhelm I was declared the first kaiser of Germany, and Bismarck was named the chancellor.

Ideology and Culture

Liberalism

Classical *Liberalism,* an offshoot of the ideals of liberty and equality of the French Revolution, set as its political goals legal equality, freedom of the press, freedom of assembly and of speech, and above all, representative government. Reacting to monarchial absolutism and to the reactionary repression (as represented by the policies of Austria's Prince Metternich, whose conservative attempt to roll back the ideals of the French Revolution amounted to a crusade against liberalism), the liberalism of the early 19th century generally opposed government intervention.

Laissez-faire, a form of economic liberalism and a principle espoused most convincingly by Adam Smith, argued for a free market system unfettered by government regulations. While this concept fostered economic growth, the theories of economists Thomas Malthus and David Ricardo (see Chapter 6) were often used to back up the predatory business practices of early capitalists and industrialists, which can be supported by Smith as well.

After the first few decades of the 19th century, liberalism was espoused mostly by the middle class and tended to ignore the rights and aspirations of the working class.

Socialism

Early *socialism* was a reaction to the gross inequities created by the Industrial Revolution. The exploitation of workers by the early capitalists convinced the *utopian socialists* (see Chapter 6) that one of the best remedies for this was to have governments intervene in the economy. Their program included government control of property, economic equality for all, and government economic planning. *Charles Fourier* (1772–1837), a Frenchman, described a scheme for a utopian community based on a socialist idea. His countryman, *Louis Blanc,* pushed a program for the democratic takeover of the state by workers to guarantee full employment.

The impracticality of their programs relegated the early *utopian socialists* to a minor political role, and modern socialism was largely founded by the theories of Karl Marx. (See Chapter 6.)

Romanticism

Romanticism, a glorification of the emotional component of human nature, was a reaction to the rationalism and restraint of the Enlightenment. The excesses of the French Revolution and the destructiveness of the Napoleonic Wars eroded faith in the "inevitable perfectability" of humankind through reason.

Romantic artists, composers, and writers shared a worldview: a willingness to express the deepest and most turbulent emotions, a fervent belief in personal freedom, awe of nature, reverence for history.

SOME REPRESENTATIVE FIGURES

William Wordsworth (1770–1850): English, a poet who glorified the beauty and solemnity of nature.

Victor Hugo (1802–1885): French, a poet and dramatist best remembered for his vibrant novels, such as *The Hunchback of Notre Dame,* which explored the darker side of the human experience.

English painter *John Constable* (1776–1837) said, "Nature is spirit visible." He painted bucolic scenes that attempted to cast rural life in an idyllic fashion, typifying the emotional examination of nature and history seen in this artistic movement.

George Sand (1804–1876): French, a countess who took a man's name as her pen name. She wrote modern, autobiographical, emotionally revealing novels about unconventional love.

Ludwig van Beethoven (1770–1827): German, his musical genius is expressed in virtually every musical form of his day, from songs to symphonies, and his evolution as a romantic is evident in the course of his composing. The symphonic music of his later period makes full use of the expanded orchestra, a romantic innovation that added three times as many instruments as the classical orchestra known to Mozart, and that expressed the profound emotionality of romantic music.

Realism

Realism, the literary movement that had replaced literary *romanticism* by the middle of the 19th century, portrayed a kind of *determinism,* the belief that human nature and human destiny are formed by heredity and environment and that human behavior is governed by natural laws that preclude free will.

Writers, such as the Frenchmen *Emile Zola* (1840–1902), *Honoré de Balzac* (1799–1850), and *Gustave Flaubert* (1821–1880), the English woman *George Eliot* (Mary Ann Evans) (1819–1880), and the Russian *Leo Tolstoy* devoted their works to a depiction of everyday life, especially of the working class and especially of its more unsavory aspects. Spurning the romantic obsession with distant times and distant places, they focused on the here and now, often shocking readers with their objective depictions of life in the cities, the slums, and the factories.

Impressionism

The advent of photography in the 19th century encouraged a group of artists, *Impressionists,* to avoid realistic depiction (better served by photography) and to capture, instead, the transitory feeling of a scene, the personal "impression." Frenchmen *Pierre-Auguste Renoir* (1841–1919) and *Claude Monet* (1840–1926) were major practitioners of the style.

Science

After the first few decades of the 19th century, and directly as a result of the technological requirements of the Industrial Revolution, "pure" scientific discoveries found application in explaining how the machinery and techniques of industrial processes worked. Physicists were able to formulate principles of *thermodynamics* applicable to a variety of technological systems, such as the operation of engines, which converted heat into motion.

The theories of biology were used by researchers, such as *Louis Pasteur* (1822–1895), to preserve food and to improve medical procedures. A burgeoning chemical industry provided a variety of new products from medicines to synthetic dyes, and the generation of electricity created whole new industries in transportation and lighting.

Charles Darwin (1809–1882) was not the first theorist to formulate the concept of evolution, but his meticulous research and voluminous specimens added weight to his idea that life evolved in its myriad forms from a common ancestor, through the process of a *struggle for survival.* The mechanism that aided this was the development of anomalies in a given species, which would actually aid in the survival of that species. His insight predates the development of the science of *genetics.* For instance, when the only foliage available for grazing was on high trees, the mutant long-neck giraffe would outlive and out-propagate his short-neck cousins. Thus, his characteristics would be more successfully passed on to later generations.

Darwin's theory had a powerful effect on the intellectual life of Europe. It was used by skeptics to attack the Biblical account of creation and religion itself. *Friedrich Nietzsche* (1844–1900), a German philosopher and contemporary of Darwin, argued that Christianity presented a "slave morality" that fettered the creativity of great individuals, the *ubermench* (superman), who must free himself from conventionality and redefine life and morality.

Herbert Spencer (1820–1903) used Darwin's theories to argue that history and human society reflect a struggle for supremacy resulting in the *survival of the fittest.*

the rich, the rulers, the powerful nations are "fit"; the poor, the downtrodden masses, the world's colonies are "weak." This *Social Darwinism* appealed to those in power and to racists and imperialists of every stripe.

Sample Essay Question

The sample thematic essay and the practice essays presented in this chapter are types found on the AP exam and they require a knowledge of causes, effects, personalities, ideas, and events.

SAMPLE QUESTION

Contrast and compare the methods of Cavour and Bismarck in unifying their respective nations.

Comments on the Sample Question

Follow the "Simple Procedures" for writing an essay. (See page 34.)

First, *What does the question want to know?* The "compare" part of this question is relatively easy; the "contrast" part is more subtle.

Second, *What do you know about it?* Both men headed the dominant states of the respective unions; both men used "power politics"—diplomacy, Machiavellian manipulations, war—to gain their ends; both viewed their roles with the kind of hardheaded realism that avoided romantic illusions about the processes and results of unification. Their contrasts: Their domestic policies differed; their methods of "power politics" differed because of the different degrees of independent strength of their states. Bismarck could rely on "Blood and Iron"; Cavour maneuvered among the giants, pitting one against the other.

Third, *How would you put it into words?* Use the question's basic structure—"contrast" and "compare"—to develop your essay. Be sure to offer specifics to back up your generalizations.

Rubric for Sample Answer

Before you read the sample answer, examine the rubric. What will the reader be looking for when he or she grades this essay? A sample rubric, shaded to show the reader's evaluation, is seen below:

9–8 POINTS

- ✔ Thesis explicitly identifies **both** Cavour and Bismarck and how the unification methods of their respective nations will be compared and contrasted. Thesis does not need to be in the opening paragraph.
- ✔ Organization is clear, consistently followed, and effective in support of the argument.

- May devote individual paragraphs to Cavour and Bismarck.
- Must identify specific methods each used to unify their nation (both used war to a degree, but Bismarck finally unified Germany by organizing the Germanic states against France, whereas Cavour negotiated with Garibaldi in the end) and compare and contrast those methods.

✔ Essay is well balanced; contrast and comparison are analyzed at some length. Essay covers the unification of both nations.

✔ Major assertions in the essay are supported thoroughly and consistently by relevant evidence.

✔ Evidence supporting the comparison and contrast may prove more specific or concrete.

✔ May contain errors that do not detract from the argument.

7–6 POINTS

✔ Thesis explicitly identifies **both** Cavour and Bismarck and how the unification methods of their respective nations will be compared and contrasted, but may not be developed fully.

✔ Organization is clear and effective in support of the argument but may introduce evidence that is not pertinent to the task.

✔ Essay covers all major topics suggested by the prompt but may analyze an aspect of Italy's unification, Germany's unification, or the comparison of them in greater depth rather than in a balanced manner.

✔ Major assertions in the essay are supported by relevant evidence.

✔ May contain an error that detracts from the argument.

5–4 POINTS

✔ Thesis identifies **both** Cavour and Bismarck and how the unification methods of their respective nations will be compared and contrasted but without any development; thesis may address only part of the question effectively; thesis may be a simple, single-sentence statement.

✔ Organization is clear but may not be consistently followed; essay may veer off task chronologically or thematically or both.

✔ Essay may not complete all tasks:
- May discuss only the comparison OR contrast of the unification of each state.
- May discuss only two or fewer aspects of the unification of each nation.
- May focus only on one nation.
- May be primarily descriptive rather than analytical.

✔ Essay offers some relevant evidence.

✔ May contain errors that detract from the argument.

3–2 POINTS

✔ Thesis may simply paraphrase the prompt OR Cavour and Bismarck and how the unification methods of their respective nations will be compared and contrasted without analyzing the extent to which they carried them out or the methods they employed to that end.

✔ Organization is unclear and ineffective; essay may focus on the personal attributes of Cavour or Bismarck rather than analyzing the unification of their nations.

✔ Essay shows serious imbalance; discussion of the unification of Italy and Germany is superficial; much of the information may be significantly out of the time period or geography of the question.

✔ Offers minimal OR confused evidence.

✔ May contain several errors that detract from the argument.

1–0 POINTS

✔ Thesis is erroneous OR irrelevant OR absent.

✔ No effective organization is evident.

✔ Discussion of Cavour and Bismarck and how the unification methods of their respective nations will be compared and contrasted is generic.

✔ Provides little or no relevant supporting evidence.

✔ May contain numerous errors that detract from the argument.

Sample Answer

The failure of the Revolutions of 1848 utilized a new diplomacy, "Power Politics," a very ungentlemanly and often ruthless application of the Machiavellian credo that "the end justifies the means." Camillo di Cavour and Otto von Bismarck became masters of the game and won the unification of two of Europe's regions that had not been unified autonomously for centuries. The methods in achieving unification that both Cavour of Italy and Bismarck of Germany used can be contrasted: One built up democracy at home while the other suppressed it; one relied on the help of stronger nation-states while the other conquered all opposition without outside help. Their methods can be compared in that they used deceit and war to achieve their ends.

Before 1861, Italy had been a well-defined geographic area—the "Boot"—made up of separate entities, one of which was independent, most of which were dominated by the Austrian Empire, all of which had long been battlegrounds in the struggle for hegemony by the larger nation-states of Europe. Before 1871, Germany was a conglomeration of nearly forty fiercely independent states, and Prussia and Austria competed for economic and political dominance within that conglomeration.

Napoleon's battlefield successes in the early 1800s and his consolidation in both regions passed on the passion of nationalism to both the Italians and the Germans. It took the right timing, the gifted leadership of the heads of the two outstanding states of each region, and war to achieve national unification.

In the decade before unification, the kingdom of Piedmont Sardinia was the only independent state of Italy. Under Cavour, its prime minister, the state became a constitutional monarchy. It was modernized by a system of roads and railroads; it was industrialized; it was reformed by the abolition of all forms of manorialism, by the reduction of the influence of the Roman Catholic Church, and by the establishment of a strong parliament. It served as a model for liberal reform and was a leader in the movement for unification.

In 1858, Cavour got Napoleon III to back him up if he could trick Austria into declaring war. The trick worked; Austria was provoked into a declaration of war in 1859; Napoleon III kept his promise; the Austrians were defeated. This was "power politics" at its most ruthless and effective.

Then the bottom dropped out of the plan. Napoleon III made a separate peace with the Austrians because of opposition to the war at home and because of fear of the Prussians, who opposed French dominance in Italy. But revolutions in a number of other Northern Italian states created governments whose electorates voted for union with Piedmont. Despite opposition from the Austrians and the Pope, who lost territory in those revolutions, the Kingdom of Piedmont was recognized by a number of powerful European states.

Unification was completed when Giuseppe Garibaldi's Red Shirts conquered Sicily from its Bourbon rulers and then Naples. The former Kingdom of the Two Sicilies was joined with the expanded Kingdom of Piedmont-Sardinia, and in March 1861 Victor Emmanuel II became king of Italy.

Prussia was the most modern and powerful of the German states. Referred to as "an army before it was a state," its efficient and fast-growing industry supported its influential military establishment. In 1862, Parliament voted down military appropriations, and King Wilhelm I appointed the tough-minded Junker Bismarck to deal with the crisis. Over the next several years, Bismarck's gap theory virtually wiped out parliamentary democracy in the country. He collected taxes over the protests of Parliament, enlarged the army, and ignored the opposition. He and Prussia were ready to lead the battle for unification.

His "realpolitik" was similar to Cavour's power politics: He used deceit, intimidation, and insult to precipitate war with national unification the goal. Bismarck nurtured a dispute between his state and rival Austria, and then isolated Austria from potential allies with promises of territory. Austria managed to get the support of the German Confederation (most of the other independent states of the region), and in 1866 they went to war against Prussia, who was without allies.

In seven weeks, the well-led, well-equipped, and well-trained Prussian army defeated Austria and her allies. Deliberately moderating the terms of the peace treaty to gain German support for his next venture, Bismarck dissolved the old German Confederation (originally set up by Napoleon) and replaced it with the North German Confederation, a watered-down constitutional monarchy, made up of the bulk of the German states and ruled by the Prussian king.

Bismarck used the issue of the succession of a German to the Spanish throne to incite France into a war he could use to unite Germany. By doctoring an account—the Ems Despatch—Bismarck provoked popular opinion in both Germany and France. In July 1870, France declared war on Prussia.

Less than six months later, France was defeated, Napoleon was humiliated, and the remaining German states had joined the North German Confederation to form the German empire. Cavour's and Bismarck's methods in unifying their countries can be contrasted.

When Cavour brought Piedmont into war with a stronger Austria, he managed to win most of his goals by manipulating an alliance with an even stronger France. Bismarck, on the other hand, used Prussian military and industrial might—*Blood and Iron*—to stand alone against all of the enemies his realpolitik set up for the kill.

Both men's methods can be compared in that they led their strongly independent states in the movement for national consolidation and that they used deception, intrigue, and war to gain their goals. Single-minded and hard-headed, they rejected the romantic appeal of mystical national bonds and hammered out unification with hardball politics, diplomatic deceit, and battlefield victories.

EVALUATE THE SAMPLE ANSWER

Now go back and look at the rubric. It is clear that this essay fulfills all of the requirements for a score of 8 or 9 on the rubric. The essay answers all parts of the question thoroughly with concrete evidence at length with a well-balanced essay. The expansive concrete support gets this essay a score of 9.

RATER'S COMMENTS ON THE SAMPLE ANSWER

9—Extremely well qualified

Not only does this essay contrast the methods of Cavour and Bismarck in unifying Italy and Germany by "showing differences" but it clearly compares their styles and means by "examining similarities." The introductory paragraphs lay out the structure of the argument. The essay then provides relevant historical background. The body of the essay demonstrates a scholarly, fact-based account of the methods of each man in operation. The conclusion sums up admirably.

Practice Essay Questions

The questions that follow are samples of the various types of thematic essays that appear on the AP exam. (See pages 21–22 for a detailed explanation of each.) Check over the **generic rubric** (see pages 58–60) before you begin any of these essays and use that rubric to score your essay if you write one.

QUESTION 1

To what extent and in what ways did Mazzini break new ground for Cavour's program of unification? Did Garibaldi help complete it?

COMMENTS ON QUESTION 1

Mazzini has been called the "poet" of Italian unification, Cavour the "architect," and Garibaldi the "cavalier." How and how much did Mazzini's proselytizing of the glories of mystical union prepare the Italian people and the world for the realpolitik of Cavour? How and how much did Garibaldi's flamboyant appeal and adventures in the two Sicilies enable Cavour to complete unification?

QUESTION 2

Explain why the political situation in Italy in the decade before unification prompted Piedmont-Sardinia to take the lead in the movement.

COMMENTS ON QUESTION 2

The Revolutions of 1848 were the kind of failures that whet the appetite for greater success and that pointed the way. Power politics grew out of the frustrations of the erstwhile reformers. Piedmont was the logical leader of unification because it was the only independent state in Italy. Most of the north was under the yoke of Austria, central Italy was controlled by the traditionalistic politics of the papacy; the south was underdeveloped and under the sway of anachronistic manorialism. When Cavour reformed and strengthened Piedmont, he was making the most of its opportunities.

QUESTION 3

Analyze Bismarck's use of war to achieve unification.

COMMENTS ON QUESTION 3

"Examine in detail" how the All-German War, the Seven Weeks' War, and the Franco-Prussian War were used by Bismarck to effect unification. It was a process of distinct stages: War with Denmark aroused a sense of German nationalism and set Austria up for the fall; the Seven Weeks' War aligned most of Germany with the loser, Austria, and against the winner, Prussia, but generous terms achieved the North German Confederation; finally, victory over France inspired a patriotic yearning for union that created the empire.

QUESTION 4

"Germany did not unite itself; rather, it was conquered by Prussia." *Assess the validity* of this statement.

COMMENTS ON QUESTION 4

To "determine the truth" of this statement, consider that Prussia stood alone against the rest of Germany in the Seven Weeks' War, that Bismarck's realpolitik united Germany by "Blood and Iron," that even the Franco-Prussian War served to draw the remaining German states into union.

QUESTION 5

Evaluate Bismarck as chancellor of the new German Empire.

COMMENTS ON QUESTION 5

Don't confuse this question of his role as chancellor of the united Germany with his role as uniter. What happened under Bismarck after 1871?

His "pluses"—his diplomacy, his mediation of the colonial rivalries in Africa, his masterful ability to maintain the delicate balance of peace despite Germany's upsetting the balance of power by its stunning victory over France, his social welfare reforms.

His "minuses"—his continued repression of democracy in Germany, *Kulturkampf* against the Catholic influence, anti-Socialist crusade.

Practice Multiple-Choice Questions

(These questions are representative of the types that appear on the AP exam.)

1. National unity was achieved in northern Italy by

   (A) diplomacy and war
   (B) the coalition between the papacy and Cavour
   (C) popular revolution
   (D) a combination of diplomacy, war, and popular rebellion
   (E) the personal wills of Cavour and Bismarck

2. Who was called "the architect of Italian unification"?

   (A) Mazzini
   (B) Garibaldi
   (C) Victor Emmanuel II
   (D) Cavour
   (E) Napoleon III

3. During Cavour's administration as prime minister of Piedmont-Sardinia, all of the following occurred EXCEPT

   (A) the influence of the Church was diminished
   (B) there was industrialization
   (C) manorialism was strengthened
   (D) constitutionalism was established
   (E) commerce was encouraged

4. Cavour's "deal" with Napoleon III at Plombieres was significant because

   (A) it was a manifestation of his "power politics"
   (B) it brought peace with Austria
   (C) it guaranteed French nonintervention in the war with Austria
   (D) it freed Napoleon III to fight Prussia
   (E) it alienated Garibaldi's "Red Shirts"

5. *Italia Irredenta* was the name given to

   (A) the process of unification
   (B) the newly united Italian constitutional monarchy
   (C) the rural south of Italy
   (D) the split between the new government and the papacy
   (E) the Italian enclaves remaining under Austrian control

6. Cavour rushed to meet Garibaldi before Garibaldi could enter the Papal States and got him to agree to

   (A) destroy the government in the Papal States and leave a power vacuum for Victor Emmanuel II
   (B) not enter the Papal States and allow Italy to become a unified republic
   (C) not enter the Papal States and allow Italy to become a unified constitutional monarchy
   (D) not enter the Papal States and allow Cavour and Victor Emmanuel to conquer the Papal States
   (E) enter the Papal States to turn Italian favor away from the formation of a republic

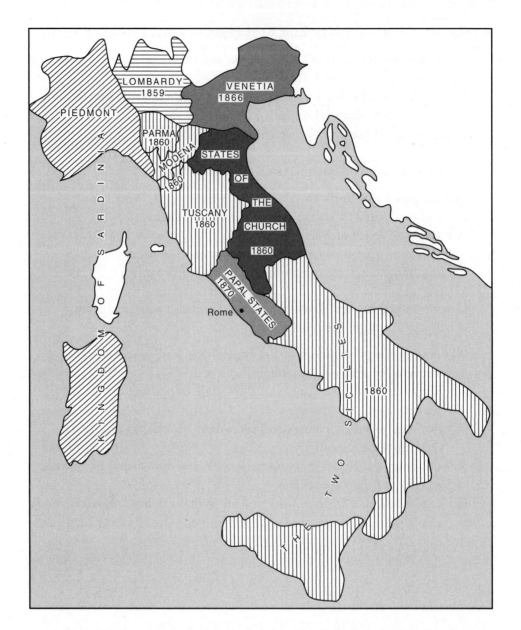

7. Which province shown on the map above was gained by the Kingdom of Italy in return for its support of Prussia in the Seven Weeks' War against Austria?

(A) Parma
(B) The states of the Church
(C) The Papal states
(D) Modena
(E) Venetia

8. The two decades following the Revolutions of 1848 saw all of the following changes in the German states EXCEPT

   (A) the German Confederation, created at the Congress of Vienna to replace the Holy Roman Empire, was revived
   (B) repression of republicans, nationalists, and liberals was common
   (C) the German population shrank due to the immigration to America of refugees from political persecution
   (D) the separate states were economically interdependent
   (E) industrial productivity rose dramatically

9. Before German unification, Prussia had instituted a series of governmental, economic, social, and military reforms in response to

   (A) the humiliating defeats by France during the Napoleonic Wars
   (B) the insurrection of peasants against landowning aristocrats
   (C) the urging of the Frankfurt Assembly
   (D) pleas from the Junkers
   (E) the threat of a unified Italy

10. The term realpolitik applies to Bismarck's

    (A) realistic support of the liberal factions in the Prussian Parliament
    (B) use of subterfuge, deceit, and military force to accomplish unification and to implement other policies
    (C) opposition to Hapsburg leadership in a united Germany
    (D) admiration of Cavour's constitutional reforms in Italy
    (E) support of Pan-Germanism

11. The struggle between King William I and the Prussian parliament revolved around

    (A) the territories of Schleswig and Holstein
    (B) universal suffrage
    (C) Austria's participation in a unified German state
    (D) the military budget and taxation
    (E) Bismarck's abuse of power to enrich himself at the expense of the state

12. All of the following were wars fought by Prussia as part of Bismarck's realpolitik to unify Germany EXCEPT

    (A) the war against Denmark, 1864
    (B) the All-German War
    (C) the Crimean War
    (D) the Seven Weeks' War
    (E) the Franco-Prussian War

"We had to avoid wounding Austria too severely; we had to avoid leaving behind in her any unnecessary bitterness of feeling or desire for revenge; we ought rather to reserve the possibility of becoming friends again with our adversary of the moment, and in any case to regard the Austrian state as a piece on the European chessboard and the renewal of friendly relations as a move open to us."

13. The individual whose memoirs are seen above was

    (A) Metternich
    (B) Garibaldi
    (C) Gladstone
    (D) Bismarck
    (E) Wilhelm II

14. The "thousand" who went with Garibaldi were also known by which of the following monikers?

    (A) The Gray Shirts
    (B) The Black Shirts
    (C) The Green Shirts
    (D) The Blue Shirts
    (E) The Red Shirts

15. The failure of Germany to develop democracy from 1871 to 1914 was due to all of the following EXCEPT

    (A) the chancellor was responsible to the kaiser rather than to the Reichstag
    (B) there was limited male suffrage
    (C) the Bundesrat represented the German states rather than the people
    (D) Bismarck's *Kulturkampf* suppressed the political activities of the influential Catholic minority
    (E) the social welfare programs created by state paternalism fostered autocracy

16. The ideology, an inheritor of the ideals of the French Revolution, that set as its political goals in the first half of the 19th century, freedom of press, assembly and speech, and the establishment of representative governments is

    (A) socialism
    (B) conservatism
    (C) liberalism
    (D) positivism
    (E) realism

17. *Laissez-faire* economic liberalism is most compatible with the theories of

    (A) Karl Marx
    (B) Adam Smith
    (C) Charles Fourier
    (D) Louis Blanc
    (E) Friedrich Engels

18. The artistic and literary movement that reacted to the rationalism of the Enlightenment by emphasizing the emotional component of humanity along with individual freedom was

    (A) Impressionism
    (B) Expressionism
    (C) Realism
    (D) Social Darwinism
    (E) Romanticism

Answers and Answer Explanations

1.	D	7.	E	13.	D
2.	D	8.	C	14.	E
3.	C	9.	A	15.	B
4.	A	10.	B	16.	C
5.	E	11.	D	17.	B
6.	C	12.	C	18.	E

1. **(D)** The Italians under Cavour used diplomacy (Napoleon III), war, and revolution as well as plebiscites to gain their national unity.

2. **(D)** Mazzini is called "the poet of unification"; Garibaldi led the Red Shirts in seizing Sicily and Southern Italy; Victor Emmanuel was king of Piedmont-Sardinia; Napoleon III was emperor of France.

3. **(C)** Manorialism was abolished in order to strengthen constitutional government and make Piedmont a model for all of Italy.

4. **(A)** He got Napoleon to back him when he provoked Austria into war.

5. **(E)** It was a bone of contention that these areas remained out of Italy's hands even after World War I.

6. **(C)** Cavour did not want Garibaldi to enter the Papal States because he did not want to lose popular support. He also got Garibaldi to agree to a constitutional monarchy rather than a republic as the form of government, which was a defeat for Garibaldi, but Garibaldi preferred unification to no government so he compromised.

7. **(E)** The Seven Weeks' War was fought in 1866.

8. **(C)** It grew due to rapid industrialization.

9. **(A)** The militarists in Prussia pushed reform in order to strengthen the army.

10. **(B)** "Blood and Iron" was the method chosen by the Iron Chancellor.

11. **(D)** The main topics of the struggle were taxation and the expansion of the military, which Bismarck pushed through without the support of the legislature and later had approved retroactively. The larger army and coffers most likely helped to unify the nation.

12. **(C)** The Crimean War was fought from 1854 to 1856 by England and France against Russian encroachments in the Black Sea area of the Ottoman Empire.

13. **(D)** The quote is from Bismarck and is typical of his *Realpolitik* outlook.

14. **(E)** Garibaldi's volunteer fighting force was the Red Shirts, who helped him invade southern Italy.

15. **(B)** There was universal suffrage, but Parliament was dominated by Prussian conservatives.

16. **(C)** *Classical Liberalism* evolved from the revolutionary goals of Liberty, Equality, Fraternity, and representative government at the core of its program.

17. **(B)** Smith's *Wealth of Nations* supported this "hands off" view of government interference in the economy. All the others were socialists.

18. **(E)** The Romantic Movement was a direct and immediate reaction to the belief in reason espoused by the Enlightenment.

CHAPTER 9

Imperialism (1870–1914)

Key Terms/People

- surplus capital
- balance of power
- white man's burden
- Social Darwinism
- Sepoy Mutiny
- Cecil Rhodes
- Open Door Policy
- Suez Canal
- The Boxer Rebellion
- Opium Wars
- Russo-Japanese War
- Colonialism
- Berlin Conference
- Mahatma Gandhi
- Ho Chi Minh
- French-Algerian War
- British East India Company
- Dutch East India Company

Overview

A contemporary definition of imperialism is any instance of a more powerful nation or group of nations acting, or being perceived to be acting, at the expense of a lesser power, usually when the more powerful nation dominates militarily or economically. Imperialism is therefore not only used to describe overt empire-building policies, such as those of the Roman Empire, the Spanish, or the British, but was also used controversially and/or disparagingly; for example, most of Europe referred to Napoleon's actions as imperialistic. The colonial power may rule the colony politically or exploit it economically or impose its culture upon it. During the so-called old imperialism of the 16th through 18th centuries, the Europeans did not acquire overseas territories—except in the Americas, where the sparse native population allowed establishment of colonies—as much as they set up trading stations. They largely respected and frequently cooperated with the local rulers in India, China, Japan, the Spice Islands (Indonesia), and the other geographic areas where a flourishing trade developed between locals and European coastal trading centers.

The new imperialism that began in 1870s colonized Asia and Africa by using military force to take control of local governments, by exploiting the local economies for the raw materials required by Europe's growing industry, and by imposing Western values to benefit the "backward" colonies. Most of Asia's rich and ancient cultures were either carved up into economic "spheres of influence" or colonized outright; virtually all of Africa was taken over by only six European nations; and Latin America was dominated by the United States.

Causes of Imperialism

1. The search for *markets* and for raw *materials*
    The rapidly industrializing and competing nations of Europe produced more manufactured goods than their own populations could consume and since favorable balance of trade was not possible for all, colonies promised potential markets. In the long run, since the non-Europeans lacked purchasing power, the promise of markets far outweighed the reality. Studies of foreign trade from 1870 to 1914 show that the best consumers of manufactured goods were other industrialized nations rather than undeveloped colonies. As the income level of Western workers rose, so did the profitablity of investing *surplus capital* into domestic ventures.

    Since many raw materials essential to the manufacturing process—from minerals to fibers—were native to the non-Western world, the Europeans were driven to acquiring the lands that produced these materials as a guarantee of a sufficient supply. They argued that unless their more advanced technologies and business methods were applied to the mining and processing of these materials, not enough would be supplied to the voracious factories of the West. Also, they claimed that they had to set up colonies in order to maintain the stability that would protect their investments.

2. Missionaries
    A burst of religious revivalism during the mid-19th century in Western Europe and the United States led to development of *worldwide missions* to convert the people of Asia and Africa to Christianity. On those rare occasions when missionaries were attacked or endangered by locals, the public sentiment in the home country was so powerful that governments often had to send military help that was the first step—sometimes a reluctant one, sometimes a pretext—in setting up a colonial administration.

3. Military and naval bases
    Once trade developed, the *home (or mother) country* felt compelled to establish a chain of naval bases to protect its overseas interests, and military outposts to stake its claim and to maintain order. This process tended to feed on itself since a *competition to acquire colonies* developed among the industrialized nations to maintain the international *balance of power* and for unvarnished *prestige*. This led to increased tensions when the "haves"—like the British Empire, which had acquired colonies for two or more centuries—clashed with the "have-nots"—like the Germans and Italians, whose late-blooming national unity gave them a slow start in the race.

4. Ideology
    The so-called "white man's burden" was a form of racist patronizing that preached that the "superior" Westerners had an obligation to bring their culture to "uncivilized" peoples in other parts of the world. *Social Darwinism,*

a half-baked philosophical application of Darwin's theory of natural selection, bolstered the idea that some races or peoples were more fit for survival than others and therefore designed by nature for rule.

Imperial adventures and adventurers appealed to the masses in the industrialized countries who felt part of some great crusade to improve people whose lot was even worse than theirs. Imperialism won votes; politicians coddled the voters.

Regions

Africa

Egypt, after winning autonomy within the Ottoman Empire in the mid-19th century, became a British protectorate in the 1880s. The British had invested in the *Suez Canal*, a vital link to India and Asia, and to maintain stability in the area, they helped Egypt take control of the Sudan and set up an *Anglo-Egyptian Administration* for both areas. Wealthy industrialists, such as Cecil Rhodes who planned to build a railroad that crossed the continent but did not build it and the DeBeers family, worked to take the natural resources from the north and south of the continent, but they did little to develop the people or any sustainable industry.

Algeria, *Tunisia*, and most of *Morocco* had fallen into French hands right before World War I. *Libya*, once part of the decrepit Ottoman Empire, was taken by the Italians.

Africa south of the Sahara was terra incognita until the 1870s, when Belgian, German, and French explorers began to lay claims. Belgium ruled the Congo in a brutal and exploitive fashion and became an example of cruel imperialism masters ruling with whips and threats. The Belgian Congo was almost thirty times the size of Belgium and was ruled solely by King Leopold until 1908, but then reports of abuses there led it to be controlled by the Belgian Administration, dominated by the Roman Catholic Church, until independence in 1960. The *Berlin Conference of 1885*, sponsored by Bismarck to prevent disputes among the imperialists, set up rules that diminished squabbles and encouraged the partition of the entire continent among the major European powers.

Asia

In 1857, the *Sepoy Mutiny*, of native troops against their Indian overlords and the *British East India Company* brought British administration to the *Indian subcontinent*. By the mid-1880s the British also took control of Burma, the Malay Peninsula, and North Borneo. Although the British did not interfere with the basic social structure of these colonies, they introduced educational reforms and technological advances, especially to India, that smoothed the way for eventual independence. Of all the colonial powers, the British proved to be most enlightened.

The Dutch expanded their hold over the *Dutch East Indies* (the islands of Indonesia); the French seized Indochina (Vietnam, Cambodia, Laos); the Germans occupied islands in the Pacific; the Russians set up a *sphere of influence* (an area under the economic and military control of one imperial power) in Persia (Iran).

China—with its teeming population, vast land area, and incredibly rich and ancient culture—was carved up into spheres of influence by the Western powers after the Opium Wars of the 1840s and 1850s. *Extraterritoriality* subjected Westerners to their home country's laws rather than China's; *leaseholds*, exclusive trading rights and limited governmental powers, were given to the Western nations; the Chinese were forced to cede outlying territories, such as Manchuria and Korea, to the Europeans. The *Open Door Policy*, sponsored by the United States in 1899 in order to open commerce to imperial latecomers like itself, urged the Europeans to allow free trade within China while respecting its territorial integrity. The *Boxer Rebellion*, a patriotic uprising by Chinese nationalists against Western encroachment, was put down by the imperial powers in 1900. Since the *Dowager Empress*, who had seized control of the government, had supported the Boxers, the *Manchu dynasty* fell into decline until it was overthrown in 1911. *Sun Yat-sen* set up a republic dedicated to modernizing China through *three principles: nationalism, democracy, livelihood.*

Japan was the only major Asian power to resist being swallowed up by the imperialists. In the mid-16th century, Portuguese traders had opened the insular Japanese to commerce and Christianity, both of which were suppressed by the *shogun*, medieval military ruler. U.S. warships, under the command of Commodore Perry, reopened the islands in 1853, and, unlike China and India, the Japanese modernized. The rule of the shogun was replaced by that of a powerful emperor, *Meiji*; feudalism was abolished; industry fostered; a central government installed; and education and the military reformed. Japan became so Westernized, while maintaining its basic social structure, that it jumped on the imperialist bandwagon by going to war with China in 1898 and winning Korea, then shocking the West by decisively defeating the Russians, in 1905, during the *Russo-Japanese War.*

The End of Colonialism

Traditional imperialist acquisitions ended before World War I when virtually the entire non-Western world was divided among the Western powers. *Colonialism*—the control of overseas colonies by imperialist powers—was shaken by World War I and collapsed in the decades following World War II.

Long-term causes for its fall were *Westernized educational systems* that preached the ideals of democracy and awakened nationalistic yearnings among the colonials; the concept of *self-determination* espoused by the Allies after World War I; the example and ideals of the *Russian Revolution* and the anti-imperialist *dogma of Communism*; the *decline of Europe* in the decades after World War II; the *example of Japan's resistance* to Western domination.

The British Empire

India, "crown jewel of the British Empire," attained independence in 1948. Decades of *nonviolent resistance*, led by *Mahatma Gandhi*, helped prepare the populace for self-rule, but bloody clashes between Hindu and Moslem factions marred the move to independence. The subcontinent was partitioned by the British into Hindu India and Moslem Pakistan. Britain's other colonies in Asia—Ceylon (Sri Lanka), Burma, Malaya—and its colonies in Africa attained independence in the two decades after World War II, and most joined the British *Commonwealth of Nations*, a loose political grouping that offered economic advantages.

When the former British mandate, Palestine, was created as a Jewish State by the United Nations in 1948, ancient rivalries between Westernized Jewish settlers and Moslem Arabs developed into a volatile and long-term conflict. Wars broke out in 1948, 1956, 1967, and 1973. Nationalization of the Suez Canal, a vital waterway to British trade, by charismatic Egyptian leader Gamal Abdel Nasser provoked war in 1956 between Egypt and allies Britain, France, and Israel. The area continues to be one of the world's most unstable.

The Dutch Empire

Early in World War II, the Japanese drove the Dutch out of the *Dutch East Indies* (originally called by the Europeans the *Spice Islands*, called *Indonesia* after independence). When the Dutch tried to resume control after the war, nationalists under the leadership of *Sukarno*—an eventual dictator until his overthrow in 1966—fought a bloody war of resistance and attained total independence in 1954.

The French Empire

After World War II, the French in Indochina (Vietnam, Cambodia, Laos) tried, like the Dutch in Indonesia, to take back the possessions that they had been driven from by the Japanese. After a costly seven-year guerrilla war, nationalists under Communist *Ho Chi Minh* (1890–1969) attained independence in 1954. The Geneva Accords recognized the independence of Vietnam, Laos, and Cambodia, and provisionally partitioned Vietnam into a northern and southern sector until nationwide elections would determine leadership. The agreement broke down into full-scale civil war between the Communist-led north and the pro-western south. By the mid-1960s the United States had sent massive military forces to aid the south. In North Africa, *Morocco* and *Tunisia* were granted independence by the French in 1956, but Algeria, considered by many French to be an integral part of France, was not. The bitter *French-Algerian War* led to independence and the mass exodus of French settlers in 1962. This war drained the French of resources and their belief in the ability of their forces to win any conflict in the developing world.

African Independence

In sub-Saharan Africa independence came suddenly from the late 1950s through the 1960s. The process was painful and costly in some places—such as the former Belgian Congo (Zaire)—and because the Europeans had ignored tribal loyalties when drawing up imperial boundaries, the newly independent states often lacked a unified heritage. The former British colonies were best prepared for self-rule, since the British had gradually transferred administration to locals.

Impact of Imperialism

The collapse of the European colonial empires was one of the modern world's most revolutionary and sudden developments. Within two decades after World War II, the European colonies, governing more than 25 percent of the earth's population, had disappeared. Most of the newly independent states, though, do not enjoy genuine freedom and democratic rule. While they often started out with democratic constitutions, poverty, ethnic conflicts, and inexperience in self-rule often led to military dictatorship or one-party rule. Freedom from foreign rule did not guarantee political freedom.

Although imperialism exploited and abused its colonial peoples, it provided them with the technological, industrial, and cultural achievements of the West and linked all the world's peoples.

Timeline of Imperialism

Year	Event
1839–1842, 1856–1860	During First and Second Opium Wars in China, the British gained the rights of extraterritoriality—to sell opium, to stay in China all year, and to trade without the co-Hong.
1854	Commodore Matthew Perry used "gunboat diplomacy" to open Japan up for trade with the Western world.
1854–1856	Crimean War—Russia lost to the Western nations and Turkey, ending its imperialist aims.
1857–1858	Sepoy Rebellion in India was led by Hindu and Muslim soldiers who believed that their ammunition was forcing them to eat pig and cow fat, contrary to their religions. Sepoys were the 200,000 Asian soldiers in the British Army.
1869	Suez Canal completed with French investment.
1871	Diamonds were discovered near Capetown, South Africa, in what will become the Kimberley diamond mines.
1871	Germany united into one nation.
1872	Henry Stanley meets Dr. David Livingstone in the African jungle.
1873	Three Emperors' League formed: Germany, Austria-Hungary, Russia.
1877	Queen Victoria crowned the "Empress of India."
1877–1878	During the Russo-Turkish War over Romania and Bulgaria, Russia thumped Turkey and gained warm water ports in Bulgaria and the Balkan Peninsula.
1879	British defeated by the Zulus at the Battle of Isandlwana.
1879	Dual Alliance between Austria-Hungary and Germany.

Year	Event
1881	Italy joined Dual Alliance forming the Triple Alliance.
1884–1885	Egypt declared a British Protectorate.
1885	**Berlin Conference** divided Africa among the European nations, but this division is on a map only. The nations did not hold the land they claimed at this point, and there are Africans there who believe that they rule themselves.
1888–1895	England and Germany created East, Central, and South African trading companies.
1896–1897	Sino-Japanese War in which Japan goes from being imperialized in 1854 to being an imperialist just 42 years later.
1898	**Battle of Omdurman** in which the British led by General Kitchener killed 10,000 Ansar warriors and injured 13,000 more while losing only 48 men.
1898	Ethiopia repelled an attempted Italian invasion.
1898	Fashoda Incident in which Kitchener goes south "up the Nile," defeated the Muslims, and met the French at *Fashoda*. The French backed down and recalled their general, Marchand. The crisis was averted.
1899	Rudyard Kipling wrote "The White Man's Burden" to encourage the United States to get into the empire business.
1899–1902	During the Spanish-American War, the Americans win independence for Cuba and control of Puerto Rico and the Philippines. Spain ends as a colonial power. The Filipinos revolted against the Americans resulting in a brutal suppression that killed between 500,000 and 1,000,000 natives.
1901	In the Boer War in South Africa, the British signed up in large numbers to fight for the right to "civilize" the people of Africa. This was a turning point in world opinion toward imperialism as the brutal tactics used to suppress the Africans were reported, and Europeans lost some of their zeal for imperialism.
1904–1905	Russo-Japanese War in which Japan defeated the Russian navy completely and demonstrated that an Asian nation could defeat a European one.
1911	Serbian *Black Hand* nationalist group formed. This group will assassinate Archduke Ferdinand in 1914.
1914	Panama Canal opened reducing the shipping mileage from Asia to Europe.
1916	**Mohandas K. Gandhi** returned to India from South Africa where he would fight tirelessly through *passive resistance* for Indian independence until the British realized that they could not rule India and left in 1948.

Sample Essay Question

The sample thematic essay and the practice essays in this chapter are types found on the AP exam and they require knowledge of causes, effects, personalities, ideas, and events.

SAMPLE QUESTION

Analyze the various motives for the "New Imperialism" and their relative importance.

Comments on the Sample Question

Follow the "Simple Procedures" for writing an essay. (See page 34.)

First, *What does the question want to know?* Why did the European world impose its economic, social, and political institutions on virtually the entire non-Western world from the last three decades of the 19th century to the beginning of World War I?

Second, *What do you know about it?* Was it the search for new markets or religious missionary fervor? Was it ethnocentrism or the need for military and naval bases? Was it to "keep up with the Joneses"? If it was all of these and more, which had the greatest pull and why?

Third, *How would you put it into words?* Remember that "to analyze" is "to examine in detail" and "to determine relationships."

Rubric for Sample Answer

Before you read the sample answer, examine the rubric. What will the reader be looking for when he or she grades this essay? A sample rubric, shaded to show the reader's evaluation, is seen below:

9–8 POINTS

✔ Thesis explicitly identifies the various motives for the "New Imperialism" and examines the analysis of those motives through a lens of relative importance. Thesis does not need to be in the opening paragraph.

✔ Organization is clear, consistently followed, and effective in support of the argument.
- May devote individual paragraphs to each motive for the New Imperialism or may devote each paragraph to how a different nation pursued the New Imperialism and the relative importance of the motives for that nation.
- Must identify specific motives for the New Imperialism (prestige, raw materials, markets, religion, profit, military outposts), and assess the relative importance of these motives.

✔ Essay is well balanced; the motives and their relative importance are analyzed at some length. Essay covers the New Imperialism throughout Europe.

✔ Major assertions in the essay are supported thoroughly and consistently by relevant evidence.

✔ Evidence supporting the motives and their relative importance may prove more specific or concrete.

✔ May contain errors that do not detract from the argument.

7–6 POINTS

✔ Thesis explicitly identifies the various motives for the "New Imperialism" and analyzes the relative importance of those motives, but may not be developed fully.

✔ Organization is clear and effective in support of the argument but may introduce evidence that is not pertinent to the task.

✔ Essay covers all major topics suggested by the prompt but may analyze an aspect of the New Imperialism or the analysis of their relative importance in greater depth rather than in a balanced manner.

✔ Major assertions in the essay are supported by relevant evidence.

✔ May contain an error that detracts from the argument.

5–4 POINTS

✔ Thesis identifies the various motives for the "New Imperialism" and examines the relative importance of those motives, but without any development; thesis may address only part of the question effectively; thesis may be a simple, single-sentence statement.

✔ Organization is clear but may not be consistently followed; essay may veer off task chronologically or thematically or both.

✔ Essay may not complete all tasks:
  • May discuss only one or two aspects of the New Imperialism.
  • May discuss only one or two nations.
  • May focus only on one motive without considering others' importance as well.
  • May be primarily descriptive rather than analytical.

✔ Essay offers some relevant evidence.

✔ May contain errors that detract from the argument.

3–2 POINTS

✔ Thesis may simply paraphrase the prompt OR examine motives for the "New Imperialism" without analyzing the motives for it or their relative importance.

✔ Organization is unclear and ineffective; essay may focus on the personal attributes of imperialist governments or rulers rather than analyzing the relative importance of the motives for the New Imperialism.

✔ Essay shows serious imbalance; discussion of the motives for the New Imperialism is superficial; much of the information may be significantly out of the time period or geography of the question.

✔ Offers minimal OR confused evidence.

✔ May contain several errors that detract from the argument.

1–0 POINTS

✔ Thesis is erroneous OR irrelevant OR absent.

✔ No effective organization is evident.

✔ Discussion of the various motives for the "New Imperialism" and analysis of the relative importance of those motives is generic.

✔ Provides little or no relevant supporting evidence.

✔ May contain numerous errors that detract from the argument.

Sample Answer

From 1870 to 1914, European nations used their superior military technology to colonize Africa, Asia, and the islands of the Pacific. The New Imperialism differed from the Old Imperialism, which was basically a trade relationship between the Europeans and local rulers, in that it took over the native governments, created often artificial markets for manufactured goods, exploited natural resources, converted the native peoples to Christianity, and measured the behavior of the locals by Western moral and social standards. Even great democracies like Britain and France denied native peoples the rights and representation of constitutional government. Why did the Europeans launch this New Imperialism?

The motives were diverse; some were more powerful than others; they often fed on each other.

It is often said that economics was the driving force. Industrialization demanded a limitless supply of raw materials for the factories and an ever-increasing market for the products. Tin, rubber, petroleum, and other natural resources abundant outside of Europe fueled the voracious appetite of industry. Billions of people, hungering for the manufactured goods of the West, promised profits. According to the "surplus capital" theory, the industrialists needed new investments outside of Europe—in mines and plantations—because there were few good ones in overdeveloped Europe.

Missionaries soon followed the traders and other profit seekers. A revival of evangelical Christianity in the latter half of the 19th century created the zeal to convert "the heathens." When missionaries got in trouble with the locals, who sometimes resorted to violence to protect their native customs or religions, the army was often sent in to protect the missionaries.

Military units required an expanded navy to get them to far-off lands; navies necessitated bases; bases had to be secured through treaties with local rulers or by takeovers of territory. Once one nation had bases in a region, other European rivals felt it was "in the interests of national security" to establish their own. The scramble became a competition between nations, and prestige was often measured in the size, riches, and numbers of colonies. The masses in the "mother countries" reveled in the contrived dramas of "heroic conquests" of "ignorant savages," the Christianization of "godless" natives, and the supremacy of Western culture. The so-called white man's burden became a rationalization for what was already being done.

The motives for the New Imperialism varied, but they were tied to one another. The push for profits started a chain of causation that led to the Europeans dividing the non-Western world among themselves.

EVALUATE THE SAMPLE ANSWER

Now go back and look at the rubric. It is clear that this essay looks like a 4 or 5 on the rubric. The essay has a weak thesis that may be relatively tangential. The subject of "New Imperialism" is poorly explained and the various motives for it are poorly examined. In this case, the details warrant a 5.

RATER'S COMMENTS ON THE SAMPLE ANSWER

5—Qualified

This is a well-organized examination of the various motives for the New Imperialism. It analyzes the importance and the relationships of each. The essay's structure is based upon a judgment that economic motives were primary and that every other motive followed the profit motive. This is a commonsensical, if somewhat conventional, analysis.

While the essay stresses the importance of seeking new markets and better investments for "surplus capital," it omits the very convincing critique of this view. In the first place, the non-Europeans simply lacked the purchasing power to buy most of the manufactured goods that the Europeans produced. In the second place, most of the surplus capital of Western Europe was actually invested in other industrialized countries: British capitalists invested heavily in North America, French capitalists in the development of Russia, and German capitalists in the Ottoman Empire.

The elegant logical clarity of the essay's structure is also one of its shortcomings. It oversimplifies the process, and there is little reference to actual instances of the operation of the New Imperialism. Was profit-seeking always the prime motive? Did missionary activity sometimes precede commercial ventures, as in equatorial Africa? If this is the exception that proves the rule, specific factual support should be given: the British policies in India, the Dutch ventures in the East Indies, the French in Indochina. Strategic considerations often came before missionary activity as when: Pacific island bases were set up to protect shipping lanes. Military intervention was used to secure a vital region, as when the British took over Egypt to protect the Suez Canal.

Practice Essay Questions

The questions that follow are samples of the various types of thematic essays that appear on the AP exam. (See pages 21–22 for a detailed explanation of each type.) Check over the **generic rubric** (see pages 58–60) before you begin any of these essays and use that rubric to score your essay if you write one.

QUESTION 1

Contrast and compare the Old Imperialism with the New Imperialism.

COMMENTS ON QUESTION 1

Sometimes called colonialism, the Old Imperialism follows the Age of Exploration of the mid-15th to the early 17th century. It was characterized by commercial ventures, coastal enclaves for the seagoing trade, and trade with the local peoples. There was little attempt, except in the New World, to encourage immigration to the colonies; there was very little attempt to impose the European social, political, or economic structures on the local population.

In contrast, the New Imperialism of the late-19th century took over the governing of its colonies; it exploited native labor and natural resources; it judged local behavior according to European mores; and it forced religious conversion.

The two forms of imperialism were similar in that the Europeans rarely attempted to absorb the culture of their colonies, nor did they encourage immigration to the mother country.

QUESTION 2

"By the end of the 19th century, European nations had divided the rest of the world among themselves." *Assess the validity* of this statement.

COMMENTS ON QUESTION 2

To "determine the truth" of this statement, consider the various regions that were targets of imperialism in the 19th century. The scramble for Africa left only two nations independent: Liberia and Ethiopia. In Asia, China was divided into spheres of influence that left a disintegrating monarchy, but one that was Chinese. Japan maintained its independence and when it was forced to open up to Western trade, Japan rapidly industrialized and was able to defeat Russia 50 years later, providing the only exception. In the Western Hemisphere, the United States regarded Latin America as its sphere of influence.

QUESTION 3

Contrast and compare the responses of China and Japan to Western encroachment.

COMMENTS ON QUESTION 3

The contrast was glaring because China resisted Westernization and was carved up into spheres of influence while Japan modernized and kept its autonomy. Why and how? Detail the Chinese response to Western militarism from the Opium War to the Boxer Rebellion to the establishment of Sun Yat Sen's republic. Trace the Japanese response from the "opening" by Commodore Perry to the Russo-Japanese War.

The comparison of similarities can be made in that both nations managed to hold onto their rich and ancient cultures, one by a stubborn adherence to tradition, the other by blending the best of the West with its own unique ways.

QUESTION 4

Evaluate the New Imperialism.

COMMENTS ON QUESTION 4

Imperialism was rampant with injustice: exploitation of people, natural resources, markets; ethnocentrism; religious and cultural intolerance; poverty and repression during and after the period of rule; two world wars caused in part by the competition for colonies.

Imperialism did introduce the non-Western world to the educational, political, economic, and social institutions of the West, many of which have been adopted by emerging nations.

This question has a broad scope, but it can be answered effectively by picking out particular peoples or regions and detailing some of their experiences under and after imperialism.

QUESTION 5

Explain why the colonial empires of Britain and France ended after World War II.

COMMENTS ON QUESTION 5

To "offer the reasons for" the disintegration of these great empires, consider the exhaustion of Europe after the devastation of the war; the promise of self-rule, India, for example; the humiliation of the "white peoples" at the hands of the Japanese in the early days of the war; the theories of self-determination and nationalistic aspirations aroused by World War I; the ideals of the Russian Revolution; the anti-imperialist dogma of Communism; the example of democratic institutions offered by many of the imperialist nations; the awakenings provided by a Western-style education.

Again, this is a question whose broad scope could be managed with specific examples of newly independent nations.

Practice Multiple-Choice Questions

(These questions are representative of the types found on the AP exam.)

1. Imperialism of the 1870 to 1914 period can best be described as

   (A) overseas mercantilism
   (B) development of a profitable trade with non-Western regions
   (C) establishment of coastal trading posts in the non-European world
   (D) the imposition by Europeans of their social, economic, and political systems upon non-Europeans
   (E) the establishment of European democratic government in the non-European world

2. The principle by which the European powers established their claim to a territory prior to the Berlin Conference was

   (A) extraterritoriality
   (B) effective occupation
   (C) proscribed negotiation
   (D) enforced subjugation
   (E) formal annexation

3. All of the following European nations were major imperial powers from 1870 to 1914 EXCEPT

   (A) France
   (B) Britain
   (C) Germany
   (D) Belgium
   (E) Austria

4. All of these could be considered major causes of imperialism EXCEPT

   (A) the search for new markets for industrial products
   (B) the acquisition of raw materials
   (C) missionary activities
   (D) the desire to absorb the culture of non-Europeans
   (E) the race for colonies

5. The Berlin Conference of 1885, sponsored by Germany's Bismarck,

   (A) determined the "rules" for the partition of Africa
   (B) set up spheres of influence in China
   (C) divided Ottoman possessions in the Middle East among six European powers
   (D) Recognized the United States' dominance in Latin America
   (E) internationalized the former Belgian Congo

THE SEPOY REBELLION, 1857–58: contemporary illustration by an anonymous native artist. The Granger Collection, New York. (0031197)

6. The picture above is of a rebellion against the British in 1857 by which of the following areas in which the British had gained dominance?

   (A) Egypt
   (B) China
   (C) India
   (D) Lebanon
   (E) Ceylon

7. Anti-imperialist leaders in Africa and Asia

   (A) typically rejected all aspects of Western culture
   (B) used Western ideologies to shape their movements
   (C) were usually of lower-class origins
   (D) rejected violence as a tool for independence
   (E) never used Marxist ideas to support their actions

8. British colonial administration of India from 1857 to 1948 was comparatively enlightened because

   (A) they supported the landlords
   (B) they completely ended the caste system
   (C) they left the entire subcontinent under local control
   (D) Indians were encouraged to serve in the colonial government
   (E) British colonial administrators adopted local customs and language

9. Which of the following avoided European colonialization and became a colonial power?

   (A) China
   (B) Japan
   (C) Persia (Iran)
   (D) Siam (Thailand)
   (E) Ethiopia

10. All of the following are valid generalizations about European imperialism in China EXCEPT

   (A) China was not directly colonized
   (B) China lost its outlying territories
   (C) Europeans residing in China were not subject to Chinese law
   (D) after the failure of a nationalist uprising, China was forced to pay indemnities to the imperialists
   (E) China was partitioned by both Europeans and Japan

11. Rudyard Kipling's stirring poems for the English to take up "the white man's burden" are compatible with which of the following?

   (A) Social Darwinism
   (B) The obligation of the West to enlighten the "benighted races" of the non-Western world
   (C) The urgings of Jules Ferry in France and Josiah Strong in the United States to "spread the culture"
   (D) None of these
   (E) All of these

12. By 1913, world trade had

   (A) increased by 25 percent over the 1800 level
   (B) almost tripled the level of 1800
   (C) more than doubled the level of 1800
   (D) grown to 25 times the level of 1800
   (E) increased to 50 times the level of 1800

13. All of these helped bring about the collapse of colonialism EXCEPT

   (A) Western-style education in the colonies
   (B) Japanese successes in World War II
   (C) the principle of self-determination first espoused at the peace conferences that ended World War II
   (D) the exhaustion of Europe after World War II
   (E) the idealism of the Russian Revolution

14. On the whole, the colonies of which European nation made the smoothest transition to independence?

    (A) the Netherlands
    (B) Britain
    (C) France
    (D) Portugal
    (E) Belgium

15. Europe's world hegemony lasted roughly

    (A) from 1870 to 1914
    (B) from 1900 to 1914
    (C) from 1870 to 1945
    (D) from 1900 to 1945
    (E) from 1870 to 1900

Answers and Answer Explanations

1.	D	6.	C	11.	E
2.	B	7.	B	12.	D
3.	E	8.	D	13.	C
4.	D	9.	B	14.	B
5.	A	10.	E	15.	C

1. **(D)** The other descriptions apply more aptly to the Old Imperialism, from the 16th to 18th centuries.

2. **(B)** The main justification for territorial claims before the Berlin Conference of 1885 was when a European power occupied the territory in a meaningful way.

3. **(E)** Austria was neither a great seapower nor, with its nationalities problem, was it interested in overseas expansion.

4. **(D)** The ethnocentrism of the Europeans ruled this out.

5. **(A)** It began the scramble for Africa by setting up guidelines acceptable to everybody but the Africans.

6. **(C)** The Sepoy Rebellion was in India, where the Sepoy soldiers revolted against the British.

7. **(B)** The anti-imperialist forces in Africa and Asia seemed to use Western ideas as the core of their ideology, which underscores the hypocrisy of imperialism after the era of the Enlightenment.

8. **(D)** Their support of the landlords against the peasants, their dismissal of the ancient and rich Indian native culture, and their failure to abolish the caste system were less than enlightened; they did not leave the entire subcontinent but only part of it to local control.

9. **(B)** Japan managed to industrialize and modernize its institutions in about fifty years by borrowing the best from the Europeans and maintaining the best of their own traditions.

10. **(E)** It was never partitioned but rather divided into spheres of influence, in which a given imperialist nation monopolized trade, set up military bases, and influenced local government.

11. **(E)** The "fittest" should rule the planet, claimed Social Darwinists; the Europeans were the most enlightened and owed the "darker races" education and religion; Jules Ferry and Josiah Ferry were imperialist birds of a feather.

12. **(D)** The value of world trade multiplied by 2,500 percent from $1.22 billion in 1800 to $38 billion in 1913.

13. **(C)** The principle of self-determination was espoused after World War I.

14. **(B)** The British prepared the subject peoples with education and a degree of self-government; it fit their constitutional nature.

15. **(C)** It began roughly around the time of German unification; it ended not long after World War II.

CHAPTER 10

World War I (1914–1918)

Key Terms/People

- Dual Alliance
- Algeciras Conference
- Militarism
- Balkan Crisis
- pan-Slavism
- Balkan Wars
- Imperialism
- Moroccan Crisis
- Schlieffen Plan
- Galliope Campaign
- *Lusitania*
- The Fourteen Points
- Treaty of Versailles
- Command economy
- Walter Rathenau

Overview

The beginning of the First World War marks the height of European power on this planet; its ending marks the beginning of the decline. Great empires fell: the Russian, Austro-Hungarian, German, and Ottoman. Others declined in power and influence: Britain and France, which had reached the zenith of imperialist expansion by 1914, saw their economies in shambles by 1918. A generation of young European men was decimated in the trenches of France, on the plains of Eastern Europe, and on global battlefronts.

It was the first "total war," involving mass civilian populations in a war effort that required rationing, employed both sexes in war plants, and pumped up popular fervor with distorted propaganda.

Narrow nationalism flourished with the fall of the old ethnically diverse empires when dominant ethnic groups formed the basis for smaller nation-states such as Yugoslavia, Czechoslovakia, Austria, and Hungary. The triumph of Communism in Russia was a direct result of the war; fascism in Italy and Nazism in Germany indirect results. The drain of Europe's resources made the United States the world's leading creditor and greatest producer, and the unresolved issues of the vindictive and haphazard peace process led inevitably to World War II.

Long-term Causes of World War I

There were *four* MAIN causes of WWI: *alliances, militarism, nationalism,* and *imperialism.* These four forces converged at a time and place that could only result in war and revolution across Europe.

Militarism

Militarism also emerged as a powerful force at the beginning of the twentieth century. An arms race emerged between Great Britain and Germany, with Germany constructing a navy with desires to rival the British navy. A massive build-up of arms and weapons, including artillery shells, bombs, rifles, and artillery, caused international pressures in Europe to worsen.

Alliances

Alliances had held Europe in a balance of power from the time of Charlemagne through Machiavelli and onward, but the alliance system in place during this period is referred to by historians as the Bismarckian Alliance System. In this system no one declared war because they knew the alliances would make war too costly. The Three Emperors League of 1873 failed when Russia and the Ottomans battled over the Balkans, and Russia was too near to Austria for their liking. Bismarck alienated Russia at the Congress of Vienna (Austria got Bosnia-Herzegovina), but he wanted peace and unity in Eastern Europe. He then created the *Dual Alliance* between Germany and Austria-Hungary, which would last from 1879–1918. He pressed Russia and Austria into the Alliance of the Three Emperors in 1881, a mutual defense pact against the Ottomans in the Balkans and France in the west. The Russians refused to renew in 1887. In the Triple Alliance (1882–1915) Bismarck tried to balance the power in his favor at the Congress of Berlin, and in so doing, arranged an alliance between Italy, Austria, and Germany. They, along with Bulgaria, would be known as the *Central Powers* in WWI. Italy switched sides in 1915. When Russia exited the Three Emperors League in 1887, Germany, in an attempt to keep peace with Russia, arranged the Russian German Reinsurance Treaty in which both promised neutrality if the other was attacked. William II did not like this friendly attitude toward Russia and dismissed Bismarck as a result of it and refused to renew the policy. France and Russia then became allies.

In 1902, the three biggest industrial powers were forming a cozy alliance. England and Japan were firmly committed in the Anglo-Japanese Alliance (1902–1915), and the United States was its usual noncommittal self, but following loyally at England's side. Anglo-French Entente seemed like a good idea to both sides by 1904. Britain was the only great power (Splendid Isolation) that had remained uncommitted to any other country during this time. After the *Boer War,* the other countries began to feel threatened by British expansion and planned to create an alliance between Austria, France, Germany, and Russia against Britain. Britain tried to resolve this problem and remain on good terms with the other countries. France's Prime Minister Theophile Déclassé also wanted better relations with Britain and arranged the Anglo-French Entente to settle any outstanding disputes between Britain and France and also gave support to Britain if the other countries decided to form an alliance against it. At the *Algeciras Conference* in 1906, the Germans tried to persuade France to turn against Britain. This brought Britain and France closer together and the conference resulted in hostile attention from Britain, France, Russia, and the United States toward Germany. This was Wilhelm II getting a wake-up call that he ignored. In 1907, the Russians, who had had their navies destroyed by the Japanese recently, asked the British to join an alliance and the Anglo-Russo Alliance began. The *Triple Entente* would finally emerge between Russia, England, and France in 1914. They, along with the United States, would be known as the *Allied powers* during WWI.

Imperialism

Imperialism was also a major factor. Each European country's population pressure, desire for wealth, and pride urged it to gain overseas possessions regardless of their population's desires. Imperialism was also vital to a capitalist economy to expand. **Some examples of how Imperialism increased international tensions follow.** The *Berlin Conference* in 1885 marked Germany's late coming into imperialism, which led Bismarck to establish rules for carving up Africa. The *Kruger Telegram* in 1902 roused British ire at Germany for congratulating the Boers on their victories over British troops in South Africa. The *Moroccan Crisis* of 1911 saw a German gunboat sent to Morocco to protest French occupation of the city of Fez. Britain supported France again, and Germany backed down for minor concessions in equatorial Africa.

Nationalism

Nationalism caused leaders and countries to do strange things for national pride. Wilhelm II of Germany was building up his navy to attempt to rival the English navy. This forced England to build its navy rather than focus on David Lloyd George's People's Budget. German nationalism was looking for another great military victory to bring glory and colonies to Germany. Nationalism was tearing the dual monarchy of Austria-Hungary apart. A good example of this is the Balkan Wars. In the *First Balkan Crisis* (1874–1878), Bosnia and Herzegovina rebelled against Ottoman rule, leading to Serbia declaring war on the Ottoman Empire in June 1876. Russia, based on the foreign policy of *pan-Slavism*, or "protector of the Balkans," declared war on the Ottoman Empire as well. Britain, interested in protecting its Mediterranean holdings that depended upon the Balkan states, supported the Turkish sultan, Hamid II. In 1878, Turkey sought peace. Greece and Bulgaria took Macedonia. This led to the *Second Balkan Crisis* (1885), a conflict between Bulgaria and Serbia over territory. Russia warned it was ready to occupy Bulgaria if it did not yield to Serbian demands. Austria-Hungary supported Bulgaria, and Germany supported Austria-Hungary. This nationalist pressure ended the Alliance of the Three Emperors.

In the *Third Balkan Crisis* (1912–1913), Italy was in conflict with the Ottoman Empire over holdings along the Adriatic Sea. In the *First Balkan War*, Serbia took Macedonia in 1912. In the *Second Balkan War* (1913), Serbia attacked Bulgaria in hopes of gaining a seaport. Russia, sympathetic to the notion of pan-Slavism, supported Serbia, while Austria-Hungary still supported Bulgaria. Britain and Germany urged peace. Serbs were enraged at Austria-Hungary for its support of Bulgaria and its continued occupation of Bosnia-Herzegovina. In the end, nationalism directly led to the **Third Balkan War**, also known as WWI.

Events Leading to the Outbreak of World War I

June 28, 1914: Archduke Francis Ferdinand, heir to the Austrian throne, was assassinated along with his wife in Sarajevo, capital of the Austrian province of Bosnia. When evidence was uncovered that high Serbian officials had plotted the murder, Austria sought German support to crush Serbia. Kaiser Wilhelm issued the infamous *blank check*, promising backing for any action Austria might take. Serbia turned to "big brother" Slav Russia, which in turn got a guarantee of French support against Germany and Austria in a similar *blank check*.

July 23, 1914: Austria presented an ultimatum to Serbia that would make Serbia a virtual protectorate of Austria.

July 28, 1914: Austria declared war on Serbia after pronouncing the Serbian response inadequate. Russia mobilized.

August 1, 1914: Germany declared war on Russia.

August 3, 1914: France declared war on Germany.

August 4, 1914: Britain declared war on Germany after German forces violated Belgium's neutrality in their attempt to invade France.

The First World War had begun.

The War

The Sides

The Allies: Britain, France, and Russia (1914) (formerly the Triple Entente)
            Italy (1915)
            United States (1917)
            Russia out (1918)

The Central Powers: Germany, Austria-Hungary (formerly the Triple Alliance) with Italy, Turkey, and Bulgaria

The Western Front

August–September 1914: The *Schlieffen Plan* failed. Since a *war of attrition* (wearing down of the resources and morale of the enemy) was to Germany's disadvantage because of the superior land mass, resources, and population of its enemies, Germany aimed for a quick victory.

THE STRATEGY OF THE SCHLIEFFEN PLAN

1. Defeat France in six weeks as in the Franco-Prussian War.
2. Hold off Russia, which the high command assumed would take six months to fully mobilize.
3. Invade France through neutral Belgium, by being granted access, in order to outflank the French armies and seize Paris.

WHY THE SCHLIEFFEN PLAN FAILED

1. The Belgians protested and put up unexpectedly stiff resistance.
2. The Russians mobilized with great speed, drawing German reserves to the Eastern Front to bolster the Austrians.
3. The French counterattacked heroically at the Battle of the Marne River (September 5, 1914) to stop the German drive to Paris.

THE WESTERN FRONT STALEMATED INTO TRENCH WARFARE

1. The trench lines extended from the North Sea to Switzerland in the south.
2. The bloody, costly fighting, after the Battle of the Marne, caused no significant breakthrough for either side.
3. Technological developments in weaponry—machine guns, poison gas, massed artillery, tanks, strafing, and bombing aircraft—were far in advance of the pitifully archaic tactics. The result was the slaughter of a generation of young Western Europeans in the trenches of France and Flanders (region of Northern France, Belgium, and the Netherlands).

The Eastern Front Remained a Mobile War

1914: German forces, under *Paul von Hindenburg* (1847–1934) (later a president of the postwar Weimar Republic) and Erich Ludendorff won important victories over the Russians; the Russians pushed the Austrians out of Galacia (Western Poland).

1915: Combined German-Austrian forces pushed the Russians out of Poland and inflicted awesome casualties. Bulgaria entered the war on Germany's side (Germany and its Allies become known as the Central Powers), and the Germans overan the Balkans. The British launched the *Gallipoli Campaign* to knock Turkey, which had joined the Central Powers, out of the war by landing at the Dardanelles, a vital control point for access between the Aegean and Black Seas.

1916: The Germans pushed deep into Russian territory. The tsar went to the front to take personal command of the troops in a battle where Russia was being outfought and outproduced. The Russians were still using single-shot rifles that had to be reloaded each shot while the Germans used machine guns. Millions of Russians were slaughtered or starved in this war. The tsar was no help, and he was now personally responsible for the ongoing defeat of his army by the Germans, who continued to advance. The people of Russia wanted peace and food. The Gallipoli Campaign failed, and its planner, Winston Churchill (1874–1965), future British prime minister, resigned his post as first lord of the admiralty.

1917: The Russian tsar abdicated in March; the provincial government under Alexander Kerensky (1881–1970) continued the war. The Bolsheviks seized power in November and eventually pulled Russia out of the war. The Russian withdrawal from the war was exactly what the allied powers did not want. This left Germany with only one front on which to fight a war, and the United States had joined the allied side just before Russia pulled out of the war, somewhat balancing the loss of Russia as an ally. If Russia had stayed in the war, the Central Powers could have been defeated faster.

Waging the War

World War I was the 20th century's first *total war*, whereby the entire civilian populations of the belligerent nations were mobilized for winning the war. Propaganda lionized the men at the front and dehumanized the enemy. News was censored. Economic production was focused on the war effort: Women replaced factory workers in uniform; rationing of food and scarce commodities was instituted; people financed the war by buying bonds. Each side aimed at "starving out" the enemy by cutting off vital supplies to the civilian population.

Naval Blockades

1. Britain used its superior fleet and sea mines to cut the Central Powers off from overseas trade.
2. Germany employed *unrestricted submarine warfare* to prevent the British from getting vital materials from their colonies. The sinking of the passenger ship *Lusitania* in May 1915 helped turn American public opinion against Germany. (Note: There is strong evidence to suggest that the *Lusitania* was carrying contraband munitions, as the Germans claimed.)

Diplomacy

1915—Neutral Italy entered the war against the Central Powers (its former Allies) with the promise of *Italia Irredenta* (unredeemed Italy) and some German colonies and Turkish territories.

1917—The infamous *Zimmerman Note* promised Mexico some of its former American holdings if it entered the war on Germany's side against the United States.

Arabs and Jews in Palestine were promised autonomy if they joined the Allies.

Eastern Europeans were promised ethnic control in return for support of the Allies.

The War Ends

Although the United States had only a small standing army, it was able to field nine divisions in France by the summer of 1918, in time to help halt the last major offensive of the exhausted German Army.

By the fall of 1918, Bulgaria and Turkey had sued for peace, Austria-Hungary had collapsed, and Germany was wracked with revolution. The kaiser abdicated, fled to neutral Holland, and a provisional German government requested negotiations on the basis of President Wilson's Fourteen Points peace plan.

On the eleventh hour of the eleventh day of the eleventh month of 1918, an *armistice* ended World War I.

(NOTE: More people died in the influenza epidemic that followed the war than died in the war itself—10 million died in combat, nearly 20 million from the disease.)

The Peace Settlements

The Fourteen Points (Wilson's peace plan that was never implemented because of the secret treaties and diplomatic maneuvering that had taken place among the Allies before the entrance of the United States in the war.)

1. End to secret treaties
2. Freedom of the seas
3. Free trade
4. Arms reduction
5. Just settlement of colonial claims
6–13. Evacuation of occupied territories *and* national self-determination
14. Establishment of a League of Nations: an international political organization to settle disputes

(NOTE: Ironically, even though it was Wilson's creation, the United States never joined the league. It was largely ineffectual, for this and other reasons, in dealing with the aggressive dictatorships of the 1930s).

The Paris Peace Conference, January 1919

The Big Four—Wilson of the United States, David Lloyd George (1863–1945) of Britain, Georges Clemenceau (1841–1929) of France, and Vittorio Orlando (1860–1952) of Italy—made all the decisions. The Central Powers were excluded; the Fourteen Points were compromised; nationality lines in Central and Eastern Europe were blurred.

The *Treaty of Versailles* ended the war with Germany but never settled the explosive issues that had led to war in the first place. Many of its provisions provided grist for Nazi propaganda mills in the 1920s and 1930s.

PROVISIONS OF THE TREATY OF VERSAILLES

1. Certain German territories were ceded to the Allies (such as Alsace to France, Schleswig to Denmark, West Prussia to Poland, control of mineral-rich Saar to France), and German overseas colonies were distributed to the Allies.
2. Germany was blamed for starting the war in the infamous "war guilt" clause.
3. The German army and navy were severely cut back to 100,000 soldiers.

4. The Rhineland (the vital strip between France and Germany) was to be demilitarized and occupied.
5. Germany had to pay *indemnities* for the civilian damage done in the war totaling $33 billion.

The Causes, Events, and Results of World War I

Causes of World War I

- The Treaty of Versailles placed blame upon Germany for the war. Germany was forced to pay huge reparations to the allied nations as a result.
- Events leading to the war include the Balkan Wars, the assassination of Archduke Franz Ferdinand and his wife, and increased bickering over colonial holdings such as the Fashoda incident and the Boer War.
- *Sidney Bradshaw Fay* and *Henry Elmer Barnes* stated that World War I was inevitable and blame rested on all the nations equally. They blamed Austria-Hungary and Serbian nationalism (Gavrillo Princip's assassination of Archduke Franz Ferdinand and his wife) as short-term causes. They saw the long-term causes as militarism (arms race and economic rivalry), the alliance system, imperialism and nationalism (*MAIN*). This view was accepted and led to the Treaty of Versailles not being enforced on Germany, which may have helped lead to World War II.
- German historian *Franz Fischer* refuted the now classic view using German secret documents as evidence in 1961. "Germany willed and coveted the Austro-Serbian war," Fischer said. Germany was worried about Russia, Germany's growing ambitions for colonies and more territory in Europe, and its attempt to distract the socialist menace at home all led to World War I.

Events of World War I

- The Germans quickly got close to Paris, but the *Battle of the Marne* stopped them before they took the capital.
- Both sides built miles of parallel trenches, leading to a stalemate in which battle after battle saw each side attempt to break through the enemies' lines.
- At the *Battle of Verdun*, the Germans again tried to break through, leading to over 700,000 deaths.
- The *Battle of the Somme* was the allied counterattack costing over 1,300,000 lives for no clear gains.
- The Eastern Front followed a similar pattern of stalemate in which nothing happened except loss of life.
- This also led to the Russian Revolution.
- In the only major naval battle, the *Battle of Jutland*, the Germans failed to break out of the British naval blockade and resorted to submarine warfare, which drew in the United States.
- American involvement decided the fate of the war due to the productive capacity of the United States, which escaped warfare at home.

Results of the War

- The war cost over $300 billion.
- The Russian, German, Austrian, and Ottoman Empires ended.
- The war strained the resources of each country as they experimented with command economies.
- National unity was reinforced for a time, but it also caused great hardship due to lack of supplies, disruption, and dislocation.
- The war contributed greatly to the increased involvement of the government in society, leading to increased propaganda, as well as to women's liberation.
- Many social customs faded out, and society became more open (at least for a time).
- There was also a rapid development of new technology.
- The economy was greatly hurt by the war, as world trade had been totally disrupted, changed to a wartime economy, and then had to transition back.
- The Russian Revolution put the world's first communist country on the map.
- A patchwork of weak, ethnically mixed states was created for political conveniences in Eastern Europe.
- Over 25 million people died as a result of the war and another 21 million soldiers were wounded, leaving a generation decimated.

World War II broke out in Europe twenty years after the signing of the Treaty of Versailles.

Sample Essay Question

The sample thematic essay question and the practice essays presented in this chapter are types found on the AP exam, and they require knowledge of causes, effects, personalities, ideas, and events.

SAMPLE QUESTION

Analyze the long-term causes of World War I.

Comments on the Sample Question

Follow the "Simple Procedures" for writing an essay. (See page 34.)

First, *What does the question want to know?* "Examine in detail," "determine relationships," and "explain" what brought about World War I. Be sure to consider the difference between a long-term cause and an immediate cause. Be sure to measure the degrees of importance of the various causes, to determine how they were related, and to explain how they are all tied together.

Second, *What do you know about it?* What was the arms race, and did it affect all the nations that eventually went to war? What was the rivalry behind the arms race? How did nationalism increase tensions and ambitions? What instabilities were caused by Pan-Slavism, by Pan-Germanism, by Italian ambition for *Italia Irredenta*? What role did imperialism play? How did the rival alliances form, and how did they set the stage for war?

Third, *How would you put it into words?* With an essay like this, that demands analysis and detailed explanation, you should organize your answer logically: rival alliances, arms race, imperialism, nationalism. Relate them and offer specifics. You are writing a short history here. There's lots to tell, and coherence can be overwhelmed by detail. Don't lose the forest for the trees!

Rubric for Sample Answer

Before you read the sample answer, examine the rubric. What will the reader be looking for when he or she grades this essay? A sample rubric, shaded to show the reader's evaluation, is seen below:

9–8 POINTS

✔ Thesis explicitly identifies the long-term causes of WWI **and** analyzes them. Thesis does not need to be in the opening paragraph.

✔ Organization is clear, consistently followed, and effective in support of the argument.
  • May devote individual paragraphs to each of the long-term causes of the war.
  • Must identify specific long-term causes of WWI (militarism, alliances, imperialism, and nationalism) and consider how each of them caused the war; does not have to present analysis by nation of long-term causes.

✔ Essay is well balanced; the long-term causes of WWI are analyzed at some length. Essay covers from the prelude to the war, 1871, through 1917.

✔ Major assertions in the essay are supported thoroughly and consistently by relevant evidence.

✔ Evidence of long-term causes of WWI may prove more specific or concrete.

✔ May contain errors that do not detract from the argument.

7–6 POINTS

✔ Thesis explicitly identifies the long-term causes of WWI and analyzes them, but may not be developed fully.

✔ Organization is clear and effective in support of the argument but may introduce evidence that is not pertinent to the task.

✔ Essay covers all major topics suggested by the prompt but may analyze a specific cause of WWI in greater depth rather than in a balanced manner.

✔ Major assertions in the essay are supported by relevant evidence.

✔ May contain an error that detracts from the argument.

5–4 POINTS

- ✔ Thesis identifies the long-term causes of WWI **and** analyzes them, but without any development; thesis may address only part of the question effectively; thesis may be a simple, single-sentence statement.
- ✔ Organization is clear but may not be consistently followed; essay may veer off task chronologically or thematically or both.
- ✔ Essay may not complete all tasks:
  - May discuss only the causes without thorough analysis of those causes.
  - May discuss only one or two long-term causes of WWI.
  - May focus only on one nation.
  - May be primarily descriptive rather than analytical.
- ✔ Essay offers some relevant evidence.
- ✔ May contain errors that detract from the argument.

3–2 POINTS

- ✔ Thesis may simply paraphrase the prompt OR identify the long-term causes of WWI **without** analysis.
- ✔ Organization is unclear and ineffective; essay may focus on the personal attributes of European leaders rather than analyzing the long-term causes of WWI.
- ✔ Essay shows serious imbalance; analysis of the long-term causes of WWI is superficial; much of the information may be significantly out of the time period or geography of the question.
- ✔ Offers minimal OR confused evidence.
- ✔ May contain several errors that detract from the argument.

1–0 POINTS

- ✔ Thesis is erroneous OR irrelevant OR absent.
- ✔ No effective organization is evident.
- ✔ Discussion of the long-term causes of WWI is generic.
- ✔ Provides little or no relevant supporting evidence.
- ✔ May contain numerous errors that detract from the argument.

Sample Answer

A complex event like the First World War is really a long-term development made up of myriad lesser events—decisions, made in response to situations, that heightened tensions, increased conflict, then exploded in a chain reaction. In the case of World War I, the most important long-term forces that caused this explosion were militarism, economic competition, nationalism, and alliances, which brought about a European conflict that enveloped the world.

First, two rival alliances, armed to the teeth and continually testing each other's strength and resolve, formed and faced off while waiting for a reason, maybe an excuse, to go at each other. France, Russia, and England were thrown into each other's arms by a common distrust of Germany and Austria, and by turns of events that submerged their tradional rivalries with each other under new needs and fears.

Second, economic competition for overseas markets between Britain, whose aged factories had grown up with the Industrial Revolution, and Germany, whose modern industry used the latest technology, degenerated into a naval arms race. British policy was to keep a navy more powerful than the combined fleets of the next two greatest powers. Their dependence on their far-flung empire seemed to necessitate this. Germany policy was a reflection of Kaiser Wilhelm II's bellicose insistence on overcoming his own inferiority complex by proving German superiority. The need for a powerful German navy was less for the protection of its growing world trade or its newly acquired colonies than for the aggrandisement of its newfound power.

The race for colonies aggravated the tensions and enmities between the rivals. Germany and Italy came late to the imperialism game and they wanted to catch up by sometimes muscling in. Britain and France had a head start on the others, and they wanted to hold onto their acquisitions. The result was a series of crises in Africa and confrontations over China.

The nationalistic urges for autonomy that had disrupted Europe since the French Revolution had awakened the idea of the uniqueness of a "people" and since the time of Napoleon had been effective in making war. The Slavs of Austria-Hungary wanted recognition and a share of power if not necessarily independence. The captive nations of the Ottoman Empire pushed and pulled and proved its weakness, adding to the overall instability. The rival nationalites of the Balkans warred with each other over ancient causes and new dominance, sucking Austria and Russia into the morass. The Italians wanted *Italia Irredenta*, enclaves still controlled by Austria, as well as territories belonging to the Turks. The Germans believed in the uniqueness of their *Kultur*, the desirability of expanding German influence, the necessity of uniting all "Germans" in Europe.

Volatile nationalism, colonial jealousies, trade wars and arms races, and a neatly arranged alignment of competitors just waited for a spark to set the whole mixture off. The assassination of the archduke could have been dealt with using rational diplomacy and good sense if conditions had been different. Smug predictions of inevitable progress for Europe and the world hid the swarming tensions underlying the relations of nations.

EVALUATE THE SAMPLE ANSWER

Now go back and look at the rubric. It is clear that this essay looks like a 6 or 7 on the rubric. In this case, the extra details warrant a 7.

RATER'S COMMENTS ON THE SAMPLE ANSWER

7—Well qualified

This was a sophisticated, well-written essay that answered the question from a broad perspective. It lacks, however, sufficient factual reference to make a totally convincing analysis of a very complex issue: What long-term developments led to World War I?

It definitely rose above the usual pat answer by connecting the events and offering insights into human behavior, the relations between nations, and the writing of history. The introductory paragraph grabs the reader's attention as well as making some philosophical observations. The body of the essay lays out the argument clearly but does fail to flesh it out with pertinent facts.

Some unanswered questions:

How and why did the rival alliances develop? Did they change, and why? Why was Britain brought out of its "splendid isolation" from the affairs of the continent?

Were there reasons other than the kaiser's mental state that encouraged the naval arms race? What were the crises and confrontations brought on by colonial rivalry? What were the Balkan crises that "sucked" the great powers into the morass? What were some of the specifics about the nationalistic urges that created conflict?

Practice Essay Questions

The questions that follow are samples of the various types of thematic essays that appear on the AP exam. (See pages 21–22 for a detailed explanation of each type.) Check over the **generic rubric** (see pages 58–60) before you begin any of these essays and use that rubric to score your essay if you write one.

QUESTION 1

"Each of the belligerents in Europe was responsible for the outbreak of World War I." *Defend or refute* this statement.

COMMENTS ON QUESTION 1

Many Americans, influenced to this day by creative Allied propaganda and by German aggression in World War II, believe that Germany was responsible for starting the First World War. Certainly the kaiser's prewar arrogance was one of the friction points, but England, France, and Russia each carried out policies that aggravated the tension. In framing your answer, consider the network of alliances that France and Germany engineered after the Franco-Prussian War; economic rivalry between Germany and Britain; the roles of Britain as well as Germany in the naval arms race; the mentalities of both "have" and "have-not" nations in the race for colonies; Russian support for Pan-Slavism in Austria-Hungary; the volatile Balkan situation.

QUESTION 2

"After the first few months of war, the combat on the Western Front was very different from anything the strategists on either side had envisioned." *Assess the validity* of this statement.

COMMENTS ON QUESTION 2

Each of the belligerents anticipated a quick, decisive victory at the outbreak of war, expecting "the boys to be home by Christmas." The end result was a war of attrition—a gradual and inexorable wearing down of the manpower, resources, and will to fight. In "determing the truth" of the assertion, consider the German Schlieffen Plan, the unexpected speed of Russian mobilization, the Battle of the Marne, the attempts at outflanking, the resulting line of trenches from Switzerland to the North Sea. Explain the importance of the development of new tactics and weaponry: sea blockades, unrestricted submarine warfare, massed artillery, poison gas, aircraft, and tanks.

QUESTION 3

Explain why the war ended the Russian, Austro-Hungarian, and German empires.

COMMENTS ON QUESTION 3

"Explain" in this context means to "offer the causes and reasons for" the collapse of those great empires. The scope of the issue is very broad, so a detailed accounting of each is not practical. Look for causes common to all three: the strains of a war of attrition—shortages; casualties; political instabilities; nationalist pressures; weakness of colonial holdings; defeats in battle. Emphasize the different characters of their problems: the Bolshevik movement in Russia; ethnic rivalries in Austro-Hungary; democratic and socialist opposition movements in Germany.

QUESTION 4

Contrast and compare the Fourteen Points with the peace settlements in Paris.

COMMENTS ON QUESTION 4

Had President Woodrow Wilson's idealistic plan for peace been implemented, the grievances that led to World War II might have been settled. The main provisions of the Fourteen Points: no secret treaties; freedom of the seas; free trade; arms reduction; settlement of colonial claims; national autonomy and adjustment of borders; establishment of a League of Nations. The Big Four Allied leaders met in Paris and drew up three treaties, without representatives of any of the Central Powers, to end the war. It is not necessary to show the differences or ascertain similarities between the Fourteen Points and each of these treaties. In general terms, show what Wilson gave up during the negotiations in order to attain his prime goal, the League of Nations.

QUESTION 5

Evaluate the Treaty of Versailles.

COMMENTS ON QUESTION 5

To "judge the worth of," "discuss the advantages and disadvantages, the pluses and minuses," examine the main provisions—border adjustments, occupation, colonial adjustments, war guilt, indemnities, German disarmament—and consider the significance and consequences. How did the reparation payments by Germany affect its economy? How well was it enforced? Why? How did Hitler use the war guilt clause in his propaganda? How did the Polish Corridor create conflict between Germany and newly independent Poland? What were the implications of Japan's receiving German Pacific colonies? How did Hitler use the remilitarization of the Rhineland and German rearmament to increase his popularity and power? Was the League of Nations effective?

Practice Multiple-Choice Questions

(These questions are representative of the types found on the AP exam.)

1. World War I had been called a "total war" for all of the following reasons EXCEPT

   (A) campaigns were fought on every continent
   (B) it involved the whole civilian population of the belligerents
   (C) the entire resources of the nations at war were marshaled for the war effort
   (D) those not serving in the military, including women, were expected to work in war plants, buy bonds to support the war, and morally back the nation's aims
   (E) there were more civilian than military casualties

2. All of the following contributed to the outbreak of World War I EXCEPT

   (A) rival alliances
   (B) conflicting colonial claims
   (C) slavic nationalism
   (D) a naval arms race
   (E) Japanese militarism

3. An important cause of the Anglo-German rivalry from the last decades of the 19th century to 1914 was

   (A) competition in world trade and territorial expansion
   (B) the declining strength of the German navy
   (C) the conflict over the Berlin to Baghdad railway
   (D) Britain's *Entente Cordial* with France
   (E) traditional enmities between the nations

4. The significance of the Algeciras Conference of 1906 was that

   (A) it granted Morocco independence from France
   (B) it gave Germany a foothold in North Africa
   (C) it demonstrated the resolve of the Triple Alliance
   (D) it solidified the rivalry of the two camps, the Triple Alliance and the *Triple Entente*
   (E) it embarrassed Kaiser Wilhelm II

5. Generally, the offensives on the Western Front

   (A) made significant territorial gains
   (B) were minor skirmishes
   (C) saw the slaughter of massed infantry units
   (D) were won by the attacking army
   (E) were fought in one or two days

6. After the assassination of Archduke Ferdinand in June of 1914, the infamous "blank check" issued by Germany to Austria

   (A) promised support in whatever action Austria took against England
   (B) was matched by a "blank check" from Russia to Serbia
   (C) encouraged Austrian military against Serbia and Russia
   (D) created a rift between Russia and France
   (E) brought an ultimatum from Britain to Germany

7. The German Schlieffen Plan failed for all of the following reasons EXCEPT

   (A) it was based on the strategy of attrition in a drawn-out war
   (B) Russian mobilization was too swift to allow the "holding action" in the east
   (C) Belgian resistance to their violated neutrality was stiff
   (D) German divisions were transferred from France to East Prussia
   (E) the French counterattack at the Marne was successful

8. Bismarck's alliance system was designed to isolate France and

   (A) expand German territory eastward
   (B) challenge Britain's dominant world position
   (C) create rival diplomatic blocs in Europe
   (D) maintain peace between Russia and Austria-Hungary
   (E) prevent Russia from moving toward a parliamentary system

9. War on the Eastern Front

   (A) quickly degenerated into static trench warfare
   (B) was similar in character to that on the Western Front
   (C) involved a defensive stand by the German armies against the numerically superior Russians
   (D) was characterized by decisive German victories, horrific Russian losses, and the German acquisition of vast territories
   (E) was marked by spectacular Austrian victories against the Turks and the Russians

10. Which was an innovation first employed in World War I?

    (A) Massed artillery
    (B) Tank warfare
    (C) Naval blockade
    (D) Large-scale infantry assaults over a broad front
    (E) Trench warfare

11. The belligerent nations directed the war effort by instituting all the following controls on their civilian populations EXCEPT

    (A) press censorship
    (B) allocation of raw materials for industry
    (C) mobilization of industrial output for war production
    (D) outlawing of labor strikes
    (E) denial of religious freedom

12. The spark that ignited the Balkan "powder keg" was the assassination of

    (A) Archduke Francis Ferdinand
    (B) Emperor Francis Joseph
    (C) Chancellor Bethmann-Hollweg
    (D) Tsar Alexander II
    (E) Tsar Nicholas II

Nash: Over the top, 1917. Painting by John Nash. The Granger Collection, New York. (0023722)

13. What was the three word phrase that described the soldiers leaving the trenches to fight the enemy?

    (A) Jumping the gun
    (B) No man's land
    (C) Duck and cover
    (D) Over the top
    (E) Facing the enemy

14. As a result of the war, all of these empires ended EXCEPT

    (A) the French
    (B) the Ottoman
    (C) the Austro-Hungarian
    (D) the Russian
    (E) the German

15. All of the following states were granted independence at the peace conferences that ended World War I EXCEPT

    (A) Poland
    (B) Czechoslovakia
    (C) Yugoslavia
    (D) Hungary
    (E) Romania

Answers and Answer Explanations

1.	A	**6.**	C	**11.**	E
2.	E	**7.**	A	**12.**	A
3.	A	**8.**	B	**13.**	D
4.	D	**9.**	D	**14.**	A
5.	C	**10.**	B	**15.**	E

1. **(A)** Although geographic totality is not a part of the definition of total war, the war was fought primarily in Europe—Western and Eastern—and in the African colonies, in parts of the Mideast, in Asia, and on both the Atlantic and the Pacific oceans. Although North Americans and Australians participated, the war did not reach the Americas or Australia.

2. **(E)** Japanese militarism helped cause World War II.

3. **(A)** Germany having come later to industrialization than the British, had more efficient factories, and the Germans took a bite out of the British world trade in the later part of the 19th and early part of the 20th centuries.

4. **(D)** The British and French hung together; only Austria backed Germany.

5. **(C)** The trench warfare saw long protracted battles with wholesale slaughter.

6. **(C)** Germany gave Austria a free hand with Serbia; France gave Russia a free hand with Austria.

7. **(A)** The Central Powers knew they hadn't the population, industry, or resources to win a drawn-out war. The Schlieffen Plan aimed for a quick victory as in the Franco-Prussian War of 1871.

8. **(B)** Bismarck's alliance system was designed to isolate France and compete with the British in trade and world dominance. Germany had no desire to expand eastward until Hitler took power, and the rival blocks were a result, not an aim, of the policies.

9. **(D)** In the first months of the war, the Germans fought a holding action; then they launched massive and successful offensives to back the Austrians against the Russians.

10. **(B)** Massed artillery was used before the time of Napoleon; naval blockade was used by the British against the American colonies and Napoleon; infantry assaults on a broad front was a tactic introduced in the American Civil War; trench warfare was a defensive tactic used in many previous wars.

11. **(E)** Since organized religion tended to back the nation's war aims, there was no need to deny religious freedom.

12. **(A)** The assassination of Archduke Ferdinand is generally accepted as the catalyst to WWI.

13.   **(D)** Soldiers went *over the top* of the trenches when they went into battle.

14.   **(A)** France was a republic without an emperor but it had colonies that it maintained until after World War II.

15.   **(E)** Romania was already an independent state.

The Russian Revolution and Communism in Russia (1917–1939)

CHAPTER 11

Key Terms/People

- Alexander III
- Constitutional Democrats (Kadet)
- Vladimir Lenin
- The Revolution of 1905
- Tsar Nicholas II
- October Manifesto
- Bloody Sunday
- Alexander Kerensky

- Rasputin
- The March Revolution
- Dictatorship of the Proletariat
- Five-Year Plans
- Farm Collectivization
- communes
- The Purge Trials

Overview

Tsarist Russia was a casualty of the First World War. What began for the Russian people—peasants, middle class, nobility—as a popular crusade, quickly became the focal point of revolution. Within a year of the start of the war, devastating defeats by the Central Powers and staggering casualties demoralized the Russian people. Military incompetence, the corruption and ineptitude of the tsarist government, and deprivations on the home front sparked the revolutionary spirit that had smoldered for decades.

Defeat in the the Russo-Japanese War (1904–1905) and the abortive Revolution of 1905 demonstrated the vulnerability of the tsarist regime. Despite accelerated industrialization in the period between 1890 and the start of the war, Russian workers were brutally exploited, and peasants—who made up the great bulk of the population—were oppressed.

The Revolution of 1917 began as an attempt at reform by the middle class and some enlightened nobles. When the moderates maintained Russia's unpopular involvement in the war, the radical Marxist Bolsheviks seized power and established the Communist regime that would change the politics of the 20th century.

Chronology

1881–1894

Tsar Alexander III (r. 1881–1894), reacting to the assassination of his predecessor by radical socialists, instituted a reactionary policy of "Russification, orthodoxy, and autocracy."

1890s

Russia industrialized, but the great mass of its population was still made up of rural peasants whose quality of life was comparable to that of farmers in the West during the Middle Ages. Since the French were eager for Russian support against the Germans, they granted loans and credits that enabled the Russians to build factories, import Western technology, and expand the railroad system. The *Trans-Siberian Railroad* linked European and Asiatic Russia.

A commercial middle class grew in influence; a proletariat of exploited workers also grew. Political parties were formed to meet the demands of these new elements. *Constitutional Democrats (Cadet)* reflected the aims of the new middle class and some liberal landowners for parliamentary government and gradual reform. Social Revolutionaries (Narodniks) stressed the glories of Slav culture (Slavophiles) and sought to keep Russia agrarian. *Marxists* urged radical revolution.

1903

A meeting of the Russian Marxist Congress resulted in a split in the party when *Vladimir Lenin* (1870–1924) favored a party of elite revolutionaries instead of an open democratic organization. When most of the attendees walked out in protest, Lenin convinced those remaining to endorse his ideas. Although his supporters made up a minority of the party, he called them Bolsheviks (majority) and referred to the actual party majority as Mensheviks (minority).

1904–1905

The Russo-Japanese War. Competing over Manchuria—a mineral rich province of China—Russia and newly modernized Japan came to blows. What the tsar hoped would be a "short, glorious war" to divert unrest in his realm was a devastating defeat, the first in modern times of a European power by a nonwhite nation. A surprise attack on the Russian fleet at Port Arthur in Manchuria, a defeat at the Battle of Mukden on Manchurian soil, and the sinking of the Russian European fleet off Tsushima Straits brought a peace mediated by President *Theodore Roosevelt.* The Treaty of Portsmouth granted Japan Russia's railroad rights in Manchuria, half of the Sakhalin Islands off Russia's Pacific coast, and guarantee of Japan's protectorate in Korea. Humiliated, Russia suffered from the Revolution of 1905 before the war was even over.

The Revolution of 1905: Faced with the growing unrest of the working class, *Tsar Nicholas II* (r. 1894–1918) commissioned a Russian Orthodox priest, *Father*

Gapon, to organize a conservative union to counteract the radical Marxists. Gapon, horrified by the conditions in St. Petersburg (the tsarist capital), led a peaceful protest march of tens of thousands of workers and their families on January 22, 1905. Troops fired on the crowd, killing hundreds. "Bloody Sunday" provoked general strikes, peasant uprisings, and the formation of workers' revolutionary councils, Soviets. In the *Zemstvos* (the provincial councils elected by landowners and peasants and set up by Tsar Alexander II (1818–1881) in 1864 as part of his great reforms), the liberals demanded reforms.

The *October Manifesto*: After a general strike was called by the Soviet of Petersburg, the tsar issued a promise for reform. Its major provisions were a constitution, civil liberties, and a Duma (legislature) to represent all classes.

1906

A Duma was elected, but did not include the Marxists, who boycotted the elections because they mistrusted the tsar's motives. Nicholas dissolved it anyway because the Duma demanded that his ministers be responsible to it.

Reforms were instituted including the strengthening of the Zemstvos, abolishing the peasant debt for the emancipation of serfs in the 1860s, and thereby creating a wealthy peasant class, the kulaks, who worked large tracts of land and hired other peasants.

1914

With the outbreak of World War I, the government suspended the Duma so that political bickering would not compromise the war effort. A national union of Zemstvos, made up of the various local elective districts, was organized to increase productivity.

Rasputin (1869–1916), "the mad monk," began to influence *Tsarina Alexandra* after he claimed to have cured the tsar's only son of hemophilia.

1915

Horrific losses at the front provoked the national union of Zemstvos and the middle class to demand that the Duma be reconvened to initiate reforms.

1916

The Duma met for the first time since its disbanding and, with support of its dominant conservatives, criticized the tsar's government.

Rasputin, whose sway over Alexandra had poisoned her advice to her easily influenced husband, was murdered by a band of young noblemen. The tsar attempted to suppress any reform.

1917

The March Revolution: Food riots broke out in Petrograd (St. Petersburg), and when the tsar ordered the Duma to dissolve and troops to suppress the disorder, neither obeyed. Workers and soldiers in Petrograd organized radical legislative bodies called Soviets. The rebellion spread throughout the country and to the troops at the front, who deserted by tens of thousands.

On March 14, the Duma formed a provisional government under *Prince Georgii Lvov (1861–1925)*. *Alexander Kerensky (1881–1970)*, a moderate member of the Soviet, played a major role.

On March 15, the tsar abdicated.

On March 17, Russia was proclaimed a republic.

Lenin and other *Bolshevik* leaders came back from exile to Petrograd in April. Their demands to the provincial government:

1. Russia withdraw from the war
2. The Petrograd Soviet run the government
3. Land be redistributed to the peasants, and factories be controlled by the Soviets (worker's committees)

After an abortive coup in July, Lenin and the Bolshevik leaders fled to Finland. Prince Lvov turned over the provincial government to Kerensky.

The October Revolution (November 1917 by the Western calendar).

Kerensky's government failed to win the support of the people because of continued shortages and because it stayed in the war against the Central Powers.

Lenin returned to Petrograd with the rallying cry of "Peace, Land, Bread."

Leninist Doctrine: According to orthodox Marxism, a social revolution is possible only in highly developed capitalist countries, such as those in the West during this period. Since Russia was virtually a feudal society and primarily agrarian, some Bolsheviks argued for a coalition with the middle classes until Russia had developed sufficiently. Lenin argued that since Western Europe was ripe for revolution, a Marxist seizure of Russia would precipitate such takeovers elsewhere, and these in turn would help Russia to bypass the capitalist stage. Lenin won the support of Leon Trotsky (1870–1940), Joseph Stalin (1878–1953), and most of the Bolshevik leaders.

October 6–7: The Bolsheviks stormed the *Winter Palace*, headquarters of Kerensky's government, and seized other key centers in Petrograd. Kerensky's provisional government fled; the Congress of Soviets, representing the local Soviets formed all over Russia, established a Council of People's Commissars with Lenin as head, Trotsky as foreign minister, and Stalin as nationalities minister. Within months, the government abolished the freely elected legislative assembly and established a secret police organization, the Cheka, also known later as the OGPU, NKVD, MVD, and KGB.

1918

The Dictatorship of the Proletariat was proclaimed in tune with Leninist doctrine:

The Bolsheviks renamed their party Communist.

Important industries were nationalized.

Russian Orthodox Church lands were seized.

Russia pulled out of World War I, surrendering Latvia, Lithuania, Estonia, Poland, and the Ukraine to Germany in the *Treaty of Brest-Litovsk*.

1918–1922

The Russian Civil War was fought for control of the remainder of the Russian Empire. Opposed by tsarists, the middle class, many peasants, and socialist factions, the Communists were able to win because their enemies could not unite. Despite the intervention of many Allied nations, including the United States, which feared the spread of Communism, the Red Army under Trotsky conquered European Russia by the end of 1920 and Siberia and central Asia by 1922. The Communist International (Comintern), to organize Communism worldwide, was organized in 1919.

1922

Nationalities Reform: The old empire was reorganized into the Union of Soviet Socialist Republics, uniting the various nation groups into a federal entity of major republics and smaller autonomous regions. Cultural identity was encouraged and toleration of various ethnic groups became an official policy.

1924

The Constitution:

1. Only workers and peasants are allowed to vote for local Soviets.
2. Local Soviets elect provincial or district Soviets which, in turn, choose a republic Soviet for each autonomous republic. A *Congress of Soviets* represents all the republics and elects a *Council of People's Commissars* (similar to a government cabinet).

Lenin died at the age of fifty-four, never fully recovering from an assassination attempt in 1920. Trotsky was at a disadvantage in becoming Lenin's successor both because he was a Jew in an anti-Semitic society and because he was considered an intellectual by the rank and file.

As secretary of the Communist party, Stalin garnered loyalty within the party by making many key appointments.

Their policy differences further alienated the men from each other: Trotsky pushed for a worldwide revolution; Stalin argued for a strengthening of Russia by industrialization before it undertook worldwide revolution—"Building socialism in one country."

1927

Stalin won the support of the party, and Trotsky fled the country. He was murdered in 1940 by a Stalinist agent.

1928

The first *Five-Year Plan* promoted rapid industrialization by centralized planning. Coal and steel production were accelerated, and a modern transportation system was developed, using the domestic resources of the U.S.S.R. since foreign nations were hostile to the new government.

Early 1930

Farm Collectivization consolidated small farms into *Communes*, modernizing agriculture but displacing many peasants, some of whom resisted the process. The kulaks, the most successful peasant farmers, were destroyed as a class, and between 5 and 12 million people, mostly in the Ukraine, perished by murder and famine.

1933

A second *Five-Year Plan* was begun that increased production of steel and heavy industry, modernized Soviet factories, created a boom when the West was in the depth of the *Great Depression,* and made Russia a leading industrial power.

1936–1937

The purge trials: Stalin's paranoid tendencies convinced him of plots within the party and the government to unseat him. Many original Bolsheviks, instrumental in carrying out the revolution, as well as high military officers, some of the most competent, were tried on trumped-up charges. As many as 1 million were executed; 5 to 7 million were sent to the gulags (Siberian labor camps) where many eventually died. Stalin strengthened his hold over the party, the government, and the nation, and became one of the century's most powerful dictators.

Figures of the Russian Revolution

Figure	When	Important Facts
Tsar Alexander II	1861–1881	He emancipated the serfs either because he felt pressure from below, it was his personal will, or he needed to react to the loss of the Crimean War; he began the process of emancipation in 1861. He was assassinated in 1881, moving Russia to the right.
Tsar Nicholas II	1894–1917	The last tsar of Russia, he was a better family man than he was a ruler. His devotion to his German wife, Alexandra, and their children, his lack of interest in affairs of state from an early age, as well as his support for his relatives ruling England and Germany were his downfall.
Russo-Japanese War	1904–1905	Japan humiliated Russia in its attempt to take parts of China by defeating the Russian navy twice, leaving them without a functioning fleet. This led to the Revolution of 1905 and the creation of the Duma, Russia's legislative body.
Father Gapon/ *Bloody Sunday*	1905	A state-appointed priest, who was supposed to help emancipated serfs adjust to their new lives, circulated a petition to the tsar. Over 200,000 people marched on the Winter Palace in St. Petersburg to give the petition to the tsar, but troops opened fire killing many. The tsar was not even there; he was with his hemophiliac son, Alexei.

Figure	When	Important Facts
Peter Stolypin	1905–1911	He oversaw the creation of the Duma as prime minister to Nicholas II. His agrarian reforms were very unpopular, and he was assassinated in 1911.
Gregori Rasputin	1905–1916	He was a peasant mystic healer whom Alexandra believed helped keep Alexei alive. His debauchery was legendary, and rumors of his influence on the Romanov family helped lead to their downfall. He predicted his own death at the hand of the Romanov family, as well as the end of their reign in a letter found after his death.
World War I	1914–1918	Russia entered World War I in 1914 to play its traditional role as protector of the Eastern Orthodox faith in defense of Serbia. Russia was not industrialized enough to be prepared for this war, which Germany and England had been stocking up for. Russia was decimated by the Germans, and even after Nicholas II took personal control of the Army, they still lost, leading to his abdication in 1917.
Alexander Kerensky	1917	He was the leader of the provisional government formed in March 1917 when Nicholas II abdicated. He and his popular Kadet (Social Democrat) Party fought for land reform while he kept the war going as a middle ground in contrast to the Bolsheviks who wanted to end the war then.
General Kornilov	1914–1918	He was an important World War I general who stayed loyal to Kerensky as his commander in chief. Described as having the "heart of a lion and the brains of a sheep," this man led the White Army during the Russian Civil War in which he was captured and killed.
Vladimir Ilyich Lenin	1917–1924	He was the Russian Bolshevik leader who was banished in 1903 and convinced the Germans to allow him back into the country in 1917. He promised the people "Peace, land and bread," and won them over to his side. He used the soviets in each town and the educated elite to foment revolution among the masses. This new take on Marxism led to a successful revolution, placing him in power of the world's first communist nation, the Union of Soviet Socialist Republics (U.S.S.R.), after a brutal civil war.
Leon Trotsky	1917–1924	He was Lenin's co-conspirator in the revolution. He helped issue *Army Order Number 1* in which companies voted whether or not to follow commands. He also took over the military and the train stations during the October Revolution that placed Lenin in power. He was pushed out by Joseph Stalin, who created a completely totalitarian regime in Russia and eventually had Trotsky killed in Mexico.
Joseph Stalin	1924–1953	He ruled the U.S.S.R. with an iron fist. He instituted five-year plans to modernize and industrialize while purging his nation of supposed enemies. Between ruining the agricultural output, which caused starvation, and imprisoning and killing political opponents, it is estimated that Stalin killed more than 50 million of his citizens. He did, however, rally his people to defeat the Germans during World War II. His actions and lack of trust with Franklin Roosevelt and Winston Churchill led directly to the Cold War.

Sample Essay Question

The sample thematic essay question and the practice questions in this chapter are types found on the AP exam, and they require knowledge of causes, effects, personalities, ideas, and events.

SAMPLE QUESTION

"Every successful revolution puts on in time the robes of the tyrant it has deposed."

Evaluate this statement with regard to the English Revolution (1640–1660), the French Revolution (1789–1815), and the Russian Revolution (1917–1930).

Comments on the Sample Question

Follow the "Simple Procedures" for writing an essay. (See page 34.)

First, *What does the question want to know?* Did the protagonists of the revolutions mentioned—Cromwell, Robespierre, Danton, Marat, Lenin, Trotsky, and Stalin—become tyrants as much as the men/regimes they deposed? This question allows you to review the three most important political revolutions covered in the course, and compare the results of these revolutions.

Second, *What do you know about it?* Examine the leaders who took power after the revolutions. In the case of England, that would be Cromwell. In France the leaders covered can range from Robespierre, Danton, and Marat to Napoleon and Louis XVIII, depending upon how you want to argue it. The Russian Revolution should compare the Romanov reign to the rule of the Bolsheviks under Lenin and Stalin. Sophisticated essays may postulate about how Trotsky could have ruled differently.

Third, *How would you put it into words?* This essay lends itself to easy paragraphs for each of the revolutions examined. If the writer writes a thesis explaining that each revolution did indeed don the robes of the tyrant to some degree and then examines the degree to which each revolution did that in the body, then the essay will be strong. It is often a good idea to contradict the proposition given on a question to distinguish the essay from others. A way to do that here is to be clear about the different degrees to which each revolution did indeed become tyrannical.

Rubric for Sample Answer

Before you read the sample answer, examine the rubric. What will the reader be looking for when he or she grades this essay? A sample rubric, shaded to show the reader's evaluation, is seen below:

9–8 POINTS

✔ Thesis explicitly evaluates the quote **and** assesses its validity in regard to all three revolutions. Thesis does not need to be in the opening paragraph.

✔ Organization is clear, consistently followed, and effective in support of the argument.
  • May devote individual paragraphs to each revolution.
  • Must evaluate the quote for each of the revolutions (The English saw Cromwell lead Parliament against an "absolutist" monarch only to instill draconian measures including closing the theaters and brothels of London. The French saw the Terror, the Committee of Public Safety, Danton, Robespierre, and finally Napoleon. The Russian Revolution replaced the tsar with Lenin's harsh rule, and eventually Stalin's paranoid purges and gulags.) Does not have to present all figures for all revolutions.

✔ Essay is well balanced; evaluates the quote **and** assesses its validity in regard to all three revolutions at some length.

✔ Major assertions in the essay are supported thoroughly and consistently by relevant evidence.

✔ Evidence may prove more specific or concrete.

✔ May contain errors that do not detract from the argument.

7–6 POINTS

✔ Thesis explicitly evaluates the quote and assesses its validity in regard to all three revolutions, but may not be developed fully.

✔ Organization is clear and effective in support of the argument but may introduce evidence that is not pertinent to the task.

✔ Essay covers all major topics suggested by the prompt but may analyze the English, French, or Russian revolutions, or the quote, in greater depth rather than in a balanced manner.

✔ Major assertions in the essay are supported by relevant evidence.

✔ May contain an error that detracts from the argument.

5–4 POINTS

✔ Thesis evaluates the quote **and** assesses its validity in regard to all three revolutions, but without any development; thesis may address only part of the question effectively; thesis may be a simple, single-sentence statement.

✔ Organization is clear but may not be consistently followed; essay may veer off task chronologically or thematically or both.

✔ Essay may not complete all tasks:
  • May discuss only the quote without applying it to each revolution, or discuss the revolutions without connecting them to the quote.
  • May discuss only two revolutions.
  • May focus only on one or more of the ways the quote is or is not verified by the revolutions.
  • May be primarily descriptive rather than analytical.

✔ Essay offers some relevant evidence.

✔ May contain errors that detract from the argument.

3–2 POINTS

✔ Thesis may simply paraphrase the prompt OR the quote OR assesses its validity in regard to two revolutions without elaboration.

✔ Organization is unclear and ineffective; essay may focus on the personal attributes of rulers rather than analyzing how the quote applies to each revolution.

✔ Essay shows serious imbalance; discussion of the quote and its validity in regard to all three revolutions is done in a superficial way; much of the information may be significantly out of the time period or geography of the question.

✔ Offers minimal OR confused evidence.

✔ May contain several errors that detract from the argument.

1–0 POINTS

✔ Thesis is erroneous OR irrelevant OR absent.

✔ No effective organization is evident.

✔ Discussion of the quote and its validity in regard to all three revolutions is done in a generic fashion.

✔ Provides little or no relevant supporting evidence.

✔ May contain numerous errors that detract from the argument.

Sample Answer

These three revolutions are pivotal points in the political history of Europe and have been much studied by historians. Crane Brinton proposed a cycle of revolutions based upon all three, that does indeed suggest that each of these revolutions did become tyrannical to some degree. The leaders of all three revolutions or their successors became more tyrannical than those they replaced to different degrees and in different arenas in each case.

Oliver Cromwell became the leader of the Puritans during the English Civil War of the mid-17th century. He led a revolt against the king because he felt that the king was forcing religious changes upon the people and was not recognizing the legal power of the English Parliament. He advocated with other members for open insurrection against the king. He molded the New Model Army into an efficient fighting machine that fought in the name of the Lord and British common law. He was able to take over Parliament after using his army to defeat King Charles I. He orchestrated a trial of the king and had him beheaded in the name of Parliament and England. Parliament became the first supreme legislature in Europe. Eventually, Cromwell became the de facto ruler of England. He controlled Parliament and eventually dismissed them with armed force. He closed the theaters and houses of ill repute and enforced strict observation of religious practices that he favored. He also instituted taxes on the people without the consent of Parliament. In the end, Cromwell died a worse tyrant than the man he deposed.

John Locke wrote about the second English political revolution in 1689 in which England gained a Bill of Rights and began the application of scientific thought to politics. His work was built upon by the French philosophes such as Montesquieu and Condorcet, which, along with a revolution in America, led to a revolution in France based upon Enlightenment ideals. The leaders of the French Revolution also came to a radical phase in which one leader, Marat, was assassinated, and another, Danton, was repudiated by the third, Robespierre, and guillotined. These leaders perpetrated a Reign of Terror upon France in which tens of thousands were killed as supposed enemies of the revolution. Eventually the Directory took over in 1795, but only for four years. Then, Napoleon took power and began his own censorship, militarism, and autocratic rule. The reign of Louis XVI had been feudal, but the revolutionaries were much more tyrannical because they did not follow their own laws and rewrote the constitution whenever it suited the government. At least the French had known what to expect before the tyrannical revolutionaries took power.

The Russians were perhaps the most oppressed Europeans in 1914. Serfdom still existed and each person was in fact the personal servant of the tsar if asked to serve. Tsar Nicholas II and his family lived a life of luxury, while the peasants starved or eked out a living. Industrialization was slow and controlled by the nobility. The revolution led first by common soldiers and Kerensky and then by the Bolsheviks ended up being more brutal and tyrannical than any Russian or other person could have imagined. Lenin came to power offering land, peace, and bread. When Stalin took over in 1924, he instituted a brutal regime that forced massive change on the nation resulting in loss and starvation. He then "purged" the country of people perceived as classist or against the revolution, killing tens of millions of his own fellow citizens. The Russian Revolution did indeed become more tyrannical than the regime it deposed.

In all three cases, the revolutions produced governments that at least for a period were more tyrannical than those they deposed. Even though they were tyrannical in different ways, with the English more concerned about religion and the Russians more concerned about class, the truth is that all three revolutions did not relieve tyranny, but increased it.

EVALUATE THE SAMPLE ANSWER

Now go back and look at the rubric. It is clear that this essay looks like a 6 or 7 on the rubric. The essay answers all parts of the question with concrete evidence but the essay focuses on one revolution and misses some major possible points. In this case, the extra details warrant a 7.

RATERS COMMENTS ON THE SAMPLE ANSWER

7—Well Qualified

This essay clearly and completely answers the question. There are some details such as the "rump parliament" or the "long parliament" missing, but the essay is strong, clear, and comprehensive. The structure makes it clear to the reader that the writer knows the events of the three revolutions and the major players in each.

The details about the closure of theaters in England were great, but the omission of censorship and the absence of an examination of how Cromwell took power, take away from this essay. The examination of the French Revolution provides enough support to make the point, but could build much more upon the importance of the tyranny of both Robespierre and Napoleon. The examination of Stalin as more tyrannical than the most tyrannical absolutist power was a powerful contrast. More detail on Stalin could have been given as support.

Practice Essay Questions

The questions that follow are samples of the various types of thematic essays that appear on the AP exam. (See pages 21–22 for a detailed explanation.) Check over the **generic rubric** (see pages 58–60) before you begin any of these essays and use that rubric to score your essay if you write one.

QUESTION 1

To what extent and in what ways did the failure of reform and abortive revolution lead to the Revolution of 1917?

COMMENTS ON QUESTION 1

"How and how much" did attempts to make the government better, improve the economy, and modernize the institutions of Russia cause the open rebellion of the people against the government and society? "How and how much" did the failed Revolution of 1905 contribute?

What were the attempts at reform? When did Russia modernize its economy and how did this lead to greater discontent among the people? Why was the Duma reconvened, and how did it precipitate events? How did the Russo-Japanese War cause discontent? What was "Bloody Sunday"? What reforms were aimed at by the marchers? What was the October Manifesto? What were Stolypin's reforms? What were the implications of his death?

QUESTION 2

Analyze Lenin's Marxism and his role as leader in establishing Communism in Russia.

COMMENTS ON QUESTION 2

"Determine the relationship" between Lenin's interpretation of Marxism and the way he defined the new Soviet government. Orthodox Marxist theory insisted that a socialist revolution can take place only under certain conditions. What were those conditions? How did that apply to the governmental shift taking place in Russia in 1917? How did Lenin disagree with the orthodox view? How did he translate that once the Bolsheviks had seized power? Was it a Marxist revolution?

QUESTION 3

Contrast and compare the methods of governing of Lenin and Stalin.

COMMENTS ON QUESTION 3

The contrast is glaring: Lenin established the basic institutions of Soviet Communism; Stalin evolved them into a grotesque parody of their original aims. Lenin ruled for about seven years; Stalin for over thirty. Lenin believed that the end justified the means; Stalin's paranoia distorted even this precept. Lenin designed the blueprint for modernization and reform; Stalin built the edifice into one of the world's worst totalitarian regimes.

The comparison, the similarities, are in their usurpation of power to gain their ends, their use of dictatorship, their methods of suppressing dissent.

This is a difficult question that requires broad statements backed by selective facts.

An examination of both of their relationships with Trotsky may add light to this subject as well.

QUESTION 4

"Despite the human cost, Russia progressed under Communism." *Defend or refute* this statement.

COMMENTS ON QUESTION 4

The impulse, if you know the cost of Soviet totalitarianism, 30-million-plus lives to start, is to refute. It is easy to overlook the modernization and industrialization of a feudal society on the facts alone without reverting to ideological biases. The first step in this question is to define "progress." Is it economic? Social? Some indefinable movement forward? You can get lost in trying to measure the improvement of the human condition from one age to another. Do the drudgery and social stagnancy of feudalism compare to the alienation and confusion of modernity?

Stick to the tangible. The Five-Year Plans—did they improve life for the Soviet people, and what was their cost? Was there a better standard of living for the Russian people under Communism or the tsar? Was Communist tyranny worse than tsarist despotism?

Remember, whether you defend or refute, it is the case you make that counts.

QUESTION 5

"The Russian Revolution of 1917 was a major force in determining the character of the 20th century." *Assess the validity* of this statement.

COMMENTS ON QUESTION 5

"Determine the truth" of this statement by considering not only the confrontation between ideologies known as the Cold War, but also the role of Soviet Communism in disrupting the world order before World War II and after. What part did it play in dismantling colonialism, as a model for new nations, as a counter to the status quo? In what ways was it a focal point for world affairs after World War I, before World War II, after World War II?

Practice Multiple-Choice Questions

(These questions represent the various types found on the AP exam.)

1. After the assassination of Russia's tsar Alexander II in 1881, his successor, Alexander III, adopted a policy of

    (A) constitutional reform
    (B) industrialization
    (C) "Orthodoxy, Russification, and Autocracy"
    (D) Westernization
    (E) modern scientific rationalism

2. All of the following were results of Russia's dramatic industrialization in the 1890s EXCEPT

    (A) the doubling of its railroad mileage
    (B) vastly increased exports
    (C) the growth of the proletariat
    (D) the growth of the commercial middle class
    (E) private ownership of all industry

3. Which is the best characterization of Lenin's program at the Russian Marxist Party Conference in Brussels and London, 1903?

    (A) Democratic socialism open to all new members
    (B) Professional revolutionaries with a small, elite leadership
    (C) Rank and file participation in policy formulation
    (D) Party division along the lines of autonomous national groups
    (E) Party cooperation with liberal and socialist parties

4. All are results of the Russo-Japanese War (1904–1905) EXCEPT

    (A) Russian forces were decisively defeated
    (B) Japan was given some of the Sakhalin Islands
    (C) Russia was forced to pay Japan an indemnity
    (D) Japan got Russia's railway concessions in Manchuria
    (E) Japan's Korean protectorate was recognized

5. Which is the most valid statement regarding the October Manifesto issued by Tsar Nicholas II in 1905?

    (A) It precipitated a general strike that paralyzed the economy.
    (B) It brought about significant constitutional reform of the government.
    (C) It created a Duma (national legislature), to which the tsar's ministers were directly responsible.
    (D) It was an expedient and temporary promise of reform in response to civil unrest.
    (E) It imposed martial law and suppressed antigovernment political activities.

6. The Russian people's support for Russian participation in World War I changed drastically

    (A) when Rasputin took virtual control of the government
    (B) after the Battles of Masurian Lakes and Tannenberg
    (C) because the Duma was reconvened in 1916
    (D) when the Germans and Austrians went on the offensive in 1915
    (E) after the Bolshevik Revolution of 1917

7. The slogan "Peace, Land, and Bread" is most closely associated with

    (A) the Duma liberals
    (B) Alexander Kerensky's moderates
    (C) Prince Lvov's coalition government
    (D) Lenin's Bolsheviks
    (E) Tsar Nicholas's cabinet

Lenin on the first day of Soviet power. The Granger Collection, New York. (0054944)

8. Why was Lenin depicted in the painting above with this group of people?

   (A) It is good propaganda to depict Lenin with common men.
   (B) These are the men Lenin took the palace with.
   (C) It is a revolution and they are military men.
   (D) It illustrated how powerful he looks in black.
   (E) It makes him look more important to be the only one wearing a tie.

9. Within a year after the October Revolution, the Bolsheviks had accomplished all of these EXCEPT

   (A) the abolition of the provisional government
   (B) the establishment of the Council of Commissars to rule Russia
   (C) the election of the National Constituent Assembly to frame a new government
   (D) the nationalization of large industries
   (E) the confiscation of Russian Orthodox Church lands

10. The organizer of the Red Army who lost the struggle for leadership of the Soviet Union to Stalin after Lenin's death was

   (A) Alexander Kerensky
   (B) Alexander Nevsky
   (C) Leon Trotsky
   (D) General Kornilov
   (E) Nikita Khrushchev

11. During the Russian Civil War, 1918–1921, all of the following opposed Bolshevik rule EXCEPT

    (A) tsarists
    (B) the middle class
    (C) peasants
    (D) urban workers
    (E) the Allied Powers of World War I

12. In 1922, after the Civil War had ended, Lenin undertook his "nationalities reform." It accomplished all of the following EXCEPT

    (A) uniting the major ethnic groups into a federation
    (B) giving smaller ethnic groups autonomous regions within the major republics
    (C) allowing schools to teach native languages
    (D) encouraging cultural uniqueness
    (E) requiring that instruction in schools be exclusively in Russian

13. Trotsky and Stalin's interpretations of Marxism differed most significantly in which way?

    (A) Trotsky wanted to foster world revolution while Stalin wanted "to build Socialism in one country."
    (B) Stalin wanted to foster revolution in Western Europe while Trotsky wanted to develop the Soviet Union first.
    (C) Stalin was a Bolshevik; Trotsky was a Menshevik.
    (D) Trotsky was deviationist; Stalin followed the party line.
    (E) Stalin believed that Russia was too backward to support Communism; Trotsky believed the opposite.

14. Stalin supported the rapid industrialization of Russia in the 1920s and early 1930s by

    (A) purging the Soviet Communist party of "deviationists"
    (B) obtaining loans from the West
    (C) slaughtering the kulaks
    (D) collectivizing agriculture to support the First Five-Year Plan
    (E) seeking international recognition of the Soviet Union

15. The original purpose of Comintern (Communist International), a congress of socialist parties in 1919, was to

    (A) combat Fascism and Nazism
    (B) foster democratic socialism worldwide
    (C) establish Moscow's leadership in fomenting Marxist revolution around the world
    (D) improve relations with the capitalist West
    (E) encourage socialists to join in coalition governments with other parties in the West

Answers and Answer Explanations

1.	C	**6.**	B	**11.**	D
2.	E	**7.**	D	**12.**	E
3.	B	**8.**	A	**13.**	A
4.	C	**9.**	C	**14.**	D
5.	D	**10.**	C	**15.**	C

1. **(C)** Tepid reform reverted to hard repression.

2. **(E)** Most industry was owned and controlled by the government, so that the government was the employer that exploited most Russian workers.

3. **(B)** Lenin believed it was the only way to effect a revolution.

4. **(C)** The indemnity was not imposed, but the effect of the war was catastrophic to the stability of the czar's government anyway. The Revolution of 1905 broke out.

5. **(D)** The czar went back on his promises as soon as the disorder ended.

6. **(B)** The terrible casualties and territorial losses turned the people against the war.

7. **(D)** A masterful slogan of masterful propagandists.

8. **(A)** The most important reason that Lenin is pictured with this group of people, who he certainly was not with on the first day of the revolution, is to show Lenin as a man of the people for propaganda purposes.

9. **(C)** The elections for a constitutional convention took place during Kerensky's regime. The Bolsheviks wanted to consolidate, not share, power.

10. **(C)** Leon Trotsky was the hero of the Red Army.

11. **(D)** Like the French Revolution before it, the Russian Revolution was largely supported by the urban workers, the vaunted proletariat.

12. **(E)** To win over the various nationalities, Lenin did the opposite of the czar's hated Russification.

13. **(A)** Trotsky had many followers among the Bolsheviks who supported his ideas. Stalin may have been right to strengthen the U.S.S.R. first, though.

14. **(D)** Consolidating small farms into communes made agriculture more productive and the party used the profits to industrialize. When the kulaks, wealthy peasant farmers, resisted, Stalin slaughtered them by the millions, but this did not contribute to industrialization.

15. **(C)** Comintern convinced the capitalists that there was a monolithic Communist conspiracy to take over the world.

CHAPTER 12

Democracy, Depression, Dictatorship, Aggression (1919–1939)

Key Terms/People

- The Irish Question
- Statute of Westminster
- Commonwealth of Nations
- Raymond Poincaré
- Daws Plan
- Young Plan
- isolationism
- tariffs
- Great Depression
- age of anxiety
- Friedrich Nietzsche
- Sigmund Freud
- Max Planck
- stream of consciousness
- James Joyce
- Virginia Woolf
- Werner Heisenberg
- uncertainty priniciple
- expressionism
- impressionism
- cubism
- surrealism

- functionalism
- cult of celebrity
- Roaring Twenties
- stock market crash
- John Maynard Keynes
- Federal Deposit Insurance Corporation (FDIC)
- The New Deal
- French New Deal
- Benito Mussolini
- Fascist
- March on Rome
- Weimar Constitution
- Adolf Hitler
- National Socialist German Workers' Party (Nazis)
- Mein Kampf
- Dachau
- Nuremberg Laws
- Kristallnacht
- Holocaust
- Anti-Comintern Pact

Overview

The fall of four great empires after World War I—Russian, German, Ottoman, and Austro-Hungarian—not only created a polyglot of smaller nations but left a political vacuum among peoples without a tradition of democracy. In the two decades between the world wars, totalitarian dictatorships were established in Russia, Italy, and Germany. For the first time in history, governments of great nations were dedicated to the total control of every area of human life, and individuals were expected to subordinate themselves to the needs of the state as defined by the single party in control. Italian fascism and German Nazism shared a common ideology of racist nationalism and the glorification of war. Russian Communism—despite its idealistic goal of the withering away of the state—imposed similar brutal repression to enforce the "dictatorship of the proletariat."

The Western democracies of England, France, and the United States came out of World War I with their heritage of democracy intact. In the 1930s, their tradition of dissent and their democratic institutions were sorely tested both by economic collapse and by the aggressions of the dictatorships. Ten years after the end of World War I, the worst depression in modern history began and lasted for over a decade. The human misery brought each of these nations close to the point of collapse and encouraged extremist movements—on the left and right—to offer simple solutions that would have destroyed democracy. Wracked by weakness and dissent, the democracies were unwilling to respond to the aggressions of the European dictators and the Japanese militarists. The policy of appeasement, which sought to placate the aggressors with concessions, only whet their appetites and led eventually to the worst war in human history.

The Western Democracies After the First World War

1920s in England

The nation did not recover, during the 1920s, from the economic losses suffered during the war. Its merchant fleet had been decimated by German submarines and its foreign trade had declined disastrously. International competition from worldwide industrialization from the proliferation of tariffs and from rival shipping nations further eroded an economic system already saddled by war debts, defaulted loans, and war relief programs.

The Liberal party, headed by David Lloyd George, fell into decline and was replaced by the Conservatives (Tory party), who favored high tariffs and welfare payments to the growing numbers of unemployed. The Labour party, whose program included a gradual nationalization of major industries, took power briefly; by 1929 and the start of the depression, an alliance of Labourites and Conservatives led by *Ramsay MacDonald* (1866–1937), then *Stanley Baldwin* (1867–1947), and finally *Neville Chamberlain* (1869–1940) ran the government until the start of World War II. Chamberlain's black umbrella became a symbol for the policy of *appeasement* (the willingness to give into the demands of the aggressive dictatorships).

British foreign policy during this period was occupied by the *Irish Question,* the granting of eventual independence to Southern Ireland after failure to suppress rebellion; the ending of the *British protectorate* in *Egypt,* although control of the Suez Canal was continued; and by the *Statute of Westminster,* which formally recognized the equality of the British Dominions—such as Canada and Australia—and set up a *Commonwealth of Nations,* which enjoyed special trading privileges.

1920s in France

The death, devastation, and debt of the First World War created economic chaos and political unrest. When the Germans defaulted on their reparations to France (which was to get 52 percent of the $33 billion), the economy nearly collapsed.

Through the 1920s, the government—a multiparty system requiring coalitions to operate—was dominated by the parties on the right, which supported the status quo and had the backing of business, the army, and the Church. In 1922, when Germany managed to pay only part of that year's reparation bill, *Raymond Poincaré* (1860–1934), prime minister, sent French troops to occupy the mineral-rich *Ruhr Valley* in Western Germany. The *Dawes Plan,* the *Young Plan,* and the *Lausanne Settlement* each, in turn, pared down German payments and diminished the ability of the French to collect. Tax and spending reforms by Poincaré's government, though, led to a temporary resurgence of prosperity until the worldwide depression hit.

French foreign policy during the decade aimed at neutralizing Germany in the event of a resurgence of militarism there. A series of alliances with buffer states such as Belgium and Poland surrounded Germany with French allies; the *Locarno Pact* of 1925 attempted to settle French-German border disputes; and the *Kellogg-Briand Pact* of 1928 aimed at outlawing war.

1920s in the United States

Disillusionment with the *Versailles Treaty* resulted in the Senate's rejection of U.S. membership in the League of Nations and the election to the presidency of *Warren G. Harding,* who promised a "return to normalcy."

Despite nostalgia for traditional *isolationism,* the United States participated in a series of naval disarmament conferences that agreed to limit the building of new battleships and fix the size of the major powers' navies.

Despite an economic boom in the United States, international trade was thwarted by a series of shortsighted *tariffs* (taxes on imports) which contributed to the *Great Depression* by diminishing foreign markets and limiting the ability of the Europeans to pay off their war debts to the United States.

Immigration quotas, which favored Northern Europeans over those from the south and east, ended the *age of immigration* that peaked at the turn of the century.

The Age of Anxiety

The carnage and disruption of World War I and the collapse of the "old order" that had defined European politics and diplomacy for nearly a century resulted in what commentators have called an "*age of anxiety*." The traditional assumption of the perfectibility of mankind through reason collapsed under the weight of events and new ideas.

Philosophy, science, the arts, and literature contributed to this crisis of confidence and conscience, but also offered new models to explain and portray humanity.

PHILOSOPHY

Friedrich Nietzsche (1844–1900), a German, attributed the decline of Western Civilization to the *slave morality* of Christian ethics. *Henri Bergson* (1859–1941), a French thinker, argued that intuition and experience are as powerful tools as science and reason for understanding the human condition. *Edmund Husserl* and *Martin Heidegger* (1889–1976), both Germans, extended the work of Nietzsche and *Soren Kierkegaard* (1813–1855), a Dane, to establish the foundations of *existentialism,* a philosophical school, popularized by *Jean-Paul Sartre* after World War II, that emphasized individual responsibility and capability for giving meaning to a meaningless universe.

PSYCHOLOGY

Sigmund Freud (1850–1939), an Austrian, portrayed human behavior as the interplay of powerful irrational and *unconscious* forces. The *id* was the driving force of the personality, a reservoir of sexual and aggressive drives; the superego, in the unconscious mind like the id, presented conflicting parental and social values that clashed with the selfish drives of the id. Individual lives and civilization itself were fragile balancing acts to keep these unconscious and potentially destructive forces in balance.

PHYSICS

Werner Heisenberg (1901–1976) developed the *uncertainty principle* that stated that a particle's velocity or position—but not both—could be calculated. This fundamental uncertainty about the nature of matter is endemic of the Age of Anxiety. The work of *Max Planck* (1858–1947), a German, demonstrated that atoms were not the basic building blocks of the universe. The theories of *relativity* of *Albert Einstein* (1879–1955), another German, further disrupted the comfortable assumptions of an orderly, rationally discoverable universe that Newton's 17th century physics had supported and encouraged *relativism* in ethics, politics, and worldviews.

LITERATURE

The aftermath of the war and intellectual trends, such as Freudianism, influenced writers to emphasize the irrational aspects of the human condition. *Stream of consciousness,* the portrayal of an individual's random thoughts and feelings, was a style perfected by *James Joyce* (1882–1941), an Irish novelist, and *Virginia Woolf* (1882–1941), an English fiction writer. It reflected the prevailing view of human life as alienated, irrational, and chaotic.

ART

Expressionism, abstract and nonrepresentational, replaced *impressionism* and was pioneered by *Vincent van Gogh* (1853–1890), *Paul Cézanne* (1839–1906), and *Paul Gauguin* (1848–1903) who painted with bold colors and images to focus on emotions and imagination. *Pablo Picasso* (1881–1973), a Spaniard, invented *cubism,* the depiction of mood through the use of geometric angles, planes, and clashing lines. *Dadaism* and *surrealism* were among the abstract styles created by artists of many nationalities, most of whom did their experimentation in postwar France. Architecture exemplified *functionalism,* buildings designed with practicality and clean lines instead of ornamentation.

MEDIA

Film and radio became major means for entertainment, information, and propaganda in the 1920s and 1930s. National broadcasting networks were set up by every major European power, and radio was employed by Adolf Hitler and other European dictators for propaganda and indoctrination. Movies became a prime medium for mass entertainment and also were employed to produce powerful propaganda. The modern *cult of celebrity*—the ironic glorification of the personalities who portrayed people other than themselves—was born with the advent of movies.

The Great Depression (1929–1939)

United States

The *economic boom* of the "Roaring Twenties" masked a deep-seated malaise. Farm prices had dropped disastrously after the peak selling during wartime; sizable segments of the population were poor; credit buying encouraged exorbitant personal debt; a dearth of new products (once the market for radios, autos, and refrigerators had been saturated) discouraged business investment.

The *stock market crash* of October 1929 was more a symptom than a cause of the depression that seized America and most of the industrialized world for the next decade. There were many contributing factors to the Great Depression, including buying stocks on large margins, a stock bubble that was not sustainable, adjustment from a wartime economy to a peaceful one, increased mechanization creating structural unemployment, changes in international patterns of trade, and declines in consumption caused by the aftermath of World War I. The Federal Reserve also exacerbated a weak economy by tightening the money supply when it needed to be loosened, thus creating deflation, which further devastated a weakened world economy that was using the dollar more than any other single currency. Since the American and European economies were interdependent through extensive investments and war debts owed to the United States, the failure of the U.S. economy led to a global breakdown. (The *command economy* of the U.S.S.R. managed to maintain and even surpass earlier productivity.) By 1932, nearly 15 million Americans were unemployed, about a quarter of the work force. Herbert Hoover's stubborn insistence that the depression was a normal fluctuation of the economy and would run its course brought the Roosevelt Democrats into the White House with a New Deal.

Franklin Delano Roosevelt (FDR) (1882–1945) and the New Deal may not have ended the depression in America, but they helped preserve capitalism and democracy in the United States by using the deficit-spending theories of *John Maynard Keynes* (1883–1946) who had predicted the Great Depression, and by establishing profound involvement of the federal government in the economy. The *Federal Deposit Insurance Corporation* protected individual depositors against bank failures; the *Agricultural Adjustment Act* provided price supports and subsidies for farmers; the *National Recovery Act* regulated industry; the *Civilian Conservation Corps* improved the ecology while providing jobs to young people; the Public Works Administration reconstructed the infrastructure of America while offering employment. The *Wagner Act* gave organized labor the right to collective bargaining and to strike. The *Social Security Act* guaranteed benefits to seniors.

Although the depression ended in the United States only when it began to rearm (1940–1941), the New Deal created a social welfare state with the obligation to relieve economic hardship while it preserved a modified and revitalized American capitalism.

England

During the 1930s, under the *National Party* (the coalition of Labourites and Conservatives) the British tried to alleviate the depression by reorganizing industry, abandoning free trade, reforming finances, and cutting government spending. Like the United States, Britain came out of the depression only through rearmament for the coming world war.

France

The depression increased class tensions and gave birth to a radical right that supported government reorganization along Fascist lines. After a financial scandal that involved high government officials in 1934, pro-Fascist riots broke out all over France. A coalition of socialists, republicans, labor unionists, and Communists responded by organizing the Popular Front, which opposed fascism, supported reform, and upheld the republic. In 1936, socialist *Leon Blum* (1872–1950) became prime minister under the *Popular Front* banner. He instituted a "*French New Deal*," which offered labor and agricultural reforms similar to those in the United States except that his measures were ineffective in ending the depression. Opposed by the conservative bloc in the Senate, the program failed to hold together the Popular Front coalition, and Blum resigned in 1937 to be replaced by conservative *Edouard Daladier* (1884–1970), who overturned the Blum reforms and practiced a policy of *appeasement* of Hitler's aggressions.

Dictatorship

Fascism in Italy

The peace settlements that ended World War I were extremely disappointing to Italian nationalists. None of the Austrian and Ottoman territories and German colonies in Africa that had been promised were received. To add to Italian discontent, a depression hit in 1919 and provoked nationwide strikes and class antagonisms. Terrified of a Communist revolution, the propertied classes looked hopefully for a strong leader to restore order.

Benito Mussolini (1883–1945), editor of a socialist newspaper and paradoxically an ardent nationalist, organized the Fascist party, a combination of socialism and nationalism, named after fasces (the rods carried by Imperial Roman officials as symbols of power). His *squadristi*, paramilitary *blackshirts*, attacked Communists, socialists, and other enemies of his program. Promising to protect private property, Mussolini won the support of the conservative classes and quickly abandoned his socialist programs.

The Fascist *March on Rome*, October 1922, caused the government to collapse and won Mussolini the right to organize a new government. King Victor Emmanuel III granted him dictatorial powers for one year to end the nation's social unrest.

The *corporate state* was the economic core of Italian fascism:

Labor unions manage and control industry.

Those unions then set the national political agenda.

Unlike socialist corporate states, where workers make decisions, authority flowed from the top.

The Fascists consolidated power through the 1920s by rigging elections and intimidating and terrorizing opponents. By 1928, all independent labor unions had been organized into government-controlled syndicates, the right to vote had been severely limited, and all candidates for the Italian parliament were selected by the Fascist party. Through the 1930s, an organization of corporations, headed by Mussolini, effectively replaced parliamentary government. Democracy was suppressed; the totalitarian state was created in Italy.

FASCIST ACCOMPLISHMENTS

Internal improvements such as electrification and roadbuilding

More efficient municipal governing

Suppression of the Mafia and improvement of the justice system (except for "enemies of the state")

Reconciliation with the papacy through the *Lateran Pact*, 1929, which gave the papacy $92 million for seized church lands in return for Pope Pius XII's recognition of the legitimacy of the Italian State

The trains in Italy ran on schedule.

FASCIST FAILINGS

- Italian democracy destroyed—press censorship, no right to strike, denial of all dissent, destruction of suffrage
- Terrorism a state policy
- Poor industrial growth due to militarism and colonialism
- Attempt to recapture the imperialistic glories of ancient Rome led to disastrous involvements in war

Nazism in Germany

In November 1918, a provisional government—socialist and democratic—was organized to negotiate a peace with the Allies. Although this government had very little input to the decisions made at the Paris Peace Conference, it did sign the Versailles Treaty and would be held responsible by conservative factions for the pact's inequities.

The *Weimar Constitution*, drafted in July 1919, set up Germany's first modern democracy by providing for a directly elected president and parliament (the *Reichstag*), by setting up a senate (the *Reichsrat*) to represent the German states, and by providing for a chancellor (prime minister), who represented the majority party of the Reichstag, and a cabinet to run the government.

After the *inflation of 1923*, Germany defaulted on its reparations to France, the French seized the Ruhr Valley, and German workers there went on a general strike. To pay these workers, the Weimar government printed paper currency and the prevalent inflation in the country became runaway. When debtors rushed to pay off their creditors with this worthless currency, the middle class was financially wiped out.

The Munich Beer Hall Putsch

The disasters for the Weimar government in 1923 encouraged *Adolf Hitler* (1889–1945) and his Nazi *Brownshirts* to seize power from the government of Bavaria, a state of Germany. Hitler, an Austrian who had fled poverty in his native land and had joined the German army at the start of World War I, helped organize the *National Socialist German Workers' Party (Nazis)* after the war. Racist, paranoid, sociopathic, and megalomaniacal, he was a brilliant orator and political strategist who played on popular discontent with the Weimar government by blaming democracy, Communism, and Jews for Germany's ills. He and *Erich Ludendorff* (1865–1937), a distinguished general who had led German troops to victory on the Eastern Front during the First World War, led the attempted coup in Munich at the end of 1923. It was suppressed, and Hitler was sentenced to five years in jail. He served only about a year of his already lenient term because many higher-ups in the justice system sympathized with his narrow nationalistic goals. While in prison, he wrote his blueprint for domination of Germany and eventually Europe, *Mein Kampf (My Struggle)*, which was a rambling, irrational, but convincing tract. It argued that Germany was never defeated in the First World War but was betrayed from within by Jews and socialists, that the Treaty of Versailles was a humiliation, that the Germans were a master race destined to expand into Eastern Europe to obtain lebensraum (living space) and to rule or exterminate inferior races such as Jews and Slavs.

After the *Dawes Plan* stabilized Germany's economy in 1924, the Nazi party's membership fell off so that by 1928 the Nazis won only twelve seats in the Reichstag. When the depression hit Germany in 1930, the Nazis won 107 seats and the Communists 77. Since the center parties—socialist and Christian Democrat—were unable to maintain a ruling coalition, many conservatives, including large landowners, industrialists, and army officers, threw their support to Hitler to avoid a Communist takeover. In January 1933, after a series of machinations, Hitler was invited by the aging president of the Weimar Republic, *Paul von Hindenburg* (1847–1934), another renowned general of the First World War, to form a government as chancellor. Hitler entered government legally, according to the constitution that he was dedicated to destroy.

The Nazi Revolution

The week before the elections of March 1933, which Hitler ordered to obtain a clear majority in the Reichstag, the *Reichstag building was destroyed by fire*. Although the Nazis almost certainly started the fire, Hitler used it as a pretext to declare emergency powers for his government. The election that followed was influenced by a suspension of freedom of the press and of speech, and by outright terrorizing of political opponents. After gaining a majority coalition in the Reichstag, the Nazis granted dictatorial powers to Hitler for four years in the Enabling Act. Within six months, all political parties but the Nazis were outlawed. When President Hindenburg died in 1934, Hitler was given a 90 percent vote of confidence by the German people to assume the presidency.

The Nazis Consolidated Power

Dachau, the first concentration camp, was opened in March 1933. Although the camps did not become death factories for mass extermination until 1941, they were brutal centers for punishing political opponents of the Nazis. During the *Night of the Long Knives*, in June 1934, Hitler purged the party by executing left-wing Nazis who had pushed for the socialist programs that Hitler had promised and leaders of the Brownshirts who had maintained autonomy within the party. The black-uniformed elite guard, the infamous *SS* (Schutzstaffel) became the party and the nation's enforcer. The *Gestapo* was the secret police force of the SS, and a rigorous selection and training process was set up for the SS, which would become the overseers of the death camps.

Labor unions were replaced, as in Fascist Italy, by a Nazi labor organization; strikes were outlawed, and factories put under the management of local Nazi officials who had dictatorial powers over the workers. Full employment resumed with arms production that thrived despite its prohibition under the terms of the Versailles Treaty.

A policy of *autarchy*, economic self-sufficiency, was developed to make Germany independent of imports and foreign markets.

The *Nuremberg Laws* of 1935 stripped Germany's half-million Jews of their rights as citizens. When Nazi mobs wrecked Jewish temples throughout Germany during *Kristallnacht* (Night of the Broken Glass) in 1938, the *Holocaust*—the systematic extermination of Jews in Germany and eventually throughout Europe—began. About 200,000 German Jews managed to escape from Germany. Of those that remained, over 90 percent were murdered.

A Collection of -ISMs

The period between the wars saw many new, some more tested ideas, movements, and philosophies compete for the beliefs of the people as the 20th century began in earnest. In many ways, that competition of ideas and ideals typifies the intellectual environment that pervades Europe today.

-ism	Definition or Explanation
absolutism	Form of government in which the monarch has complete control. Examples include Russia under Peter the Great and France under Louis XIV.
anarchism	The belief and political movement holding that the absence of government is better than any form of government yet conceived.
anti-Semitism	A belief that Jewish people are inferior and worthy of discrimination
Austro-Slavism	The idea that all the Slavs are better off protected by Austria than being conquered by Russia or exterminating each other was popular in the early 20th century.
capitalism	Economic system in which the means of production is controlled by private individuals who engage in business to earn a profit and whose competition created the best mix of output for consumers. This is the development of Adam Smith's laissez-faire principles outlined in his definition of capitalism, *An Inquiry into the Nature and Causes of the Wealth of Nations*.
colonialism	An idea tied to imperialism in which a mother country controls colonies for economic growth, political power, and military bases.
communism	An economic system that puts all power in the hands of the government ostensibly to manage the country for the good of the "people." The original ideas were Karl Marx's. It was butchered in Russia by Lenin and his successors who built a "communist" society that diverged greatly from Marxism and had not met Marx's requirements before the revolution.

-ism	Definition or Explanation
conservatism	The idea that change is bad and should be slowed or fought completely.
cubism	Artistic movement that succeeded impressionism and surrealism, led by Pablo Picasso and Georges Braque in which subjects were morphed into geometric shapes on the canvas.
deism	The belief that an all-powerful entity created the universe with rules and stepped back to watch it work.
enlightened despotism	Absolute rule justified by the monarch's paternalistic outlook for the best interests of his or her people. It was used to rationalize and organize several states from the top down during the age of the Enlightenment. Examples include Catherine the Great, Frederick the Great, and Joseph II of Austria.
existentialism	Twentieth-century philosophy wherein each individual is thought to be responsible for adding meaning to his or her existence.
fascism	A governmental nationalist system in which the state and big business partners eliminate worker rights and any resistance to governmental or corporate power. It is also sometimes called nationalism on steroids.
futurism	Artistic movement observed in pre–World War I Italian painting and sculpture. Sometimes identified with fascism, it opposed traditionalism and tried to depict dynamic movement through the elimination of conventional form, balance, and rhythm; it also stressed the violence and speed of the machine age.
humanism	The ideal of human possibilities that came from the revival of Greco-Roman literature and other artistic works was an important influence in the Renaissance and continues to influence the liberal view today.
idealism	Plato first defined this as a system of belief that relies on the mental plane rather than the material one. It has come to mean belief in the idea that one can make the world better and that things can work out well.
imperialism	The doctrine that states that more powerful nations can dominate less powerful ones militarily, economically, politically, and spiritually, as seen in England's actions toward India and Belgium's actions in the Congo.
impressionism	Artistic movement beginning in France with Monet in which an impression of the scene infused with the painter's emotion was depicted; it was a reaction to realism and the invention of photography.

-ism	Definition or Explanation
individualism	The idea that the desires of each person are important and that every person is important and that neither the state nor other individuals have the right to subvert any individual's desire.
liberalism	Political philosophy originating in the 19th century based upon the idea that political change can make society better than what it has been. This idea originally supported democratic rule, laissez-faire economic practices, and the removal of the Corn Acts, and also led to utilitarianism and the reform movement.
Marxism	The adherence to the communist theory devised by Marx and Engels in which the state owns the means of production and citizens contribute what they are capable of to society while society gives to each citizen what he or she needs.
materialism	The philosophical belief that only the tangible is real.
mercantilism (sometimes called bullionism)	The economic system of trade based upon a belief that a national economy must be strong and self-sufficient. It focused on a "favorable" balance of trade in which a nation exports more than it imports. It was meant to result in an accumulation of bullion. Government participation was imperative so mercantilism was opposed by the capitalists who wanted freedom from all government involvement in the economy.
nationalism	The idea that people with the same language, traditions, ideas, ideals, culture, heritage, and beliefs should have their own nation and love that nation.
naturalism	A literary movement of the early 20th century that recognized the human struggle with nature and humans as typified by Emile Zola.
nihilism	The idea that nothing but science exists supported by the 19th century Russian intellectual elites such as Turgenev.
pan-Slavism	The idea that there should be a nation for the Slavic peoples which was supported by Russia.
positivism	Auguste Comte's contribution to philosophy states that ideas must be tested and became the basis for modern critical thinking in the social sciences.
realism	Artistic movement of the late 19th century that depicted the horrors of everyday life for the common person. Grew out of romanticism.
radicalism	Movement that began in England where people called for immediate universal male suffrage, but it eventually came to be associated with any movement calling for rapid significant change.

-ism	Definition or Explanation
relativism	The idea that truth is not absolute but rather subjective; it maintains that the basis for judgment depends on the events, people, or circumstances surrounding a given situation.
republicanism	Idea that people should be ruled through representative democracy in a republic.
romanticism	Artistic movement of the mid to late 19th century that depicted the beauty of nature and lamented its passing as the Industrial Revolution began; scenes of industrial waste as well as common workers ravaged by the pace of change were popular in graphic and written arts alike. The emotionality and "storm and stress" of nature were emphasized.
Social Darwinism	The ideas of Darwin's evolution applied to the classes, implying that those at the top were more fit rather than better connected.
socialism	Idea that the government should manage the economy or aspects of the economy for the good of the people. Nineteenth-century socialists agreed that workers were unfairly treated. They opposed competition as a principle of economic behavior, rejected laissez-faire, and questioned the validity of the concept of private property.
totalitarianism	The idea that the government can and should control all aspects of the lives of its citizens, leaving them few choices in life. It was practiced by Stalin and Hitler.
utilitarianism	Jeremy Bentham's idea of the "greatest good for the greatest number" led to running water throughout England and eventually the world.
Zionism	The idea that the Jewish people should have a national homeland in Israel.

Sample Essay Question

The sample thematic essay question and the practice questions that appear in this chapter are types found on the AP exam, and they require a knowledge of causes, effects, personalities, ideas, and events.

SAMPLE QUESTION

Explain how, during the Great Depression, traditionally democratic European governments maintained their democracy while some of the newer European democracies fell under dictatorship.

Comments on the Sample Question

Follow the "Simple Procedures" for writing an essay. (See page 34.)

First, *What does the question want to know?* You must "offer the reasons for" and "detail" why democracy survived in some European nations and failed in others.

Second, *What do you know about it?* In England and France, the institutions and impulses of democracy prevailed over the crisis. In England, a coalition reformed the economic system. In France, the socialist "French New Deal" matched Roosevelt's policies in the United States. In Germany, the weak Weimar Republic crumbled with the election of a plurality of Nazis. In Spain, the Republican government—lacking popular support—was crushed by Franco's Falange. In Italy, Mussolini's Fascists completed the "corporate state" in response to the depression.

Third, *How would you put it into words?* Be sure to explain why democracy prevailed or failed.

Rubric for Sample Answer

Before you read the sample answer, examine the rubric. What will the reader be looking for when he or she grades this essay? A sample rubric, shaded to show the reader's evaluation, is seen below:

9–8 POINTS

- ✔ Thesis explicitly explains **both** how traditional European democracies maintained their democracy AND how some of the newer European democracies fell under dictatorship. Thesis does not need to be in the opening paragraph.
- ✔ Organization is clear, consistently followed, and effective in support of the argument.
  - • May devote individual paragraphs to an examination of traditional and newer European democracies.
  - • Must assess specific reasons for traditional democracies' stability and for the dictatorships emergence in newer democracies (traditional democracies had strong state functions when the Depression hit, experience with dissent, and met the basic needs of the populace while the newer democracies had weaker state apparatus, and traditions of democracy and tolerance).
- ✔ Essay is well balanced; how traditional European democracies maintained their democracy AND how some of the newer European democracies fell under dictatorship are analyzed at some length. Essay covers the inter-war period through 1939.
- ✔ Major assertions in the essay are supported thoroughly and consistently by relevant evidence.
- ✔ Evidence of the successes and failures of newer and older democracies may prove more specific or concrete.
- ✔ May contain errors that do not detract from the argument.

7–6 POINTS

- ✔ Thesis explains **both** how traditional European democracies maintained their democracy AND how some of the newer European democracies fell under dictatorship, but may not be developed fully.
- ✔ Organization is clear and effective in support of the argument but may introduce evidence that is not pertinent to the task.
- ✔ Essay covers all major topics suggested by the prompt but may analyze an aspect of the preservation of European democracies or their failure in greater depth rather than in a balanced manner.
- ✔ Major assertions in the essay are supported by relevant evidence.
- ✔ May contain an error that detracts from the argument.

5–4 POINTS

- ✔ Thesis explains **both** how traditional European democracies maintained their democracy AND how some of the newer European democracies fell under dictatorship, but without any development; thesis may address only part of the question effectively; thesis may be a simple, single-sentence statement.
- ✔ Organization is clear but may not be consistently followed; essay may veer off task chronologically or thematically or both.
- ✔ Essay may not complete all tasks:
  - May only explain how traditional European democracies maintained their democracy OR how some of the newer European democracies fell under dictatorship.
  - May discuss only one or two democracies.
  - May be primarily descriptive rather than analytical.
- ✔ Essay offers some relevant evidence.
- ✔ May contain errors that detract from the argument.

3–2 POINTS

- ✔ Thesis may simply paraphrase the prompt OR explain how traditional European democracies maintained their democracy OR how some of the newer European democracies fell under dictatorship.
- ✔ Organization is unclear and ineffective; essay may focus on the personal attributes of inter-war rulers rather than analyzing how democracies fared.
- ✔ Essay shows serious imbalance; explanation of the survival of the traditional democracies and the dictatorships emerging in newer democracies is superficial; much of the information may be significantly out of the period or geography of the question.
- ✔ Offers minimal OR confused evidence.
- ✔ May contain several errors that detract from the argument.

1–0 POINTS

- ✔ Thesis is erroneous OR irrelevant OR absent.
- ✔ No effective organization is evident.

✔ Explanation of the survival of the traditional democracies and the dictatorships emerging in newer democracies is generic.

✔ Provides little or no relevant supporting evidence.

✔ May contain numerous errors that detract from the argument.

Sample Answer

The economic disaster of the Great Depression shattered international trade, resulted in unemployment rates as high as 30 percent in the capitalist world, and tested the political systems of the traditional democracies and those created after World War I. Britain and France—among the world's three great constitutional governments, which included the United States—relied on their "habits" of democratic problem-solving to deal with the crisis. Germany, Spain, and, to some degree, Italy fell under the yoke of dictatorship during the depression.

Britain's well-established parliamentary system came to the fore during the depression, when a coalition of the Labour and Conservative parties developed a program to regulate commerce and industry and to extend the social welfare system that had its foundations in the pre-World War I period. A responsiveness to the electorate had been achieved gradually through the course of British history, and it prevailed over the extremist promises of the right and left.

The strong Socialist segment in France's political life came through with a "French New Deal" patterned after the programs of America's Franklin Delano Roosevelt. Labor legislation and farm subsidies, put through the assembly by a coalition led by the Socialists, offered hope to the electorate. Although the program was largely unsuccessful, rather than falling under the sway of the growing Communist party or French Fascists, the people returned the government to conservative factions. The hard-won republican democracy of the French seemed to have ingrained a sense of moderation and mistrust of extremism.

The Weimar Republic was a creation of the peace conferences at the end of World War I. Resented by the conservatives for its part in accepting the harsh Versailles Treaty, mistrusted by the masses for its haphazard responses to the runaway inflation of the mid-1920s and to the hardships of the depression, it was destroyed from within. When his Nazis won a plurality of Reichstag seats in 1932, Hitler was appointed chancellor and within less than two years he had laid the foundations for one of the world's most terrible totalitarian regimes. Democracy had been imposed on the Germans by their enemies; their history had not developed democratic institutions. The monarchies of the separate states, the despotism of Bismarck's new empire, and the virtual absolutism of Kaiser Wilhelm II's aggressive "fatherland" were the only prelude to the messy and inefficient coalition governments of the Weimar Republic. Hard times nurtured extremists, like the Nazis, that promised simplistic solutions. The Nazis were elected by the very democracy they destroyed.

Since its unification in the late 15th century, Spain has been the bulwark of Catholic, monarchical conservatism. When a republic was set up in 1931, after the king was ousted, leftists tried to diminish the influence of the Roman Catholic Church by secularizing the schools, seizing church lands, and abolishing the Jesuits.

This attempt, along with their land redistribution program, alienated the conservative faction—the military, the church, the monarchists—and Falangists (Spanish Fascists) organized a government. When the popular election in 1936 put a coalition of leftists back in power, General Francisco Franco started a civil war against the republican government. Backed by a sizable segment of the populace and by the arms and men of the Italian Fascists and the German Nazis, while the Republicans were backed by the Soviet Communists, Franco won the bloody and costly civil war and seized power in 1939. He ruled Spain as the world's longest reigning Fascist dictator until his death in 1975.

Mussolini used the Great Depression as an excuse to impose his plan for the "corporate state" on Italy. He and his party had been in power since 1922, and he completed his restructuring of the government by about 1934. In essence, labor unions managed industry and set the national political agenda. Of course, the unions were unrepresentative of the workers' real needs and they were dominated by the Fascists.

The failure of democracy during the Great Depression in Germany, Italy, and Spain resulted from the lack of adaptable democratic institutions and from the peoples' general mistrust of an unaccustomed form of government. Its success in Britain, France, and the United States came from their well-established constitutional systems.

EVALUATE THE SAMPLE ANSWER

Now go back and look at the rubric. It is clear that this essay fulfills all of the requirements for a score of 8 or 9 on the rubric. The essay answers all parts of the question thoroughly with concrete evidence at length with a well-balanced essay. The extra concrete support gets this essay a score of 9.

RATER'S COMMENTS ON THE SAMPLE ANSWER

9—Extremely well qualified

The essay more than fulfills the requirements of the question. It offers the two most important examples of European democracy's resilience during the depression and three of the most important instances of its failure. The essay is supported by accurate information, although its tone is generalized. Specific mention might have been made of the personalities and parties that led the British and French governments during this crisis: Labourite Ramsey MacDonald, Conservatives Stanley Baldwin and Neville Chamberlain for Britain; rightist Raymond Poincaré, socialist Leon Blum, conservative Edouard Daladier, the Fascist-type party, *Action Francaise,* and the prorepublican coalition, *Popular Front* for France. The Fascist movements in Eastern Europe, Latin America, and Asia could also have been mentioned, including Ioannis Metaxas in Greece, the Arrow Cross in Hungary, the Green Shirts in Ireland, Brazil's Vargas, Hideko Tojo and his Imperial Way faction in Japan, Novo and Ante Pavelić of Croatia, the Iron Guard of Romania, or the Slovak People's Party in Slovakia.

Practice Essay Questions

The questions that follow are samples of the various types of thematic essays that appear on the AP exam. (See pages 21–22 for a detailed explanation.) Check over the **generic rubric** (see pages 58–60) before you begin any of these essays and use that rubric to score your essay if you write one.

QUESTION 1

Evaluate the successes and failures of fascism in Italy.

COMMENTS ON QUESTION 1

A system as heinous as fascism makes an objective evaluation difficult, but Mussolini stayed in power as long as he did—1922 to 1943—because he and his party appealed in some way to the Italian people. Even if the minuses far outweigh the pluses, consider the domestic policy of the regime. For instance, did the corporate state increase employment while it destroyed unionism? How did Italy fare during the Great Depression? What internal improvements were made? Mussolini's aggressive foreign policy was costly to both the Italians and targets of his grandiose colonizing, but he did play the peacemaker during some of the early crises caused by Hitler.

QUESTION 2

"Nazi totalitarianism was a different breed from ordinary dictatorship." *Assess the validity* of this statement.

COMMENTS ON QUESTION 2

To "determine the truth" of this statement, you have to consider the phrase "different breed." It implies that that the Third Reich was far more encompassing and repressive than the usual military dictatorship. The task is to explain how. How did the Nazis use state-sponsored terrorism to gain and hold power? How did their racist theories lead to genocide? What was the structure of their police state? How did they use propaganda and education to inculcate their program? How was war an integral part of their ideology? This essay cannot be complete without comparing and contrasting Hitler's regime with that of Stalin or other totalitarian rulers.

QUESTION 3

"The Versailles Treaty gave birth to the Nazis; the Great Depression gave them power."
Defend or refute this statement.

COMMENTS ON QUESTION 3

A few crucial questions point the way when answered. How did the Nazis and other rightist extremists grow in membership after Germany's defeat in World War I? What part did the war guilt clause of the treaty play in their propaganda? How did the indemnity payments destabilize the German economy? What was happening to Nazi party membership during the late 1920s and how did the emergence of the Great Depression affect that trend?

QUESTION 4

Explain how, in order to gain their foreign policy goals during the 1930s, the "have-not" nations used force while the "have" nations refrained from its use.

COMMENTS ON QUESTION 4

Who were the "haves"? Britain, France, the United States. The "have-nots"? Germany, Italy, Japan. How did the peace settlements after the First World War make them that way? What acts of aggression did the "have-nots" perpetrate in the name of international justice? What was the response—or lack of it—from the "haves"? Aggression and appeasement are the story here. This essay must examine the use of economic and political policy used by the "winners" of the First World War as opposed to military policy utilized by those without imperialist holdings such as Italy and Japan.

QUESTION 5

Contrast and compare German Nazism and Italian fascism.

COMMENTS ON QUESTION 5

The similarities are easier to lay out: the means by which Hitler and Mussolini got into office, gained control of the state, and used propaganda, education, and force to subdue internal enemies; the ideology of war for the glorification of the state; the subversion of the institutions of society to serve the state.

The differences are of kind and degree: the Fascists never preached or practiced the poisonous racism that led to genocide; their military never achieved the kind of power that enabled the Nazis to impose their murderous policies all over the continent; their program and ideology were never digested by the Italian people with the relish with which the Germans swallowed Nazism.

Practice Multiple-Choice Questions

(These questions represent the various kinds found on the AP exam.)

1. Britain failed to recover economically after the First World War for all of the following reasons EXCEPT

    (A) its merchant fleet had been decimated by German U-boats
    (B) its Commonwealth trading partners had industrialized considerably during the war
    (C) other maritime nations had entered the competition for overseas shipping
    (D) German wartime bombing had devastated its cities
    (E) its Allies defaulted on war loans

2. In the first decade and a half after World War I, British foreign policy focused on

    (A) the "Irish question" and problems in the Middle East
    (B) Mussolini's overseas expansionism
    (C) Japanese aggression in mainland Asia
    (D) the rise of Nazism
    (E) Communism in Russia

3. The French post-World War I economy was in chaos for all of these reasons EXCEPT

    (A) the tremendous loss of life and property damage inflicted by the war
    (B) the economic policies of Raymond Poincaré
    (C) the Russian default on prewar investments by the French
    (D) the cost of fighting the war
    (E) the failure of the Germans to pay expected reparations

4. The goal of French foreign policy in the interwar years was

    (A) a prevention of the Japanese takeover of French Indochina
    (B) a return to isolation
    (C) the containment of potential German and Russian expansion
    (D) to check aggression by Fascist Italy
    (E) to aid the republican government against Franco's Spanish Fascists

5. In 1925, Germany's democratic Weimar government signed the Locarno Pacts which

    (A) set a ten-year moratorium on naval construction
    (B) guaranteed the territorial integrity of the Chinese Republic
    (C) outlawed war
    (D) recognized the French-Belgium-German boundaries set at Versailles
    (E) allied Germany with Fascist Italy

Munich Conference photograph. The Granger Collection, New York. (0006119)

6. The man on the left, pictured here with Hitler, was which of the following world leaders who said that he had "preserved peace?"

    (A) Edouard Daladier
    (B) Winston Churchill
    (C) William Gladstone
    (D) Benito Mussolini
    (E) Neville Chamberlain

7. The United States and Britain came out of the depression largely because of

    (A) social welfare programs of the American New Deal and the British National party
    (B) high tariff barriers to foreign competition
    (C) currency manipulation
    (D) raised taxes and lowered spending
    (E) rearmament for the coming war

8. American foreign policy regarding Europe in the 1930s was primarily directed toward

    (A) maintaining U.S. neutrality
    (B) containing the spread of Soviet Communism
    (C) blocking Fascist aggression
    (D) guaranteeing the safety of the democracies that had emerged after World War I
    (E) supporting the Loyalists in the Spanish Civil War

9. Totalitarianism includes all of the following characteristics EXCEPT

    (A) the state has the right to control the lives of its citizens from cradle to grave
    (B) total control by the state is essential to society
    (C) the state has an existence apart from the individuals who comprise it
    (D) every citizen owes the state absolute obedience unless the government violates individual rights
    (E) war brings glory and the state must arm for it while the citizen must train for it

10. The Scandinavian response to the Great Depression represented the

    (A) fascist response
    (B) capitalist response
    (C) Communist response
    (D) middle path between capitalist and communist responses
    (E) rejection of the Young and Dawes plans

11. Despite its totalitarian suppression of political freedom and human rights, fascism appealed to many Italians for all these reasons EXCEPT

    (A) the improvement of municipal government under centralized control
    (B) the electrification of rural Italy
    (C) overseas colonization
    (D) the Lateran Pact with the Pope, 1929
    (E) the suppression of the Mafia in Southern Italy

12. In January of 1933, Adolf Hitler assumed the post of Reichschancellor

    (A) by means of the Munich Beer Hall Putsch
    (B) by seizing control of the government
    (C) after his party received a plurality of votes in the democratic elections
    (D) after he overthrew the Weimar Republic
    (E) by staging a coup against Paul Hindenburg, president of the republic

13. The Weimar Republic (1919–1933), despite a valiant attempt to introduce democracy to Germany, failed to gain support of the German people mainly because

    (A) the Nazis maintained a wide following throughout the 1920s and 1930s
    (B) Von Hindenburg's presidency was marred by his personal corruption
    (C) monarchists, supporters of the abdicated kaiser, and militarists, humiliated by defeat in World War I, opposed it from the start
    (D) the government was unable to stabilize the economy or maintain law and order
    (E) a conspiracy of Jewish-capitalist-Communist bankers weakened the government

14. Hitler's Nazi program for Germany, as explained in his rambling autobiography *Mein Kampf,* included all of the following EXCEPT

    (A) Germany was defeated in World War I not on the battlefield but rather by traitors and revolutionaries
    (B) Germany was in the process of being destroyed from within by Jews, Communists, and democrats
    (C) the Germans were a master race destined to rule Europe
    (D) Germany must acquire lebensraum (living space) in Western Europe
    (E) "inferior races" must be enslaved or exterminated

15. European thought in the early 20th century was LEAST influenced by which of the following?

    (A) The concept of existentialism proffered by Nietzsche
    (B) The Darwinist concept of evolution
    (C) The Enlightenment works of Voltaire and Montesquieu
    (D) Wittgenstein's ideas of logical positivism
    (E) The uncertainty principle of Heisenberg

Answers and Answer Explanations

1.	D	**6.**	E	**11.**	C
2.	A	**7.**	E	**12.**	C
3.	B	**8.**	A	**13.**	C
4.	C	**9.**	D	**14.**	D
5.	D	**10.**	D	**15.**	C

1. **(D)** Massive bombing of British cities took place during the "Blitz" in the Battle of Britain during World War II. Lighter-than-air Zeppelins did only minimal damage during World War I.

2. **(A)** The independence of Ireland, the status of Northern Ireland, and issues in the Middle East, such as the Palestine Question, were major concerns.

3. **(B)** Poincaré's policies helped reform and stabilize the economy.

4. **(C)** The traditional enemy, Germany, was an inevitable threat given the Treaty of Versailles, inequities; Russia under Communism was a renewed threat.

5. **(D)** Germany signed the Locarno pacts, accepting the boundary settlements made at Versailles, in an attempt to improve its international relations.

6. **(E)** Neville Chamberlain was the one pictured here—he offered up the Sudetenland in exchange for "Peace in our time."

7. **(E)** War brings full employment.

8. **(A)** The depression aggravated the isolationist policies that World War I had encouraged.

9. **(D)** Individual rights do not exist in a totalitarian state; there is no right of revolution.

10. **(D)** The Scandinavians found a middle path of socialism between Communism and capitalism that has left them among the most successful and educated countries in the world.

11. **(C)** Mussolini's ill-fated attempts to recapture the glories of ancient Rome led to his overseas debacles in Libya, Albania, Ethiopia, and Greece, and it drew Italy into World War II.

12. **(C)** Von Hindenburg appointed Hitler after the Nazis won a plurality of votes in the 1932 elections and a coalition government had fallen. The Beer Hall Putsch took place in 1923; the Weimar Republic was never overthrown since Hitler took power legally.

13. **(C)** The Weimar government restored order and economic stability from 1924–1929; therefore C is the best answer since these influential "interest groups" opposed the Republic from the start.

14. **(D)** Eastern Europe, especially the vast spaces of the U.S.S.R., was the draw; Western Europe was already among the most densely populated areas on earth.

15. **(C)** While all of the others listed did figure prominently in early 20th century thought, Montesquieu and Voltaire did not.

World War II: Its Causes, Course, and Aftermath

CHAPTER 13

Key Terms/People

- Lebensraum
- League of Nations
- Axis Powers
- ghettos
- blitzkrieg
- Nonagression Pact
- Gestapo
- Red Army
- Battle of Britain
- Luftwaffe
- Royal Air Force (RAF)
- Franklin Delano Roosevelt
- Atlantic Charter
- Winston Churchill
- Auschwitz-Birkenau
- Erwin Rommel
- Joseph Stalin
- Big Three
- D-Day Invasion
- Yalta Conference
- United Nations
- Potsdam Conference
- superpowers
- Third World
- Iron Curtain
- Cold War
- Marshall Plan

Overview

As many as 70 million people perished in World War II, and for the first time in history the majority of the casualities were noncombatants. Saturation bombing of enemy cities, widespread starvation caused by war damage and displacement of people, and state-sponsored murder to exterminate a people (*genocide*) contributed to the terrible losses.

The war was fought on every continent but the Americas; it was global in scale; it was made up of separate conflicts, each with an identifiable beginning and end; it was a series of strategic improvisations rather than the result of carefully laid plans; it began at various times, as early as 1931 for the Manchurians and Japanese, as late as 1941 for the Russians and Americans.

It began over the issues never resolved after World War I: the failure of the Versailles Treaty to settle the problems of nationalistic yearnings for autonomy, of economic security, of blame for the First World War. The "have-not" nations—

Germany, Italy, and Japan—under the rule of repressive dictatorships, sought to redress what they saw as the inequities of the peace settlements after World War I. The "have" nations—the United States, France, and England—were absorbed in dealing with economic depression and with avoiding another costly war. When the Western democracies' policy of appeasement failed to stop the aggressions of the Axis powers, war resulted. It was officially declared in Europe in September 1939, after Germany's invasion of Poland. It ended with the unconditional surrender of Nazi Germany to the Russians, British, Americans, and French in May 1945, and with the surrender of Japan in September 1945.

It not only changed the balance of power in Europe with an international "balance of terror" created by nuclear weapons, but it gave rise to a nonmilitary conflict between the world's two superpowers, the Cold War.

Prelude to War

The rise of nationalist, industrialist, and imperialist single-party states, discussed in Chapter 12, was a significant factor contributing to the outbreak of the Second World War. One political factor was the personal will of Adolf Hitler, which many historians credit with being a major cause of the war. Another was the weakness of the Treaty of Versailles, which did not fix the underlying pressures in Western Europe, leaving the continent ripe for another war. The failure of the League of Nations to intervene in many instances when Hitler or Hideki Tojo (r. 1941–1945) broke the Treaty of Versailles made the dictators more brazen. Finally, the policy of appeasement as outlined below led to more and more aggression from the *Axis Powers* of Germany, Italy, and Japan.

Aggression and Appeasement

1931

Japan invaded Manchuria and the League of Nations did not intervene in any meaningful way. Japan and China were involved in a struggle over Japanese imperialism in China. The Japanese occupation of Manchuria lasted until the end of the war.

1933

Hitler pulled Germany out of the League of Nations.

1935

Hitler began rebuilding the German armed forces in open violation of the Treaty of Versailles. The Western powers, immersed in the Great Depression, objected but did not act. The Saar Plebiscite returned the Saar Valley back to Germany.

Mussolini attacked the independent kingdom of Ethiopia in East Africa; the League ordered *sanctions* (an embargo on trade in arms and raw materials) but the sanctions were not enforced.

1936

Hitler's troops occupied the *Rhineland,* which the Treaty of Versailles had made into a demilitarized zone between France and Germany. France and England failed to act, giving birth to the policy of *appeasement* (the submission, by default or deliberately, to the demands of the dictators).

1936

General *Francisco Franco* and his Spanish Falangists (Fascists) began an insurrection against the democratically chosen republican government of Spain. The Fascist dictators, Mussolini and Hitler, supported Franco with men, arms, and money. Stalin backed the Republicans, a significant number of whom were Communists. The brutal and destructive *Spanish Civil War,* which lasted for over three years and claimed the lives of 600,000, became a testing ground for the war machines of the dictatorships. The Fascists won, and Franco remained as the longest reigning Fascist dictator, his regime ending when he died in 1975.

1937

The second Sino-Japanese War began in earnest as the Japanese launched a full-scale attack, made significant territorial gains, and committed atrocities on the Chinese people, such as the Rape of Nanking. The League of Nations again did not respond.

Germany, Italy, and Japan signed the *Anti-Comintern Pact* to oppose international Communism. It marked the beginning of their alliance, the *Axis.*

Japan invaded mainland China, quickly conquering the seacoast and driving *Chiang Kai-shek's Nationalists* deep into the interior, where they waged a guerrilla war that proved costly to the Japanese.

1938

Hitler engineered the *Anschluss* (the forced union of Germany and Austria), again in violation of the Versailles Treaty. Once again the Western powers failed to act.

Hitler prepared to annex the *Sudetenland* (a part of Czechoslovakia that had been German territory). France and England, at the urging of the U.S.S.R., issued warnings. After tensions and talks, a conference was called, at Mussolini's suggestion, in which *Chamberlain,* prime minister of Britain, and *Daladier,* prime minister of France, met with Hitler and Mussolini. The infamous *Munich Conference* ceded the Sudetenland to Germany and marked the pinnacle of appeasement.

1939

Hitler seized the rest of Czechoslovakia, abandoned by the West, and the western part of Lithuania.

Mussolini invaded Albania.

Hitler and Stalin signed a *Nonaggression Pact,* which cleared the way for Hitler's *invasion of Poland.*

Triumph of the Axis Powers (1939–1942)

Although Germany, Italy, and Japan were often referred to as Fascists, their dictatorships were significantly different. The German Nazis and to a lesser degree the Italian Fascists imposed totalitarian systems upon their people. The Japanese, whose constitutional government was loyal to the emperor—a "living god," they believed—had a military dictatorship imposed in the 1930s. The term "Axis" came from the *Rome, Berlin, Tokyo Axis*, a pledge of mutual cooperation between the three nations that led to virtually no combined military ventures between the two European powers and Japan.

In addition to the military attacks on nations, wars against the ethnic and other minorities, waged more by Germany and Japan than by Italy, were a separate front. The Japanese dominated the areas they conquered economically and militarily. The Japanese turned the civilians into a slave labor force, including hundreds of thousands of women forced into prostitution for Japanese soldiers, commonly referred to as "comfort women." It is believed that almost 20 million Chinese were killed in the course of World War II. In addition, the Japanese performed medical experimentation on the Chinese civilians with biological agents.

The Nazis created a systematic method for enslaving the peoples they conquered. They had a system for deciding a civilian's fate by ethnicity. Germanic people held all positions of importance or power. Slavs and Russians were sent to forced work camps and factories. Jewish people, the Roma, homosexuals, handicapped people, known communists, and dissidents were sent to concentration camps to be exterminated.

The Jewish people were a special target for genocide. Jews were first ostracized and forced from positions of authority by the racist *Nuremberg Laws*. Then, all Jewish people in Nazi occupied territories were sent from their homes without their possessions to *ghettoes* to live in squalid conditions. After the *Wannsee Conference* of 1942, the Germans decided on a *Final Solution* in which all of the Jews would be killed, the ghettoes liquidated, and all Jewish people would be sent to death camps such as *Auschwitz*.

1939

September 1: Hitler invaded Poland, ostensibly to get back the part of East Prussia that the Versailles Treaty had ceded to Poland for access to the Baltic Sea, the *Polish Corridor*. The Germans used the *blitzkrieg* technique for this invasion with a massive air strike at a directed area of the enemy lines, followed by a reinforced rapid massive mechanized attack at the point of the air strike. The Germans penetrated enemy lines and divided the enemy, who could then be eliminated in sections by the superior firepower of the German war machine. The tanks and mechanized infantry swept in at lightning speed, giving the *blitzkrieg* its name of lightning war. The Germans also used their *Einsatzgruppen*, a special military force dedicated to killing leaders of Jewish people, communists, and the Roma during the invasion.

September 3: England and France declared war against Germany to honor their treaty with Poland.

October: Poland fell, occupied by the Germans in the West and the Russians in the East as part of the 1938 *Nonaggression Pact* between the two dictatorships. Russia also annexed the Baltic states of *Latvia, Lithuania,* and *Estonia,* which had been granted autonomy by the Versailles Treaty.

1940

The time period from the fall of Poland to April 1940 was called the sitzkrieg because the French sat behind their supposedly impregnable *Maginot Line,* a series of fortresses on the German border, the *British Expeditionary Force* in France made no moves, and the Germans prepared secretly for a spring offensive.

In a matter of days, Nazi forces overran and occupied Denmark and Norway.

The German Army cut through neutral Belgium and Luxembourg to outflank the Maginot Line. Within six weeks, the Nazi tactics of *blitzkreig* caused France to fall. Isolated and surrounded, the 250,000 man British Expeditionary Force was evacuated from Dunkirk in Belgium to England along with about 100,000 *Free French* fighters but without most of its heavy equipment. Mussolini invaded Southern France, an invasion that was ineffectual militarily but symbolic of Nazi-Fascist solidarity.

France surrendered on June 22. Germany occupied the north and west, and here, as in all the Nazi-occupied lands, terror and repression reigned. A puppet government, under World War I French *Marshal Philippe Petain,* known as the Vichy Regime, controlled the south and the North African possessions. General Charles De Gaulle (1880–1970), however, led the Free French, who continued to fight the Nazis under the guise of the Provisional Government of France, and the French Resistance undermined the Nazis from inside of France.

The *Battle of Britain,* an air war for supremacy of the skies over England, began in August. The industrial cities of Southern England, including massive London, were subjected to nightly bombings called "the Blitz."

1941

This was a pivotal year for the war. It looked like Great Britain was the last hold out at the beginning of the war when the war moved to Africa, but due to German and Japanese invasions, the U.S.S.R. and the United States joined the British effort by the end of the year. The United States had been supporting the British through a lend-lease program that allowed the British to use American war materials such as ammunition and ships. Russia was invaded and looked like it too might fall quickly, but the Germans were caught in the Russian winter just as the Americans declared war on the Axis powers. President Franklin D. Roosevelt, Prime Minister Winston Churchill, and Soviet Premier Joseph Stalin became the "Big Three" who made Allied policy.

1942

By June, the Axis powers in Europe controlled virtually the entire continent from the Atlantic in the west to the gates of Moscow in the east, from Scandinavia in the north to a good part of North Africa in the south. The Nazis set up extermination camps in Poland, Austria, and Germany, and they transported millions of Jews, other minorities, Soviet prisoners of war, and political enemies there for systematic murder. Auschwitz-Birkenau was the most infamous of these new extermination camps. Almost 12 million people were slaughtered inside concentration camps in accord with Nazi racist doctrine; 6 million of those were European Jews (about 60 percent of the prewar Jewish population). The Asian Axis partner, Japan, had seized the cities of coastal China, Indochina from the French, Indonesia from the Dutch, Malaya and Burma from the British, and the Philippines from the United States.

General *Erwin Rommel*, the Desert Fox, had managed to push the British in North Africa deep into Egypt, and the Suez Canal, lifeline of the British Empire, was threatened.

The Tide of War Turns (mid-1942–1943)

1942

June: Rommel's *Afrika Corps*, the elite mechanized force that spearheaded the Axis forces in this theater of war, was stopped at El Alamein in Egypt by British Forces under General Montgomery.

American aircraft carriers won a stunning victory against a superior Japanese naval force at the *Battle of Midway*.

Summer to winter: The Russian city of *Stalingrad*, controlling the lower Volga River, stood against German invaders and the fierce battle there marked the end of Nazi advances in the Soviet Union.

November: A joint Anglo-American force landed on the shores of Axis-held territory in *North Africa*.

1943

The Axis was cleared from North Africa.

The Russians began the advance that would lead them ultimately into Germany itself. (About 80 percent of German casualties in World War II were inflicted by the Soviets. Between 25 and 30 million Russians died during the war.)

Allied war leaders Roosevelt, Churchill, and representatives of Stalin met at *Casablanca* in North Africa and agreed to demand *unconditional surrender* of the Axis powers.

Allied Victory (1943–1945)

1943

American, British, and Canadian forces invaded the island of Sicily off the boot of Italy. Mussolini was overthrown, and the Allies landed in Italy proper and fought against determined German resistance.

At the *Teheran Conference* the Big Three agreed that they would only accept unconditional surrender from all three of the Axis powers, and that after the war was won, Germany would be occupied by the Allied powers and demilitarized.

1944

The *D-Day Invasion* of the French coast at *Normandy* marked the beginning of the end of Nazi domination of the continent. Paris was liberated by August. The last German offensive took place at the *Battle of the Bulge* in Belgium during December. From that point on, the Germans were in retreat on all fronts. In Dresden, firebombs were used to decimate the Germans and force them to surrender unconditionally.

1945

The Red Army smashed into East Prussia, Hungary, and Czechoslovakia while the Americans crossed the Rhine River. Hitler committed suicide; encircled Berlin was seized by the Russians; Germany surrendered, unconditionally, on May 8.

August 6: The United States dropped the *first atomic bomb* on the Japanese city of *Hiroshima.* (70,000 people died immediately; tens of thousands suffered after-effects.)

August 9: A second atomic bomb was dropped on the city of *Nagasaki*, and Japan surrendered.

September: Japan signed an official surrender and agreed to occupation by U.S. forces. Under the supervision of *General Douglas MacArthur* (1880–1964), commander of Allied forces in the Pacific theater, the emperor denied his own divinity, an antiwar constitution was imposed, under the Marshall Plan, wartime destruction was repaired, technical and financial assistance was given for further industrialization and modernization, and a democratic government was set up.

Aftermath of the War

Crucial Conferences for Postwar Europe

The *Yalta Conference*, among the Big Three in February of 1945, drew up a plan for the postwar settlement in Europe. Its main provisions:

Eastern Europe—Bulgaria, Czechoslovakia, Hungary, Poland, and Romania—would be set up with coalition governments of Communists and non-Communists until free elections could be held.

Germany would be partitioned into four zones of occupation—American, British, French, Russian.

Russia would enter the war against Japan in return for territories in Asia and islands north of Japan.

A *United Nations* was set up as a successor to the defunct League of Nations, with a *General Assembly* to represent all member nations in deliberations and a *Security*

Council of fifteen members dominated by five permanent members, the Great Powers—the United States, the U.S.S.R., Britain, France, and China—each of which would have veto rights over any proposal for involving the organization in preserving international peace.

The *Potsdam Conference*, July 1945, was attended by Churchill, Stalin, and Harry S. Truman, who had become president after Roosevelt's sudden death in April. Already cracks showed in the alliance between the Western democracies and Communist Russia when Truman and Churchill criticized Stalin for not allowing free elections in Soviet-occupied Eastern Europe.

Millions of refugees from concentration camps and from the war itself attempted to return home or to make new lives for themselves. Many tried to reconnect with families and friends with varying degrees of success. Thousands of refugees from the Soviet Union and Yugoslavia were returned to those nations by the western powers.

The Marshall Plan gave financial aid to any of the countries devastated by World War II that wanted to accept it. The money came in the form of loans that had to be spent on American goods, helping to transition economies from wartime to peacetime. The Marshall Plan also helped draw the lines between the capitalist countries that were tied together through the financial web of trade, symbolized by the Marshall Plan, and the communist nations that rejected Marshall Plan aid. This also led to greater interconnectedness between the economies of Western Europe and the dissolution of trade barriers that had plagued prewar Europe.

The Conflict for Control of Europe

At the end of World War II, only two great powers remained with the resources, land mass, population, industrial capacity, and military strength to affect world events. The United States, virtually untouched by the war, and the U.S.S.R., devastated but industrially and militarily powerful, became *superpowers*. Since the 17th century, there had been powerful single nations in Europe—Spain, France, England, Germany—but six or seven other great states had managed, through alliances, to maintain a balance of power. Soon after the war, two competing blocs would emerge: the *Soviet Bloc* with its *satellites* of puppet governments in Eastern and Central Europe and the *Western Bloc* or "Free World" made up, primarily, of the democracies. With the collapse of the colonial empires (see Chapter 9, "Imperialism"), a third bloc would emerge: the *Third World*, consisting of newly independent nations.

In a speech in Fulton, Missouri, in 1946, former prime minister Winston Churchill described Stalin's expansion of Communist totalitarianism as an *Iron Curtain* separating the captive peoples of Eastern and Central Europe from the rest of the world. A competition began between the *superpowers* to win Europe, its cities in ruins, its population decimated and displaced, but still a great industrial and population center of the world.

The *Cold War* had begun.

Casualties of World War II by Country

Country	1939 Population	Military Death Totals	Civilian Death Totals	Total Jewish Holocaust Deaths	Death Totals	Deaths as Percentage of 1939 Population
Albania	1,073,000	30,000		200	30,200	2.63%
Australia	6,998,000	40,500	700		41,200	0.57%
Austria	6,653,000		40,500	65,000	105,500	5.5%
Belgium	8,387,000	12,100	49,600	24,400	86,100	1.02%
Bulgaria	6,458,000	22,000	3,000		25,000	0.38%
China	517,568,000	3,800,000	16,200,000		20,000,000	3.86%
Czechoslovakia	15,300,000	25,000	43,000	277,000	345,000	2.25%
Denmark	3,795,000	2,100	1,000	100	3,200	0.08%
Dutch East Indies	69,435,000		4,000,000		4,000,000	5.76%
Estonia	1,134,000		50,000	1,000	51,000	4.50%
Finland	3,700,000	95,000	2,000		97,000	2.62%
France	41,700,000	217,600	267,000	83,000	567,600	1.35%
Germany	69,623,000	5,533,000	1,540,000	160,000	7,233,000	8.6%
Greece	7,222,000	20,000	220,000	71,300	311,300	4.31%
Hungary	9,129,000	300,000	80,000	200,000	580,000	6.35%
Iceland	119,000		200		200	0.17%
Italy	44,394,000	301,400	145,100	8,000	454,500	1.02%
Japan	71,380,000	2,120,000	580,000		2,700,000	3.78%
Latvia	1,995,000		147,000	80,000	227,000	11.38%
Lithuania	2,575,000		212,000	141,000	353,000	13.71%
Luxembourg	295,000		1,300	700	2,000	0.68%
Netherlands	8,729,000	21,000	176,000	104,000	301,000	3.44%
Norway	2,945,000	3,000	5,800	700	9,500	0.32%
Poland	34,849,000	240,000	2,760,000	3,000,000	6,000,000	17.2%
Romania	19,934,000	300,000	64,000	469,000	833,000	4.22%
(Soviet Union) U.S.S.R.	168,500,000	10,700,000	11,400,000	1,000,000	23,100,000	13.71%
United Kingdom	47,760,000	382,700	67,100		449,800	0.94%
United States	131,028,000	416,800	1,700		418,500	0.32%
Yugoslavia	15,400,000	446,000	514,000	67,000	1,027,000	6.67%
World Totals	**1,963,205,000**	**25,282,100**	**42,168,400**	**5,752,400**	**73,169,900**	**3.71%**

Sample Essay Question

The sample thematic essay question and the practice essays in this chapter are types found on the AP exam, and they require a knowledge of causes, effects, personalities, ideas, and events.

> ## SAMPLE QUESTION
>
> *To what extent did the Second World War weaken the influence of Europe on the rest of the world?*

Comments on the Sample Question

Follow the "Simple Procedures" for writing an essay. (See page 34.)

First, *What does the question want you to explain?* This essay is asking you to measure the extent to which the Second World War weakened the international influence of Europe. This essay must present evidence and evaluate how much Europe's influence around the world was weakened by the Second World War.

Second. *What do you know about it?* Be sure to include details about the continent being destroyed and production being reduced as rebuilding became a priority. The growing influence of the Soviet Union and the United States must also be assessed as a factor. The Marshall Plan must be examined. A thorough investigation of decolonization, as well as the Cold War, should be displayed. The rise of communism in Asia should also be addressed.

Third, *How do you want to write about it?* Create a thesis that states how great that influence was. It is advisable to mention French, German, and British influence before and after the war. Give supporting details about how the Second World War did or did not affect the decline of European power internationally, and finish with an overall evaluation of the extent of that influence.

Rubric for Sample Answer

Before you read the sample answer, examine the rubric. What will the reader be looking for when he or she grades this essay? A sample rubric, shaded to show the reader's evaluation, is seen below:

9–8 POINTS

- ✔ Thesis explicitly identifies the extent to which the Second World War weakened the influence on the rest of the world for **both** Western and Eastern Europe. Thesis does not need to be in the opening paragraph.
- ✔ Organization is clear, consistently followed, and effective in support of the argument.
  - • May devote individual paragraphs to an examination of the extent to which the Second World War weakened the influence on the rest of the world for both Western and Eastern Europe.

- Must identify factors of weakening influence (rise of American power, the Marshall Plan, European economic malaise in the 1950s–1970s, retreat of European powers in India, China, Indochina, Algeria, Afghanistan, and throughout Africa, and the end of direct imperialism through colonial holdings should be mentioned), factors of retaining dominance (economic power and influence around the globe, Soviet power during the Cold War, the common market and the European Union and the return of German industry, NATO, and British banking), and consider the extent to which Europe's influence was weakened after WWII.
- ✔ Essay is well balanced; the extent to which the Second World War weakened the influence on the rest of the world is analyzed at some length. Essay covers the postwar period to present.
- ✔ Major assertions in the essay are supported thoroughly and consistently by relevant evidence.
- ✔ Evidence of the spread of these ideas may prove more specific or concrete.
- ✔ May contain errors that do not detract from the argument.

7–6 POINTS

- ✔ Thesis explicitly identifies the extent to which the Second World War weakened the influence on the rest of the world for **both** Western and Eastern Europe, but may not be developed fully.
- ✔ Organization is clear and effective in support of the argument but may introduce evidence that is not pertinent to the task.
- ✔ Essay covers all major topics suggested by the prompt but may analyze an aspect of Europe's weakening influence, or the extent to which it occurred in one geographic locale in greater depth rather than in a balanced manner.
- ✔ Major assertions in the essay are supported by relevant evidence.
- ✔ May contain an error that detracts from the argument.

5–4 POINTS

- ✔ Thesis identifies the extent to which the Second World War weakened the influence on the rest of the world for Western and Eastern Europe, but without any development; thesis may address only part of the question effectively; thesis may be a simple, single-sentence statement.
- ✔ Organization is clear but may not be consistently followed; essay may veer off task chronologically or thematically or both.
- ✔ Essay may not complete all tasks:
  - May discuss only the extent to which Western or Eastern Europe's influence was weakened.
  - May discuss only one or two nations.
  - May focus only on the 20th century.
  - May be primarily descriptive rather than analytical.
- ✔ Essay offers some relevant evidence.
- ✔ May contain errors that detract from the argument.

3–2 POINTS

✔ Thesis may simply paraphrase the prompt OR identify the extent to which the Second World War weakened the influence on the rest of the world for **both** Western and Eastern Europe without analyzing the extent to which that weakening occurred.

✔ Organization is unclear and ineffective; essay may focus on one nation rather than analyzing the extent to which all of Europe's power was affected.

✔ Essay shows serious imbalance; discussion of the ways and extent to which European power changed as a result of WWII is superficial; much of the information may be significantly out of the time period or geography of the question.

✔ Offers minimal OR confused evidence.

✔ May contain several errors that detract from the argument.

1–0 POINTS

✔ Thesis is erroneous OR irrelevant OR absent.

✔ No effective organization is evident.

✔ Discussion of the extent to which European power changed as a result of WWII is generic.

✔ Provides little or no relevant supporting evidence.

✔ May contain numerous errors that detract from the argument.

Sample Answer

The period before World War II saw Europeans, such as the British and the French, dominate much of the world through trade and political and military policies, but World War II significantly reduced the influence of European nations in the world, with the exception of the Soviet Union, which engaged in the Cold War with the United States. Although other factors, such as increasing political awareness and industrialization, affected the decline of European, and particularly British, influence, the Second World War was a major contributing factor to that loss.

The destruction of much of the productive capacity of Europe, as factories were either bombed or converted to military use, did impact the decline of European influence in the rest of the world. The Europeans had gained power because they brought trade goods to people all over the world. As the primary shipping nations, they influenced the world through trade negotiations and supplying manufactured products. As the Second World War ended, the Europeans had been devoted to fighting the war and lost their trade connections in part because they had no goods to supply. The British and French still held political control over India and many other colonial possessions at the end of the war, but those possessions would want independence as the Europeans were not as helpful. Instead, the Americans became dominant in many of these areas by increasing trade and supplying Marshall Plan money to rebuild the world destroyed by war. The United States had not been ravaged by war, and thus still had a strong productive capacity, which was applied to trade and reconstruction directly after the Second World War. In this way, the

United States gained prominence as the European powers of old lost it. The Soviet Union also provided aid to countries in order to encourage communism there, and thus increased its influence in Eastern Europe as that region was subject to soviet control. This could be seen in Vietnam and Eastern Europe.

Decolonization was another major factor that reduced the international power of most of Europe. The French gave up many of their possessions, such as Indochina and eventually Algeria. The French defeat in Algeria is symbolic of the decline of European power after the Second World War. The British also gave up holdings in the Middle East, India, Latin America, and Africa, as well as their South Pacific holdings. The loss of India significantly reduced the international influence of Great Britain, and it occurred mostly as a result of WWII and the Indian support for that war.

The rise of the United Nations gave all nations a more egalitarian mode of interacting after World War II. This, along with the knowledge that European tensions had drawn the entire world into armed conflict costing close to 70 million lives, also reduced the international influence of those perceived to have begun the war, such as Germany, Great Britain, and France. With the exception of the superpowers, nations gained a more even playing field after the Second World War, and this further reduced the influence of the old European powers.

The emergence of the Cold War after the Second World War greatly increased the international influence of the United States and the Soviet Union, while decreasing the influence of formerly powerful nations such as Britain, France, and Belgium, which ruled a territory almost thirty times the size of the mother country before World War II. The Cold War can be seen as a direct result of World War II, so it could be argued that this change in the patterns of international influence resulted from the Second World War. The power struggle between the two superpowers created alliances such as NATO and the Warsaw Pact, which further increased the influence of the superpowers. The superpowers gained power as they vied for the attention of rulers around the world in order to spread their ideologies of capitalism and communism. The American dominance of the World Bank and the International Monetary Fund were also results of the Cold War, and further increased American power, while reducing European influence. Soviet financial and military aid also increased their international influence in the second half of the twentieth century.

While many factors came together to increase the international influence of the Soviet Union and the United States after the Second World War such as exploitation of vast natural resources, the war played a significant role in increasing the influence of those two superpowers while also contributing to the declining influence of the other European nations such as Britain and France.

EVALUATE THE SAMPLE ANSWER

Now go back and look at the rubric. It is clear that this essay fulfills all of the requirements for a score of 8 or 9 on the rubric. The essay answers all parts of the question thoroughly with concrete evidence at length with a well-balanced essay. The lack of extra concrete support gets this essay a score of 8.

RATER'S COMMENTS ON THE SAMPLE ANSWER

8—Extremely well qualified

This essay is clearly written with a strong structure that presents a clear analysis of the impact of the Second World War on the international influence of European nations. It also clearly states that the *extent to which* the Second World War impacted that influence was *significant* and uses facts to support that thesis. The analysis of the superpowers gaining influence while other European nations lost influence was cogent and addressed the subtlety of power inherent in the question. The division of European nations into the Soviet Union and Western European nations helped address the extent to which that influence was diminished. This essay could have been improved by discussing the composition of the United Nation's Security Council as an example of "Old Europe's" loss of international power and by using quotes to support the ideas and using specific examples from more nations.

Practice Essay Questions

The questions that follow are samples of the various types that appear on the AP exam. (See pages 21–22 for a detailed explanation.) Check over the **generic rubric** (see pages 58–60) before you begin any of these essays and use that rubric to score your essay if you write one.

QUESTION 1

"The Berlin-Rome-Tokyo Axis was more an ideological than an actual alliance." *Assess the validity* of this statement.

COMMENTS ON QUESTION 1

To "determine the truth" of this statement, you have to consider the ways in which the Axis partners aided each other's war efforts. Did the Italians and the Germans actually coordinate battlefield strategy? Recall Mussolini's "stabbing France in the back" in 1940; the North African campaign; the "Balkans Rescue"; the invasion of Sicily. Did the European Axis partners ever coordinate battle plans, send or receive war materials, plan overall strategy with the Japanese? How were they united in aims, ideology, political methods?

QUESTION 2

To what extent and in what ways did the United States, the U.S.S.R., and Britain coordinate war aims and strategies?

COMMENTS ON QUESTION 2

"How and how much" is the issue here. In dealing with Russian and Western cooperation, consider the Big Three conferences: Teheran, Yalta, Potsdam (after the death of Roosevelt); the second-front controversy; the material aid from the United States to Russia.

The American-British alliance is more tangible: Lend-Lease; the Atlantic Charter; North Africa, Sicily, Italy, Normandy, the bombing and invasion of Germany; the Pacific War.

QUESTION 3

The Allied decision to demand "unconditional surrender" of the Axis powers lengthened the war needlessly." *Defend or refute* this statement.

COMMENTS ON QUESTION 3

This has been an issue much argued, "a hypothesis contrary to fact." Would the war have ended sooner if the Allies had negotiated with the Axis governments or even with antigovernment military factions? In framing your answer, consider that despite the saturation bombing of Germany's cities, the Nazis maintained an iron grip until the end; despite assassination attempts, Hitler ruled until his suicide when the Russians were at the gates of Berlin; despite firebombing and the dropping of the first A-bomb, the Japanese refused to surrender.

QUESTION 4

Contrast and compare the results of the war on both the United States and the U.S.S.R.

COMMENTS ON QUESTION 4

"Show differences": What was the destruction to the homelands of each? What political, social, or economic changes took place for each? What were the human losses? What were the war gains?

"Examine similarities": They were the only two powers—superpowers—with the strength left to influence European and world events; they had established parallel spheres of influence; both were brought into the war through sneak attack; they had simultaneously solidified their competing ideologies and launched the Cold War.

This is an abstract question that requires crisp organization and thoughtful presentation.

QUESTION 5

Analyze the way the wartime cooperation of the United States and the Soviet Union degenerated, within a few years after the end of the war, into the Cold War.

COMMENTS ON QUESTION 5

The wartime alliance between the West and the Soviet Union was the cooperation of competing systems in order to defeat a common enemy. Strains showed early in the Russian push for a second front, manifested themselves in the tensions at Yalta and at Potsdam in the Russian refusal to allow free elections in Russian-occupied Eastern Europe. The geographic expansion of Communism because of the war frightened the West. The presence of massive American forces in Europe frightened the Soviets.

Practice Multiple-Choice Questions

(These represent the types of questions that appear on the AP exam.)

1. The shaded area of the map on the following page shows

   (A) the belligerent nations at the start of World War II in Europe
   (B) the furthest extent of Axis conquest in Europe and Africa
   (C) the Nazi Empire
   (D) the gains of the Red Army at the end of World War II
   (E) the Axis-occupied territory right before the D-Day Normandy invasion

2. The regimes of Nazi Germany, Fascist Italy, and the Stalinist Soviet Union all shared a

   (A) complete rejection of private property
   (B) violently racist ideology
   (C) goal of complete economic transformation
   (D) profound hatred of Western liberalism
   (E) state support of private industry

3. The period of relative military inaction in Europe between the fall of Poland and the fall of France is called
   (A) the Russo-Finnish War
   (B) the Vichy period
   (C) the Battle of Britain
   (D) the Blitzkrieg
   (E) the Sitzkrieg

"More grain for the home front." The Granger Collection, New York. (0044506)

4. The illustration on page 345 from a Second World War era Soviet poster suggests that women should

   (A) work inside of the home
   (B) save grain and not be wasteful
   (C) join the army for their family and for Mother Russia
   (D) contribute to the war effort by taking on traditionally male jobs
   (E) keep the farms in good shape for when their husbands return home

5. The Atlantic Charter—issued by President Roosevelt and Prime Minister Churchill in 1941 and drawn from the principles of Woodrow Wilson's Fourteen Points—formed the basis for the Allied war aims and pledged all EXCEPT
   (A) the restoration of governments conquered by Germany and Italy
   (B) free trade and fair access to resources
   (C) freedom from tyranny and want
   (D) freedom of thought and religion
   (E) a U.N. organization to ensure peace after the war

6. The tide of war turned from Axis conquests to Allied victories in all EXCEPT

   (A) the Battles of Midway and Guadalcanal in the Pacific
   (B) the Battle for Stalingrad in Soviet Russia
   (C) the evacuation at Dunkirk in Europe
   (D) the Battle of El Alamein in Egypt
   (E) Operation Torch in North Africa

7. A major issue of contention between the Western Allies—Britain, the United States, and the Soviet Union—before 1944 was

   (A) the opening of a second front in Europe
   (B) whether or not to demand the unconditional surrender of the Axis
   (C) the fate of democracy in Eastern Europe after the war
   (D) promised U.S. military aid to Communist Russia
   (E) British occupation of Iran, which bordered the U.S.S.R.

8. Which of the following is true of the Allied D-Day invasion of "Fortress Europe" on June 6, 1944?

   (A) It was the largest seaborne invasion in human history.
   (B) It inflicted 50 percent of the casualties the German Army suffered during the war.
   (C) It landed at the "soft underbelly" of Europe.
   (D) After the landing the Germans were unable to launch another major offensive during the course of the war.
   (E) It was a joint operation of American, British, and Russian forces.

9. The agreements of Roosevelt, Stalin, and Churchill at Yalta in 1945 are controversial for all of the following reasons EXCEPT

   (A) they gave Stalin a free hand in dominating the liberated states of Eastern Europe
   (B) they gave the Russians control of a sizable segment of Germany
   (C) they lacked provision for the de-Nazification of Germany
   (D) they gave the U.S.S.R. Japanese territories in Asia
   (E) they gave the U.S.S.R. Polish territory

10. During World War II, most of the damage to cities in Western Germany was caused by

    (A) seige cannons of the Russian army
    (B) search-and-destroy tactics of the Americans
    (C) the scorched-earth policy of the retreating Nazis
    (D) sabotage by anti-Nazi Germans
    (E) saturation bombing by American and British air forces

11. The Grand Alliance was cemented by all of the following policies EXCEPT

    (A) a commitment to unconditional surrender
    (B) U.S. adoption of the "Europe first" principle
    (C) postponement of a discussion of the eventual peace settlement
    (D) the decision to exclude France from the Alliance
    (E) patriotic desires to defeat the aggressive Axis powers

12. In 1945, the war left only these nations with the economic and military strength to significantly influence world affairs

    (A) United States, U.S.S.R., Great Britain, France, China
    (B) United States, U.S.S.R., Great Britain, China
    (C) United States, U.S.S.R., Great Britain, France
    (D) United States, U.S.S.R., Great Britain
    (E) United States, U.S.S.R.

13. Which was NOT a feature of the Cold War between the United States and the U.S.S.R.?

    (A) A series of confrontations short of direct military conflict
    (B) A competition of productivity between differing economic systems
    (C) A number of direct and open military clashes between U.S. and Soviet forces
    (D) An ideological conflict that involved espionage, propaganda, and military and economic support for erstwhile Allies
    (E) A division into blocs of politically and ideologically aligned nations

14. Soviet and Western wartime cooperation had already degenerated into serious tensions at the Potsdam Conference in July 1945 because

    (A) Harry S. Truman, who had succeeded to the presidency after the death of Roosevelt in April, plainly expressed his dislike of Stalin
    (B) Winston Churchill had strained relations with his claims of Soviet empire building in Eastern Europe
    (C) the Soviets had reneged on their promise to enter the war against Japan
    (D) Stalin had reneged on his promise to allow free elections in Soviet-occupied Eastern Europe
    (E) the U.S. A-bomb attacks on Japan had intimidated the Soviets

15. The phrase "iron curtain," used by Winston Churchill in his 1946 speech at Fulton, Missouri, refers to

    (A) the security measures employed by Stalin's bodyguards
    (B) the Berlin Wall
    (C) Stalin's policy of holding firm in negotiations with the West
    (D) the Kremlin's veil of secrecy
    (E) Soviet domination of Eastern Europe

Answers and Answer Explanations

1.	B	**6.**	C	**11.**	D
2.	D	**7.**	A	**12.**	E
3.	E	**8.**	A	**13.**	C
4.	D	**9.**	C	**14.**	D
5.	E	**10.**	E	**15.**	E

1. **(B)** The Mediterranean was an Italian Lake; Western Europe was in Hitler's hand; the Nazis had reached the suburbs of Moscow.

2. **(D)** The only aspect that all three did share was a profound hatred of Western liberalism. The Fascists and Nazis supported private industry and the Nazis were racist while the Soviets rejected private property and wanted complete economic transformation.

3. **(E)** This lull is often called the Phony War.

4. **(D)** The women were depicted doing traditionally male jobs as was needed during the Second World War in order to keep up production and fight the war well. Women in the Soviet Union were soldiers as well as tractor drivers.

5. **(E)** It was not part of the Atlantic Charter but was proposed during the wartime Big Power conferences.

6. **(C)** A tactical victory, it was still a retreat.

7. **(A)** The Russians, under attack by the Germans, wanted the pressure taken off.

8. **(A)** It was the largest seaborne invasion; over a million troops were landed within the first week or so. The largest land invasion force was the 2 million plus Nazi Operation Barbarossa, the invasion of the U.S.S.R. in June 1941.

9. **(C)** De-Nazification was carried out by all four of the occupying powers. The United States, especially, was rigorous in its pursuits of Nazi war criminals and in its reconstruction of the political and social institutions of Nazism.

10. **(E)** The bombing of these cities was indiscriminate in its choice of targets—military, industrial, civilian. The theory was that the enemy's will and capacity to make war would be destroyed. By early 1945, the Germans were producing more in the occupied countries than they had before the bombing had started, and there is evidence that bombing strengthened German resolve and German willingness to swallow the Nazi line.

11. **(D)** The only thing that did not help cement the "Big Three" was dislike for the French. The Soviets and Americans as well as the British had no reason to care about the exclusion of the French except for the fact that there was a puppet government there controlled by the Nazis.

12.   **(E)**   That is how they became superpowers.

13.   **(C)**   There was no direct war between the United States and the U.S.S.R.

14.   **(D)**   Truman and Churchill berated him for this, but could do little.

15.   **(E)**   The Soviet Empire was forming.

CHAPTER 14

Postwar Europe: Recovery, Communism, and Cold War (1945–1970)

Key Terms/People

- Morgenthau Plan
- The Marshall Plan
- North Atlantic Treaty Organization (NATO)
- Schuman and Monnet Plan
- Warsaw Pact
- European Economic Community
- Common Market
- Sputnik
- Brezhnev Doctrine
- Truman Doctrine

- blockade of Berlin
- Berlin Airlift
- Korean War
- Douglas MacArthur
- The Geneva Summit
- Fidel Castro
- Paris Summit
- Bay of Pigs
- Berlin Wall
- Cuban Missile Crisis
- brain drain

Overview

The destruction of Europe after World War II was far more extensive than that at the end of the First World War. The technology and tactics of the First World War had limited the damage to specific regions of Europe: Flanders, which consisted of Northeastern France and parts of Belgium, Poland and sections of European Russia, some provinces of Northern Italy and Southern Austria; some areas of the Balkans.

During the Second World War, the mass bombing of industrial and population centers severely damaged virtually all the cities of the European belligerents and it left Germany in ruins. The German destruction and the scorched-earth policy of the Soviets leveled tens of thousands of villages, towns, and cities in the Western Soviet Union. Ruined transport systems, factories, and housing shattered the economies of Western and Eastern Europe.

The economic recovery of Western Europe was so amazing, it was referred to as "the miracle." Within a decade, productivity had reached prewar levels; within two, unparalleled prosperity prevailed. Germany, defeated, demoralized, and divided, had been the key to recovery. The United States infused massive aid through the **Marshall Plan** to rebuild not only its former Allies but also its former enemies— Germany and Italy. By the end of the 1950s, Western Europe had made the first moves toward economic and, perhaps, political union. The United States also aided Japan and set up a viable democratic government.

The rebuilding of the U.S.S.R. was no less spectacular. Under Stalin's Five-Year Plans, most of the war damage had been repaired within a decade. A vastly expanded Soviet Empire, established by the successes of the Red Army against the Nazis, included most of the countries of Eastern Europe, which became satellites of the brutally repressive Stalinist Soviet Union. After the death of Stalin in 1953, new leaders redefined the role of Soviet Communism but kept an iron grip on the U.S.S.R. and Eastern Europe.

The emergence of the United States and the U.S.S.R. as superpowers at the end of the war created a new balance of power in Europe and in the world. Europe quickly became divided into the Western and Communist blocs, the West dedicated to the containment of Soviet expansionism, the Communists intent on both spreading their philosophy and defending their gains against the "capitalist conspiracy." The Cold War—the ideological, economic, and, at times, military rivalry between the two blocs—was all the more dangerous for the development of nuclear weapons. The peaks of tension, during which the superpower confrontations almost led to war or even nuclear holocaust, alternated with "thaws" until a policy of "peaceful coexistence" emerged.

Western European Recovery (1945–1957)

The 1940s After the War

Since Germany's *Ruhr Basin* was the industrial center of a devastated Europe, the Western Allies decided that Germany would have to be rebuilt. The Soviets had hoped to use German reparations for reconstruction of their own massive war damage, and the *Morgenthau Plan* had been developed by the U.S. secretary of the treasury to transform Germany back into an exclusively agricultural society. Led by the Americans, the British and French agreed that in order for Western Europe to recover, Germany would have to be rebuilt.

Joint administration of the *four occupation zones* broke down in 1946. The American, British, and French sectors eventually became West Germany; the Russian sector, East Germany.

Agitation by Communist parties in France and Italy worsened relations between the democracies of Western Europe and the Soviet Union. In 1948 the Czech Communists seized power in Prague and set up a government.

The Marshall Plan, developed by Secretary of State and former military chief of staff *George Marshall* (1880–1959), was put into operation. Billions of dollars in grants went to Western Europe and Germany to rebuild housing, transportation systems, and industrial plants.

The United States and eleven other nations formed the *North Atlantic Treaty Organization* (NATO) to rearm non-Communist Europe and safeguard it against invasion. Soon after, West Germany (the *Federal Republic of Germany*), Greece, and Turkey joined. Eventually Germany was encouraged to organize a national army under NATO command.

The 1950s in Western Europe

Productivity in those countries that were aided had exceeded prewar rates, and the United States urged the Europeans to develop a European free-trade zone similar to that among the various American states. The Marshall Plan combined self-interest—Communism in Europe would be contained and markets for U.S. goods opened—with altruism. Under the French-sponsored *Schuman and Monnet Plan,* six industrial countries on the continent—Belgium, France, Holland, Italy, Luxembourg, and West Germany—formed the *European Coal and Steel Community* to pool their resources in 1952. The *Warsaw Pact* was formed as an alliance by the Soviet Union and its Eastern European satellite nations as an answer to the formation of NATO by Western Europe. The *European Economic Community,* the *Common Market,* was created by the same six nations that formed the European Coal and Steel Community. It aimed at an end to internal tariffs and the free exchange of money and workers between members. By 1968, its plan would be in full effect. By 1973, Britain, previously denied membership by France, joined as a full partner along with Ireland and Denmark. By 1960, many of the best scientists and engineers left Europe to go to the United States for higher salaries. This movement was the "brain drain."

Decolonization

France, Belgium, Great Britain, Italy, the Netherlands, and Portugal all gave up their colonial empires in the period after the Second World War. By 1975, most of Africa and Asia was back under African and Asian rule, with a few minor exceptions. The horrors of the world wars had destroyed much of the confidence the western powers had that they were better than those they ruled and allowed Europeans to see that the rest of the world deserved self rule.

Britain lost India first in 1947; then much of Africa was relinquished after 1960. The British also gave up possessions in the Middle East that are now Syria, Iraq, and Israel. A Jewish homeland was created in Israel in 1948. There was little or no bloodshed in British decolonization.

The French gave up Indochina after their resounding defeat at Dien Bien Phu in 1954 but fought very hard to keep Algeria. It was a long and brutal conflict that sapped France of resources and forced it to fight against guerilla tactics and a native nationalist movement. The conflict ended with a French Commonwealth that included most of the African area France had fought to keep.

Belgium had ruled a portion of Africa that was thirty times the size of Belgium. The Democratic Republic of the Congo was formed in 1960, ending more than a century of Belgian rule there.

There are some scholars who argue that the proliferation of European languages in education and finance, as well as Cold War political pressures, led to an era of *neocolonialism* in which nations were dominated financially and politically rather than militarily.

Communism: The Soviet Union and Its Satellites (1945–1968)

Immediately after World War II

Backed by the Red Army, local Communist parties in Eastern Europe—Bulgaria, Czechoslovakia, Poland, and Romania—took over the coalition governments and fell into the Soviet orbit. East Germany, under occupation, also became a satellite. *Albania* and *Yugoslavia*, under Communist party rule, managed to maintain independence from Moscow since they had not been liberated from the Nazis by Soviet troops.

The Soviets Consolidate Power (1945–1953)

Communist governments in the satellite nations carried out land distribution reforms and nationalization of industry. Forced *collectivization* of agriculture was only moderately successful. Soviet-type five-year plans helped reconstruction and built up heavy industry at the expense of consumer goods. Police state methods were used—domestic spying, arbitrary imprisonment, censorship, torture—to silence opposition parties and to remove the influence of the Roman Catholic Church.

Repression was tightened to the breaking point in the U.S.S.R. itself during the last years of Stalin. His achievements—industrialization of Europe's backward giant, victory in the *Great Patriotic War* against the Nazis, post-war reconstruction accomplished in a decade, and the spread of a Soviet Communist empire to Eastern Europe—had to be measured against the brutal repression he imposed on the Russian people. Over the course of his totalitarian regime he was responsible for the slaughter of perhaps 30 million of his citizens, for denying basic civil rights, for establishing forced labor camps (gulags), for repressing any and every form of free expression.

Stalin died in 1953, and there was a power struggle in the Soviet Union. The party leadership executed *Lavrenti Beria*, head of the secret police, to prevent a coup, and it set up a figurehead premier.

Riots against Soviet domination broke out in East Berlin, a precursor of greater resistance from the satellites.

The Era of Khrushchev (1956–1964)

Nikita S. Khrushchev (1894–1971), a former deputy of Stalin and by 1954 head of the Soviet Communist party, made a speech to the Central Committee on the *crimes of Stalin*. Stalin, he said, had built a *cult of personality*, created terror among citizens and party leaders alike, and had even been responsible for the dismal failure of Soviet troops to stop the initial advances of the Nazi invaders in 1941.

De-Stalinization encouraged resistance in the satellites; *revolts* broke out *in Poland and Hungary.* In Poland, *Wladysaw Gomulka* (1905–1982) managed to win concessions from Soviet leaders and to liberalize the government. In Hungary, armed revolt in Budapest and other cities threatened the existence of the Communist regime, and the Soviets brutally crushed all resistance.

The launching of the first artificial earth satellite, *Sputnik*, in 1957, pointed out the considerable technological achievements of the Soviets. In 1949, they had tested *their first atomic bomb*; in 1953, they had developed their first *hydrogen bomb.* Their work on rocketry, aided by German scientists captured after the war, enabled them to eventually develop *intercontinental missiles* capable of striking the United States.

Khrushchev was ousted in 1964. *Centralized economic planning (Gosplan)* had developed the five-year plans that reconstructed the U.S.S.R. after World War II and had raised the Soviet gross national product from 30 percent of the American in 1950 to about 50 percent in the mid-1960s. Agriculture performed badly, though, partly because of the failure of collectivized farms to provide incentives for production and partly because of bad decisions by Khrushchev. Party rivals resented his personal power, and they found an excuse to oust him.

The Conflicts of 1968

In August, Soviet leaders sent a massive military force to end the *liberalization of Czechoslovakia*, a threat to both the Warsaw Pact and Soviet domination. The *Brezhnev Doctrine*, formulated by the head of the Soviet Communist party and future premier Leonid Brezhnev (1906–1982), stated that the *U.S.S.R. had the right to intervene* in the internal affairs of any satellite nation if Communism was threatened. This doctrine and the intervention in Czechoslovakia ended Soviet leadership of the Communist world and its role as a model for Communist governments.

Cold War

The *Cold War* was the economic, cultural, ideological, political, diplomatic, and, under certain circumstances, military struggle between the Western and Communist blocs. It took place, in varying degrees of severity, over decades after the end of World War II. The two superpowers that led the opposing blocs—the United States and the U.S.S.R.—allocated great portions of their military might toward defeating each other in a projected war but never did directly confront each other militarily.

The initial phase of the Cold War involved a struggle for the control of war-devastated Europe. By the late 1940s, U.S. aid had shored up the exhausted democracies of Western Europe against Soviet encroachments, and the Red Army had installed Communist governments in Eastern Europe under Moscow's domination.

The next phase involved the **containment** of Communism by the West in the Third World, those regions that had emerged from colonialism after World War II. Wars involving the European democracies or the United States against Marxist nationalists broke out in Asia, Africa, and Latin America. Foreign aid and regional alliances, primarily provided and engineered by the United States, countered the influence of Moscow. A nuclear arms race created a "balance of terror" between the two superpowers while cracks in their systems of alliances aggravated the overall conflict. The world was saved from nuclear holocaust only by the fact that both sides knew that either side could literally destroy all human life on earth, and, therefore, they could not afford to come into open conflict. This balance of power, dubbed *Mutually Assured Destruction*, is credited by many historians for preventing a nuclear conflict between the superpowers. The role of the United Nations, however controversial, expanded as more newly independent nations joined and the superpowers realized the limitations of their might.

With the collapse of the Soviet Union in the 1990s, the Cold War is said to have ended. The United States, after the dissolution of the Soviet Union, became the sole Superpower with no opposing power to temper U.S. foreign policy goals. The Cold War gave a focus to the amorphous conflicts and competitions among the earth's peoples, and decades of waging it seemed to establish some rational limitations to winning it. (The two main protagonists managed to keep the peace between themselves for nearly a half century.) Despite its repressiveness and creaky inefficiencies, Soviet Communism helped to restrain the uglier expressions of narrow nationalism and ethnic rivalry. The world may be a more dangerous place until people settle into new definitions.

Détente prevailed in the years that followed. Splits in the ranks of both the Western and Communist blocs had changed relations between the two superpowers, which in the late 1940s and through the 1950s had faced off with the support of allies or satellites. DeGaulle's France had questioned the leadership of the United States in European affairs just as Mao's China had questioned that of the Soviet Union in the Communist world. The suppression of Czechoslovakia had tarnished the Soviet image just as the Vietnam War had the American. A prosperous and independent Western Europe took more and more charge of its own affairs, and nationalist resistance in Eastern Europe diminished Soviet influence. The Cold War between the United States and the U.S.S.R. began to "thaw."

Timeline for the Cold War

What follows is a detailed timeline of the Cold War that covers the era with more than enough information to answer any questions that may appear on the AP exam.

Year	Event
1945–1947	• Communist agitated strikes in Western Europe and takeovers of governments in Eastern Europe. • Contrary to Stalin's previous promises, worsened relations between the former World War II Allies, the United States and the U.S.S.R.
1947	• The *Truman Doctrine* was announced, pledging military aid to Greece, Turkey, and any other nation threatened with Communist aggression and expansion.
1948	• A Soviet *blockade of Berlin*—the former capital city administered by the four occupying powers but deep within the Russian zone. • Countered by the *Berlin Airlift*. • The Soviets had initiated the blockade to retaliate for the unification of the American, British, and French zones into West Germany.
1948	• The *European Recovery Plan* (Marshall Plan) went into effect, and the Soviets, although invited, declined to participate and forbade their satellites to do so.
1949	• *NATO* was established along with regional military alliances in the Middle East, Southeast Asia, and the Southwest Pacific. • After nearly two decades of civil war, the Chinese Communists led by *Mao Zedong* (1893–1976) and aided by the U.S.S.R., defeated the corrupt regime of *Chiang Kai-shek's Nationalists*, despite massive U.S. military aid. • Drove them from the Chinese mainland to the Island of *Formosa (Taiwan)*. • The United States opposed the recognition of the Communist regime in the United Nations.
1950	• The *Korean War* (1950–1953) was the first major military conflict between the West and the Communists. After the Japanese had been driven from the peninsula, south of Manchuria, the country had been occupied in the north by the Soviets and south of the 38th parallel by the United States. • The Soviets rejected free elections in a unified Korea and, instead, supported a satellite regime under *Kim Il Sung*. • Elections in South Korea in 1948 brought *Syngman Rhee* into power. In June 1950, a powerful North Korean army, supported by Soviet aid, invaded south of the 38th parallel and expected quick victory. • President Truman, fearful of repeating the pre-World War II policy of appeasement, convinced the United Nations' Security Council to condemn North Korean aggression and oppose it militarily. • Since the Russians were boycotting the United Nations for failing to recognize Communist China, they could not veto the proposal, and a U.N. force led by *General Douglas MacArthur* (1880–1964) made up of mostly U.S. troops landed in South Korea. Fifteen nations provided mostly token contingents. • Hundreds of thousands of Chinese Communist troops attacked the U.N. force in November 1950, driving them back to the 38th parallel.

Year	Event
	• General MacArthur insisted on attacking China. • President Truman, fearful of involving the United States in an Asian land war, removed MacArthur from command.
1951	• A cease-fire ended serious fighting in July 1951; an armistice, returning the Koreas to the situation before the war, was signed in 1953.
1953	• The war pitted United States forces against a Communist foe supported and aided by the Soviet Union, and despite the losses—54,000 U.S. dead, 2.5 million Koreans and Chinese—it convinced the United States that military might could contain the spread of Communism. • Neither the European democracies, preoccupied with rebuilding their shattered nations, nor the large, non-Communist Asian nations of India, Burma, and Indonesia, mistrustful of a new kind of Western imperialism, shared the U.S. enthusiasm. • The death of Stalin *thawed* the Cold War. Tensions rose and relaxed and then returned again, but *peaceful coexistence* seemed possible.
1955	• *The Geneva Summit* between President *Dwight Eisenhower*, the British and French prime ministers, and Soviet leaders led to a conciliatory atmosphere.
1956	• War in the Middle East, between Israel and its Arab neighbors, renewed tensions between the Soviets, who aided the Arab states, and the West, which supported Israel. (France and Britain made military moves against Egypt for nationalizing the Suez Canal.) • The Geneva Accords divided Vietnam into the Communist North and the non-Communist South.
1959	• U.S. and Soviet relations soured further when *Fidel Castro*, an avowed Marxist, was openly aided by Soviet and Chinese Communists in his overthrow of Cuban dictator *Fulgencio Batista*.
1960	• The *Paris Summit* ended when Khrushchev proved that the United States had been making spy flights over the U.S.S.R. after a *U-2* high-altitude reconaissance plane had been shot down over Soviet territory. • The U.S.S.R. became capable of launching direct nuclear attacks against the United States.
1961	• The *Bay of Pigs invasion* of Cuba by anti-Castro Cuban refugees was a total disaster and a humiliation for newly elected president *John F. Kennedy*, whose administration had supported it. • The infamous *Berlin Wall*, as powerful a symbol of Soviet tyranny as the Bastille had been of royal abuses, was erected to keep East Berliners from fleeing to the West.
1962	• The first U.S. troops, "military advisers," arrived in South Vietnam to shore up its anti-Communist government against attacks by Communist North Vietnamese infiltrators and *Vietcong* guerrillas. • The *Cuban Missile Crisis* brought the world to the brink of nuclear war when President Kennedy demanded that Premier Khrushchev remove nuclear missiles that the Soviets had installed in Cuba. • The "eyeball-to-eyeball" confrontation ended when the bases were dismantled.

Year	Event
1963	• A *nuclear test ban treaty* to stop atmospheric explosions was signed by three of the world's four nuclear powers: the United States, the U.S.S.R., and Britain. France refused. • A *hotline* or direct communication phone was installed between the Kremlin and the White House to prevent accidental nuclear war. • A *rift between the Soviets and Chinese Communists* led to growing tensions and a parting of the ways between the two giants.
1964	• Communist China became the fifth member of the "nuclear bomb club."
1965	• *Lyndon Johnson*, who succeeded to the presidency after the assassination of Kennedy, bolstered American involvement in the Vietnam conflict by continuing bombing raids against North Vietnam and by sending a massive ground force. • The Soviets and Chinese Communists supplied great quantities of arms and other aid to help the northerners maintain the fight against an eventual U.S. force of well over a half-million troops.
1968	• *Prague Spring* in Czechoslovakia occurred when the reformist Alexander Dubcek was elected and tried to give his people more civil and economic rights. • The other Warsaw Pact nations, led by the U.S.S.R., invaded with tanks and occupied the country until 1990.
1969	• During the administration of President *Richard Nixon*, an avowed anti-Communist in his early political career, he and his secretary of state, Henry Kissinger, pursued a policy of *détente*, peaceful coexistence between the Western and the Communist blocs. Leaders exchanged visits, and the *SALT* negotiations (Strategic Arms Limitations Talks) began. • The United States landed a manned expedition on the moon.
1970	• A *nonproliferation treaty* to limit the spread of nuclear weapons was signed by the United States and the U.S.S.R. Unfortunately, nations with nuclear power plants proved it was possible to reprocess spent fuel in order to make nuclear bombs. (India became the sixth member of the "nuclear bomb club" this way in 1974.)
1972	• *Nixon's dramatic visit to Communist China*—followed by scientific and cultural exchanges—resumed relations between the two former enemies.

Sample Essay Question

The sample thematic essay question and the practice questions presented in this chapter are types found on the AP exam, and they require a knowledge of causes, effects, personalities, ideas, and events.

SAMPLE QUESTION

Explain the significance of the Marshall Plan.

Comments on the Sample Question

Follow the "Simple Procedures" for writing an essay. (See page 34.)

First, *What does the question want to know?* What did the Marshall Plan do? What intended and unintended consequences did it have?

Second, *What do you know about it?* The significance of the Marshall Plan (European Recovery Program) is in three areas: it marked the commitment of the United States to European affairs, a turnabout from its traditional policy of postwar isolationism; it was the keystone to the rebuilding of war-devastated Western Europe; it was the first economic weapon used in the containment of Soviet Communism.

Third, *How would you put it into words?* The task here is to "make clear" and to "detail" how. Why was the United States willing to commit billions of dollars to the restoration of Europe? Why did it help even its former enemies, Germany and Italy? What prompted fear of the spread of Soviet Communism?

Rubric for Sample Answer

Before you read the sample answer, examine the rubric. What will the reader be looking for when he or she grades this essay? A sample rubric, shaded to show the reader's evaluation, is seen below:

9–8 POINTS

✔ Thesis explicitly explains the significance of the Marshall Plan. Thesis does not need to be in the opening paragraph.

✔ Organization is clear, consistently followed, and effective in support of the argument.
  - May devote individual paragraphs to an examination of the Marshall Plan for Eastern and Western Europe as well as the world.
  - Must assess specific pieces of significance of the Marshall Plan, (rebuilt Western Europe while communists in Eastern Europe refused funds, were to be paid back in currency, built an economic miracle in Western Europe).

✔ Essay is well balanced; significance of the Marshall Plan is analyzed at some length. Essay covers the post-WWII Reconstruction period into the early Cold War.

✔ Major assertions in the essay are supported thoroughly and consistently by relevant evidence.

✔ Evidence of the spread of these ideas may prove more specific or concrete.

✔ May contain errors that do not detract from the argument.

7–6 POINTS

✔ Thesis explains the significance of the Marshall Plan, but may not be developed fully.

✔ Organization is clear and effective in support of the argument but may introduce evidence that is not pertinent to the task.

✔ Essay covers all major topics suggested by the prompt but may analyze an aspect of the Marshall Plan in greater depth rather than in a balanced manner.

✔ Major assertions in the essay are supported by relevant evidence.

✔ May contain an error that detracts from the argument.

5–4 POINTS

✔ Thesis explains the significance of the Marshall Plan, but without any development; thesis may address only part of the question effectively; thesis may be a simple, single-sentence statement.

✔ Organization is clear but may not be consistently followed; essay may veer off task chronologically or thematically or both.

✔ Essay may not complete all tasks:
  • May only explain the significance of the Marshall Plan partially.
  • May discuss only one or two nations.
  • May focus only on one or two effects of the Marshall Plan.
  • May be primarily descriptive rather than analytical.

✔ Essay offers some relevant evidence.

✔ May contain errors that detract from the argument.

3–2 POINTS

✔ Thesis may simply paraphrase the prompt OR explain the significance of the Marshall Plan.

✔ Organization is unclear and ineffective; essay may focus on the personal attributes of postwar rulers rather than analyzing the importance of the Marshall Plan.

✔ Essay shows serious imbalance; explanation of the significance of the Marshall Plan may be significantly out of the period or geography of the question.

✔ Offers minimal OR confused evidence.

✔ May contain several errors that detract from the argument.

1–0 POINTS

✔ Thesis is erroneous OR irrelevant OR absent.

✔ No effective organization is evident.

✔ Explanation of the significance of the Marshall Plan is generic.

✔ Provides little or no relevant supporting evidence.

✔ May contain numerous errors that detract from the argument.

Sample Answer

"Get the boys home in time for Christmas." It seems to be the habitual response of America after its foreign wars are won. After World War I, the United States participated in the partial and very temporary occupation of Germany and in an ill-fated expedition against the Red Army during the civil wars that followed the Russian Revolution of 1917. The troops—well over a million who served in Europe during the First World War—soon went home. The U.S. Congress—following a tradition established by Washington—slipped back into isolation, and the Senate refused to join Wilson's League of Nations. Twenty years later, 12 million Americans were back in uniform to fight the Axis.

The policies of isolation, neutrality, and appeasement had not worked against the Fascist dictators, and the United States had learned. Not only did the U.S. military occupy Germany in 1945—along with British, French, and Russian forces—but the United States realized that only it and Stalin's Soviet Union were strong enough to make a difference in European affairs. In 1947, at an address at Harvard University, George Marshall, U.S. secretary of state and, during the war, chief of staff of the military, proposed the European Recovery Plan to rebuild wartorn Europe.

By 1948, eighteen European nations, excluding Fascist Spain, which was not invited to join, and Russia and its East European allies, which refused to participate, formed the Organization for European Economic Cooperation. It was designed to first rebuild the cities, factories, energy sources, housing, and transport systems of Europe and then to increase productivity and reduce trade barriers.

From 1948 to 1952, the United States spent about $14 billion on the Marshall Plan, most of it in the form of U.S.-produced nonmilitary machinery, raw materials, and food. The aim of the United States in spending this money was more than altruistic. There seemed to be no precedent in modern history for the victor-nation to build not only an enemy country but those that would be potential economic competitors. But the United States understood that if the non-Communist nations of Western Europe remained weak, they would be vulnerable to Soviet expansionism. Already Eastern Europe was part of the satellite empire. Also, the United States had another realistic motive: to create potential markets in a prosperous and free Western Europe.

The significance of the Marshall Plan was threefold. It marked the commitment of the United States to "winning the peace as well as the war." It helped to rebuild the shattered states of Western Europe and to keep them from falling under Communism. It also marked the beginning of European economic cooperation that has evolved into the European Union, an international economic powerhouse.

EVALUATE THE SAMPLE ANSWER

Now go back and look at the rubric. It is clear that this essay looks like a 6 or 7 on the rubric. The essay answers all parts of the question with concrete evidence but the essay focuses on one, Western Europe, and misses some major possible points. In this case, the lack of extra details warrants a 6.

RATER'S COMMENTS ON THE SAMPLE ANSWER

6—Well qualified

This is a good compact summary of the significance of the Marshall Plan. In general terms, it explores the plan's importance to U.S. foreign policy in marking the departure from traditional isolationism by helping to rebuild shattered Western Europe and "contain" Communism in Europe.

Suggestions for improvement:

The thesis statement did not occur until the conclusion. While an alert reader may score this essay correctly, it is always advised to place the thesis in the first paragraph, usually as the second sentence. It could have been made clearer that the Marshall Plan was an economic branch of battle in the Cold War. Reference could have been made to other U.S. economic and military assistance programs like Point Four technical assistance to underdeveloped nations and the Truman Doctrine to help Greece and Turkey to fight Communist insurgents. A brief discussion of the enormity of U.S. involvement in world affairs would have been useful. A consideration of why the U.S.S.R. and its satellites did not avail themselves of the plan would have been relevant: they saw it as a form of "American imperialism." A further exploration of the role of the Organization for European Economic Cooperation in the movement for consolidation was called for.

Practice Essay Questions

The questions that follow are samples of the various types of thematic essays that appear on the AP exam (see pages 21–22). Check over the **generic rubric** (see pages 58–60) before you begin any of these essays and use that rubric to score your essay if you write one.

QUESTION 1

Explain the major confrontations of the Cold War before the death of Stalin.

COMMENTS ON QUESTION 1

To "detail" is the task. First, determine what is meant by "confrontation." The very essence of the Cold War was that the superpowers never directly confronted each other militarily.

Before 1953 and the death of Stalin, one of the most serious confrontations involved the United States and the U.S.S.R. over the Berlin Blockade. Through the winter of 1948–1949, mostly American aircraft flew over Soviet-held East Germany to supply West Berlin. The forces of each of the superpowers were within easy shooting distance, but moderation prevailed on both sides.

The Korean War (1950–1953) brought the United States and other U.N. forces into a shooting war with the new Communist China, which was considered a close ally of the Soviets and was supplied with Russian arms and aided by Russian "volunteers." President Truman's sacking of General MacArthur limited the scope of the war.

The Truman Doctrine and NATO, the West's responses to the Communist threat in Europe, could be considered elements of the overall confrontation.

QUESTION 2

Evaluate the role of NATO in the defense of Western Europe.

COMMENTS ON QUESTION 2

"What minuses?" you ask. Did its establishment in 1949 increase tensions between the West and the Soviets? Should West Germany have been rearmed by 1950? Should it have been authorized to create a "national army" by 1954? Did its role in NATO exaggerate the importance of the United States in Europe? Would the Warsaw Pact have been consummated if not for the existence of NATO? Were there alternatives?

The pluses? It seems to have averted an invasion of Western Europe after its inception. The stationing of hundreds of thousands of American troops on European soil not only aided the Western Europeans in their defense, but it enabled them to invest in their economies the huge sums needed for defense. The United States also gave billions of dollars to other NATO powers to build up their military forces, and U.S. bases boosted their local economies.

QUESTION 3

Analyze the movement toward economic union in Western Europe.

COMMENTS ON QUESTION 3

Recall that the Marshall Plan inspired the Organization for European Economic Cooperation. Did this set the tone for the Schumann and Monnet Plan? What was the European Coal and Steel Community? How did it evolve into the Common Market? Who were the Common Market's first members? Why wasn't Britain one of them? What was the role of the French in delaying British membership? How has European consolidation gone beyond the economic? How did all of this lead to the creation of the European Union and the euro? How did the Treaty of Maastricht (formerly the Treaty of the European Union) come about? How has the development of the euro strengthened the European Union?

QUESTION 4

Contrast and compare the status of the Eastern European satellites before and in the two decades after the death of Stalin.

COMMENTS ON QUESTION 4

Eastern Europe before the Soviet takeover after World War II was an agricultural, not an industrial, region. How did land redistribution and Soviet-type Five-Year Plans change this? What was the political situation for the satellites? How did the East Berlin riots of 1953 set a new precedent in the relations between the Soviets and their satellites?

How did "de-Stalinization" help precipitate revolts in Poland and Hungary in 1956? How did these revolts affect the political and economic reform of Eastern Europe? How did the suppression of Czechoslovakia in 1968 diminish the Soviet reputation as anti-imperialistic in the Third World? What changed, what remained the same after Stalin's death?

QUESTION 5

Analyze how and why the Cold War gradually thawed.

COMMENTS ON QUESTION 5

Again, the death of Stalin cannot be underestimated as an influence. Be aware, though, that while the "cult of personality" disappeared from Soviet political life, the edifices of the totalitarian state remained. The so-called thaw involved a number of "quick-freeze" crises. The realization that any nuclear confrontation would destroy humanity (or at least reduce the global standard of living) and the Mutually Assured Destruction (MAD) theory led both powers to be more conciliatory.

The summit meetings played an invaluable role in decreasing superpower tensions. The Cuban Missile Crisis may have alerted the United States and the U.S.S.R. to the ultimate disaster that "brinksmanship" could lead to. The year 1963 was significant in that the Test Ban Treaty was signed and the monolithic Communist Bloc cracked with the Soviet-Chinese rift. Nixon's policy of détente, despite the Vietnam War, was a giant step. The Nonproliferation Treaty and the SALT treaties were significant.

The growing gap between the standard of living enjoyed in western capitalist countries compared to the standard of living enjoyed by communist nations, was another cause of the thaw in the Cold War. The broadcast of the capitalist standard of living on television and radio around the world also helped entice those living in communist nations that capitalism was a better system of production.

Practice Multiple-Choice Questions

(These questions represent the various types found in the AP exam.)

1. By late 1945, the Western Allies had decided that in order for Western Europe to recover from the devastation of war, Germany would have to be rebuilt because this area of Germany was still the industrial center of Europe.

   (A) Berlin
   (B) the Rhineland
   (C) the Ruhr Basin
   (D) East Prussia
   (E) Bavaria

2. Tensions between the West and the Soviets manifested themselves in 1946 when the joint administration of which of the following broke down?

   (A) The de-Nazification program
   (B) The four zones of occupied Germany
   (C) Berlin
   (D) The trials of Nazi war criminals
   (E) The reconstruction of German industry

3. A definitive break from the United States' traditional policy of isolationism was marked by its

   (A) criticism of Stalin's establishment of repressive governments in Eastern Europe
   (B) participation in the Nuremberg War Crimes trials
   (C) growing anti-Communism at home
   (D) commitment to the reconstruction and defense of Western Europe
   (E) generosity to its former enemies

4. Politicians such as Alcide de Gaspari, Robert Schuman, and Konrad Adenauer exemplified the

   (A) resurgent nationalism in Europe in the 1960s
   (B) leadership of Christian Democratic parties in postwar Europe
   (C) resistance to the political unity of Europe
   (D) increased influence of the far left in European politics
   (E) despotic control that was exercised in Eastern Europe

5. Under the Schuman and Monnet Plan, the first move toward economic union in Europe was made in 1952 when six industrial countries in the West pooled what resources?

   (A) Coal and steel
   (B) Hydroelectric power
   (C) Military equipment
   (D) Uranium and plutonium
   (E) Skilled labor

6. The primary reason the United States and Great Britain agreed to Stalin's demands for "friendly" governments in the Eastern European states liberated by the Red Army was

   (A) to reward the Soviet Union for its role in World War II
   (B) their fear of communist revolution at home
   (C) their fear of resurgent Nazism
   (D) the presence of the Red Army in those states
   (E) lack of resources in those areas made them less attractive to capitalists

7. Which two Communist nations were not considered Soviet satellites because they were not liberated from the Nazis by the Red Army?

   (A) Poland and Czechoslovakia
   (B) Bulgaria and Romania
   (C) Albania and Yugoslavia
   (D) Yugoslavia and East Germany
   (E) Albania and Austria

8. All of the following are true of the Soviet satellites in Eastern Europe from 1945 to 1953 EXCEPT

   (A) land-distribution programs were carried out
   (B) agriculture was forcibly collectivized
   (C) industrialization was discouraged
   (D) Soviet police state methods silenced opposition to the regimes
   (E) the influence of the Roman Catholic Church was removed

9. Which of the following policies associated with Stalin survived Khrushchev's de-Stalinization?

   (A) Stringent control over society and culture
   (B) The collective system of agriculture
   (C) Continuous purges of dissidents and minority ethnic groups
   (D) The monopoly on power of the communist party
   (E) Stalin's cult of personality

10. After the death of Stalin in 1953, the new party leadership, headed by Nikita Khrushchev, did all of the following EXCEPT

    (A) leave intact most of the basic structure of Stalinist totalitarianism
    (B) grant the satellites of Eastern Europe greater autonomy
    (C) denounce the "crimes of Stalin" in victimizing the people and the party
    (D) accuse Stalin of failing to respond effectively against the initial advances of the Nazi invaders
    (E) accuse Stalin of creating a "cult of personality"

11. Despite the spectacular Soviet reconstruction successes of the postwar Five-Year Plans developed by centralized economic planning (Gosplan), production of which of the following lagged far behind the rest of the economy by the 1960s?

(A) Military weaponry
(B) Heavy machinery
(C) Automobiles
(D) Food
(E) Spacecraft

Berlin Wall: Children, 1962. Dieter Ottoullstein bild. The Granger Collection, New York. (0072844)

12. The picture above is of a barrier between two countries known as

(A) the Berlin Airlift
(B) the West Bank
(C) the Berlin Wall
(D) the Maginot Line
(E) the Line of Demarcation

13. The Cold War "thawed" because of all of the following EXCEPT

    (A) the U-2 incident
    (B) summit diplomacy
    (C) the SALT negotiations
    (D) the Soviet-Chinese rift
    (E) Nixon's policies toward the U.S.S.R. and China

14. A serious flaw of the Nonproliferation Treaty of 1970 was

    (A) that the Soviets continued to export nuclear weapons technology
    (B) the United States provided its allies with tactical nuclear weapons
    (C) China was eager to develop nuclear weapons
    (D) Britain and France refused to honor it
    (E) many nations with nuclear power plants were able to reprocess spent fuel in order to produce bombs

15. Which of the following did NOT contribute to the split during the 1960s and 1970s within the ranks of both the Western and Communist Blocs?

    (A) DeGaulle's questioning of U.S. leadership of a restored Europe
    (B) Mao Zedong's charge of "revisionism" against Soviet leaders
    (C) nationalism in Eastern Europe
    (D) the tarnished images of both superpowers
    (E) the policy of détente

Answers and Answer Explanations

1.	C	**6.**	D	**11.**	D
2.	B	**7.**	C	**12.**	C
3.	D	**8.**	C	**13.**	A
4.	B	**9.**	D	**14.**	E
5.	A	**10.**	B	**15.**	E

1. **(C)** The Ruhr Valley in Western Germany was and is one of the world's most important industrial centers.

2. **(B)** The three zones administered by the United States, Britain, and France became West Germany (the Federal Republic of Germany) in 1949; the Russian sector became East Germany (the People's Democratic Republic of Germany).

3. **(D)** The Marshall Plan and NATO signaled the United States' global commitment.

4. **(B)** All of the leaders mentioned in the question were Christian Democrat leaders and were not overtly nationalistic; rather, they got along with other nations and were mainstream democrats.

5. **(A)** It all started with a sharing of these two basic raw materials of industrial production.

6. **(D)** The presence of the Red Army and their battle-seasoned troops was the most important deterrent of American and British involvement in that area.

7. **(C)** Albania was liberated by the Western Allies and Yugoslavia, under Marshal Tito, maintained a fierce independence from Moscow.

8. **(C)** The Soviets did, under Five-Year Plans, industrialize the region, which had been primarily agricultural.

9. **(D)** The Soviets maintained their monopoly on power in the Soviet Union until the Soviet Union fell in 1989.

10. **(B)** The basic structure and institutions, such as the secret police, of Stalinist totalitarianism were kept intact.

11. **(D)** A crisis in agriculture because of the failure of collectivized farming—it lacked incentives, a basic problem in Communist economies—led to the downfall of Khrushchev.

12. **(C)** The Berlin Wall is depicted, separating East and West Berlin.

13. **(A)** The downing of the U.S. U-2 high-flying spy plane derailed the Paris Summit between President Eisenhower and Premier Khrushchev in 1960.

14. **(E)** Many "have-not" nations of the Third World gained and continue to strive for more status and self-importance by belonging to the once exclusive "nuclear club."

15. **(E)** This policy was made easier by the split in the once solid ideological blocs.

CHAPTER 15

Trends in Contemporary Europe

Key Terms/People

- The Common Market
- Arab-Israeli War of 1973
- Stagflation
- European Community
- Pure and Applied Science
- Big Science
- European Union

- Euro
- Glasnost
- Perestroika
- Commonwealth of Independent States
- baby boomers
- 9/11 Terrorist Attacks

Overview

In the 1970s, high energy prices resulting from instability in the Middle East and the disintegration of the American-dominated global monetary system brought about a worldwide recession. Western Europe suffered stagflation and huge government deficits.

During this decade, détente, a relaxation of tensions between East and West, was furthered by West Germany's attempts to reconcile with Eastern Europe and by the Helsinki Agreements, and it was strained by the U.S. involvement in Vietnam, the Soviet involvement in Afghanistan, and a massive American arms buildup.

The most important and dramatic developments of the 1980s and early 1990s were the largely peaceful anti-Communist revolutions in Eastern Europe and the collapse of Soviet Communism that led to the dismantling of the Soviet Union. The Solidarity movement in Poland, liberalization in Hungary and Czechoslovakia, and the unification of East and West Germany marked the end of Soviet domination of Eastern Europe. The gradual decline of Soviet economic strength under Brezhnev and Andropov led Gorbachev to initiate profound political and social reform (glasnost) and economic restructuring (perestroika). In 1989, the first free elections were conducted since the 1917 revolution. A military coup against Gorbachev in the summer of 1991 faced popular opposition and failed, many Soviet republics declared independence, and with the promise of reform Boris Yeltsin was elected president of the Russian Republic. Vladimir Putin replaced Yeltsin in 2000, and oversaw the privatization of the Soviet state possessions such as oil companies and other industry. Dmitri Medvedev replaced Putin in 2008 as his handpicked successor. Putin still holds power as the Russian prime minister.

The entrance of great numbers of women into the workplace and the feminist movement altered the lives of women in Europe and the United States. The birthrate dropped, the divorce rate rose, and sexual and social attitudes toward women changed.

At the beginning of the 20th century women could not vote, and at the time of publication of this book women have been elected as prime ministers to Great Britain, Germany, India, Portugal, Norway, Yugoslavia, Lithuania, Pakistan, France, Poland, Turkey, and many other nations. The 20th century was the century of the woman in many ways. Women gained intellectual and professional freedom and increased earning power. Widespread use of contraception led to increased emancipation in industrialized nations allowing women to participate more equally in society as their roles changed from caretakers to wage earners in many cases. By the 1990s, laws preventing wage and other forms of discrimination against women were prevalent in Europe and America. Women have risen to the highest positions of power in Europe and elsewhere as they have gained more legal, political, and economic freedom than at any time in European history.

Economics

Through the 1960s, Europe, led by the *Common Market*, accounted for a quarter of the world's industrial output. West Germany alone was third behind the United States and Japan in gross national product. In 1970, twenty-five years after World War II had ended, prosperity and democracy in Western Europe submerged centuries of national rivalry and promised peace and even greater economic progress and political cooperation.

The *oil embargo of 1973* helped change this rosy picture. The *Arab-Israeli War of 1973* incited Arab oil-producing nations to stop the flow of oil to those nations that had supported Israel. Since over 70 percent of Western Europe's petroleum came from the Middle East, the embargo and the resulting price rise threatened to destroy not only Europe's economy but the world's economy. *Stagflation,* a combination of slowdown and inflation that developed into a worldwide recession, had already been a problem that the oil embargo only aggravated. Western Europe's unparalleled economic growth and prosperity in the postwar period—as well as that of the United States and the rest of the industrialized world—was threatened.

Although the recession, the most severe since the Great Depression of the 1930s, improved by early 1976, and while unionism and welfare benefits enabled working people to cope with it more easily, economic growth rates slowed.

By late 1991, the twelve members of the *European Community*—the Common Market—had completed a plan to integrate economically and to consolidate politically. The *Maastricht Treaty* that went into force in November 1993 was the first major step toward European unification into the European Union, which now shares a common currency, central bank, and set of trade regulations. There are no tariffs or restrictions between the twenty-seven member states that comprise the economic entity with one of the largest GDPs in the world at over $14 trillion.

The European Union with 27 member states has become a prominent political as well as economic force on the world stage. Sixteen of these nations use the Euro as their currency, but all of them participate in a mixture of supranational and intergovernmental cooperation that holds this confederation of European states together. The member states are Austria, Belgium, Bulgaria, Cyprus, the Czech Republic, Denmark, Estonia, Finland, France, Germany, Greece, Hungary, Ireland, Italy, Latvia, Lithuania, Luxembourg, Malta, the Netherlands, Poland, Portugal, Romania, Slovakia, Slovenia, Spain, Sweden, and the United Kingdom. Member states are responsible for their own defense, but many belong to NATO. The presidency of the European Union rotates currently, but there is some discussion about an elected president for the European Union.

This union has allowed cooperation on many fronts from the financial sector to the law enforcement sector, to planning common infrastructure and energy policy, to cooperation in engineering and science. The European Space Agency and Airbus, the world's second largest airplane manufacturer, are joint European projects demonstrating that the European Union is a study in international cooperation. The expansion of the European Union into Eastern Europe and the Baltic states has caused tensions with Russia, but has also modernized the economies of those areas. Turkey has made gestures at joining the European Union, but so far that has not come to fruition.

This economic and political union has helped revive Europe as an economic powerhouse during the transition from the 20th to the 21st century. The Euro has become one of the most important currencies in the world in less than a decade, gaining value on other world currencies such as the dollar. There is some talk in financial circles about the dollar and the pound being replaced by the Euro as the standard of value.

Science

World War II changed the way scientists did their work, how they were funded, and where their research was directed. Scientists the world over were employed by their various governments to aid the war effort and their work led to technological advances, such as the use of atomic energy, the development of radar and jet aircraft, the advent of computers. New discoveries, inventions, and industries spurred research after the war in both *pure and applied science.*

New means of funding and organization of the increasingly specialized fields of research led to the advent of *Big Science*, which stressed teamwork, the combining of theoretical research with engineering techniques, and complex research facilities with professional managers and expensive, sophisticated equipment. The United States took the lead in this area after World War II and by the mid-1960s most scientific research (which doubled the sum of human knowledge every decade) was funded by the federal government, whose principal aim was defense. Many of the best scientists from Europe went to the United States for better wages and budgets in a phenomenon known as the *brain drain.* A "space race" between the United

States and the U.S.S.R. led to Russia's development of the first artificial satellite in 1957, *Sputnik*, and to a manned moon landing in 1969 by the United States. To stem the *brain drain* of their best scientists to the United States, European nations began funding their own research programs. The European Union gaining prominence and focusing on cooperation did much to stem the *brain drain*. Cooperative endeavors such as the international laboratory at CERN, creator of the world's largest particle collider, the Large Hadron Collider, drew scientists back to Europe in order to use the most advanced tools in the trade. Other international projects have led to retention of the best minds in science. Many scientists are coming from America and Asia to work on government-supported projects in Europe thanks in large part to the European Union.

Population and Poverty

Industrialization, urbanization, attitude changes, and modern contraception had lowered the birthrate during this century in Europe and other areas with developed economies. In the *Third World*, including newly independent nations that had been colonial possessions, the population exploded in the second half of the 20th century. Cultural and religious attitudes and economic dependence on large families maintained a high birthrate. Better food production and distribution, and modern medical and sanitation practices led to a decline in the death rate. Investments that could have been made to improve the standard of living in these areas was used instead to support the burgeoning population. Even with population control programs and a growing women's movement, the problem continues to get worse.

The gap between the rich industrialized nations and the less developed countries of the Third World widened. When the worldwide recession of the early 1970s caused the West to reduce its aid to the Third World, the less developed nations became more militant in demanding a more equitable share of the world's resources and industrial production. The result is a revolution of rising expectations that helps create worldwide political instability.

The Collapse of Communism and the End of the Cold War

In 1985, the election of *Mikhail Gorbachev* (1931–) by the Soviet Communist party leadership to serve as party general secretary promised fresh blood to reform the ailing economy and to invigorate the party after the stagnation of the Brezhnev era. His policies of *glasnost*, or openness, and *perestroika*, or restructuring, gave the peoples of Eastern Europe hope for a better life, and the façade of Soviet power crumbled, leaving the people ready for bigger changes. An intended reformer, Gorbachev became the agent of an unintended and unexpected revolution that led to the collapse of Communism and the dissolution of the world order that had reigned since the end of World War II.

In 1987, two years after he took office, Chairman Gorbachev and President Ronald Reagan signed the *INF Treaty*, which began the delicate and dangerous process of nuclear disarmament with the destruction of all short- and intermediate-range nuclear missiles. Two years after that, the U.S.S.R. withdrew from the *War in Afghanistan*, its "Vietnam." Gorbachev's perestroika or restructuring of the economy and his policy of glasnost seemed to be moving Soviet Communism toward reform.

The *collapse of the Soviet Union* in 1989 marked a very important change in the European balance of power. The Soviet regime was overturned throughout Eastern Europe in mostly bloodless revolutions. The Supreme Soviet lost power to the *Congress of People's Deputies*, and the new body demanded greater reforms. The Soviet Union was dissolved and may have seen a bloody coup if Moscow mayor, *Boris Yeltsin* (1931–2007), had not intervened to ease tensions. Many nations were formed from the former Soviet Union, such as Turkmenistan, Ukraine, and Georgia. Communism was rejected as a failure throughout the continent, and China was left as the only major communist power. The United States was left as the world's only superpower.

Solidarity, the Polish trade-union movement, led by Lech Walesa (1943–), who had opposed the rigid Communist government and been suppressed under martial law, was swept into office by the first free elections since before World War II. Changes in the Communist governments of Hungary, Bulgaria, and Czechoslovakia took place over the next several months. In November of 1989, the *Berlin Wall*, symbol of Communist oppression, was breached. It marked the beginning of the downfall of the Communist East German government. A violent revolution in Romania overthrew the longtime Communist dictatorship. Free elections established non-Communist governments in many of the old East European satellites.

In October of 1990, *Germany reunited*. Despite fears of a resurgent and aggressive united Germany, Gorbachev had allowed the union of West and East Germany without the promise of its neutrality. Germany joined NATO, and less than a year later the Warsaw Pact, its Communist counterpart, was dissolved. *The Cold War officially ended* in November, when Soviet, U.S., and Western European leaders signed the *Charter for a New Europe*.

In mid-1991, *Boris Yeltsin*, an outspoken and charismatic political rival of Gorbachev, was elected as president of the Soviet Republic of Russia. He had run as an independent candidate on a platform of drastic economic and political reform. During that same month, June, *Croatia and Slovenia declared their independence from Yugoslavia* and a civil war, made more brutal by ancient ethnic rivalries, broke out.

START, the Strategic Arms Reduction Treaty, was signed in July of 1991 by Gorbachev and President George Bush to reduce the long-range nuclear missiles of both nations.

One month later, old-line party and military leaders launched a coup against the vacationing Gorbachev as they sent military units towards Moscow. Within days, the coup collapsed in the face of massive public demonstrations against its leaders. *Latvia, Lithuania, and Estonia* declared their independence from the Soviet Union. By late 1991, Russia, Ukraine, and Belarus formed the *Commonwealth of Independent States* and the Soviet Union effectively ceased to exist.

By 1993, ethnic rivalries among the former Soviet republics, the bloody war pitting Serbia and Croatia against their former Yugoslavian brothers Bosnia and Herzegovina, and the division of Czechoslovakia has created a dangerous and fluid political situation in Europe. Despite initial reluctance to get involved in the Balkan crisis, the United States and Western European nations have imposed a settlement on the warring factions and have prosecuted war criminals in the World Court.

The collapse of Communism in Europe created a *fluid* political situation worldwide that is similar to the disruptions of the old orders after World Wars I and II. Power has shifted; the rules have changed. The end of the Cold War has diminished the prospects of nuclear war but has created new rivalries and unleashed bloody ethnic conflicts to test the resolve of NATO. The allies of the Gulf War alliance have adopted varying policies in the Middle East that often reflect their own economic interests. The birth of a new international order will, as always, be difficult.

Society

After World War II, European class distinctions blurred due to unprecedented economic growth in the West and its accompanying opportunities in jobs and in higher education. Western Europeans enjoyed a new social mobility and a greater democratization of their governments. Education and ability outweighed family connections. Health care and other social security programs alleviated traditional class conflicts and promoted greater economic equality. General prosperity promoted a *consumer culture*, making big businesses out of such products and services as food, leisure, entertainment, and travel.

Powerful social changes occurred after World War II. Prosperity and increased educational opportunities swelled the middle classes in both Europe and the United States. With science and technology wedded by war, *big science*, which was funded by government and industry, created new products and new career opportunities. With greater educational opportunities available to women, more females sought careers outside the home. Cities grew as agricultural workers left the farms in search of new vocations.

In the 1960s, a youth culture, which grew first in the United States from the great numbers of *baby boomers*, the unparalleled prosperity, and the increased enrollment in higher education, spread globally. Rebellion against the status quo manifested itself in rock music, widespread use of illegal drugs, and less rigid sexual attitudes. The materialism of the West encouraged a revolutionary idealism among young people who participated in the antiwar movement in the United States and in the student radicalism of Europe. Student revolts against rigid educational practices in universities broke out in France and in other European countries.

Economic setbacks in the 1970s and 1980s spurred changes in family life. In order to maintain the family's standard of living, many women in Europe and the United States went into the work force. Income independence enabled more women to get divorces; birth control allowed them to plan their families and resulted in a decreased birthrate. This newfound independence and a number of gifted female writers, such as Simone de Beauvoir in France and Betty Friedan in the United States, helped launch a new feminism that attacked gender inequalities in all aspects of society and that used political action and attitude alteration. The dissolution of the Soviet Union and its Communist satellites also led many women, who had lived in those more emancipated cultures, to encourage further emancipation of Western European women. The increasing prevalence of scientific, business, and political leaders who are women, from Rosalind Franklin to Oprah Winfrey to Margaret Thatcher, has also done much for the feminist cause. The 21st century is witness to common bumper stickers that state that feminism is the radical notion that women are people.

Recent Developments

The 1990s marked powerful political and economic changes in Europe, comparable in magnitude to those at the end of World Wars I and II. After the collapse of Communist governments in the former Soviet Union and its Cold War satellites, a new order emerged.

- Western Europe, with the exception of Britain, instituted a *monetary union,* a natural evolution from the political and economic ties of the European Union, creating the euro, one of the most powerful and stable currencies in the world.
- Germany, completely and peacefully united (although with unforseen complications that came from the need to absorb the former Communist East), set up its capital in Berlin once again, and became the most powerful country in Europe, a status it had not held since the end of World War II.
- Poland, Hungary, and the Czech Republic established democratic governments, instituted capitalist reforms of their economies, and joined NATO.
- Independence movements from the Serb-dominated Yugoslavian government in Belgrade degenerated into bitter and bloody struggles between various ethnic groups (Serbs, Croats, Bosnians, Kosovars, Montenegrins, Albanians) and revived the specter of *genocide* in the form of *"ethnic cleansing."* The intervention of NATO resulted in a precarious peace and in the prosecution of Slobodan Milosevic, Serbian president, and other Serbian leaders for war crimes.
- Russia, the largest, richest, and most populous republic of the former Soviet Union, grappled with a faltering economy, a fitful start to democratization (widespread corruption during Boris Yeltsin's presidency tainted the effort), and a bloody ethnic war with Chechnya. The replacement of Yeltsin by Vladimir Putin as president promised reform, a renewed *détente* with the West, and a more enlightened role for Russia in regional and world affairs. That promise was not kept. Putin used power as a tool to enrich himself and his cronies. These *oligarchs* became immensely rich businessmen with ties to the former Communist Party. Putin is widely regarded as decreasing freedom and opportunity in Russia as he and his former KGB connections enriched themselves through corruption. He was replaced as president in 2008 by Dmitri Medvedev, but remains, as prime minister, a key power holder.

The *9/11 Terrorist Attacks* against the United States in 2001 marked the beginning of a new international era, one more dangerous to world peace and stability than at any time since the height of the Cold War. Widespread poverty in the Third World and ethnic rivalry all over the globe have fostered religious fanaticism and conflict, such as that in the Middle East between Israelis and Palestinians, and both the United States—as the world's only *superpower*—and the European states must respond to the challenge.

Sample Essay Question

The sample thematic essay question and the practice questions presented in this chapter are types found on the AP exam, and they require a knowledge of causes, effects, personalities, ideas, and events.

SAMPLE QUESTION

Assess the validity of the following statement. *The collapse of Communism in Europe has created a more dangerous world.*

Comments on the Sample Question

Follow the "simple procedures for writing an essay." (See page 34.)

First, *What does the question want to know?* It is highly unlikely that an FRQ question will be asked on this era. Is the world safer after the fall of the Communist governments of Eastern Europe and the USSR, or have the drastic changes created hazardous instabilities?

Second, *What do you know about it?* The fall of the Communist governments in Eastern Europe and the U.S.S.R. ended the military threat to NATO and the Cold War. The possibility of nuclear war between the United States and U.S.S.R. seemed more remote than ever. But the ethnic rivalries and weak democracies that have resulted could encourage nationalistic dictatorships that might use nuclear weapons to resolve their conflicts.

Third, *How would you put it into words?* To "assess the validity" of the statement, you must evaluate whether the global situation was more or less stable before the collapse of European Communism. You could argue against the statement or agree wholly or partially.

Rubric for Sample Answer

Before you read the sample answer, examine the rubric. What will the reader be looking for when he or she grades this essay? A sample rubric, shaded to show the reader's evaluation, is seen on page 380:

9–8 POINTS

- ✔ Thesis explicitly assesses the validity of the statement in regard to the current world. Thesis does not need to be in the opening paragraph.
- ✔ Organization is clear, consistently followed, and effective in support of the argument.
  - May devote individual paragraphs to assessing the statement in regard to world war, economic security, personal security, and individual and societal prosperity.
  - Must identify the factors affecting the danger level in the world including world war, economic security, personal security, and individual and societal standards of living seen throughout the world.
- ✔ Essay is well balanced; assesses the statement at some length.
- ✔ Major assertions in the essay are supported thoroughly and consistently by relevant evidence.
- ✔ Evidence may prove more specific or concrete.
- ✔ May contain errors that do not detract from the argument.

7–6 POINTS

- ✔ Thesis explicitly assesses the statement but may not be developed fully.
- ✔ Organization is clear and effective in support of the argument but may introduce evidence that is not pertinent to the task.
- ✔ Essay covers all major topics suggested by the prompt but may analyze some factors in greater depth rather than in a balanced manner. Must discuss both more and less dangerous factors.
- ✔ Major assertions in the essay are supported by relevant evidence.
- ✔ May contain an error that detracts from the argument.

5–4 POINTS

- ✔ Thesis assesses the statement; thesis may address only part of the task effectively; thesis may be a simple, single-sentence statement.
- ✔ Organization is clear but may not be consistently followed; essay may veer off task chronologically or thematically or both.
- ✔ Essay may not complete all tasks:
  - May discuss the statement only as it applies to a few factors.
  - May discuss only the more or less dangerous factors.
  - May focus only on one or two nations involved.
  - May be primarily descriptive rather than analytical.
- ✔ Essay offers some relevant evidence.
- ✔ May contain errors that detract from the argument.

3–2 POINTS

- ✔ Thesis may simply paraphrase the prompt OR assesses the statement partially.
- ✔ Organization is unclear and ineffective; essay may focus on the other factors rather than analyzing how the fall of communism affected world security.
- ✔ Essay shows serious imbalance; discussion of the statement may be significantly out of the time period or geography of the question.
- ✔ Offers minimal OR confused evidence.
- ✔ May contain several errors that detract from the argument.

1–0 POINTS

- ✔ Thesis is erroneous OR irrelevant OR absent.
- ✔ No effective organization is evident.
- ✔ Discussion is done in a generic fashion.
- ✔ Provides little or no relevant supporting evidence.
- ✔ May contain numerous errors that detract from the argument.

Sample Answer

"Nature abhors a vacuum." The vacuum created by the fall of Communism in Europe has been filled by weak democracies and by ugly nationalism. Russia, the most powerful and populous autonomous republic of the former Soviet Union, is suffering economic breakdown and social dislocation. Its underpaid and poorly housed military may someday overthrow the parliamentary government that has no tradition of democracy. The Soviet Republics of Azerbaijan and Armenia gained independence and waged bitter "tribal war" against each other. The civil war between the regions of the former Yugoslavia involved atrocities and "ethnic cleansing" genocide not seen in Europe since the defeat of the Nazis. The instability in the Balkans could lead to a regional or even worldwide war as it did in 1914.

EVALUATE THE SAMPLE ANSWER

Now go back and look at the rubric. It is clear that this essay looks like a 2 or 3 on the rubric. The essay has a weak thesis that may be completely tangential. The question is not fully answered; the lack of facts warrants a score of 2.

RATER'S COMMENTS ON THE SAMPLE ANSWER

2—Not qualified

This was a one-sided and somewhat simplistic approach to a very complex issue. The writer has overstressed remote possibilities of "danger" while ignoring the significant and tangible risks that have ended with the fall of the Eastern Bloc. This is a paragraph, not an essay. The ideas are poorly developed, and there is a complete absence of factual support. No one should write a FRQ answer with so little information and analysis.

Suggestions for improvement:

The validity of the statement could be argued much more convincingly if future dangers had been weighed against past risks. Does the danger posed by a possible military takeover of the Russian government measure up to the risks of nuclear war during the Cold War? Is the suffering caused by ethnic and nationalistic rivalries equivalent to the miseries of life under Communist totalitarianism? What about the dangers of terrorism from stray nuclear or biological weapons? What about another developing conflict in Afghanistan? Is the world more stable with two rival ideologies aligned against each other or with fractious states struggling to establish democracy and capitalism?

Practice Essay Questions

The questions that follow are samples of the various types of thematic essays that appear on the AP exam. (See pages 21–22 for a detailed description.) Check over the **generic rubric** (see pages 58–60) before you begin any of these essays and use that rubric to score your essay if you write one.

QUESTION 1

To what extent and in what ways did Gorbachev's reforms bring about the dissolution of the U.S.S.R.?

COMMENTS ON QUESTION 1

How important were his reforms in the process? Which ones affected it? Consider both perestroika and glasnost. Be sure to show how their degree of success or failure provoked the final breakdown. Consider his repudiation of the Brezhnev Doctrine. Would the U.S.S.R. have dissolved without Gorbachev's reforms?

QUESTION 2

Analyze the causes of the economic crises in Europe during the 1970s.

COMMENTS ON QUESTION 2

Trace the causes and determine the relationships of the world monetary crisis and the OPEC oil embargoes in bringing about the regional stagflation of the 1970s. This essay must examine the changing structures of the world economy and financial system seen in the 1970s.

QUESTION 3

Describe the Eastern European Revolutions of 1989.

COMMENTS ON QUESTION 3

Explain the patterns of revolution in the various East European states during 1989. Consider the role of Solidarity in Poland, the liberalization policies in Hungary, the bloody uprising in Romania, the opening of the Berlin Wall in Germany, and the role of Gorbachev and the dissolution of the Soviet Union.

QUESTION 4

Discuss how the entrance of great numbers of women into the workplace has altered European society.

COMMENTS ON QUESTION 4

Relate the "big picture" and offer specific effects of this powerful trend. How has life changed for the mass of European women? How has the trend affected family, birthrate, divorce, and marriage? How have wages and leisure time been affected?

QUESTION 5

Explain how the Solidarity movement in Poland evolved from a trade union movement to a force for national democratization.

COMMENTS ON QUESTION 5

Offer reasons for, and make clear why, a trade union was able to democratize a Communist dictatorship. Be sure to examine origins; leadership on both sides; the role of the Roman Catholic Church; the nature of Polish society; and the gains, losses, and final triumphs of the movement.

Practice Multiple-Choice Questions

(These questions represent the various types found on the AP exam.)

1. All of the following contributed to the global economic recession of the 1970s and early 1980s EXCEPT

    (A) the collapse of the American-dominated world monetary system
    (B) the OPEC oil embargo of 1973
    (C) President Reagan's elimination of federal deficits
    (D) President Nixon's refusal to sell American gold
    (E) An end to cheap oil

2. An important reason why the widespread unemployment and inflation of the 1970s and 1980s did not lead to profound political instability in Western Europe was

    (A) the existence of welfare systems set up after World War II
    (B) the imposition of martial law
    (C) the austerity measures pioneered by Britain's Thatcher
    (D) the kind of nationalization and public investment introduced by France's Mitterand
    (E) the European-wide investment in *big science*

3. The *second wave* of feminism began in

    (A) the later 19th century
    (B) right before World War I
    (C) during the 1920s
    (D) right after World War II
    (E) in the 1960s

4. Willy Brandt's most important contribution as a leader of West Germany was

    (A) the construction of the autobahn
    (B) the initiative for reconciliation with the Eastern Bloc
    (C) the unification of West and East Germany
    (D) the demolition of the Berlin Wall
    (E) the banning of the Communist party from all elective office

Boris Yeltsin giving a speech from atop a tank. ullstein bild/The Granger Collection, New York. (0085615)

5. The man speaking in this picture is trying to

(A) incite the crowd to riot
(B) encourage the crowd to disperse
(C) deliver a decision from the court
(D) get control of the assembled mob
(E) prevent a military coup without bloodshed

6. The U.S.S.R.'s invasion of, and stalemate in, what country has been likened to the U.S. failure in Vietnam?

(A) Czechoslovakia
(B) Poland
(C) Afghanistan
(D) Hungary
(E) Germany

7. The world monetary system adopted at Bretton Woods in 1944 and upon which postwar recovery progressed was based on

(A) The Japanese yen
(B) The German mark
(C) The French franc
(D) The American dollar
(E) Gold

8. When Communism fell in Eastern Europe in 1989, bloody revolution took place in

   (A) East Germany
   (B) Poland
   (C) Romania
   (D) Hungary
   (E) Czechoslovakia

9. All of the following contributed to the success of the Solidarity movement in Poland EXCEPT

   (A) a lack of Soviet-style collectivization
   (B) the independence of the Polish Roman Catholic Church
   (C) a booming economy
   (D) the leadership of Lech Walesa
   (E) the Gdansk Agreement

10. An important reason for the failure of Gorbachev's perestroika was

    (A) the continuance of rigid price setting
    (B) the refusal of the government to allow private profit seeking
    (C) failure to allow state enterprises some independence
    (D) the centrally planned economy's failure to adapt to free market mechanisms
    (E) the resentment of the Soviet people of attempts at reform

11. Gorbachev's repudiation of the Brezhnev Doctrine

    (A) accelerated the peaceful revolutions in Eastern Europe
    (B) enabled the U.S.S.R. to invade Afghanistan
    (C) caused a diplomatic confrontation with the United States
    (D) increased East-West tensions
    (E) suppressed nationalist demands in the Soviet Republics

12. Her book *The Second Sex* was the first and one of the major intellectual influences on the second wave of feminism

    (A) Betty Friedan
    (B) Olympe de Gouges
    (C) Mary Wollstonecraft
    (D) Margaret Thatcher
    (E) Simone de Beauvoir

13. The diplomatic initiative to relax Cold War tension around the globe was

   (A) the policy of détente
   (B) the Brezhnev doctrine
   (C) the Warsaw Pact
   (D) glasnost
   (E) the Pentagon Papers

14. One of the most significant trends in the life of women in Europe over the last three decades is that

   (A) Motherhood is occupying a greater part of their total life span
   (B) Many are foregoing careers in order to raise their children
   (C) Motherhood is occupying less of their total life span
   (D) Most are opting for large families
   (E) Their span of fertility has diminished

15. Glasnost is best characterized as

   (A) a form of re-Stalinization
   (B) an openness of expression
   (C) a restructuring of the economy
   (D) a form of central planning
   (E) a guarantee of human rights

Answers and Answer Explanations

1.	C	**6.**	C	**11.**	A
2.	A	**7.**	D	**12.**	E
3.	E	**8.**	C	**13.**	A
4.	B	**9.**	C	**14.**	C
5.	E	**10.**	D	**15.**	B

1. **(C)** Reagan's fiscal policies tripled the U.S. deficit.

2. **(A)** Social welfare programs maintained the political stability in Western democracies, preventing the kind of dictatorships that grew after WWII.

3. **(E)** Although De Beauvoir's classic, *The Second Sex*, was published in the late 1940s, the movement it helped inspire came to fruition in the 1960s.

4. **(B)** His peace initiative prompted Nixon and his advisors to push for global détente.

5. **(E)** Boris Yeltsin was in the process of preventing a military coup without a military confrontation.

6. **(C)** The Soviet Union's failure in Afghanistan, like that of the United States in Vietnam, was the case of a superpower ground to a halt by a Third World, agrarian nation.

7. **(D)** At the time the U.S. currency was the world's most stable.

8. **(C)** A bloody repression by the Communist government led to a bloody overthrow.

9. **(C)** The lagging Polish economy gave the movement its impetus.

10. **(D)** The reforms did not go far enough to transform the moribund Soviet economy.

11. **(A)** The revolutions of 1989 in Eastern Europe were fostered by Gorbachev's pledge not to interfere in the internal affairs of those nations.

12. **(E)** It was published nearly twenty years before Friedan's work.

13. **(A)** Inspired by Brandt's peace initiatives in Europe, it was designed largely by Nixon's secretary of state, Henry Kissinger.

14. **(C)** The social implications of this are staggering; the structure of family life has changed; the role of women in society and the economy has broadened.

15. **(B)** It was the more successful of Gorbachev's reforms.

PART THREE

MODEL EXAMS

Answer Sheet

MODEL TEST 1

SECTION I

1 Ⓐ Ⓑ Ⓒ Ⓓ Ⓔ   21 Ⓐ Ⓑ Ⓒ Ⓓ Ⓔ   41 Ⓐ Ⓑ Ⓒ Ⓓ Ⓔ   61 Ⓐ Ⓑ Ⓒ Ⓓ Ⓔ
2 Ⓐ Ⓑ Ⓒ Ⓓ Ⓔ   22 Ⓐ Ⓑ Ⓒ Ⓓ Ⓔ   42 Ⓐ Ⓑ Ⓒ Ⓓ Ⓔ   62 Ⓐ Ⓑ Ⓒ Ⓓ Ⓔ
3 Ⓐ Ⓑ Ⓒ Ⓓ Ⓔ   23 Ⓐ Ⓑ Ⓒ Ⓓ Ⓔ   43 Ⓐ Ⓑ Ⓒ Ⓓ Ⓔ   63 Ⓐ Ⓑ Ⓒ Ⓓ Ⓔ
4 Ⓐ Ⓑ Ⓒ Ⓓ Ⓔ   24 Ⓐ Ⓑ Ⓒ Ⓓ Ⓔ   44 Ⓐ Ⓑ Ⓒ Ⓓ Ⓔ   64 Ⓐ Ⓑ Ⓒ Ⓓ Ⓔ
5 Ⓐ Ⓑ Ⓒ Ⓓ Ⓔ   25 Ⓐ Ⓑ Ⓒ Ⓓ Ⓔ   45 Ⓐ Ⓑ Ⓒ Ⓓ Ⓔ   65 Ⓐ Ⓑ Ⓒ Ⓓ Ⓔ
6 Ⓐ Ⓑ Ⓒ Ⓓ Ⓔ   26 Ⓐ Ⓑ Ⓒ Ⓓ Ⓔ   46 Ⓐ Ⓑ Ⓒ Ⓓ Ⓔ   66 Ⓐ Ⓑ Ⓒ Ⓓ Ⓔ
7 Ⓐ Ⓑ Ⓒ Ⓓ Ⓔ   27 Ⓐ Ⓑ Ⓒ Ⓓ Ⓔ   47 Ⓐ Ⓑ Ⓒ Ⓓ Ⓔ   67 Ⓐ Ⓑ Ⓒ Ⓓ Ⓔ
8 Ⓐ Ⓑ Ⓒ Ⓓ Ⓔ   28 Ⓐ Ⓑ Ⓒ Ⓓ Ⓔ   48 Ⓐ Ⓑ Ⓒ Ⓓ Ⓔ   68 Ⓐ Ⓑ Ⓒ Ⓓ Ⓔ
9 Ⓐ Ⓑ Ⓒ Ⓓ Ⓔ   29 Ⓐ Ⓑ Ⓒ Ⓓ Ⓔ   49 Ⓐ Ⓑ Ⓒ Ⓓ Ⓔ   69 Ⓐ Ⓑ Ⓒ Ⓓ Ⓔ
10 Ⓐ Ⓑ Ⓒ Ⓓ Ⓔ   30 Ⓐ Ⓑ Ⓒ Ⓓ Ⓔ   50 Ⓐ Ⓑ Ⓒ Ⓓ Ⓔ   70 Ⓐ Ⓑ Ⓒ Ⓓ Ⓔ
11 Ⓐ Ⓑ Ⓒ Ⓓ Ⓔ   31 Ⓐ Ⓑ Ⓒ Ⓓ Ⓔ   51 Ⓐ Ⓑ Ⓒ Ⓓ Ⓔ   71 Ⓐ Ⓑ Ⓒ Ⓓ Ⓔ
12 Ⓐ Ⓑ Ⓒ Ⓓ Ⓔ   32 Ⓐ Ⓑ Ⓒ Ⓓ Ⓔ   52 Ⓐ Ⓑ Ⓒ Ⓓ Ⓔ   72 Ⓐ Ⓑ Ⓒ Ⓓ Ⓔ
13 Ⓐ Ⓑ Ⓒ Ⓓ Ⓔ   33 Ⓐ Ⓑ Ⓒ Ⓓ Ⓔ   53 Ⓐ Ⓑ Ⓒ Ⓓ Ⓔ   73 Ⓐ Ⓑ Ⓒ Ⓓ Ⓔ
14 Ⓐ Ⓑ Ⓒ Ⓓ Ⓔ   34 Ⓐ Ⓑ Ⓒ Ⓓ Ⓔ   54 Ⓐ Ⓑ Ⓒ Ⓓ Ⓔ   74 Ⓐ Ⓑ Ⓒ Ⓓ Ⓔ
15 Ⓐ Ⓑ Ⓒ Ⓓ Ⓔ   35 Ⓐ Ⓑ Ⓒ Ⓓ Ⓔ   55 Ⓐ Ⓑ Ⓒ Ⓓ Ⓔ   75 Ⓐ Ⓑ Ⓒ Ⓓ Ⓔ
16 Ⓐ Ⓑ Ⓒ Ⓓ Ⓔ   36 Ⓐ Ⓑ Ⓒ Ⓓ Ⓔ   56 Ⓐ Ⓑ Ⓒ Ⓓ Ⓔ   76 Ⓐ Ⓑ Ⓒ Ⓓ Ⓔ
17 Ⓐ Ⓑ Ⓒ Ⓓ Ⓔ   37 Ⓐ Ⓑ Ⓒ Ⓓ Ⓔ   57 Ⓐ Ⓑ Ⓒ Ⓓ Ⓔ   77 Ⓐ Ⓑ Ⓒ Ⓓ Ⓔ
18 Ⓐ Ⓑ Ⓒ Ⓓ Ⓔ   38 Ⓐ Ⓑ Ⓒ Ⓓ Ⓔ   58 Ⓐ Ⓑ Ⓒ Ⓓ Ⓔ   78 Ⓐ Ⓑ Ⓒ Ⓓ Ⓔ
19 Ⓐ Ⓑ Ⓒ Ⓓ Ⓔ   39 Ⓐ Ⓑ Ⓒ Ⓓ Ⓔ   59 Ⓐ Ⓑ Ⓒ Ⓓ Ⓔ   79 Ⓐ Ⓑ Ⓒ Ⓓ Ⓔ
20 Ⓐ Ⓑ Ⓒ Ⓓ Ⓔ   40 Ⓐ Ⓑ Ⓒ Ⓓ Ⓔ   60 Ⓐ Ⓑ Ⓒ Ⓓ Ⓔ   80 Ⓐ Ⓑ Ⓒ Ⓓ Ⓔ

Model Test 1

SECTION 1
MULTIPLE-CHOICE QUESTIONS

TIME—55 MINUTES FOR 80 QUESTIONS

Directions: Each of the following questions has five suggested answers. Choose the one that is best in each case.

1. Which of the following is a significant difference between medieval and Renaissance sculpture?

   (A) The shift from Old Testament to New Testament themes
   (B) The use of stone rather than wood
   (C) Renaissance sculpture was devoid of religious subjects
   (D) Renaissance art represented the visible world rather than conventional symbolism
   (E) Renaissance sculpture was no longer commissioned by the popes

2. Regiomontanus and Nicholas of Cusa helped lay the foundations for Copernicus's radical theory of astronomy by their work in

   (A) telescopic observation
   (B) physics
   (C) mathematics
   (D) empirical science
   (E) philosophical disputation

3. Which of the following is NOT a major tenet of Lutheranism?

   (A) Salvation is by faith and faith only
   (B) The Bible is the final authority for Christian Doctrine
   (C) Absolution from sin comes only through the grace of God
   (D) Baptism is the only valid sacrament
   (E) Only the inner grace of God, not indulgences or absolution, can free one from sin

4. The Massacre of St. Bartholomew's Day in 1572

   (A) marked the renewal of religious civil war in France
   (B) resulted in the slaughter of Catholic leaders
   (C) marked the end of Protestantism in France
   (D) restored religious toleration in France
   (E) was perpetrated by Huguenot mobs

5. "The church is not subordinate to the state, but rather must be ruled according to God's plan. The chosen few should not only govern the church but also the state." An adherent of what religious group is likely to have believed this in the 16th century?

   (A) Lutheran
   (B) Calvinist
   (C) Roman Catholic
   (D) Millennarian
   (E) Anabaptist

6. During the 16th century, which dynasty ruled a dominion that stretched from the Atlantic to Eastern Europe, from the Baltic to the Mediterranean?

   (A) Valois
   (B) Hohenzollern
   (C) Bourbon
   (D) Tudor
   (E) Hapsburg

7. Religious toleration by the English government from 1534, when the English Reformation began, to 1689, when the Toleration Act was passed

   (A) guaranteed the right to worship to all Christian sects
   (B) denied the right to worship to all except Anglicans
   (C) denied only the right to worship to atheists
   (D) periodically denied to Catholics the right to worship
   (E) was varied, at times denying then guaranteeing freedom of worship to different sects

8. Which of the following is NOT true of the "Glorious Revolution" of 1689?

   (A) It established, once and for all, the right of Parliament to levy taxes.
   (B) It established that the monarchy and Parliament ruled England together.
   (C) It reflected the theories of government of Thomas Hobbes.
   (D) It was supported by the theories of John Locke.
   (E) It marked the supremacy of constitutionalism in England.

9. In the 14th and 15th centuries, mystics, such as Meister Eckhart, Thomas à Kempis, and the founder of Brothers of the Common Faith, Gerard Groote

   (A) preached rebellion against the papacy
   (B) stressed the importance of the sacraments
   (C) laid the foundations for Protestantism's personal approach to worship
   (D) argued the necessity of adhering to dogma
   (E) had a universal and popular appeal

10. Which was NOT a goal of Christian humanists like Erasmus and Thomas More?

   (A) To recapture the moral force of early Christianity
   (B) To reform the Roman Catholic Church
   (C) To criticize the pomposities of leaders and inequities of society
   (D) To support Protestantism
   (E) To emphasize the religious aspects of classical literature

11. Machiavelli's *The Prince* offered which of the following pieces of advice?

   (A) Know your enemy and know yourself and you cannot be defeated.
   (B) Behave like a weasel and a bear to be smart and ferocious.
   (C) Allow a strong minister to help you run your nation.
   (D) Do not conquer your enemies too harshly.
   (E) Be loved or feared, but never hated.

12. Calvinism in France

   (A) often served as a cloak for noble independence
   (B) was rejected by the peasants
   (C) had little impact on the nobility
   (D) was rejected by the middle class and artisans
   (E) became the official state religion

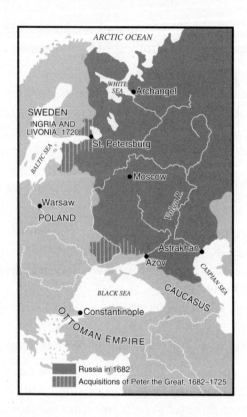

13. The above map shows acquisitions of Peter the Great from 1682 to 1715. The territories gained

   (A) were of great strategic importance because Russia gained the ability to spy better on Prussia
   (B) were of great economic importance due to the vast mineral resources there
   (C) included many large cities and generally had a high population density
   (D) were mostly owned by Austria before Russia acquired them
   (E) allowed Peter the Great to build a port as his window to the west

14. Prussia has been called "a state built around an army," meaning that

   (A) the kings were recruited from the High Command
   (B) in a nation of separate states, the army was a unifying force
   (C) the Junkers were militarists
   (D) the army ruled the monarchy
   (E) universal conscription was the rule

15. An important accomplishment of the Treaty of Utrecht (1713–1714) was

   (A) that it allowed a Bourbon monarch to rule both Spain and France
   (B) it established a French empire in North America
   (C) it set up an independent and unified Netherlands
   (D) it ousted the Austrians from Italy
   (E) it helped restore the balance of power on the continent

16. Why is it significant that Napoleon crowned himself as emperor of the First French Empire in 1804?

    (A) He was the first of his line.
    (B) It was a symbolic gesture to show his independence.
    (C) Because of the Concordat of 1801, the clergy refused to participate.
    (D) Because the Senate had named him "Emperor of the French" rather than "Emperor of France."
    (E) It had no significance.

17. Philip II of Spain (1556–1598)

    (A) championed religious toleration of Spanish Jews and Moslems
    (B) granted independence to the Spanish Netherlands
    (C) abolished the Alcabala, a 10 percent tax on all sales that inhibited commerce
    (D) dedicated his reign to establishing Catholic orthodoxy
    (E) was defeated by the Turks at Lepanto

18. The Enclosure Movement is best assessed by which of the following statements?

    (A) A peasant movement demanding special courts for nobles who were accused of fur collar crime
    (B) A set of naval maneuvers perfected by Sir Francis Drake
    (C) A set of military fortifications separating Alsace Lorraine from Germanic lands
    (D) A set of rules governing trade between the Germanic states involved in the Zollverein.
    (E) The slow movement away from the open field system as the nobility fenced in their land and moved the peasants off it

19. All of the following were results of the Industrial Revolution EXCEPT

    (A) it created two new social classes
    (B) it displaced the landed aristocracy as the dominant social class
    (C) it brought great wealth to factory owners
    (D) it subjected workers and their families to low wages, long working days, and oppressive living conditions
    (E) it created poverty much worse than that in the countryside

20. Joseph II of Austria (1780–1790) has been called the "ideal Enlightened Despot" for all of the following EXCEPT

    (A) he abolished serfdom
    (B) he fostered freedom of the press
    (C) he granted religious freedom to most Christian sects and to Jews
    (D) he abolished the secret police
    (E) he suppressed the influence of the Roman Catholic Church

21. Louis XVI of France convened the Estates General in 1789 for the first time in over 150 years because

    (A) he wanted to show support for the growing democratic movement
    (B) he wanted approval to exempt the First and Second Estates from taxation
    (C) he wanted approval for taxing all landowners in the realm
    (D) he needed funds to help support the American cause against the British
    (E) he needed a legislative body to check the powers of Parlement of Paris

22. How did Edward Jenner's development of a vaccine against smallpox influence the Industrial Revolution?

    (A) It increased the food supply by protecting farmers from developing the disease through exposure to infected cows.
    (B) It led indirectly to a population increase that provided more workers for urban factories.
    (C) It improved the health of milkmaids and increased the supply of dairy products.
    (D) Used on cattle, it increased the yield of meat.
    (E) It had no influence.

23. According to Ricardo's Iron Law of Wages

    (A) workers in pig iron production must earn subsistence wages
    (B) population will outrun the food supply
    (C) a ten-hour workday was most productive
    (D) variations in the supply and demand of labor will lead to eventual mass starvation
    (E) poverty will end only with the public ownership of the means of production

24. A revolution in psychology at the end of the 19th century popularized the notion that human behavior springs from irrational forces and unconscious urges. It was pioneered by

    (A) Auguste Comte
    (B) Leopold von Ranke
    (C) Sigmund Freud
    (D) William James
    (E) Carl Gustave Jung

25. All of the following are accurate depictions of the Thirty Years' War (1618–1648) EXCEPT

    (A) it was fought mostly in Germany
    (B) it involved the major states of Europe
    (C) it was a religious struggle between Protestants and Catholics
    (D) it was a political struggle between the German princes and the Holy Roman Empire
    (E) it allied the French with the Austrian Hapsburgs

26. When the French people drew up cahiers (lists of grievances) in 1789 for the Estates General to consider, which of the following would NOT have been likely?

    (A) The peasants wanted relief from feudal dues.
    (B) The bourgeoisie called for access to high office in the military and government.
    (C) Shopkeepers wanted an end to unnecessary taxes on commerce.
    (D) The nobles wanted an expansion of royal power.
    (E) The clergy wanted protection of monastic lands.

John Constable's Flatford 1817. The Granger Collection, New York. (0026525)

27. The painting above would most likely adhere to the themes of the movement that included which of the following?

    (A) Marx and Engels
    (B) Charles Darwin
    (C) Byron and Goethe
    (D) Edmund Burke
    (E) Freud

28. Monet, Renoir, and Pissarro pioneered which style of painting?

    (A) Romanticism
    (B) Impressionism
    (C) Realism
    (D) Abstractionism
    (E) Cubism

"The Age of Reason diminished the human spirit by denying the emotionality that flows from the soul. Miracles are acts of God, not illusions for the senses. Mystery is at the core of existence. The tiller of the soil is purer at heart than the factory laborer, and science will never uncover the ultimate meaning of life."

29. The passage above would most likely have been written in the first half of the 19th century by

    (A) a Socialist
    (B) a materialist
    (C) a Romantic
    (D) a rationalist
    (E) a liberal

30. Who was the most influential statesman in Europe for the two decades before 1890, and why was he so powerful?

    (A) Prime Minister Cavour because a united Italy had become a major player on the world stage
    (B) Kaiser Wilhelm I because Germany had become the world's leading industrial power
    (C) Chancellor Bismarck because the unification of Germany had upset the European balance of power
    (D) Emperor Franz Joseph because he headed the rejuvenated monarchy of Austria-Hungary
    (E) Prime Minister William Gladstone because England had acquired an empire upon which "the sun never set"

31. The transition from colonialism to independence was LEAST chaotic in which of the following?

    (A) The Philippines
    (B) The Belgian Congo
    (C) The Dutch East Indies (Indonesia)
    (D) Algeria
    (E) Indochina

32. All of the following are accurate assessments of the New Imperialism EXCEPT

    (A) it degraded the subject peoples
    (B) it created immensely profitable markets for European goods in the colonies
    (C) it introduced progressive economies to the non-Western world
    (D) it helped precipitate World Wars I and II
    (E) it encouraged the non-West to modernize its social and political systems

33. Which of the following were strongholds of Protestantism by 1600?

    (A) Northern Italy and Southern Germany
    (B) Poland and Austria
    (C) Hungary and Northern Germany
    (D) Scandinavia and Northern Germany
    (E) Austria and Germany

The Defenestration of Prague. The Granger Collection, New York. (0008853)

34. The event depicted here marked the start of which armed conflict?

    (A) The Thirty Years' War
    (B) The War of the Roses
    (C) The War of the Three Henrys
    (D) The Hapsburg-Valois Wars
    (E) The War of Spanish Succession

35. As a result of the revolt by the Czech nobility in 1618

    (A) Bohemia gained independence from the Habsburgs
    (B) the Habsburgs allowed Protestant worship
    (C) the native nobility was wiped out
    (D) the Bohemian parliament gained power over taxation
    (E) the Czechs gained independence after the Battle of White Mountain

36. New industries, such as railroads, chemical production, and electricity generation advanced most rapidly in which of the following European countries during the last years of the 19th century?

    (A) Belgium
    (B) Russia
    (C) Germany
    (D) England
    (E) France

37. All were weapons first employed in combat during World War I EXCEPT

    (A) armored tanks
    (B) poison gas
    (C) observation balloons
    (D) diesel-powered submarines
    (E) fighter aircraft

38. Which was NOT a provision of the Treaty of Versailles?

    (A) Germany accepted sole responsibility for starting World War I.
    (B) Austria was required to pay reparations to the Allies.
    (C) Germany was effectively disarmed.
    (D) The Rhineland was demilitarized.
    (E) Germany was to pay the cost of damage done to the property of Allied civilians.

39. All are important reasons for the failure of the League of Nations EXCEPT

    (A) each member nation of the Assembly got one vote regardless of its power
    (B) the United States never joined
    (C) economic sanctions could be ignored by member nations
    (D) the league could but never did raise an international force to repel aggression
    (E) Italy and Japan's defiance of league mandates in the 1930s reduced its credibility

40. Cultural relativism—that the validity of a society's values depend upon its political and economic context—was encouraged in the 20th century by the theories of

    (A) Herbert Spencer
    (B) Sigmund Freud
    (C) Albert Einstein
    (D) Thomas Huxley
    (E) Isaac Newton

41. The Glorious Revolution of 1688 was a turning point in British history because

    (A) the Roundheads defeated the Cavaliers and executed the king, making Parliament the supreme power in the nation
    (B) it marked Roman Catholicism's return to both England and Scotland as an official state religion
    (C) the French vowed to stay out of British international affairs as a result of the Glorious Revolution of 1688
    (D) Puritans gained supreme power throughout the country and they threatened another civil war if Oliver Cromwell's reforms were not reinstated
    (E) it was accompanied by the English Bill of Rights that limited monarchical authority significantly

42. The impact of Napoleon's Grand Empire included all of the following EXCEPT

    (A) the abolition of serfdom
    (B) legal and administrative reform
    (C) the popular belief in Napoleon as the enlightened liberator
    (D) resentment against foreign domination
    (E) massive conversions to Catholicism all over Europe

43. All of the following are valid generalizations about the rise of Communism in Russia from 1917 to 1939 except

    (A) corruption in the tsar's government and war reverses brought Communism to power
    (B) the disunity of both their internal and their foreign enemies solidified the original successes of the Communists
    (C) central economic planning and brutal repression industrialized Russia's agrarian economy within two decades
    (D) royal excess of the Romanov family diminished respect for the tsar and his family
    (E) the Soviet system of rule was embraced by all of the people

44. The peace settlements at the end of World War I helped cause World War II for all the following reasons EXCEPT

    (A) the newly established independent states of Eastern Europe left a power vacuum in the region
    (B) the establishment of Communism in Russia led to eventual conflict between Germany and the U.S.S.R.
    (C) reparations and the war guilt clause provided grounds for Hitler's propaganda
    (D) Italy's and Japan's resentments of the settlements created international instability
    (E) the collapse of the Ottoman Empire created a belligerent and aggressive independent Turkey

45. What was the condition of the Soviet economy on the eve of World War II?

   (A) It was in a shambles due to the political repression of the labor force.
   (B) It was one of the world's most productive.
   (C) It had been ravaged by depression, unemployment, and underproduction.
   (D) It depended heavily on foreign investment and imports.
   (E) While healthy, its technology and productivity were far behind that of the capitalist nations of the West.

WONDER HOW LONG THE HONEYMOON WILL LAST?

Nazi/Soviet Pact by Clifford K. Berryman. The Granger Collection, New York. (0036907)

46. The cartoon above depicts Hitler and Stalin after their 1939 nonaggression pact, which Hitler signed primarily to

   (A) avoid a Soviet invasion of Germany due to Hitler's anticommunist policies
   (B) unite their forces in order to jointly invade the rest of Europe
   (C) swap German technology for Russian manpower to increase the power of both nations
   (D) keep Stalin close to him as an ally so that he could not be surprised by him later
   (E) be certain that he would not face a war on two fronts when Germany invaded Poland.

47. During the economic crisis of the Great Depression, Hitler addressed his promises of economic and political salvation to all of the following groups EXCEPT

    (A) young people
    (B) upper and middle classes
    (C) big businessmen and army leaders
    (D) workers
    (E) Germans who wanted more land

48. The emergence of the "second wave" women's movement in the 1960s has been attributed to all of the following reasons EXCEPT

    (A) changes in the patterns of work and motherhood
    (B) the work of a vanguard of feminist intellectuals
    (C) the organization of dissatisfied women to demand changes
    (D) new methods of birth control gave women more freedom over their own lives
    (E) fewer opportunities for women existed outside the home

49. The photo above is of a structure that has been called the greatest monument to absolutism and self-aggrandizement. It was

    (A) the Hermitage of Catherine the Great
    (B) the Schonbrunn Palace of the Hapsburgs
    (C) the Palace at Versailles of Louis XIV
    (D) Sans Souci of Frederick the Great
    (E) The Blenheim Palace of the Duke of Marlborough

50. Hapsburg rule in the Austro-Hungarian Empire prior to World War I was most threatened by

    (A) the growth of socialism
    (B) liberal reformers
    (C) German aggression
    (D) the Pan-Slavic movement
    (E) a decline of the fine arts

51. What is the social significance of women working in factories during World War I?

    (A) Due to the wartime shortage of male workers, even the supervisiors were women.
    (B) Women were found to be more adept than men at close detail work.
    (C) Universal suffrage had been granted with the outbreak of war, and women used the vote as leverage for getting industrial jobs.
    (D) The vital contribution of women to the war effort helped in their liberation from narrow social roles.
    (E) Only women in those days would accept such tedious, menial work.

52. After Lenin's death, how was Stalin able to succeed to the leadership of Communist Russia?

    (A) His heroic exploits during the Civil War of 1918 to 1922 earned him universal respect.
    (B) He was Lenin's heir apparent.
    (C) As secretary of the Soviet Communist party, he had appointed many of his supporters to positions of power.
    (D) He had his closest rival, Leon Trotsky, assassinated soon after Lenin died.
    (E) Most party members supported his policy of "building socialism in one country."

53. Adolf Hitler became chancellor of Germany in 1933 by

    (A) engineering a putsch against the Weimar Republic
    (B) setting fire to the Reichstag Building and using it as a pretext to restore order
    (C) being invited by the president to form a coalition government after the Nazis won a plurality of Reichstag seats
    (D) being directly elected by a clear majority
    (E) assassinating the chancellor of the Weimar Republic and seizing the office

54. The Nuremberg Laws of 1935

    (A) imprisoned known Communists in concentration camps
    (B) denied the Jews of Germany all their rights as citizens
    (C) outlawed labor unions and strikes in Germany
    (D) made Hitler German president for life
    (E) repealed the Treaty of Versailles

55. When they rejected Western aid in the form of the American Marshall
    Plan in order to rebuild their war-torn land, the Soviets

    (A) were unable to repair the damage for decades
    (B) commandeered the tools of industry from their satellites in order to
        rebuild their own damaged factories and left an agrarian economy in
        Eastern Europe
    (C) scoured the Third World for investors
    (D) repaired the damage within a decade under Stalin's Five-Year Plans
    (E) never did fully rebuild after the war

56. The first European country to grant women suffrage, in 1906, was

    (A) Britain
    (B) France
    (C) Germany
    (D) Norway
    (E) Finland

"'God is on our side,' each claimed and fervently believed as they
marched off in 1914. They denied themselves the freedom to learn the
truth and speak out against the insanity of it all, and they sent a whole
generation of their young men to the slaughter."

57. The "they" in the passage above refers to

    (A) the kaiser's military High Command
    (B) the British General Staff
    (C) the leaders of the Central Powers
    (D) the czarist government of Russia
    (E) the belligerent nations of World War I

58. Which of the following nations consistently urged the world community
    to take up "collective security" in the 1930s?

    (A) The United States
    (B) Britain
    (C) France
    (D) China
    (E) The U.S.S.R.

59. There is strong evidence that the German Army might have toppled Hitler from power if the Western democracies had made a firm stand in 1936

(A) against the *Anschluss* with Austria
(B) at the Munich conference against the German annexation of the Sudetenland
(C) against the Nazi-Soviet Nonaggression Pact
(D) against the remilitarization of the Rhineland
(E) against the invasion of Poland

60. What is the best estimate of the total cost in human lives of World War II?

(A) 55 million, of whom approximately two thirds were civilians
(B) 40 million, of whom approximately half were civilians
(C) 30 million, of whom three quarters were civilians
(D) 25 million, of whom two fifths were civilians
(E) 15 million, of whom one third were civilians

61. The devastation of Europe after World War II was far worse than after World War I for all of the following reasons EXCEPT

(A) the technology and tactics of the First World War limited the damage to specific regions
(B) saturation bombing of cities during World War II destroyed or severely damaged nearly all the major industrial areas of the belligerents
(C) the scorched-earth policy leveled hundreds of thousands of structures in the U.S.S.R. during World War II
(D) more refugees relocated during World War II
(E) more poison gas weapons were used in World War II

62. Which is the most valid generalization about the response of the Soviet satellites to the de-Stalinization program of the Soviet Communist party after Stalin's death?

(A) They branded it as revisionist and rejected it.
(B) They followed the "party line."
(C) They responded in varying degrees; some were encouraged to openly revolt against Soviet domination.
(D) They demanded and were granted liberalization of their Soviet-dominated governments.
(E) They turned to the West for guidance.

American U-2 plane. The Granger Collection, New York. (0076771)

63. An airplane like the one pictured above was

    (A) awarded a world speed record with Gary Powers piloting it
    (B) awarded a world altitude record with Gary Powers piloting it
    (C) flown around the world nonstop with Gary Powers piloting it
    (D) shot down while spying on the Soviet Union with Gary Powers piloting it
    (E) used to support combat missions in Korea when it was shot down with Gary Powers piloting it

"You can no more win a war than you can win an earthquake."
—Jeanette Rankin

64. Had the above quote been written in 1914 in one of the warring countries, its writer would likely have been

    (A) published in the mainstream press
    (B) applauded by the general public
    (C) publically debated by an official of the government
    (D) ostracized and censored
    (E) a member of Parliament

65. Hitler's rule in Germany was popular with most of the German people until

    (A) the Nuremberg Laws were enacted
    (B) Dachau concentration camp was opened
    (C) Germany suffered serious reversals in World War II
    (D) the abuses of the SS were publicized
    (E) Germany entered World War II

66. The German blitzkrieg tactic, used against Poland in 1939 and France in 1940, included all EXCEPT

(A) frontal infantry assaults against heavily fortified positions
(B) a spearhead of fast armor on a narrow front
(C) tactical air support of ground forces
(D) mobile infantry units transported by motorcycles and fast vehicles
(E) the clearing of enemy mines and obstacles by combat engineers

67. The Soviets were able to repel and defeat the Nazi invaders in World War II for all of these reasons EXCEPT

(A) the Germans were never prepared for combat in the brutal Russian winter
(B) the Russians mounted heroic resistance
(C) the enormous front overextended German defenses and supply lines
(D) Soviet war production surpassed that of the Germans
(E) the Soviets moved most of the industry of European Russia hundreds of miles east out of range of the Germans

68. Which was the MOST important contribution of the United States to the defeat of the Axis?

(A) The superiority of its aircraft
(B) The development of atomic weapons
(C) The brilliance of its military commanders
(D) The productivity of its industries
(E) The abundance of its natural resources

69. In 1957, the West grudgingly accepted the technological advancement of the Soviets, who

(A) tested their first atomic bomb
(B) perfected an intercontinental missile capable of striking the United States
(C) developed a hydrogen bomb
(D) launched the world's first artificial satellite
(E) installed indoor plumbing in all public housing in the U.S.S.R.

70. Which was NOT true of the Brezhnev Doctrine?

(A) It stated that the U.S.S.R. had the right to intervene in the internal affairs of any of its satellites where Communism was threatened.
(B) It was applied to suppress the Hungarian Uprising of 1956.
(C) Its promulgation marked the end of Soviet leadership of the Communist world.
(D) It diminished the role of the U.S.S.R. as a model for other Communist states.
(E) It alienated many Third World nations.

71. The policy of détente—the peaceful coexistence of the Western and Communist blocs—was most actively pursued during the administration of which of the following U.S. presidents?

    (A) Harry Truman
    (B) Dwight Eisenhower
    (C) John Kennedy
    (D) Lyndon Johnson
    (E) Richard Nixon

72. The militant contemporary phase of the women's movement that began in the 1960s

    (A) sought an end not only to legal but also to social barriers to gender equality
    (B) had the greatest appeal in the Third World
    (C) argued that gender differences were inborn
    (D) found that gender discrimination was a problem rarely found in Communist societies
    (E) originated in the United States and had little appeal in Europe

73. "Functionalism," founded by Walter Gropius and taught at the German *Bauhaus* was

    (A) a philosophical movement espousing the expansion of women's roles in modern society
    (B) a style of clothing that dispensed with frills
    (C) a trend in postmodern painting that used limited colors and set modes of execution
    (D) a school of literary critique that argued for precision in language in the age of "doubletalk"
    (E) a style of architecture that argued that beauty will follow once a building is well designed to serve its purpose

74. By the 1920s, the theories of Sigmund Freud, developed before World War I, had become widely known and by mid-century all of the following were true EXCEPT

    (A) his emphasis on the sex urge had been modified by his successors
    (B) new schools of psychology offered vastly different explanations of human behavior
    (C) Freud was criticized for his less than rigorously scientific methods
    (D) his theories were criticized for interpreting male behavior by standards more appropriate to females
    (E) watered-down versions of his creative and complex theories had crept into the popular culture

Picasso's *Guernica*, 1937. The Granger Collection, New York. (032522)

75. The painting above is a cubist piece protesting the brutality of the fascist actions during the Spanish Civil War painted by which of the following artists?

    (A) Salvador Dali
    (B) Juan Gris
    (C) Marcel Duchamp
    (D) Edvard Munch
    (E) Pablo Picasso

76. All of the following are valid generalizations about academic philosophy in the period before World War II EXCEPT

    (A) it attempted to adopt the methodology of science
    (B) it was often limited to linguistic analysis
    (C) it attempted to answer the traditional problems posed by philosophers
    (D) it was detached and remote from the ethical concerns of modern life
    (E) its concerns were remote for most people

77. All of the following are true of organized religion after World War II EXCEPT

    (A) Protestantism attempted a closer understanding with Roman Catholicism through ecumenicalism
    (B) Christianity adjusted to new challenges such as secularism and Communism
    (C) the newly created state of Israel received support from Jews all over the world in response to the Holocaust
    (D) Hinduism, Buddhism, and Islam drew new adherents in the West
    (E) most Christian sects incorporated scientific research and support into their theology

78. The youth rebellion that developed worldwide in the 1960s had all of the following characteristics EXCEPT

    (A) it tended to point out the failings of modern technological society and underplay its advantages
    (B) it glorified rebels against the status quo such as Fidel Castro and Ho Chi Minh
    (C) it attacked materialism and tradition
    (D) it looked to Soviet Communism for guidance
    (E) it drew on neo-Marxist theories and often resorted to violence to further its programs

79. The policy of glasnost in the Soviet Union was

    (A) a crackdown on dissident leaders
    (B) a reason for the United States to escalate the Cold War
    (C) associated with openness and freedom of speech
    (D) the policy that Boris Yeltsin used as the first president
    (E) an excuse to increase corruption there

80. The European Union member nations must

    (A) use the same currency
    (B) restrict national debt to set a percentage of GDP
    (C) allow the Swiss Franc to be spent within EU borders
    (D) construct tariffs for Asian trade
    (E) no longer trade with the United States

STOP

END OF SECTION I

SECTION II

FREE-RESPONSE QUESTIONS

Part A: Document-Based Essay Question (DBQ)

WRITING TIME—2 HOURS AND 10 MINUTES TO COMPLETE
THIS PART OF THE EXAM, 50 PERCENT OF TOTAL GRADE

Suggested time:
15 minutes reading time for part A
45 minutes to complete part A
35 minutes for ONE question from Group 1
35 minutes for ONE question from Group 2

You may take 15 minutes to look over the documents and make comments on them. You will then have 1 hour and 55 minutes to complete all three essays.

Directions: The following question is based upon documents 1–12. (These documents may have been edited in order to engage the student.) The DBQ is designed to test your ability to read and interpret documents. Show your mastery of this skill by analyzing the content and the <u>point of view and validity of the source's author</u>. Answer the question fully by utilizing your analysis of the documents and the time period discussed to support a well-constructed essay.

1. Assess the various reactions and responses to the rise of socialism in Europe 1800–1989.

   Historical background: During the Industrial Revolution, the underside of capitalism was revealed. Workers labored in backbreaking conditions for long hours and lived in unsanitary, crowded tenements. A competing economic and social system evolved from the ideas of Charles Fourier, Louis Blanc, Robert Owen, Henri Saint-Simon, Pierre-Joseph Proudhon, and other French thinkers. Socialism emerged and was embraced by intellectuals at first, then the masses, and finally governments. Revolutions were undertaken in the name of socialism, and conservatives rallied against it.

Document 1

Source: Henri Saint-Simon, early French socialist, *Letters of a Geneva Inhabitant to his Contemporaries*, 1803.

Compared with those who do not own property you are numerically very small. Why, then, are they willing to obey you? It is because you combine your powers against them, and this is usually enough to give you the advantage in the struggle which always exists between you and them. As long as you do not adopt my proposal, gentlemen, each of you will be exposed to such calamities as have befallen those members of your class living in France.

Document 2

Source: Charles Fourier, early French Socialist, *Theory of Social Organization*, 1820.

Under a true organization of commerce, property would be abolished, the mercantile classes become agents for trade of industrial goods and commerce would then be the servant of society. There will be no idlers, all will earn more than they consume. They will render industry attractive and end the evil distinction between producers and consumers.

Document 3

Source: Chartist movement, *People's Petition*, England, 1838.

Our slavery has been exchanged for an apprenticeship to liberty, which has aggravated the painful feeling of our social degradation, by adding to it the sickening of still deferred hope. The capital of the master must no longer be deprived of its due reward; that taxation must be made to fall on property, not on industry; that the good of the many, as it is the only legitimate end, so must it be the sole study of the government.

Document 4

Source: Sidney Webb, British socialist and Fabian, *The Historic Basics of Socialism*, 1889.

But it will not long be possible for any man to persist in believing that the political organization of society can be completely altered without corresponding changes in economic and social relations. In the present socialist movement these two streams are united: advocates of social reconstruction have learnt the lesson of democracy, and know that it is through the slow and gradual turning of the popular mind to new principles that social reorganization bit by bit comes.

Document 5

Source: *Socialist Allegory*, an English illustration supporting the International Socialist & Trade Union Congress of 1896, showing the nations of Europe and America represented by workers, 1896.

English illustration by Walter Crane. The Granger Collection, New York. (0078717)

Document 6

Source: Rosa Luxemberg, A German socialist in the working class, *The War and the Workers*, 1916.

The fall of the socialist proletariat in the present world war is unprecedented. It is a misfortune for humanity. But socialism will be lost only if the international proletariat fails to measure the depth of this fall, if it refuses to learn from it. German Social Democracy always took the lead and blindly bestowed its confidence upon the admired leadership of the mighty German Social Democracy: the pride of every socialist and the terror of the ruling classes everywhere.

Document 7

Source: Harry W. Laidler, *Platform of the British Labour Party*, 1945.

1. Public Ownership of the fuel and power industries.
2. Public Ownership of inland transport
3. Public Ownership of iron and steel
4. Public supervision of monopolies and cartels

Document 8

Source: Winston Churchill, former British prime minister, *Conservative Party Principles*, 1946.

We oppose the establishment of a Socialist State, controlling the means of production, distribution and exchange. We are asked, "What is your alternative?" Our Conservative aim is to build a property-owning democracy, both independent and interdependent. In this I include profit-sharing schemes in suitable industries and intimate consultation between employers and wage-earners. In fact we seek so far as possible to make the status of the wage-earner that of a partner rather than of an irresponsible employee.

Document 9

Source: Albert Einstein, *Why Socialism*, 1949

I am convinced there is only *one* way to eliminate these grave evils, namely through the establishment of a socialist economy, accompanied by an educational system which would be oriented toward social goals. In such an economy, the means of production are owned by society itself and are utilized in a planned fashion. A planned economy, which adjusts production to the needs of the community, would distribute the work to be done among all those able to work and would guarantee a livelihood to every man, woman, and child.

Document 10

Source: Hungarian Building Industry University Students, *Sixteen Political, Economic, and Ideological Points*, October 22, 1956.

We demand the re-organization of the entire economic life of Hungary, with the assistance of specialists. Our whole economic system based on planned economy should be re-examined with an eye to Hungarian conditions and to the vital interests of the Hungarian people.

Document 11

Source: Nikita Khrushchev, *Telegram to the U.S. State Department*, October 16, 1962.

It was one thing when U.S. was very powerful, but now there is a force as great as yours. We will never agree to your capitalistic way of thinking. Our policy is, let us live in peace. Let us have our socialism and you can have your capitalism. Let's respect internal affairs of other countries and not interfere with life of other countries.

Document 12

Source: Margaret Thatcher, conservative prime minister of Great Britain, *Speech to the Church of Scotland*, May 21, 1988.

We are told we must work and use our talents to create wealth. "If a man will not work he shall not eat," wrote St. Paul to the Thessalonians. Indeed, abundance rather than poverty has a legitimacy which derives from the very nature of Creation. It is not the creation of wealth that is wrong, but love of money for its own sake. Any set of social and economic arrangements which is not founded on the acceptance of individual responsibility will do nothing but harm. We simply cannot delegate the exercise of mercy and generosity to others.

SECTION II

FREE-RESPONSE QUESTIONS

Part B: Two Essay Questions

WRITING TIME—70 MINUTES FOR TWO ESSAYS;
55 PERCENT OF SECTION II SCORE

Directions: Answer two of the following, one from Group A and one from Group B. Be sure to cite relevant historical information to support your answer. Number your answer as the question below is numbered. Use extra time to check your work.

GROUP A

2. Assess the reasons for the split between the Anglican and Roman Catholic Churches in light of the fact that the Anglicans had not adopted any of the tenets of Protestantism when the split occurred.

3. "The Congress of Vienna aligned the European balance of power effectively, but it restored the old order clumsily." Assess the validity of this statement.

4. To what extent and in what ways had Western Europe recovered economically from the effects of World War II a decade after it had ended?

GROUP B

5. Assess the reasons for the similarities and differences between the French Revolution of 1789 and the Russian Revolution of 1917.

6. "The most profound revolutions are in the realm of ideas." Analyze this statement by making reference to the influence upon their age of TWO of the following thinkers: Copernicus, Calvin, Newton, Adam Smith, Darwin, Freud, Einstein.

7. "Japan's successes up to 1942 served as a model for subject peoples in the European colonial empires." Defend or refute this statement.

END OF SECTION II

Answer Key
MODEL TEST 1

SECTION I

1. D	11. E	21. C	31. A	41. E	51. D	61. E	71. E
2. C	12. A	22. B	32. B	42. C	52. C	62. C	72. A
3. D	13. E	23. A	33. D	43. E	53. C	63. D	73. E
4. A	14. B	24. C	34. A	44. E	54. B	64. D	74. D
5. B	15. E	25. E	35. C	45. B	55. D	65. C	75. E
6. E	16. B	26. D	36. C	46. E	56. E	66. A	76. C
7. E	17. D	27. C	37. C	47. B	57. E	67. A	77. E
8. C	18. E	28. B	38. B	48. E	58. E	68. D	78. D
9. C	19. E	29. C	39. A	49. C	59. D	69. D	79. C
10. D	20. D	30. C	40. C	50. D	60. A	70. B	80. B

Scoring the Practice Exam

Once you have completed the exam with 55 minutes for the multiple-choice questions and 130 minutes to read and interpret the documents and finish all three essays, you can score your exam.

The multiple-choice test is scored with one point given for each correct answer. *There is no penalty for guessing as of May 2011,* so students should attempt to answer every question on the exam.

The test taker should use the DBQ rubric and the FRQ rubric seen after the multiple-choice explanations for this exam to assess their DBQ and FRQ essays, respectively.

To attain a final AP score for a student, he or she should plug his or her scores into the chart below and calculate a final score:

AP European History Exam Composite Score Conversion Chart	
Score Range	**AP Score**
119–180	5
100–118	4
71–99	3
60–70	2
0–59	1

Multiple Choice Score × 1.125 = _____

+

DBQ Score × 4.5 = _____

+

FRQ 1 Score × 2.75 = _____

+

FRQ 2 Score × 2.75 = _____

**Total of all above scores
is composite score = _____**

Answers Explained

1. **(D)** It shows emotion, anatomic accuracy, humanity. It was religious but lacked the symbolic representation of medieval art.

2. **(C)** Their work allowed Copernicus to develop a more elegant and simple model of the universe than that of Ptolemy.

3. **(D)** Baptism and Holy Communion were both considered sacraments by Luther.

4. **(A)** Catholic plotters and Catholic mobs slaughtered Huguenot leaders, and the religious civil war broke out with renewed fervor and brutality.

5. **(B)** Theocracy was a feature of only Calvinism, which argued that religious morality should influence the state.

6. **(E)** The fabled Hapsburg family was one of the oldest and most powerful in Europe.

7. **(E)** Catholics and some Protestant sects were denied religious freedom at various times.

8. **(C)** Hobbes's works are the only ones cited that supported absolutism.

9. **(C)** The mystics' personal approach to communion with God and the simple piety preached by Groote set the tone for Luther's tenets.

10. **(D)** They wanted to reform but not dismantle Roman Catholicism.

11. **(E)** Machiavelli advised for a ruler to be loved or feared but never hated.

12. **(A)** The peasants, nobility, middle class, and artisans all converted to Calvinism in Huguenot areas of France, often as a cloak for rebellion against the monarchy.

13. **(E)** The most important impact of these land acquisitions was the construction of St. Petersburg as a port city and a "window to the west."

14. **(B)** A Protestant buffer state between the West and the Russians, its army was always its focal point.

15. **(E)** France's overwhelming strength and Louis's penchant for war had disturbed the balance of power for decades.

16. **(B)** Beholden to no one and nothing but his own abilities. That was his point.

17. **(D)** He forcibily converted or expelled the Jews and the Moors, Spain's most productive and educated groups; he crushed resistance in the Spanish Netherlands; he put a restrictive tax on all sales; he helped defeat the Turkish invaders.

18. **(E)** The Enclosure Movement was a slow movement to end feudal landholding practices and introduce the concept of private property.

19. **(E)** Poverty was a normal condition before the generalized prosperity of the 20th century. Country people were as poor as urban dwellers, sometimes more so. The difference was that the Industrial Revolution concentrated the poverty in the city slums so it could not be ignored and had to be dealt with.

20. **(D)** The secret police actually helped Joseph to extend his reforms by making centralization of his government easier.

21. **(C)** The high court, the Parlement of Paris, declared it was necessary if he was to initiate a tax on the exempted First and Second Estates.

22. **(B)** Healthier people work harder, live longer. His original experimental innoculation of a diluted solution containing a cowpox scab was into the arm of a small boy.

23. **(A)** He tried to explain why Adam Smith's "natural law" economy did not bring about the general prosperity that he had promised in *Wealth of Nations*. Ricardo's Iron Law of Wages says that all labor will be paid subsistence wages in the long run.

24. **(C)** Freud's view of human irrationality revolutionized attitudes.

25. **(E)** Cardinal Richelieu got into the war in order to nullify Austria's power and influence among the German states.

26. **(D)** The battle for power between a centralized monarchy and the nobility was a familiar theme all during the growth of the nation-state.

27. **(C)** Lord Byron, the English poet, and Johann von Goethe, the great German poet and dramatist, personified the Romantic movement as did Constable.

28. **(B)** The invention of the camera and the harshness of the 19th century led to a new movement in painting that gave an impression of the emotions along with the image, known as impressionism.

29. **(C)** The Romantic movement was a reaction to the rationalism of the Enlightenment.

30. **(C)** Head of a powerful united Germany, victor over France, he was the most influential man in Europe during that period. His masterful diplomacy kept a balance but helped incite World War I decades after his death because he tried to isolate France with a network of alliances.

31. **(A)** It was slated for independence in 1946, and, despite the ravages of World War II, which ended in 1945, the schedule was kept.

32. **(B)** The non-European peoples in the colonies did not have wealth enough to provide a rich market for European manufactured goods. The most profitable trade was between industrialized nations.

33. **(D)** England was also an important center. Poland, Austria, and Italy have always been predominantly Catholic.

34. **(A)** The Defenestration of Prague began the Thirty Years' War.

35. **(C)** The Hapsburgs destroyed the Czechs at the Battle of White Mountain, replaced the nobility with Catholics loyal to the Hapsburgs, and banned Protestant forms of worship.

36. **(C)** Germany's industrialization during this period far surpassed any of the other nations listed.

37. **(C)** Observation balloons were used as far back as the U.S. Civil War.

38. **(B)** It was required to pay indemnities but not under the Treaty of Versailles. The Treaty of Saint-Germaine settled the peace with Austria.

39. **(A)** The big powers got representation in the council.

40. **(C)** It was another of those broad applications of a revolutionary theory in a specific field, like social Darwinism following along on the coattails of natural selection.

41. **(E)** The English Bill of Rights was a cornerstone in British political growth.

42. **(C)** Napoleon reformed Europe through the Napoleonic Code, which provided for abolition of serfdom and religious toleration, but the people of Europe did not see him as an enlightened liberator, but a tyrannical conqueror.

43. **(E)** There were many who were killed or sent to Gulags because they rejected Soviet rule.

44. **(E)** Turkey modernized, regained some territory lost after the peace settlements, but then maintained its neutrality during World War II, even though it leaned toward the Axis.

45. **(B)** Stalin's Five-Year Plans had made it so despite the appalling costs to the people in terms of political repression.

46. **(E)** Hitler made a pact with Stalin and the Soviet Union to ensure that he would not have to fight them when he invaded Poland.

47. **(B)** Hitler did appeal to the poor, the industrialists, the soldiers, but not to the middle class.

48. **(E)** More opportunities existed for women outside of the home.

49. **(C)** The Palace at Versailles of Louis XIV cost huge sums of money that severely drained the French treasury. It was a monument to Louis XIV's glorified view of himself and his position.

50. **(D)** Of the many non-German minorities that were part of the empire, the Slavs were most vocal in their anti-German, anti-Hungarian nationalism which led to the outbreak of World War I.

51. **(D)** War expediency drastically altered the idea that women—even middle-class women—belonged in the home. Their efficiency and dedication helped win them the vote in many European nations.

52. **(C)** Trotsky was the organizer of the victorious Red Army and Lenin's heir apparent, despite Stalin's claims to the contrary in the creative propaganda and historical revision after he had gained power. Stalin had Trotsky assassinated in 1940, more than a decade and a half after ascending to power. The party was split on the issue of expanding the revolution outside the U.S.S.R.

53. **(C)** He won the leadership of the democracy he swore to destroy, democratically.

54. **(B)** They couldn't hold office, vote, own newspapers, marry non-Jews, work for the government, or carry on most business. It was the first step in the "final solution."

55. **(D)** It was a spectacular feat considering the destruction and death caused by the war.

56. **(E)** Finland and then Norway granted women the vote before World War I. Britain and Germany instituted women's suffrage soon after World War I. France did not do it until after World War II.

57. **(E)** They all believed that God supported their cause.

58. **(E)** The U.S.S.R. feared the Fascist militarists to the point of supporting the republican cause in the Spanish Civil War. Since the democracies were both afraid of Communism and absorbed by the depression, they ignored Soviet pleas.

59. **(D)** Hitler gambled that the French, with thousands of well-armed troops, would not oppose his token force. Anti-Nazi commanders in the Wehrmacht intended to depose him if the gamble had failed. The French sat behind their defenses and let him violate the Treaty of Versailles.

60. **(A)** There is new evidence that the toll was even higher.

61. **(E)** There was less gas used in World War II.

62. **(C)** Armed resistance broke out in Poland and Hungary in 1956. Accommodations were made by the Soviets with the Communist government of Poland; the Hungarian Revolt was brutally and ruthlessly crushed.

63. **(D)** A U-2 plane was shot down on an espionage mission in the Soviet Union with Gary Powers piloting it.

64. **(D)** Pacifists were not only publically reviled; they were often jailed.

65. **(C)** When the bombs began to drop on their cities, they began to question the regime. By then, it was too late.

66. **(A)** This was the deadly and futile tactic of the First World War.

67. **(A)** After suffering the ravages of the winter of 1941–1942, the German military trained and equipped their troops and adopted tactics appropriate to the severe weather conditions.

68. **(D)** It was the "arsenal of democracy" and its industrial output surpassed that of all the other belligerents put together.

69. **(D)** Sputnik shook the West out of its complacency.

70. **(B)** It was used as a pretext to suppress the Czechoslovakian Uprising in 1968.

71. **(E)** Despite, or maybe because of, his ardent anti-Communism, Nixon used personal diplomacy to improve U.S. relations with not only the U.S.S.R. but with Communist China.

72. **(A)** The gender issues in the Third World are powerful effects of tradition and poverty; subtle conditioning was identified as an important cause of sexual stereotyping; gender discrimination respects neither national boundaries nor ideology; it had wide appeal throughout the industrialized world.

73. **(E)** "Form follows function" was the idea.

74. **(D)** The opposite is true; Freud was known for interpreting female behavior by male standards.

75. **(E)** This work was by Pablo Picasso.

76. **(C)** According to Ludwig Wittgenstein, philosophy could not deal with "God, death, and what is higher."

77. **(E)** Most sects of Christianity do not incorporate science into theology.

78. **(D)** It rejected the Soviet leadership as encrusted bureaucrats out of touch with the real issues facing the planet, the Third World, and humanity.

79. **(C)** Glasnost was translated as openness, and this policy allowed for increased freedom of speech and communication.

80. **(B)** Not all EU member nations have to accept the Euro, but they must restrict their debt to a certain percentage of GDP.

Comments on the DBQ

A note on scoring DBQ essays: Due to the importance of grouping and point of view in the DBQ essay, the DBQ explanations will present a possible thesis and an explanation of the possible groupings. Each grouping will then be explained in terms of what is required for core elements and what is required for an expanded core score (best essays).

For an essay to meet all core elements, the following must be completed:

1. The essay must provide an appropriate, explicitly stated thesis that directly addresses all parts of the question. *Thesis may not simply restate the question.*
2. The essay discusses a majority of the documents individually and specifically.
3. The essay demonstrates understanding of the basic meaning of a majority of the documents (may misinterpret no more than one).
4. The essay supports the thesis with appropriate interpretations of a majority of the documents.
5. The essay analyzes point of view or bias in at least three documents.
6. The essay analyzes documents by explicitly organizing them in at least three appropriate groups.

All essay explanations give the basic requirements for the essay. If all of the basic requirements are fulfilled, the essay receives a core score of 6. The top tier or best essays will meet expanded core requirements and earn a score of 7–9 depending on how many of the elements described in the DBQ chapter are contained in the essay and to what extent they are supported.

The Expanded Core Elements are as follows:

1. The thesis is clear, analytical, and comprehensive.
2. The essay uses all or almost all documents.
3. The essay addresses all parts of the question thoroughly.
4. The essay uses documents persuasively as evidence.
5. The essay shows understanding of nuances in the documents.
6. The essay analyzes point of view or bias in at least four documents cited in the essay.
7. The essay analyzes the documents in additional ways—additional grouping or other.
8. The essay brings in relevant "outside" historical content.

A graphical representation of the rubric for the DBQ can be seen on the next page.

The structure and thesis of this essay will vary depending upon which groups the author uses in the essay. The essay should have a thesis that addresses all groups within the essay (3 groups for core, 4–5 for expanded core). The essay should then have a separate paragraph for each grouping of documents that examines why the document belongs within that group and the point of view of the authors of the documents. A concluding paragraph should then restate the thesis and indicate that it has been justified.

This DBQ essay must begin with a thesis paragraph that has one sentence setting the scene and one sentence that addresses the entire question such as: "The theory of socialism was first embraced by Europeans (1, 2, 3, 4, 5, 6, 7, 9, 11), whose reactions to socialism can also be examined by looking at the authors, including French and British socialists (1, 2, 4, 5), workers and their associations (3, 6, 10), and rulers (8, 7, 11, 12), but this theory was later rejected by rulers and some workers (10, 8, 12)." The essay should define socialism as the economic system in which people own private property, but the government controls the means of production.

It is usually best to present arguments in the same order as the thesis statement, so documents in favor of socialism will be examined first. *Listing the documents either in the thesis or within the paragraph is recommended.* The essay should use the documents as described below to craft an explanation of the various reactions of socialists to industrialization and the rise of capitalism into a paragraph that illustrates those reactions and responses. *Although they should not be presented in the order presented in the question, the documents will be addressed in that fashion here.* Each document will be analyzed for how the essay author should use it. Documents in this group are documents 1, 2, 3, 4, 5, 6, 7, 9, and 11. The essay should present document 1 as the ideas of a founder of socialism. The point of view of a founding thinker of socialism can be used to show a preoccupation with class existing in 1803. Document 2 is also supportive of socialism. This document can be used to show further support for socialism from its founders. It can also be used to help define socialism. The point of

DBQ Rubric

Score one point if accomplished	**Basic Core:** If any one of the following tasks is not performed, *the essay cannot get a score higher than 6.* The basic core points are objective like a checklist with one point for each.

1. Provides an appropriate, explicitly stated thesis that directly addresses all parts of the question—**thesis may not simply restate the question**.
2. Discusses a majority of the documents individually and specifically.
3. Demonstrates understanding of the basic meaning of a majority of the documents (may misinterpret no more than one).
4. Supports the thesis with appropriate interpretations of a majority of the documents.
5. Analyzes point of view or bias in at least three documents.
6. Analyzes documents by explicitly organizing them in at least three appropriate groups.

Sum of Scores Above:	*Only* **if all six of the above criteria are met**, then the writer may attain a score of 7–9 if the writer can accomplish the expanded core elements. The more thoroughly the writer completes any of the following elements, the higher the additional score will be.

Expanded Core: If all core requirements are met, the writer may score points in any of the criteria below. *Very thorough application of any element below can score multiple points.* A **maximum** of 3 points may be awarded on the expanded core area. Scoring here is more subjective, and this section is not a checklist; to be awarded points writers must clearly accomplish any of the additional scoring criteria:

The thesis is clear, analytical, and comprehensive.

The essay uses all or almost all documents.

Addresses all parts of the question thoroughly.

Uses documents persuasively as evidence.

Shows understanding of nuances in the documents.

Analyzes point of view or bias in at least four documents cited in the essay.

Analyzes the documents in additional ways, or groupings.

Brings in relevant "outside" historical content.

Total sum of core plus any expanded points	If core score was 6, then add any expanded points to the core to get a final score from 0–9.

view of this document is that of a founding father of socialism. Document 3 can be best used to illustrate the workers' early support for socialist ideas. Point of view for this document can be attributed to the workers who wanted a better life. Document 4 can be used to illustrate British support for socialism and its slow adoption so as not to scare those in the bourgeois class. The fact that the author is a socialist explains point of view. Document 5 is further support from the British for socialism and can be used to demonstrate the proselytizing nature of socialism. The support for socialism is fine for point of view for this document. The support of workers as seen in document 6 is also important to show in this essay. Luxemberg's presentation of the strength of socialism is also good to use. Even after the Second World War, the importance of socialism is demonstrated by the program of the British Labour Party in document 7. The greatest scientific mind of the twentieth century perhaps was Albert Einstein, who adds his support to socialism in document 9. His weight as a world thinker can be used to show just how widely supported socialism was. Khrushchev's support of socialism is to be expected in document 11. He is the leader of a communist country that claims to be socialist and to support socialists, which can be used to illustrate point of view. The best essays will include point of view on two or more documents, include explanations for why most documents belong in this group, and explain why the documents that could possibly fit into this group may belong there or why others do not.

Documents authored by socialists also make up a group that can gain a "point of view" point for grouping them. The essay should use the documents as described below to craft an explanation of the various reactions of socialists to industrialization and the rise of capitalism into a paragraph that illustrates those reactions and responses. *Although they should not be presented in the order presented in the question, the documents will be addressed in that fashion here.* Each document will be analyzed for how the essay author should use it. Documents in this group are 1, 2, 4, and 5. The essay should present document 1 as the ideas of a founder of socialism. The point of view of a founding thinker of socialism can be used to show a preoccupation with class existing in 1803. Document 2 is also supportive of socialism. This document can be used to further support socialism from the point of view of its founders. It can also be utilized to help define socialism. The point of view of this document is also that of a founding father of socialism. Document 4 can be used to illustrate British support for socialism and its slow adoption so as not to scare those in the bourgeois class. The fact that the author is a socialist explains point of view. Document 5 is further support from the British for socialism and can be used to demonstrate the proselytizing nature of socialism. The support for socialism is fine for point of view for this document. The best essays will include point of view on two or more documents, include explanations for why most documents belong in this group, and explain why the documents that could possibly fit into this group may belong there or why others do not.

The documents by workers make a small group and are 3, 6, and 10. The essay should use the documents as described below to craft an explanation of the various reactions of laborers to industrialization and the rise of capitalism into a paragraph that illustrates those reactions and responses. *Although they should not be presented in the order presented in the question, the documents will be addressed in that fashion here.* Each document will be analyzed for how the essay author should use it. Document 3 can be best used to illustrate the workers' early support for socialist ideas. Point of view for this document can be attributed to the workers, who wanted to get a better life. Document 6 is also important to show how the working class supported socialism in this essay. Luxemberg's presentation of the strength of socialism is also good to use. Her ardent socialism would add to point of view. Outside information about her publishing many socialist works would add to this part. Document 10 can be used to show that some workers working within the socialist system criticized it later. This shows a change over time and that not all workers were united in opinion. The point of view of this document may be affected by the authors' residence in a totalitarian communist state. The best essays will include point of view on two or more documents, include explanations for why most documents belong in this group, and explain why the documents that could possibly fit into this group may belong there or why others do not.

The documents that should be listed in the grouping of those who ruled and their governments are 7, 8, 11, and 12. The essay should use the documents as described below to craft an explanation of the various reactions of rulers to industrialization and the rise of capitalism into a paragraph that illustrates those reactions and responses. *Although they should not be presented in the order presented in the question, the documents will be addressed in that fashion here.* Each document will be analyzed for how the essay author should use it. After the Second World War, the importance of socialism is demonstrated by the program of the British Labour Party in document 7. This document can be used to indicate that the government of Great Britain was adopting socialism. Document 8 expresses the propagandistic message of Winston Churchill, the British prime minister during World War II, and can be used to show his rejection of socialism. His status as a member of the upper classes may be used to demonstrate point of view. Khrushchev's support of socialism is to be expected in document 11. He is the leader of a communist country that claims to be socialist and to support socialists, which can be used to illustrate point of view. Document 12 should be used to show that as time passes more leaders rejected socialism in Europe. The fact that the prime minister of a previously socialist nation rejected the tenets of socialism can be used. Thatcher's point of view as a conservative leader can be used. The best essays will include point of view on two or more documents, include explanations for why most documents belong in this group, and explain why the documents that could possibly fit into this group may belong there or why others do not.

Another grouping of documents is those opposed to socialism, including documents 10, 12, and 8. These are all documents indicating that opposition to socialism did not manifest strongly until later. The essay should present document 8 as it expresses the propagandistic message of Winston Churchill, the British prime minister during World War II, and can be used to show his rejection of socialism. His status as a member of the upper classes may be used to demonstrate point of view. Document 10 can be used to show that some workers working within the socialist system criticized it later on. This shows a change over time and that not all workers were united in opinion. The point of view of this document may be affected by the authors' residence in a totalitarian communist state. Document 12 should be used to show that as time passes more leaders rejected socialism in Europe. The fact that the prime minister of a previously socialist nation rejected the tenets of socialism can be used. Thatcher's point of view as a conservative leader can be used. The best essays will include point of view on two or more documents, include explanations for why most documents belong in this group, and explain why the documents that could possibly fit into this group may belong there or why others do not.

The best essays will have a clear, comprehensive, and concise thesis, address all responses and reactions to socialism presented, as well as the change over time of those responses and reactions, and demonstrate point of view in at least eight documents and/or groupings. They will have four or more groups of documents, and use all fourteen documents to create a cogent essay that persuasively presents specific evidence for how the documents support the conclusions of the essay, brings in relevant outside information, and flows well.

Comments on the Essay Questions

In answering these questions, be sure to follow the "Simple Procedures" for writing an essay:

First, ask yourself what the question wants to know.

Second, ask yourself what you know about it.

Third, ask yourself how you would put it into words.

Use this generic rubric to help you or a friend or a tutor score each of the two essays you answered for this exam, one from Group A and one from Group B.

Generic Essay Scoring Rubric

9–8 POINTS

- ✔ Thesis explicitly addresses **all parts of the question**. Thesis does not need to be in the opening paragraph.
- ✔ Organization is clear, consistently followed, and effective in support of the argument.

  - May devote individual paragraphs to an examination of each part of the question.
  - Must identify major terms associated with the question and put them into context for the question; does not have to present every detail for every part.

- ✔ Essay is well balanced; the issues are analyzed at some length. Essay covers all chronological requirements of the question to some extent.
- ✔ Major assertions in the essay are supported thoroughly and consistently by relevant evidence.
- ✔ Evidence may prove more specific or concrete.
- ✔ May contain errors that do not detract from the argument.

7–6 POINTS

- ✔ Thesis explicitly identifies **all parts of the question**, but may not be developed fully.
- ✔ Organization is clear and effective in support of the argument but may introduce evidence that is not pertinent to the task.
- ✔ Essay covers all major topics suggested by the prompt but may analyze an aspect in greater depth rather than in a balanced manner.
- ✔ Major assertions in the essay are supported by relevant evidence.
- ✔ May contain an error that detracts from the argument.

5–4 POINTS

- ✔ Thesis identifies **all parts of the question**, but without any development; thesis may address only part of the question effectively; thesis may be a simple, single-sentence statement.
- ✔ Organization is clear but may not be consistently followed; essay may veer off task chronologically or thematically or both.
- ✔ Essay may not complete all tasks:

  - May discuss only …
  - May discuss only …
  - May focus only on …
  - May be primarily descriptive rather than analytical.

- ✔ Essay offers some relevant evidence.
- ✔ May contain errors that detract from the argument.

3–2 POINTS

- ✔ Thesis may simply paraphrase the prompt OR identify the parts of the question without analyzing.
- ✔ Organization is unclear and ineffective; essay may focus on personal or national attributes rather than analyzing.
- ✔ Essay shows serious imbalance; discussion is superficial; much of the information may be significantly out of the time period or geography of the question.
- ✔ Offers minimal OR confused evidence.
- ✔ May contain several errors that detract from the argument.

1–0 POINTS

- ✔ Thesis is erroneous OR irrelevant OR absent.
- ✔ No effective organization is evident.
- ✔ Discussion is generic.
- ✔ Provides little or no relevant supporting evidence.
- ✔ May contain numerous errors that detract from the argument.

GROUP A ESSAYS

> 2. Assess the reasons for the split between the Anglican and Roman Catholic Churches in light of the fact that the Anglicans had not adopted any of the tenets of Protestantism when the split occurred.

What does the question want to know? Assess the reasons for and details of why the Church of England declared its independence from Rome and the papacy before it had adopted any of the dogmas of Protestantism.

What do you know about it? In 1512, Henry VIII was awarded the title "Defender of the Faith" by Pope Clement VII for his anti-Lutheran tract. Six years later, when he decided to divorce Catherine of Aragon—to get a male heir and because he loved Anne Boleyn–the Pope denied him. Why did he deny him? What was his personal response? What was the role of Thomas Cranmer? Why did Parliament pass the Act of Supremacy in 1534? Why can it be said that the Statute of Six Articles, 1539, completed the break with Rome?

How should you put it into words? The Anglican Church is the only Protestant sect to break with Rome before adopting Protestant ideas. Use a chronological approach to the events in order to explain why it happened.

> 3. "The Congress of Vienna aligned the European balance of power effectively, but it restored the old order clumsily." *Assess the validity* of this statement.

What does the question want to know? "Determine the truth of" whether the Congress of Vienna laid out a design for peace better than it provided for a return to the systems of government that ruled European nations before the French Revolution.

What do you know about it? There was no continent-wide war in Europe for nearly a century after the Congress of Vienna. What is a balance of power? How had France upset it during the Wars of the Revolution and the Napoleonic Wars? How did the Congress nullify future French aggression with a system of "buffer states"?

What was the old order? How had the ideals of the French Revolution conflicted with absolutism, and how had they been spread over Europe? How did the Revolutions of 1832 and 1848 manifest many of these new ideals of government, such as nationalism, liberalism, republicanism?

How would you put it into words? Decide whether the statement is true or not. Build your essay accordingly. If you think it is true, demonstrate how the Congress designed the balance of power but failed to complete and maintain a restoration of the old governmental order.

> 4. *To what extent and in what ways* had Europe recovered economically from the effects of World War II a decade after it had ended?

What does the question want to know? "How and how much" had Europe rebuilt its devastated cities, factories, transport systems, housing by the mid-1950s?

What do you know about it? What was the role of the United States in this reconstruction? What were the goals, accomplishments, and limitations of the Marshall Plan? How did the Soviet Bloc rebuild? How did the Five-Year Plans transform not only the U.S.S.R. but Eastern Europe? What part did the policy of containment play? What were the first steps taken toward a European economic union? What measures were there of economic revival?

How would you put it into words? Explain how Europe rebuilt and how far the reconstruction had gotten by 1955. Describe the progress, the agents of that progress, the innovations, the limitations.

GROUP B ESSAYS

> 5. Assess the reasons for and the similarities and differences between the French Revolution of 1789 and the Russian Revolution of 1917.

What does the question want to know? Explain the reasons for the similarities and differences between the two revolutions. Is there a cycle that many revolutions go through? Were there similar conditions leading to both? Were the societies similar or different?

What do you know about it? Both revolutions replaced monarchies with governments disliked by the rest of Europe. Both were revolutions led by elites who stirred the masses who had suffered unfair and oppressive conditions exacerbated by bad harvests and depressions. Both had oppressive phases that oppressed all opposition to the revolution. Both had to fight wars to preserve their revolutions. Both redistributed property and increased government intervention in society and the economy. The differences lie in the sustainability of the revolutions and the sophistication of the societies both after and before the revolutions. Russia was involved in an unpopular war when its revolution began, but France was simply bankrupt.

How would you put it into words? Explain why the different conditions apparent in both countries before the revolutions and the personalities of the figures involved in the revolutions and their aftermath, such as Louis XVI, Danton, Robespierre, Marat, Napoleon, Trotsky, Lenin, Nicholas II, and Kerensky, account for the similarities and differences in the revolutions.

---

6. "The most profound revolutions are in the realm of ideas." Analyze this statement by making reference to the influence on their age of TWO of the following thinkers: Copernicus, Calvin, Newton, Adam Smith, Darwin, Freud, Einstein.

What does the question want to know? It requires you to "examine in detail" and to "explain" how new ideas create great revolutions. You have no choice here of evaluating the statement; you must show how a "profound revolution" can occur without a political change. Determine the meaning of "revolution" in this context, and then demonstrate how two of the thinkers helped bring one about in their respective historical periods.

What do you know about it? Copernicus developed the heliocentric view; Calvin formulated a new dogma of Protestantism; Newton described the universe according to "natural law"; Smith described the perfect laissez-faire economy; Darwin formulated the theory of natural selection; Freud defined human behavior by introducing the concept of the unconscious; Einstein introduced the theories of relativity.

How would you write about it? Each of these thinkers came up with ideas that shattered age-old assumptions or deeply held attitudes. What were these? What new perspective did the thinkers provide? How did it effect a revolution of belief, a crisis of belief?

---

7. "Japan's successes up to 1942 served as a model for subject peoples in the European colonial empires." *Defend or refute* this statement.

What does the question want to know? Argue for or against the idea that Japan was a role model for colonial peoples up to the time when it began to lose World War II.

What do you know about it? How was Japan's response to European imperialism different from that of most non-European nations? How were its industrialization, modernization, and maintenance of tradition an inspiration to the captive peoples of colonialism? How did its initial successes in World War II foster nationalism in the colonial world? How did its own colonial policies toward the Asians it conquered—the Co-Prosperity Sphere—alienate them? How did their wars against the Japanese invaders foster later independence?

How would you put it into words? Make your choice to argue for or against. The case for is very strong and easily defended. The case against has little to support it.

Answer Sheet

MODEL TEST 2

SECTION I

1 Ⓐ Ⓑ Ⓒ Ⓓ Ⓔ	21 Ⓐ Ⓑ Ⓒ Ⓓ Ⓔ	41 Ⓐ Ⓑ Ⓒ Ⓓ Ⓔ	61 Ⓐ Ⓑ Ⓒ Ⓓ Ⓔ
2 Ⓐ Ⓑ Ⓒ Ⓓ Ⓔ	22 Ⓐ Ⓑ Ⓒ Ⓓ Ⓔ	42 Ⓐ Ⓑ Ⓒ Ⓓ Ⓔ	62 Ⓐ Ⓑ Ⓒ Ⓓ Ⓔ
3 Ⓐ Ⓑ Ⓒ Ⓓ Ⓔ	23 Ⓐ Ⓑ Ⓒ Ⓓ Ⓔ	43 Ⓐ Ⓑ Ⓒ Ⓓ Ⓔ	63 Ⓐ Ⓑ Ⓒ Ⓓ Ⓔ
4 Ⓐ Ⓑ Ⓒ Ⓓ Ⓔ	24 Ⓐ Ⓑ Ⓒ Ⓓ Ⓔ	44 Ⓐ Ⓑ Ⓒ Ⓓ Ⓔ	64 Ⓐ Ⓑ Ⓒ Ⓓ Ⓔ
5 Ⓐ Ⓑ Ⓒ Ⓓ Ⓔ	25 Ⓐ Ⓑ Ⓒ Ⓓ Ⓔ	45 Ⓐ Ⓑ Ⓒ Ⓓ Ⓔ	65 Ⓐ Ⓑ Ⓒ Ⓓ Ⓔ
6 Ⓐ Ⓑ Ⓒ Ⓓ Ⓔ	26 Ⓐ Ⓑ Ⓒ Ⓓ Ⓔ	46 Ⓐ Ⓑ Ⓒ Ⓓ Ⓔ	66 Ⓐ Ⓑ Ⓒ Ⓓ Ⓔ
7 Ⓐ Ⓑ Ⓒ Ⓓ Ⓔ	27 Ⓐ Ⓑ Ⓒ Ⓓ Ⓔ	47 Ⓐ Ⓑ Ⓒ Ⓓ Ⓔ	67 Ⓐ Ⓑ Ⓒ Ⓓ Ⓔ
8 Ⓐ Ⓑ Ⓒ Ⓓ Ⓔ	28 Ⓐ Ⓑ Ⓒ Ⓓ Ⓔ	48 Ⓐ Ⓑ Ⓒ Ⓓ Ⓔ	68 Ⓐ Ⓑ Ⓒ Ⓓ Ⓔ
9 Ⓐ Ⓑ Ⓒ Ⓓ Ⓔ	29 Ⓐ Ⓑ Ⓒ Ⓓ Ⓔ	49 Ⓐ Ⓑ Ⓒ Ⓓ Ⓔ	69 Ⓐ Ⓑ Ⓒ Ⓓ Ⓔ
10 Ⓐ Ⓑ Ⓒ Ⓓ Ⓔ	30 Ⓐ Ⓑ Ⓒ Ⓓ Ⓔ	50 Ⓐ Ⓑ Ⓒ Ⓓ Ⓔ	70 Ⓐ Ⓑ Ⓒ Ⓓ Ⓔ
11 Ⓐ Ⓑ Ⓒ Ⓓ Ⓔ	31 Ⓐ Ⓑ Ⓒ Ⓓ Ⓔ	51 Ⓐ Ⓑ Ⓒ Ⓓ Ⓔ	71 Ⓐ Ⓑ Ⓒ Ⓓ Ⓔ
12 Ⓐ Ⓑ Ⓒ Ⓓ Ⓔ	32 Ⓐ Ⓑ Ⓒ Ⓓ Ⓔ	52 Ⓐ Ⓑ Ⓒ Ⓓ Ⓔ	72 Ⓐ Ⓑ Ⓒ Ⓓ Ⓔ
13 Ⓐ Ⓑ Ⓒ Ⓓ Ⓔ	33 Ⓐ Ⓑ Ⓒ Ⓓ Ⓔ	53 Ⓐ Ⓑ Ⓒ Ⓓ Ⓔ	73 Ⓐ Ⓑ Ⓒ Ⓓ Ⓔ
14 Ⓐ Ⓑ Ⓒ Ⓓ Ⓔ	34 Ⓐ Ⓑ Ⓒ Ⓓ Ⓔ	54 Ⓐ Ⓑ Ⓒ Ⓓ Ⓔ	74 Ⓐ Ⓑ Ⓒ Ⓓ Ⓔ
15 Ⓐ Ⓑ Ⓒ Ⓓ Ⓔ	35 Ⓐ Ⓑ Ⓒ Ⓓ Ⓔ	55 Ⓐ Ⓑ Ⓒ Ⓓ Ⓔ	75 Ⓐ Ⓑ Ⓒ Ⓓ Ⓔ
16 Ⓐ Ⓑ Ⓒ Ⓓ Ⓔ	36 Ⓐ Ⓑ Ⓒ Ⓓ Ⓔ	56 Ⓐ Ⓑ Ⓒ Ⓓ Ⓔ	76 Ⓐ Ⓑ Ⓒ Ⓓ Ⓔ
17 Ⓐ Ⓑ Ⓒ Ⓓ Ⓔ	37 Ⓐ Ⓑ Ⓒ Ⓓ Ⓔ	57 Ⓐ Ⓑ Ⓒ Ⓓ Ⓔ	77 Ⓐ Ⓑ Ⓒ Ⓓ Ⓔ
18 Ⓐ Ⓑ Ⓒ Ⓓ Ⓔ	38 Ⓐ Ⓑ Ⓒ Ⓓ Ⓔ	58 Ⓐ Ⓑ Ⓒ Ⓓ Ⓔ	78 Ⓐ Ⓑ Ⓒ Ⓓ Ⓔ
19 Ⓐ Ⓑ Ⓒ Ⓓ Ⓔ	39 Ⓐ Ⓑ Ⓒ Ⓓ Ⓔ	59 Ⓐ Ⓑ Ⓒ Ⓓ Ⓔ	79 Ⓐ Ⓑ Ⓒ Ⓓ Ⓔ
20 Ⓐ Ⓑ Ⓒ Ⓓ Ⓔ	40 Ⓐ Ⓑ Ⓒ Ⓓ Ⓔ	60 Ⓐ Ⓑ Ⓒ Ⓓ Ⓔ	80 Ⓐ Ⓑ Ⓒ Ⓓ Ⓔ

Model Test 2

SECTION 1

MULTIPLE-CHOICE QUESTIONS

TIME—55 MINUTES FOR 80 QUESTIONS

Directions: Each of the following questions has five suggested answers. Choose the one that is best in each case.

1. Which is true of Humanism?

    (A) It set limits on what human beings could accomplish in this world.
    (B) It emphasized the study of Greek and Roman classical literature.
    (C) It sought to understand human nature exclusively by means of studying the writings of the early Christian philosophers.
    (D) It promoted a medieval lifestyle.
    (E) It discouraged a study of pagan writers.

2. During the early 16th century the need for reform within the Roman Catholic Church was indicated by all of the following EXCEPT

    (A) clerical immorality
    (B) the lack of education of the ordinary clergy
    (C) the growth of The Brethren of the Common Life
    (D) the extravagant lifestyle of prelates and popes
    (E) clerical pluralism

3. One of the tenets of Protestantism as stated in the Confession of Augsburg was that religious authority rests with

    (A) the pope
    (B) the Bible
    (C) the Ecumenical Councils
    (D) the Holy Roman Emperor
    (E) the German princes

4. Which was one of the most important accomplishments of The Council of Trent (1545–1563)?

   (A) Reconciliation with the Protestants.
   (B) Reforms led to a spiritual renewal of the Roman Catholic Church.
   (C) The sale of indulgences was encouraged.
   (D) Simony and pluralism were established.
   (E) The Roman Inquisition was instituted.

5. One of the most significant long-term effects of Spain's establishment of a New World empire was that New World gold and silver

   (A) helped make Spain militarily superior in Europe
   (B) gave the Portuguese hegemony in the Atlantic
   (C) created a massive inflation that ended Spain's European empire
   (D) created a glut of precious metal jewelry among the upper classes in Europe
   (E) ruined manufacturing in the Spanish Netherlands

Line engraving *Witches' Sabbath*, 17th century. The Granger Collection, New York. (0005418)

6. The Great European Witch Hunt, typified by the engraving above, was a result of all of the following EXCEPT

   (A) the religious struggles of Europe during the 16th and 17th centuries
   (B) the increased social and religious conformity of the 16th and 17th centuries
   (C) a general misogynistic movement in society
   (D) a rise in the belief of the evil power of witches
   (E) the decline of most superstitions in common European society at the time

7. What is the most significant difference between absolutism and modern totalitarianism?

   (A) Totalitarian dictators lacked the political power of the absolutist kings.
   (B) Absolutism sought to subordinate only the nobility.
   (C) Absolutist states lacked the total control of their citizens "from cradle to grave."
   (D) State bureaucracies were absent in absolutist states.
   (E) Standing armies are an invention of modern totalitarianism.

8. His *Second Treatise on Government* justified the Glorious Revolution of 1689.

   (A) Thomas Hobbes
   (B) Bishop Laud
   (C) Oliver Cromwell
   (D) James II
   (E) John Locke

9. Secularism during the Renaissance can best be described as

   (A) a repudiation of the Roman Catholic faith
   (B) a concern with the nature of individuality
   (C) an emphasis on money and pleasure
   (D) a belief in individual genius
   (E) a literary movement centered primarily in the Northern states of Europe

10. The artistic brilliance of the *quattrocento* and the *cinquecento* was spurred in both Florence and Rome by

    (A) the patronage of both civic groups and the Church
    (B) artist guilds
    (C) the Medicis
    (D) the *popolo*
    (E) foreign financiers

11. One of Calvin's central ideas in *The Institutes of Christian Religion* was that

    (A) the Church was subordinate to the state
    (B) all Christian sects should be tolerated
    (C) "man is the measure of all things"
    (D) Calvinism should be confined to the theocratic city of Geneva
    (E) salvation is predestined

12. The religious conflicts of the 1500s and 1600s led to

    (A) religious toleration between Roman Catholicism and the major Protestant sects
    (B) a unified Christian society in Europe
    (C) unremitting religious riots and civil war in Spain
    (D) a virtual end to Hapsburg hegemony in Germany
    (E) the establishment of Roman Catholicism as the state religion of the United Provinces of the Netherlands

13. Constitutionalism in BOTH 17th-century England and the Netherlands

    (A) was established with the formation of long-lasting republics in both states
    (B) was protected exclusively by unwritten constitutions
    (C) limited the powers of the state by law
    (D) came about as the result of bloody revolutions in both countries
    (E) lacked protection of the rights of individual citizens

14. He said he had seen further than others because he had stood on the shoulders of giants when explaining how he revolutionized the way humans viewed the universe in 1687.

    (A) Kepler
    (B) Newton
    (C) Galileo
    (D) Tycho Brahe
    (E) Bacon

15. Which is the most accurate statement pertaining to the *philosophes* of the 18th century?

    (A) They were exclusively French.
    (B) They promoted radical revolution in the political sphere.
    (C) They were primarily reformers.
    (D) They were universally condemned by the monarchs of Europe.
    (E) They appealed only to the intellectual elite.

16. All of the following were causes of explosive growth in the population of Europe during the 18th century EXCEPT

    (A) disappearance of the plague
    (B) improvements in sanitation
    (C) better nutrition
    (D) fewer deaths
    (E) immigration from North America

17. Renaissance culture

   (A) was enjoyed by most Europeans
   (B) was rejected by the Church for its secularism
   (C) was that of a small business elite
   (D) mirrored the attitudes of the urban population
   (E) stressed Greco-Roman ideals of gender equality

18. Which is NOT true of the Northern Renaissance?

   (A) It was focused more on religion than on the Italian Renaissance.
   (B) It stressed social reform based on Christian teachings.
   (C) It began in the last three decades of the 15th century.
   (D) It preceded the Italian Renaissance.
   (E) Its art was more religious and less influenced by classical themes than Italian art.

19. Which of the following reforms of Louis XIV most helped him to take direct control of the local political and economic administration?

   (A) The *intendant* administrative system
   (B) The Palace at Versailles as a "gilded cage" for the nobility
   (C) A policy of regional wars for state aggrandizement
   (D) The Revocation of the Edict of Nantes to establish a state religion
   (E) Creation of a powerful standing army

20. The trend seen in 17th-century absolutism is best characterized as

   (A) the power of the monarchy being challenged and constitutionalism gaining ground on the continent
   (B) monarchical power being challenged by the nobility who kept it in check
   (C) monarchs consolidating power on the continent by subjugating the nobility through force or bribe
   (D) the English Stuarts subjugating the parliament and reigning as absolute monarchs without challenge
   (E) the example of Louis XIV being followed in England and the Netherlands

21. Cardinal Richelieu extended the power of French royalty with the *intendant system*:

   (A) a centralized administrative system
   (B) a medal of honor for the *musketeers*
   (C) a series of fortified cities in France
   (D) a tax that local nobles could levy
   (E) a standing army of 400,000 trained troops

22. Which revolution caused the greatest change in the world view and in the evolution of Western society?

   (A) The French Revolution
   (B) The Russian Revolution of 1917
   (C) The American Revolution
   (D) The Scientific Revolution of the 17th century
   (E) The Price Revolution of the 16th century

23. The Enlightenment

   (A) was based upon the assumption that science and reason can explain all things
   (B) was diametrically opposed to the Newtonian concept of natural law
   (C) was widely attacked by the royalty and nobility of Europe
   (D) regarded human progress as an impossibility "in this best of all possible worlds"
   (E) rejected the claims of modern science

Parisian women marching to Versailles on 5 October 1789: contemporary colored engraving. The Granger Collection, New York. (0009827)

24. The women depicted above are marching on Versailles to seek relief from which of the following causes of the French Revolution?

   (A) The bankruptcy of the nation
   (B) The suppression of Enlightenment ideas
   (C) The corruption of the ruling class throughout the country
   (D) The ostentatious wardrobe indulgences of Marie Antoinette
   (E) Famine and hunger that were ravaging France

25. What was the political impact of the Protestant Reformation on Germany?

   (A) It thwarted the designs of the French kings.
   (B) It strengthened the hold of the Hapsburgs over the region.
   (C) It aroused nationalism in Germany.
   (D) It enabled the Holy Roman Emperor to determine the religion of the various German principalities.
   (E) It led to a more united Germany.

26. As a result of the scientific theories developed through the 16th and 17th centuries, Europeans developed a conception of the universe

   (A) as governed by natural laws
   (B) as geocentric
   (C) as guided in every physical realm by a personal God
   (D) as chaotic, reflective of chance
   (E) as Aristotelian in makeup

OLIVER CROMWELL (1599–1658). Lord Protector of England (1653–1658). Cromwell dissolving the Long Parliament in 1653. Mezzotint by John Sartain after Benjamin West. The Granger Collection, New York. (0013247)

27. The Long Parliament, which Oliver Cromwell is pictured dissolving

   (A) was dismissed because Cromwell believed they might not fund his army
   (B) sat from 1638 to 1658
   (C) was continually in power from 1640 to 1660
   (D) ordered Charles II beheaded for treason
   (E) was composed mostly of farmers

28. Peter the Great of Russia incorporated all of the following in his effort to modernize his states EXCEPT

    (A) a standing professional army
    (B) new taxation policies
    (C) a bureaucracy based on merit
    (D) the disbanding of the Cossacks
    (E) a new capital city with a port

29. Premarital sex in preindustrial Europe

    (A) was rampant
    (B) resulted in a high percentage of illegitimate births
    (C) was more common than it is today
    (D) was suppressed by the social controls of village life
    (E) did not exist

30. Which best describes the Third Estate prior to the French Revolution?

    (A) It consisted of the peasantry.
    (B) The First and Second Estates outnumbered it in terms of population.
    (C) It included the middle class, peasants, and urban workers.
    (D) It had the right to tax peasants for its own profit.
    (E) It was exempt from the tithe.

31. Napoleon has been characterized as a "son of the Enlightenment" because during his reign

    (A) he supported freedom of speech and the press
    (B) his civil code granted legal equality to the middle class
    (C) he conquered most of the autocratic regimes in Europe
    (D) the Napoleonic code established women's rights
    (E) he was a liberal emperor

32. All are important reasons for the Industrial Revolution beginning in England EXCEPT

    (A) agricultural improvements
    (B) increased demand for manufactured goods
    (C) adequate transportation
    (D) sufficient oil reserves
    (E) a banking system

33. The putting-out system

    (A) created the urban craft industry
    (B) reduced rural poverty
    (C) eliminated the need for merchant-capitalists
    (D) destroyed cottage industry
    (E) replaced factory manufacturing

A late 17th-century engraving of the old observing room at the Greenwich Observatory, England. The Granger Collection, New York. (0003758)

34. The illustration above demonstrates what principle crucial to the emerging field of science?

   (A) The air of Eastern England is best for observing stars.
   (B) Science can be practiced best with royal patronage.
   (C) Many assistants were necessary to do scientific research.
   (D) Science is only as good as the tools it produces.
   (E) Science should proceed from an empirical collection of data and analysis.

35. Monarchial absolutism

   (A) was absent from Eastern Europe during the 17th century
   (B) lasted longer in Western than in Eastern Europe
   (C) abolished serfdom in 16th-century Eastern Europe
   (D) lasted longer in Eastern Europe than in Western Europe
   (E) ended in Prussia and Russia by the early 1700s

36. The Enlightenment concept of a remote God who does not interfere in the operations of his creation is

   (A) theism
   (B) pantheism
   (C) deism
   (D) atheism
   (E) Protestantism

37. Many philosophes, such as Voltaire, believed that governmental reform would be accomplished by

    (A) the introduction of democracy
    (B) benevolent absolutist monarchs
    (C) empowering the nobles at the expense of the kings
    (D) revolution
    (E) trusting the masses

38. "Liberty," in 18th century thought, can best be described as

    (A) human rights and the sovereignty of the people
    (B) equality of opportunity
    (C) an offshoot of the divine right of kings
    (D) generally opposed by the intellectual elite
    (E) receiving widespread popular support before the French Revolution

39. Which event occurred during the radical stage of the French Revolution?

    (A) Formation of the national assembly
    (B) The Great Fear
    (C) Napoleon's military dictatorship
    (D) The Terror
    (E) The Storming of the Bastille

40. He believed that charity and medicine made matters worse because he saw the central human problem as one of population versus production.

    (A) Thomas Malthus
    (B) David Ricardo
    (C) Adam Smith
    (D) Karl Marx
    (E) Jeremy Bentham

41. The agricultural revolution of the late 17th and 18th centuries came about because of all of the following EXCEPT

    (A) crop rotation
    (B) the Enclosure Movement
    (C) establishment of the open field system
    (D) establishment of capitalist farming
    (E) disappearance of common land

42. What new sexual division of labor emerged as a result of industrialization in the 19th century?

    (A) Women became the family's primary wage earner.
    (B) Married women with children were most likely to work in factories.
    (C) Women were confined to low-paying jobs with little chance for advancement.
    (D) "Mr. Moms" often provided child care while their wives worked.
    (E) African slavery was introduced in the newly industrialized nations of Europe.

43. All of the following are important British literary romantics EXCEPT

    (A) William Wordsworth
    (B) George Sand
    (C) Walter Scott
    (D) Percy Shelley
    (E) Samuel Taylor Coleridge

44. Which is the most accurate appraisal of the Revolutions of 1830 and 1848?

    (A) They established democratic republics in both Britain and France.
    (B) They overthrew the conservative regimes of central Europe.
    (C) They were largely unsuccessful.
    (D) They brought about German unification.
    (E) They established parliaments in both Russia and Austria.

45. Before the work of Pasteur, Koch, and Lister, the prevailing theory of disease in the 19th century was that

    (A) it was caused by bad odors
    (B) it could be controlled by vaccination
    (C) it was caused by microorganisms
    (D) it could be prevented by the sterilization of wounds
    (E) it was brought about by an imbalance of the humors

46. In the latter half of the 19th century, the preindustrial pattern of women working outside of the home continued primarily for which group?

    (A) Middle-class women
    (B) Social elites
    (C) The wives of urban professionals
    (D) Working-class women
    (E) Young urban professionals

47. The scientific theory that all life had evolved from a common origin, by a process of struggle for survival, and was applied by social thinkers to human affairs was developed by

    (A) Charles Darwin
    (B) Gregor Mendel
    (C) Herbert Spencer
    (D) Jean Baptiste Lamarck
    (E) Auguste Comte

48. Which of the following empires did NOT collapse as a result of World War I?

    (A) The Russian
    (B) The British
    (C) The German
    (D) The Austro-Hungarian
    (E) The Ottoman Turk

49. Which of the following ideologies had its roots in the French Revolution and the conquests of Napoleon?

    (A) Marxian socialism
    (B) *Laissez-faire* economic liberalism
    (C) Political conservatism
    (D) Nationalism
    (E) Utopian socialism

50. Which is the best characterization of the romantic movement?

    (A) It emphasized order and reason.
    (B) It stressed individualism, emotionality, and imagination.
    (C) It viewed nature as a force to resist.
    (D) It rejected the study of history.
    (E) It reflected the ideals of the Enlightenment.

CHILD LABOR, 1871. Paying children for their labor in the brickyards. Wood engraving, English, 1871. The Granger Collection, New York. (0042385)

51. Scenes like the one above in which young children were being paid for work in factories and mines

   (A) were common in Germany until after 1900
   (B) were more prevalent in Russia during the 19th century
   (C) were perceived as demonstrating the work ethic of the British people
   (D) are still seen in Europe today
   (E) became a scarcity in England after 1842

52. Which literary movement, stressing the influence of heredity and environment on human behavior, replaced romanticism in the last decades of the 1800s?

   (A) Humanism
   (B) Rationalism
   (C) Relativism
   (D) Utopianism
   (E) Realism

53. Between 1850 and 1914, which principle of organization became supreme by appealing to all of Europe's social classes?

    (A) Urbanization
    (B) Socialism
    (C) Nationalism
    (D) Industrialization
    (E) Internationalism

54. The "new imperialism" by Europeans from 1880 to 1914 differed from the imperialism of earlier periods in that

    (A) it was primarily economic
    (B) its goal was the establishment of peaceful trading empires
    (C) it involved the political domination of masses of people in Asia and Africa
    (D) it was limited to the Pacific region
    (E) it focused mainly on the Middle East

55. During World War I, mobilization for war and planned economies helped set the stage for which of the following?

    (A) Post-war democratic gains
    (B) An increase in wartime strikes by unions
    (C) The entrance of women into the workplace after the war
    (D) Totalitarianism
    (E) The establishment of laissez-faire economies in Europe

56. The work of Max Planck and Albert Einstein undermined belief in the natural laws and rational worldview of what earlier scientist?

    (A) Ernest Rutherford
    (B) George Orwell
    (C) Werner Heisenberg
    (D) Isaac Newton
    (E) Soren Kierkegaard

The violent repression of the working-class demonstration in St. Peter's Fields, Manchester, August 1819, caused this incident to be ironically called the Peterloo Massacre. The Granger Collection, New York. (0006130)

57. The demonstration in Manchester, illustrated above, was fomented to address which of the workers' concerns of the Industrial Revolution?

   (A) Low wages and bad working conditions
   (B) Unsanitary living conditions
   (C) A lack of housing in Manchester
   (D) The need for medical reforms
   (E) Fair parliamentary representation

58. The failure of the Frankfurt Conference in 1848 to unify what nation encouraged the growth of authoritarianism and militarism?

   (A) France
   (B) Germany
   (C) Italy
   (D) Austria
   (E) Russia

59. All of the following are considered causes for the "new imperialism" EXCEPT

   (A) a search for markets for European manufactured goods
   (B) European racism
   (C) acquisition of colonies for prestige and national security
   (D) missionary zeal
   (E) the rising power of industrializing nations

60. Which is the best characterization of the Treaty of Versailles that ended World War I?

    (A) In the League of Nations, it established an effective deterrent to future wars.
    (B) It rejected the principle of national self-determination.
    (C) It sowed the seeds for the growth of Nazism.
    (D) It served as a foundation for the post-war alliance between Britain and France.
    (E) It ended European imperialism.

61. Which is not considered a long-term cause of World War I?

    (A) The assassination of the Austrian Archduke
    (B) A system of rival military alliances
    (C) Nationalism
    (D) A naval arms race between Germany and Britain
    (E) Competition for colonies and markets

62. The modern style of painting that focused on mood and imagination rather than on portraying nature or real objects was

    (A) baroque
    (B) expressionism
    (C) impressionism
    (D) romantic
    (E) functionalism

63. The deficit spending theories of this economist were employed by governments attempting to boost GNP during the Great Depression:

    (A) Gustav Stresemann
    (B) John Maynard Keynes
    (C) Charles C. Dawes
    (D) Bertrand Russell
    (E) Aristide Briand

64. German military victories from 1939 to 1940 were largely attributable to which of the following?

    (A) The naval supremacy that Germany created for surface ships such as *The Bismarck*
    (B) The power of the soviet forces was not strong enough to resist the German onslaught
    (C) The weakness of the spirit of the British people caused them to surrender in large numbers
    (D) The German population was far greater than that of the territories they invaded
    (E) Blitzkrieg warfare that included strategic and overwhelming use of armor and air power

65. The rulers of these ethnically diverse empires regarded nationalism within their borders as a threat:

    (A) Britain and France
    (B) Germany and Austria
    (C) Italy and Russia
    (D) Russia and Austria
    (E) Prussia and Russia

66. The Second Empire from 1852 to 1870 of which leader demonstrated how the programs of a national state could have an appeal by cutting across class and political lines?

    (A) Otto Von Bismarck
    (B) Camillo Cavour
    (C) David Lloyd George
    (D) Giuseppe Garibaldi
    (E) Louis Napoleon

"The Red Wedge Breaks Through." Russian Revolution propaganda poster, 1917. The Granger Collection, New York. (0037077)

67. The event that occurred after the Bolshevik takeover of Russia that is propagandized in the poster above is

    (A) the takeover of the Russian army
    (B) the defeat of Germany
    (C) the surrender of Tsar Nicholas II
    (D) the communist takeover of the government
    (E) Russian civil war

68. Because World War I tested the belief in traditional ideas and institutions, the post-war period is often referred to as

    (A) "the roaring 20s"
    (B) "the age of anxiety"
    (C) "The Great Depression"
    (D) "the era of angst"
    (E) "the age of appeasement"

69. All of the following mass media were used both for entertainment and pro-paganda in the period between World Wars I and II EXCEPT

    (A) newspapers
    (B) television
    (C) radio
    (D) motion pictures
    (E) popular journals and magazines

70. The pessimism and alienation of the Age of Anxiety influenced writers such as James Joyce and Virginia Woolf to experiment with a literary technique in which emotions and thoughts from the unconscious surfaced randomly. It was called

    (A) dadaism
    (B) surrealism
    (C) stream of consciousness
    (D) Bauhaus functionalism
    (E) Ashcan realism

71. Which of the following marked a post–World War II move toward European unity?

    (A) establishment of the League of Nations
    (B) the Warsaw Pact
    (C) the six-nation Coal and Steel Community
    (D) the policies of Charles de Gaulle
    (E) a resurgence of nationalism in the 1960s

72. Reform and "de-Stalinization" in the U.S.S.R. was begun in 1956 when this Soviet leader denounced Stalin's "cult of personality":

    (A) Mikhail Gorbachev
    (B) Nikita Khrushchev
    (C) Leonid Brezhnev
    (D) Yevgeny Yevtushenko
    (E) Leon Trotsky

73. The psychoanalytical theories that fostered the belief that human behavior is basically irrational belonged to

(A) Sigmund Freud
(B) Aristotle
(C) Charles Darwin
(D) Jean-Paul Sartre
(E) Oswald Spengler

74. The philosopher whose ideas that Christian humility and rationalism had caused a decline in Western Civilization was

(A) Friedrich Nietzsche
(B) Henri Bergson
(C) Ludwig Wittgenstein
(D) Max Planck
(E) Georges Sorel

Germany, 1924. The Granger Collection, New York. (0073034)

75. The line seen above is forming to obtain loans after what occurred in Germany from 1922 to 1924?

(A) A takeover by the Russian army
(B) The defeat of Germany in World War I
(C) The failure of the electricity industry
(D) The communist takeover of the government
(E) The destruction of the currency through inflation

76. The radical dictatorships that grew in Europe during the 1920s and '30s and were characterized by a rejection of democratic ideals and by extreme control over every aspect of their citizens' lives were known as

    (A) communistic
    (B) fascistic
    (C) conservative authoritarian
    (D) totalitarian
    (E) militaristic

77. The economic programs that brought about dramatic gains in productivity and enabled the U.S.S.R. to catch up with the West in the growth of heavy industry during the 1930s were called

    (A) five-year plans
    (B) collectivization
    (C) the New Economic Policy (NEP)
    (D) the Russian New Deal
    (E) the Young Plan

78. All of the following are examples of decolonization following World War II EXCEPT

    (A) the work of Mahatma Gandhi and the Indian Congress Party
    (B) the political aims of Ho Chi Minh
    (C) Nasser's nationalization of the Suez Canal
    (D) the struggle between the communists and nationalists in China
    (E) the Pan-Arab movement

79. Which has been the most significant outcome of the collapse and breakup of the Communist governments in the U.S.S.R. and Yugoslavia?

    (A) The establishment of vibrant democratic governments among the new republics
    (B) Ethnic conflict
    (C) A dramatic increase in the standard of living
    (D) The re-establishment of conservative authoritarianism in the newly independent states
    (E) The universal adoption of Russian cultural institutions

80. The movement led by Lech Walesa in Poland that challenged Soviet authority

    (A) was the solidarity movement led by Communist Party leaders as a way to regain control from the U.S.S.R.
    (B) was the solidarity movement led by laborers who wanted more of a voice in government and workplace decisions
    (C) was the Destalinization of Poland led by the Communist Party leaders
    (D) was a policy allowing the farm workers to share tools and technology
    (E) helped to stabilize Eastern Europe in the 1980s

Model Test 2

STOP

END OF SECTION I

SECTION II
FREE-RESPONSE QUESTIONS
Part A: Document-Based Essay Question (DBQ)

WRITING TIME—2 HOURS AND 10 MINUTES TO COMPLETE
THIS PART OF THE EXAM, 50 PERCENT OF TOTAL GRADE

Suggested time:
15 minutes reading time for part A
45 minutes to complete part A
35 minutes for ONE question from Group 1
35 minutes for ONE question from Group 2

You may take 15 minutes to look over the documents and make comments on them. You will then have 1 hour and 55 minutes to complete all three essays.

Directions: The following question is based upon documents 1–12. (These documents may have been edited in order to engage the student.) The DBQ is designed to test your ability to read and interpret documents. Show your mastery of this skill by analyzing the content and the point of view and validity of the source's author. Answer the question fully by utilizing your analysis of the documents and the time period discussed to support a well constructed essay.

1. Analyze the various reactions and responses to the practice of total war and assess the change of these reactions and responses throughout the 20th century (1910–1965).

   Historical background: After the Industrial Revolution, society was organized in a more efficient and productive fashion, which affected how wars were fought, particularly during the first half of the 20th century. The increased productive capacity and the new machinery that resulted from the Industrial Revolution helped create European societies that could engage in Total War. Total War is when every aspect of the society comes together to support the war effort. The two world wars are the best examples of total war.

Document 1

Source: V. Bourtzeff, Russian Socialist leader *Letter to the Editor of the London Times*, 1914.

Even we, the adherents of the parties of the Extreme Left, and hitherto ardent antimilitarists and pacifists, even we believe in the necessity of this war. This war is to protect justice and civilization. It will, we hope, be a decisive factor in our united war against war.

Document 2

Source: French World War I Propaganda Poster, 1916.

"WOMEN, HELP YOUR MEN WIN THE WAR! WORK IN A WAR PLANT!"

Document 3

Source: German governmental edict, 1916.

All male workers between the ages of 17 and 60, as well as able-bodied women, are henceforth ordered to perform labor essential to the war effort

Document 4

Source: Wilfred Owen, British soldier killed in World War I, *Dulce Et Decorum Est: Disillusionment*, describing a gas attack, 1918

If you could hear, at every jolt, the blood
Come gargling from the froth-corrupted lungs
Obscene as cancer, bitter as the cud
Of vile, incurable sores on innocent tongues,
My friend, you would not tell with such high zest
To children ardent for some desperate glory

Document 5

Source: Naomi Loughnan, *Munitions Work*, 1918.

We little thought when we first put on our overalls and caps and enlisted in the Munitions Army how much more inspiring our life was to be than we had dared to hope. Though we munitions workers sacrifice our ease, we gain a life worth living.

Document 6

Source: His Majesty's Stationery Office, *Women in Industry of the War Cabinet Committee on Women in Industry*, London, 1918.

Women in the British Labor Force (1914–1918)	1914	1918	Difference between Women Employed in 1914 and 1918	Estimated Number of Male Jobs Replaced by Females
Total Women Employed in the Labor Force	23,710,000	24,538,000	817,000	n/a
Women Employed in Industry	2,178,600	2,970,600	792,000	704,000
Women Employed in Metal Working	170,000	594,000	424,000	195,000
Women Employed in the Chemical Industry	40,000	104,000	64,000	35,000
Women Employed in Government	2,000	225,000	223,000	197,000

Document 7

Source: Anna Eisenmenger, *Blockade: The Diary of an Austrian Middle-Class Woman 1914–1924*, 1932.

Already in 1914 we housewives began to suffer from measures of economy, which were not improved when the military authorities took over the control of supplies. We submitted uncomplainingly when we received news of victories, but at the end of the fourth year of war we are like a besieged fortress cut off from all external supplies without any hope of breaking through the hunger blockade.

Document 8

Source: Winston Churchill, *Speech before Commons*, after the retreat at Dunkirk, June 4, 1940.

We shall fight in France and on the seas and oceans; we shall fight with growing confidence and growing strength in the air. We shall defend our island whatever the cost may be; we shall fight on beaches, landing grounds, in fields, in streets and on the hills. We shall never surrender and even if, which I do not for the moment believe, this island or a large part of it were subjugated and starving, then our empire beyond the seas, armed and guarded by the British Fleet, will carry on the struggle.

Document 9

Source: Stefan Zweig, Austrian novelist and pacifist, from his *Autobiography*, written about World War I, 1941.

There were parades in the streets, flags, ribbons, and music burst forth everywhere, young recruits were marching triumphantly, their faces lighting up at the cheering. I must acknowledge that there was a majestic, rapturous, and even seductive something in that first outbreak of the people. In spite of my hatred and aversion to war, a nation of fifty million felt that they were participating in world history, and that each one was called upon to throw their infinitesimal selves into the glowing mass.

Document 10

Source: Russian propaganda poster from World War II, 1942.

"'Follow This Worker's Example
Produce More for the Front."

WWII: Russian Poster, 1942. The Granger Collection, New York. (0028555)

Document 11

Source: United Nations, *Charter of the United Nations*, 1945.

The purposes of the United Nations are:

1. To maintain international peace and security, and to that end: to take effective collective measures for the prevention and removal of threats to the peace ...
2. To develop friendly relations among nations based upon respect.
3. To achieve international cooperation in solving international problems of economic, social, cultural or humanitarian character.

Document 12

Source: Treaty to create a partial ban on nuclear testing, United Nations, 1963.

The Governments of the United States, the Soviet Union and Great Britain proclaim that it is their aim to achieve an agreement on disarmament, under United Nations control, to put an end to the armaments race and eliminate the incentive to the production and testing of all kinds of weapons, including nuclear weapons.

SECTION II
FREE-RESPONSE QUESTIONS
Part B: Two Essay Questions

WRITING TIME—70 MINUTES FOR TWO ESSAYS;
55 PERCENT OF SECTION II SCORE

Directions: Answer two of the following, one from Group A and one from Group B. Be sure to cite relevant historical information to support your answer. Number your answer as the question below is numbered. Use extra time to check your work.

GROUP A

2. "During the *Age of Anxiety,* the 1920s and 1930s, both psychology and the new physics contributed to the breakdown of traditional values." Assess the validity of this statement.

3. Assess the reasons for the similarities and differences between the Italian Renaissance and the Northern Renaissance.

4. How and why did the *Opening of the Atlantic* lead to a shift of political and economic power from the Mediterranean Basin to Western Europe.

GROUP B

5. To what extent and in what ways was Romanticism in art, literature, and music a reaction against the Enlightenment?

6. Describe how the public health movement and urban planning during the latter half of the 19th century changed life in Europe's cities.

7. "Religious differences caused the greatest disruption in 16th-century Europe, ideological differences the greatest disruption in 20th-century Europe." Defend or refute this statement.

END OF SECTION II

Answer Key
MODEL TEST 2

SECTION I

1. B	11. E	21. A	31. B	41. C	51. E	61. A	71. C
2. C	12. D	22. D	32. D	42. C	52. E	62. B	72. B
3. B	13. C	23. A	33. B	43. B	53. C	63. B	73. A
4. B	14. B	24. E	34. E	44. C	54. C	64. E	74. A
5. C	15. C	25. C	35. D	45. A	55. D	65. D	75. E
6. E	16. E	26. A	36. C	46. D	56. D	66. E	76. D
7. C	17. C	27. A	37. B	47. A	57. E	67. E	77. A
8. E	18. D	28. D	38. A	48. B	58. B	68. B	78. D
9. C	19. A	29. D	39. D	49. D	59. E	69. B	79. B
10. A	20. C	30. C	40. A	50. B	60. C	70. C	80. B

Scoring the Practice Exam

Once you have completed the exam with 55 minutes for the multiple-choice questions and 130 minutes to read and interpret the documents and finish all three essays, you can score your exam.

The multiple-choice test is scored with one point given for each correct answer. *There is no penalty for guessing as of May 2011*, so students should attempt to answer every question on the exam.

The test taker should use the DBQ rubric and the FRQ rubric seen after the multiple-choice explanations for this exam to assess their DBQ and FRQ essays, respectively.

To attain a final AP score for a student, he or she should plug his or her scores into the chart below and calculate a final score:

AP European History Exam Composite Score Conversion Chart	
Score Range	**AP Score**
119–180	5
100–118	4
71–99	3
60–70	2
0–59	1

Multiple Choice Score × 1.125 = _____

+

DBQ Score × 4.5 = _____

+

FRQ 1 Score × 2.75 = _____

+

FRQ 2 Score × 2.75 = _____

Total of all above scores is composite score = _____

Answers Explained

1. **(B)** The secular literature of the ancient world was "rediscovered" by European thinkers.

2. **(C)** The Brethren of the Common Life, which supported the idea of living "a life based upon that of Jesus," was itself a reform movement.

3. **(B)** Replacing the "final authority" of the Pope and Church Council with the Bible was one of the basic tenets of Protestantism.

4. **(B)** Both doctrinal and administrative reforms of the Council inspired renewal.

5. **(C)** The influx into Spain and Europe of New World precious metals created a demand for goods that the limited productivity could not match.

6. **(E)** Superstitions were still common in Europe.

7. **(C)** Limited technology and the autonomy of traditional institutions, such as the Church, curtailed the power of the absolutist monarchs.

8. **(E)** Locke's political philosophy served as the doctrinal basis for constitutionalism and was written to justify the Glorious Revolution of 1689.

9. **(C)** While the people and elites of the Italian Renaissance were by and large committed to Roman Catholicism, a life of activity was stressed, as opposed to the medieval ideal of monastic contemplation.

10. **(A)** Both the Church and civic groups, often led by powerful families, sponsored the artists of the Renaissance.

11. **(E)** Predestination—the idea that God has "chosen" the few who will attain salvation at the beginning of time—is central to Calvinism.

12. **(D)** The wars of religion evolved into national struggles and the HRE lost power and influence.

13. **(C)** This is the essence of constitutionalism.

14. **(B)** Newton was the great synthesizer: "If I have seen further . . ."

15. **(C)** While they railed against the social, economic, political, and religious institutions of their day, they did not advocate revolution.

16. **(E)** There was not a statistically significant emigration from North America to Europe.

17. **(C)** Renaissance culture was an elitist movement that was enjoyed only by the wealthy new merchant classes and the aristocracy. The urban commoners rejected the ideals of the Renaissance and the Pope had to flee Rome when Dominican Friar Girolamo Savonarola encouraged the people to revolt against Renaissance excesses.

18. **(D)** The Northern Renaissance borrowed from the Italians and gave Renaissance ideals religious flavor and national interpretations.

19. **(A)** The intendant system took the oversight of regional economic and political affairs from the nobility and gave it to Louis XIV through his local administrators called intendants.

20. **(C)** The 17th century saw the monarchies in continental Europe consolidate power, subjugating the nobility. Great Britain and the Netherlands were the only exceptions to this rule with constitutional systems that had strong legislatures.

21. **(A)** This extended the power of the monarchy over the nobles and local institutions.

22. **(D)** The Scientific and concomitant Technological Revolution continue to affect the nature and quality of life.

23. **(A)** A direct descendant of Newton's "natural laws," the Enlightenment assumed that humans could progress through reason and the scientific method.

24. **(E)** The Bread March depicted was ostensibly to get food for the poor, who were starving.

25. **(C)** It gave a focus to the aspirations of the German princes against the Holy Roman Emperor.

26. **(A)** A direct result of Newton's physics.

27. **(A)** Cromwell believed the Long Parliament might not fund his army.

28. **(D)** Peter I did not disband the Cossacks, but he did create a meritocracy, set up new taxation policies, establish a standing army, and build St. Petersburg as a new capital on the Baltic.

29. **(D)** Restraints were encouraged and enforced by local communities.

30. **(C)** It made up more than 90 percent of the total pre-revolutionary population of about 24 million.

31. **(B)** an autocrat and self-proclaimed emperor, he put this aspect of the *philosophes'* program into law.

32. **(D)** Petroleum was not a significant energy source in the 18th and 19th centuries.

33. **(B)** The rural workers, who produced goods from the raw materials provided by merchant-capitalists, found work.

34. **(E)** The scientific concept illustrated is that empiricism is the key scientific principle.

35. **(D)** The absolutist traditions of Eastern Europe help explain the roots of contemporary economic, social, and political issues in that region.

36. **(C)** Voltaire, who was not an original thinker, promoted this idea as an antidote to the biases and intolerance of the organized religion of his day.

37. **(B)** Absolutism was still a powerful institution on the continent, and the so-called "enlightened despots" cultivated the *philosophes* while paying lip service to their ideals.

38. **(A)** These were the very specific 18th century meanings of the term.

39. **(D)** It was precipitated by war and the perceived threat of counter-revolution.

40. **(A)** After Malthus, economics was referred to as "the dismal science."

41. **(C)** The replacement of the traditional open field system increased productivity through an efficient competitive system.

42. **(C)** The shared labor of the farm and of the cottage industry was replaced.

43. **(B)** Sand, a woman, was French.

44. **(C)** They were suppressed, thousands of revolutionaries were killed, jailed, or exiled, but their nationalistic and socialistic aims were largely realized in subsequent decades.

45. **(A)** It was the "miasmatic theory."

46. **(D)** Low family incomes required working class women to supplement their husband's pay.

47. **(A)** Like Newton before him, Darwin was a pure scientist whose theories were applied and misapplied to the social sciences.

48. **(B)** Its economic and social institutions were weakened, but its governmental system survived.

49. **(D)** Napoleon's successes inspired emulators of French nationalism among other peoples.

50. **(B)** It broke with the Enlightenment's optimistic investment in reason.

51. **(E)** After the Factory Act of 1833 and the Mines Act of 1842, child labor was outlawed in Great Britain.

52. **(E)** The "new" sociology and psychology promoted its growth.

53. **(C)** Nationalism cut across class lines in its appeal.

54. **(C)** The "new imperialism" imposed European political, religious, and social institutions on non-European peoples.

55. **(D)** Planned economies and national war efforts prepared many European states for the mass mobilization of totalitarianism.

56. **(D)** Newton's "natural laws" inspired the Age of Reason.

57. **(E)** The Peterloo demonstration was ostensibly held to improve the representation of urban areas in Parliament.

58. **(B)** Prussia, with its military and autocratic traditions, led the movement for German unification.

59. **(E)** The growing power of industrializing nations was not a major factor in "new imperialism."

60. **(C)** In failing to address the issues that precipitated World War I, and in blaming the Germans for the war, it gave the Nazis a political lever for gaining popular support.

61. **(A)** It was an *immediate cause.*

62. **(B)** Picasso is perhaps the most famous exponent of this school.

63. **(B)** His deficit spending policies were to be employed in the United States as well as in Europe.

64. **(E)** The Blitzkrieg tactic was the single most important reason for German success in 1939 and 1940.

65. **(D)** Both were polyglot empires whose dynastic rulers were threatened by ethnic separatism.

66. **(E)** He is in many ways the first "modern" politician with a program to appeal to the masses.

67. **(E)** The Russian civil war is symbolized by the *red* wedge breaking the *white* circle.

68. **(B)** This pervasive anxiety manifested itself in art and literature, and it was exacerbated by the findings of physics and psychology.

69. **(B)** Invented between the wars, TV came into popular use in the 1950s and 1960s.

70. **(C)** The character's train of association enabled the writer to delve into his/her unconscious.

71. **(C)** It was the forerunner of the Common Market and the European Union.

72. **(B)** While his policies failed and he was ousted from power, Khrushchev started the liberalization that reached full fruition under Gorbachev.

73. **(A)** His theories fit and fostered "the age of anxiety."

74. **(A)** He is one of the most misinterpreted philosophers of modern times.

75. **(E)** The massive inflation of 1922–1923 decimated middle-class wealth, leading many to line up for loans, as seen in the photograph.

76. **(D)** "From cradle to grave."

77. **(A)** The emphasis on heavy industry was at the cost of the ordinary Russian's standard of living.

78. **(D)** This was a civil war.

79. **(B)** The West's dream of the collapse of Communism has created a fluid and even more dangerous world.

80. **(B)** The Solidarity movement led by Lech Walesa challenged Soviet authority in Poland through a movement of workers who wanted better conditions and rights, which was embarrassing for the Communists.

Comments on the DBQ

A note on scoring DBQ essays: Due to the importance of grouping and point of view in the DBQ essay, the DBQ explanations will present a possible thesis and an explanation of the possible groupings. Each grouping will then be explained in terms of what is required for core elements and what is required for an expanded core score (best essays).

For an essay to meet all core elements, the following must be completed:

1. The essay must provide an appropriate, explicitly stated thesis that directly addresses all parts of the question. *Thesis may not simply restate the question.*
2. The essay discusses a majority of the documents individually and specifically.
3. The essay demonstrates understanding of the basic meaning of a majority of the documents (may misinterpret no more than one).
4. The essay supports the thesis with appropriate interpretations of a majority of the documents.
5. The essay analyzes point of view or bias in at least three documents.
6. The essay analyzes documents by explicitly organizing them in at least three appropriate groups.

All essay explanations give the basic requirements for the essay. If all of the basic requirements are fulfilled, the essay receives a core score of 6. The top tier or best essays will meet expanded core requirements and earn a score of 7–9, depending on how many of the elements described in the DBQ chapter are contained in the essay and to what extent they are supported.

The Expanded Core Elements are as follows:

1. The thesis is clear, analytical, and comprehensive.
2. The essay uses all or almost all documents.
3. The essay addresses all parts of the question thoroughly.
4. The essay uses documents persuasively as evidence.
5. The essay shows understanding of nuances in the documents.
6. The essay analyzes point of view or bias in at least four documents cited in the essay.
7. The essay analyzes the documents in additional ways—additional grouping or other.
8. The essay brings in relevant "outside" historical content.

A graphical representation of the rubric for the DBQ can be seen on the next page.

The structure and thesis of this essay will vary depending upon which groups the author uses in the essay. The essay should have a thesis that addresses all groups within the essay (3 groups for core, 4–5 for expanded core). The essay should then have a separate paragraph for each grouping of documents that examines why the document belongs within that group and the point of view of the authors of the documents. A concluding paragraph should then restate the thesis and indicate that it has been justified.

This DBQ essay must begin with a thesis paragraph that has one sentence setting the scene and one sentence that addresses the entire question such as: Total

DBQ Rubric

Score one point if accomplished	**Basic Core**: If any one of the following tasks is not performed, *the essay cannot get a score higher than 6.* The basic core points are objective, like a checklist, with one point for each.

1. Provides an appropriate, explicitly stated thesis that directly addresses all parts of the question—**thesis may not simply restate the question**.
2. Discusses a majority of the documents individually and specifically.
3. Demonstrates understanding of the basic meaning of a majority of the documents (may misinterpret no more than one).
4. Supports the thesis with appropriate interpretations of a majority of the documents.
5. Analyzes point of view or bias in at least three documents.
6. Analyzes documents by explicitly organizing them in at least three appropriate groups.

Sum of Scores Above:	*Only* **if all six of the above criteria are met**, then the writer may attain a score of 7–9 if the writer can accomplish the expanded core elements. The more thoroughly the writer completes any of the following elements, the higher the additional score will be.

Expanded Core: If all core requirements are met, the writer may score points in any of the criteria below. *Very thorough application of any element below can score multiple points.* A **maximum** of 3 points may be awarded on the expanded core area. Scoring here is more subjective, and this section is not a checklist; to be awarded points writers must clearly accomplish any of the additional scoring criteria:

The thesis is clear, analytical, and comprehensive.

The essay uses all or almost all documents.

Addresses all parts of the question thoroughly.

Uses documents persuasively as evidence.

Shows understanding of nuances in the documents.

Analyzes point of view or bias in at least four documents cited in the essay.

Analyzes the documents in additional ways, or groupings.

Brings in relevant "outside" historical content.

Total sum of core plus any expanded points	If core score was 6, then add any expanded points to the core to get a final score from 0–9.

Warfare elicited many responses from laborers (4, 5, 7), women (2, 6, 5, 7), and those who ruled through government (1, 3, 8, 11, 12), which changed over time as the practice of Total War was accepted by the majority at the beginning of the 20th century (1, 2, 3, 5, 6, 8, 9, 10), and although some opposed it earlier, it fell out of favor after World War II (4, 7, 11, 12). This essay could also have groupings according to social documents (1, 2, 3, 4, 5, 6), political (1, 3, 7, 11, 12), and economic (2, 3, 5, 6, 8, 9, 13). An additional grouping of propaganda documents is also possible (2, 3, 8, 10).

It is usually best to present arguments in the same order as the thesis statement, so documents related to laborers will be examined first. *Listing the documents either in the thesis or within the paragraph is recommended.* The essay should use the documents as described below to craft an explanation of the various reactions of laborers to total war into a paragraph that illustrates those reactions and responses. *Although they should not be presented in the order presented in the question, the documents will be addressed in that fashion here.* Each document will be analyzed for how the essay author should use it. Documents in this group are documents 4, 5, and 7. The essay should present document 4 as the reaction of a soldier in the First World War. As a soldier, he is the ultimate laborer in a total war. His point of view as a soldier must be utilized. This document should also be used to indicate that some of those involved in total war were opposed to it early in the 20th century. Document 5 is much more supportive of total war. This document can be used to illustrate the difference in attitudes between workers on the home front and those on the battlefields. It can also be utilized to indicate that women were supportive of the war effort, further supporting World War I as a total war. The point of view of this document may be attributed to a woman laborer, who feels pride in her work. Document 7 can be best used to illustrate the sacrifices for the total war on the home front. It is attributable to another woman laborer who felt a compelling urge to work for the war effort. It also is somewhat critical of what total war did to the population of Europe. The best essays will include point of view on two or more documents, include explanations for why most documents belong in this group, and explain why the documents that could possibly fit into this group may belong there or why others do not.

Documents authored by or about women also make up a good group to examine. The essay should use the documents as described below to craft an explanation of the various reactions of women to total war into a paragraph that illustrates those reactions and responses. *Although they should not be presented in the order presented in the question, the documents will be addressed in that fashion here.* Each document will be analyzed for how the essay author should use it. Documents in this group are 2, 6, 5, and 7. Document 2 can only be included because it is a propaganda plea for women to join the war effort. It should be used to show how propaganda posters put pressure on women to support the war effort, and calling it propaganda poster is enough for point of view here, although it could also be attributed to a government in need of laborers. Document 6 is from a study conducted in England at the end of the war to determine the impact of women on the war effort. It can be used to indicate that that effect was substantial. The point of view attributed to this document must be that of the British government. Document 5 can be utilized to indicate that women were supportive of the war effort, further supporting World War I as a total war. The point of view of this document may be attributed to a woman laborer who feels pride in her work. Document 7 can be used to demonstrate the other side of total war for women by illustrating the sacrifices for the total war on the home front. It is attributable to a woman laborer who felt a compelling urge to work for the war effort. It also is somewhat critical of what total war did to the population of Europe. The best essays will include point of view on two or more documents, include explanations for why most documents belong in this group, and explain why the documents that could possibly fit into this group may belong there or why others do not.

The documents that should be listed in the grouping of those who ruled and their governments are 1, 3, 8, 11, and 12. The essay should use the documents as described below to craft an explanation of the various reactions of those who ruled and their governments to total war into a paragraph that illustrates those reactions and responses. *Although they should not be presented in the order presented in the question, the documents will be addressed in that fashion here.* Each document will be analyzed for how the essay author should use it. The essay should present document 1 as the reaction of a Russian socialist who probably was a pacifist for point of view. It can be used to demonstrate the unity of those in government when it came to total war. Document 3 is further evidence of lengths to which governments went to utilize total war in order to win. The only possible point of view is that of a desperate government facing defeat. This would also gain credit for outside info by using 1916 to show the desperation of Germany. Document 8 expresses the propagandistic message of Winston Churchill, the British prime minister during World War II, and can be used to show the efforts of the government to goad the populations into supporting total war. The point of view of a nationalist prime minister is sufficient here. Documents 8 illustrates the commitment of governments to total war during World War II. Document 11 should be used to show that after World War II, nations saw that total war was not worth the cost. It should also be indicated that as a document of the United Nations, it was approved by all of the parties to World War II, and thus is a government document supported by the most important governments. Document 12 should be utilized to further support the rejection of total war by many nations as it is a limitation on war. It is another United Nations document and can be attributed to that body, as was the last, for point of view. The best essays will include point of view on two or more documents, include explanations for why most documents belong in this group, and explain why the documents that could possibly fit into this group may belong there or why others do not.

The documents in favor of total war also make up an impressive group and include documents 1, 2, 3, 5, 6, 8, 9, and 10. The essay should use the documents as described below to craft an explanation of the various reactions of proponents of total war into a paragraph that illustrates those reactions and responses. *Although they should not be presented in the order presented in the question, the documents will be addressed in that fashion here.* Each document will be analyzed for how the essay author should use it. Document 1 should be cited as the reaction of a Russian socialist who probably was a pacifist for point of view. It can be used to demonstrate the unity of those in government when it came to total war. Document 2 is a propaganda poster supporting the war, and thus is certainly in favor of the use of total war. Calling it propaganda is enough for point of view. Document 3 is further evidence of lengths to which governments went to utilize total war in order to win the war. The only possible point of view is that of a desperate government facing defeat. This would also gain credit for outside info by using 1916 to show the desperation of Germany at that point. Document 5 can be utilized to indicate that women were supportive of the war effort, further supporting World War I as a total war. The point of view of this document may be attributed to a woman laborer who feels pride in her work. Document 6 is from a study conducted in England at the end of the war to determine the impact of women on the war effort. It can be used to indicate that that effect was substantial. The point of view attributed to this document must be that of the British government. Document 8 illustrates the commitment of governments to total war during World War II. Document 9 can be used to show support for the war efforts in total war from the least suspected person, a pacifist. His point of view as a pacifist author should be used to show that the feeling of total war was very contagious. The Soviet propaganda poster that is document 10 is further support for total war on the home front. The best essays will include point of view on two or more documents, include explanations for why most documents belong in this group, and explain why the documents that could possibly fit into this group may belong there or why others do not.

Another grouping of documents is those opposed to total war, including documents 4, 7, 11, and 12. The essay should present document 4 as the reaction of a soldier in the First World War. As a soldier, he is the ultimate laborer in a total war. His point of view as a soldier must be utilized. This document should also be used to indicate that some of those involved in total war were opposed to it early in the 20th century. Document 7 can be best used to illustrate the sacrifices for the total war on the home front. It is attributable to another woman laborer who felt a compelling urge to work for the war effort. It also is somewhat critical of what total war did to the population of Europe. It also illustrates early opposition to total war, but only from the fringes of society. Documents 11 and 12 can be used to show a more mainstream rejection of total warfare, with the United Nations rejecting the practice as well as journalists. Document 11 should be used to show that after World War II, nations saw that total war was not worth the cost. It should also be indicated that, as a document of the United Nations, it was approved by all of the parties to World War II, and thus is a government document supported by the most important governments. Document 12 should be utilized to further support the rejection of total war by many nations as it is a limitation on war. It is another United Nations document and can be attributed to that body, as was the last, for point of view. The best essays will include point of view on two or more documents, include explanations for why most documents belong in this group, and explain why the documents that could possibly fit into this group may belong there or why others do not.

Four more groups could be formed, which would use the documents much as they were used above. These groups are social documents (1, 2, 3, 4, 5, and 6), political (1, 3, 7, 11, and 12), economic (2, 3, 5, 6, 7, and 10), and propaganda documents (2, 3, 8, and 10). If these were used, see how documents were used above to determine if you used them properly.

Demonstration of change over time is also important to this essay. **If it is not accomplished, the student cannot achieve a score over 5.** This may be done within the groups as presented here, or a separate paragraph may be dedicated to illustrating change over time.

The best essays will have a clear, comprehensive, and concise thesis, address all responses and reactions to the emergence of total war presented, as well as the change over time of those responses and reactions, and demonstrate point of view in at least eight documents and/or groupings. They will have four or more groups of documents and use all sixteen documents to create a cogent essay that persuasively presents specific evidence for how the documents support the conclusions of the essay, bring in relevant outside information, and flow well.

Comments on the Essay Questions

In answering these questions, be sure to follow the "Simple Procedures" for writing an essay:

First, ask yourself what the question wants to know.

Second, ask yourself what you know about it.

Third, ask yourself how you would put it into words.

Use this generic rubric to help you or a friend or a tutor score each of the two essays you answered for this exam, one from Group A and one from Group B.

Generic Essay Scoring Rubric

9–8 POINTS

- ✔ Thesis explicitly addresses **all parts of the question**. Thesis does not need to be in the opening paragraph.
- ✔ Organization is clear, consistently followed, and effective in support of the argument.

  - • May devote individual paragraphs to an examination of each part of the question.
  - • Must identify major terms associated with the question and put them into context for the question; does not have to present every detail for every part.

- ✔ Essay is well balanced; the issues are analyzed at some length. Essay covers all chronological requirements of the question to some extent.
- ✔ Major assertions in the essay are supported thoroughly and consistently by relevant evidence.
- ✔ Evidence may prove more specific or concrete.
- ✔ May contain errors that do not detract from the argument.

7–6 POINTS

✔ Thesis explicitly identifies **all parts of the question**, but may not be developed fully.

✔ Organization is clear and effective in support of the argument but may introduce evidence that is not pertinent to the task.

✔ Essay covers all major topics suggested by the prompt but may analyze an aspect in greater depth rather than in a balanced manner.

✔ Major assertions in the essay are supported by relevant evidence.

✔ May contain an error that detracts from the argument.

5–4 POINTS

✔ Thesis identifies **all parts of the question**, but without any development; thesis may address only part of the question effectively; thesis may be a simple, single-sentence statement.

✔ Organization is clear but may not be consistently followed; essay may veer off task chronologically or thematically or both.

✔ Essay may not complete all tasks:

- May discuss only …
- May discuss only …
- May focus only on …
- May be primarily descriptive rather than analytical.

✔ Essay offers some relevant evidence.

✔ May contain errors that detract from the argument.

3–2 POINTS

✔ Thesis may simply paraphrase the prompt OR identify the parts of the question without analyzing.

✔ Organization is unclear and ineffective; essay may focus on personal or national attributes rather than analyzing.

✔ Essay shows serious imbalance; discussion is superficial; much of the information may be significantly out of the time period or geography of the question.

✔ Offers minimal OR confused evidence.

✔ May contain several errors that detract from the argument.

1–0 POINTS

✔ Thesis is erroneous OR irrelevant OR absent.

✔ No effective organization is evident.

✔ Discussion is generic.

✔ Provides little or no relevant supporting evidence.

✔ May contain numerous errors that detract from the argument.

GROUP A ESSAYS

> 2. "During the Age of Anxiety, the 1920s and 1930s, both psychology and the new physics contributed to the breakdown of traditional values." Assess the validity of this statement.

What does the question want to know? Decide whether these "new" sciences did, indeed, help to erode peoples' fundamental beliefs, then describe how.

What do you know about it? This period followed World War I and was characterized by the dissolution of great empires, economic boom and bust, a disruption of class and gender roles, the rise of radical dictatorships. How and why did Freudian psychology and the physics of Einstein help shake peoples' faith in the traditional values and institutions of European civilization?

How should you put it into words? Describe the political, economic, and social disruption caused by the war; explain how the scientific theories contributed to a climate of cynicism.

> 3. Assess the reasons for the similarities and differences between the Italian Renaissance and the Northern Renaissance.

What does the question want to know? Explain the reasons for the similarities and differences between the Italian Renaissance and the Northern Renaissance.

What do you know about it? The emphasis placed upon religion and the common person was the basic difference between the Northern Renaissance and the Italian Renaissance. Both shared themes of secularism, individualism, and humanism, but the ways they expressed them were quite different. In the North the relationship between the individual and God or the individual's community was examined more, whereas in Italy the wealthy and the Roman Catholic Church patronized the arts, making them more grandiose through images of religion and personal status. The Italian Renaissance was earlier, and many of those who began the Northern Renaissance traveled to Italy and corresponded with Italians during the later Northern Renaissance. It never hurts to mention thinkers of each region mentioned in the Renaissance Characters chart seen in Chapter 1 and compare their ideas and reasons for those ideas. Was Luther a Northern Renaissance thinker?

How would you put it into words? Explain why the Renaissance was expressed differently in each region. Here it is best to construct a strong thesis noting similarities and differences and/or some reason for them. From here, the writer can either dedicate a paragraph to each region or a paragraph to similarities and one to differences.

> 4. How and why did the Opening of the Atlantic lead to a shift of political and economic power from the Mediterranean Basin to Western Europe?

What does the question want to know? How and why did exploration and colonization in the 15th and 16th centuries enable the countries that bordered the Atlantic Ocean to achieve economic, political, and military dominance in Europe?

What do you know about it? "Geography is destiny." For centuries, Italy dominated European trade with the Far East due to its strategic location on the Mediterranean. New trade routes with Asia established by Portuguese explorers and the discovery of the New World by Spanish and other explorers whose nations had Atlantic access offered new routes and new products. Explain how the Columbian Exchange gave Spain and eventually England and the Netherlands huge economic power. The importance of Northern European advances in naval technology and knowledge as factors in shifting power further north can also be examined.

How would you put it into words? With "geography is destiny" as your theme, describe how and why the power shifted in the 15th and 16th centuries.

GROUP B ESSAYS

> 5. To what extent and in what ways was Romanticism in art, literature, and music a reaction against the Enlightenment?

What does the question want to know? What were the values, expressions, and accomplishments of the Enlightenment and how much did Romanticism repudiate these in the various arts?

What do you know about it? The Enlightenment was characterized by a climate of progress and a fervid faith in reason as the tool for humanity to move to its highest fruition. The Romantic Movement emphasized emotion, glorified nature, and looked to the past.

How would you put it into words? Identify the assumptions and aims of the Enlightenment; show how Romantic art, literature, and music repudiated these.

> 6. Describe how the public health movement and urban planning during the latter half of the 19th century changed life in Europe's cities.

What does the question want to know? What was the condition of Europe's cities in the 19th century? What were the public health movement and urban planning? How did they improve life in the cities?

What do you know about it? Haphazard growth and industrialization had resulted in overcrowded, filthy, unhealthy urban centers built on or around Europe's ancient cities. Reformers—in the health field and in urban planning—put their new theories into practice, thereby transforming many of Europe's cities into more livable, economically viable, and beautiful centers.

How would you put it into words? Describe the squalor and chaos that prevailed. Identify specific reformers and their theories. Detail specific improvements. If you have the facts, you could use a specific city as an illustration.

---

7. "Religious differences caused the greatest disruption in 16th-century Europe, ideological differences the greatest disruption in 20th-century Europe." Defend or refute this statement.

What does the question want to know? Is the statement true or false? Make an argument that is supported by facts.

What do you know about it? The schism of the Christian world brought about by the Protestant Reformation and the subsequent political, social, cultural, and economic upheaval lasted for well over a century. The collapse of the political order that followed World War I affected every sphere of life in Europe, almost to the end of the 20th century.

How would you put it into words? The statement is most easily defended. Compare the realms of disruption in both centuries; contrast the religious issues of the 16th century with the ideological issues of the 20th.

Index

How to Use the CD-ROM

The software is not installed on your computer; it runs directly from the CD-ROM. Barron's CD-ROM includes an "autorun" feature that automatically launches the application when the CD is inserted into the CD-ROM drive. In the unlikely event that the autorun feature is disabled, follow the manual launching instructions below.

Windows®

1. Click on the Start button and choose "My Computer."
2. Double-click on the CD-ROM drive, which will be named **AP_European_History.exe**.
3. Double-click **AP_European_History.exe** to launch the program.

MAC®

1. Double-click the CD-ROM icon.
2. Double-click the **AP_European_History** icon to start the program.

SYSTEM REQUIREMENTS

(Flash Player 10.2 is recommended)

Microsoft® Windows®	**MAC® OS X**	**Linux® and Solaris™**
Processor: Intel Pentium 4 2.33GHz, Athlon 64 2800+ or faster processor (or equivalent). Memory: 128MB of RAM. Graphics Memory: 128MB. Platforms: Windows 7, Windows Vista®, Windows XP, Windows Server® 2008, Windows Server 2003.	Processor: Intel Core™ Duo 1.33GHz or faster processor. Memory: 256MB of RAM. Graphics Memory: 128MB. Platforms: Mac OS X 10.6, Mac OS X 10.5, Mac OS X 10.4 (Intel) and higher.	Processor: Intel Pentium 4 2.33GHz, AMD Athlon 64 2800+ or faster processor (or equivalent). Memory: 512MB of RAM. Graphics Memory: 128MB. Platforms: Red Hat® Enterprise Linux (RHEL) 5 or later, openSUSE® 11 or later, Ubuntu 9.10 or later. Solaris: Solaris™ 10.